TEN THOUSAND YEARS OF INEQUALITY

AMERIND STUDIES IN ANTHROPOLOGY

Series Editor **Christine Szuter**

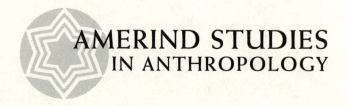

TEN THOUSAND
YEARS OF INEQUALITY

THE ARCHAEOLOGY OF
WEALTH DIFFERENCES

EDITED BY
Timothy A. Kohler and Michael E. Smith

THE UNIVERSITY OF
ARIZONA PRESS
TUCSON

The University of Arizona Press
www.uapress.arizona.edu

© 2018 The Arizona Board of Regents
All rights reserved. Published 2018

ISBN-13: 978-0-8165-3774-7 (cloth)

Cover design by Leigh McDonald
Cover art: Hathor as a cow breastfeeding Amenhotep II as a young man, Deir-el-Bahari, Egypt, 15th century BC. Just as the Pharaoh was nourished by milk, so too were early wealth inequalities in the Old World stimulated by the availability of large domesticated animals, particularly for traction. Lacking such animals, post-Neolithic New World societies had lower wealth levels than their Old World counterparts. DEA / G. DAGLI ORTI / Granger, NYC—All rights reserved.

Library of Congress Cataloging-in-Publication Data
Names: Kohler, Timothy A., editor. | Smith, Michael Ernest, 1953– editor.
Title: Ten thousand years of inequality : the archaeology of wealth differences / edited by Timothy A. Kohler and Michael E. Smith.
Other titles: Amerind studies in anthropology.
Description: Tucson : The University of Arizona Press, 2018. | Series: Amerind studies in anthropology | Includes bibliographical references and index.
Identifiers: LCCN 2017047626 | ISBN 9780816537747 (cloth : alk. paper)
Subjects: LCSH: Social archaeology. | Equality—Economic aspects. | Prehistoric peoples—Social conditions.
Classification: LCC CC72.4 .T44 2018 | DDC 930.1—dc23 LC record available at https://lccn.loc.gov/2017047626

Printed in the United States of America
♾ This paper meets the requirements of ANSI/NISO Z39.48-1992 (Permanence of Paper).

CONTENTS

PREFACE

As we write this, the Republicans in the U.S. Senate are debating whether to revoke tax increases on the wealthy imposed by Obamacare in tandem with their plan to reduce federal health spending for the poor. We have not heard "Ginis" mentioned in this context, but they are relevant, since Obamacare, though primarily a system of health care, also entailed a small transfer of wealth from rich to poor. While this particular issue will soon be decided, we assume, the underlying tension about whether such transfers should be allowed and how large they should be has long vexed democracies.

Many find disturbing statistics such as that reported by Oxfam in early 2017. The world's eight richest men, by their calculation, now own as much combined wealth as the entire poorest half of humankind ("Economy of the 99 Percent," www.oxfam.org). But others say, in effect, that what really matters is the standard of living and the well-being of all; if the economy today produces so much surplus that some become extremely wealthy, that's OK so long as everyone is doing well. To which many would then respond that in fact not everyone is doing well.

However one feels about these debates, we believe they badly need some historical perspective. If the Gini coefficient measuring wealth concentration in the United States stands around 0.8, as the National Bureau for Economic Research reported in 2008, how anomalous, or how normal, is such a number? True, it appears to be among the highest (most unequal) in the world today, but as archaeologists, we suggest that our inquiry should begin not with conditions today, or in 1950, or even at the onset of the Industrial Revolution, but at the dawn of the Holocene some 12,000 years ago. The great age of hunting and gathering, with its largely equal wealth distributions, was then rapidly drawing to a close. As people settled into a way of life dominated by farming and herding, did wealth inequalities develop suddenly or slowly? Why did they increase at all—or did they? How recent are the high levels of wealth inequality now experienced in many developed nations? How would we as archaeologists even be able to tell?

The editors of this volume have been concerned about such issues for many years, and individually we have published some relevant studies (see chapter 1). Yet we have been frustrated by the relative lack of attention to these topics among our colleagues and by the spotty nature of the relevant data from prehistory. So we decided to join forces and organized a symposium titled "Measuring and Explaining Household Inequality in Antiquity: Inequality from the Bottom Up" at the 2016 Society for American Archaeology meetings in Orlando. We invited all the archaeologists we knew who were doing relevant research to participate.

Perhaps we put on a good show; in any case, the Amerind Foundation kindly invited us to revisit the topic in a more leisurely fashion on their beautiful Dragoon, Arizona, campus in fall 2016. The volume now in your hands is the immediate result. We hope that a longer-term result will be the establishment of a rigorous research program on the creation and distribution of wealth in prehistory, the relationship of wealth to broader measures of well-being, and related large-scale questions on the prehistory of the human condition. These issues are too frequently left to philosophers, novelists, and economists.

We editors have more people to thank than your patience as a reader would permit, but let us begin with the Amerind Foundation and its executive director, Christine Szuter, an enthusiastic advocate for this project and a delightful host; our authors, who have been graceful under strict time constraints; and Laura Ellyson, a PhD student in anthropology at Washington State University (WSU), who provided editorial support all along the way. The University of Arizona Press could not have selected more capable outside reviewers than Tim Earle and Ian Morris; their comments helped at several junctures. Kohler also thanks the Department of Anthropology, WSU, and the Santa Fe Institute both for their support and for providing occasions to try out some of the ideas presented in chapters 5 and 11, and Marilyn Von Seggern, for her patience and good humor as the volume was being assembled. Smith tried out some of his ideas on these topics at a lecture at the University of Bonn, Germany, for the Research Training Group in the Archaeology of Pre-Modern Economies in 2014. He does not contribute an empirical chapter here, because his main contribution was published in 2014 (Smith, Dennehy,

Kamp-Whittaker, Colon, and Harkness 2014: "Quantitative Measures of Wealth Inequality in Ancient Central Mexican Communities," *Advances in Archaeological Practice* 2:311–23). Smith thanks his co-authors on that paper for their contributions. Some of the Gini data from the project Access to Service in Premodern Cities, co-directed by Smith, were used in chapter 11; they were prepared and analyzed by Timothy Dennehy, also a member of that project. Smith and Dennehy thank fellow project members Benjamin Stanley, Barbara Stark, Abigail York, Sharon Harlan, and April Kamp-Whittaker for help in measuring inequality in a sample of premodern cities.

TEN THOUSAND YEARS OF INEQUALITY

Studying Inequality's Deep Past

Michael E. Smith, Timothy A. Kohler,
and Gary M. Feinman

They should have been complete strangers, these societies that had exchanged neither word nor material for over ten millennia. Yet they seemed oddly familiar. The Spanish could recognize kings, priests, warriors, merchants, markets, and many other organizational features of Aztec society.

But looking the other way was stranger. The Spanish ships seemed so implausible that the Aztec likened them to mountains or towers. The first Aztec messengers fainted upon seeing Spanish cannons fired. They marveled at the "stags" the Spanish rode, tall as the roof of a house; the enormous dogs, tireless and powerful, with yellow eyes flashing fire and shooting off sparks; and the soldiers' trappings, swords, and shields of iron. Yet the Spanish fixation on gold was puzzling: "[T]hey hungered [for it] like pigs . . . fingered it like monkeys" (Leon-Portilla 1962:30, 31, 51).

The dramatic encounter between the Spanish conqueror Hernando Cortés and the Aztec emperor Motecuhzoma II in 1519 initiated a series of catastrophic transformations of Mesoamerican societies. Accompanying the conquest, subjugation, exploitation, and disease, the level of social inequality rose dramatically. In fact, though the Aztec empire was socially complex, politically powerful, and densely populated at its core with a strongly entrenched elite class (Smith 2012), its level of wealth inequality was relatively modest (Smith et al. 2014). By 1790, toward the end of the colonial period in Mexico, however, the degree of inequality had almost doubled (Williamson 2010:239).

How could the concentration of wealth nearly double in colonial central Mexico when rising wages at this time (Scheidel 2017:314–19) should logically have resulted in *reduction* in wealth inequality? Especially given the simultaneous influx of contagious diseases causing Native populations to crater, we would expect decreases in wealth differences. The imposition of a new set of social institutions and technologies by colonial authorities proved to be even more powerful than these population changes. Private property, Spanish imperial rule, an export-driven economy, and the encomienda system regulating race, class, and allocating virtual slave labor to Spanish conquistadors and other leaders—these all worked to favor the concentration of wealth in the hands of a small portion of society despite countervailing changes.

This book is about how numerous factors interacted in often complex ways to affect wealth inequality in a variety of societies over the past 10,000 years. This transformation of Mexico from Aztec to Spanish rule is part of a deeper historical story of social inequality and its changes across time and space. That inequality was greater in sixteenth-century Spain than in Aztec Mexico may be surprising. But one of the many new findings emerging from the case studies presented in this book is that levels of wealth inequality were generally higher in the ancient and historical agrarian state societies of the Old World than in their New World counterparts. We have assembled archaeological data from many parts of the world to estimate wealth concentrations for societies that have never before been part of the conversation on wealth and inequality. Prior comparisons of inequality have focused on societies that produced written documents (Milanovic 2011; Milanovic et al. 2011; Scheidel 2017) but here we extend our gaze deep into the archaeological past. We have encountered unexpected results. Some small-scale societies—often considered egalitarian—exhibit considerable wealth concentration, whereas wealth inequality in some complex polities was apparently surprisingly low.

Our most wide-ranging new finding, though, is a previously unrecognized contrast in levels of inequality between the later Neolithic through Iron Age societies of Eurasia and the developed societies of the pre-Hispanic Americas. Although there is some variability, these Old World societies exhibit much greater wealth differences than their counterparts in North America and Mesoamerica. (We have yet to estimate wealth inequalities for any pre-Hispanic society in South America.) In chapter 11 we endeavor to explain these differences using a combination of technological and institutional factors.

But perhaps the greatest value of the case studies assembled here is the way in which they advance a consistent analytical logic and empirically grounded methods to study wealth inequality in the deep past. Our approach in this book is data driven. Nevertheless, theory helps us know where to look for meaningful data, and so we begin by considering how researchers have explained the origins and growth of inequality, concentrating particularly on approaches developed over the past few decades.

DIVERGENT VIEWS ON INEQUALITY

Socioeconomic inequality is pervasive in the world today. Life chances diverge greatly in rich versus poor nations and between elites and others within most nations; gender-based wage disparities are almost universal; and the concentration of wealth by the super-rich is growing nearly everywhere (Krugman 2014; Pringle 2014; Reeves 2017). These pronounced inequalities are not created solely by the actions of a few powerful individuals, and they are certainly not hardwired into our brains or our culture. Rather, they result from the interpersonal interactions of individuals shaped by the constraints of resources, technology, and institutions, including stable social systems promoting inheritance of wealth from one generation to the next. Inequalities develop through historical processes that operate on many levels, from the individual to the society, from the kin group and neighborhood to the state. Today globalization is adding its own distinct impetus to these processes.

But just how pervasive has inequality been throughout history around the world? This question has been answered in an astonishing variety of ways by social scientists over the years. Sociologists used to think that all human societies had social classes (Davis and Moore 1945), until anthropologists pointed out that this is not at all the case (Smith 1966). Anthropologists at one time believed that all hunter-gatherers were egalitarian (see discussion in Flanagan 1989) until both archaeological and ethnographic fieldwork proved them wrong (Arnold 1996; Flanagan 1989). Many scholars once thought that inequality grew following an orderly sequence of social types—from bands to tribes to states (Service 1966) or from communal society through slavery and castes to class systems (Kerbo 2011:47–54)—until archaeological fieldwork revealed a far more complex human past (Flannery and Marcus 2012; Trigger 2006).

Some scholars have claimed that all early state societies were highly unequal, with severe exploitation, downtrodden peasants, and slave labor (Ste. Croix 1981; Wittfogel 1957), while others identify numerous states that were more "collective"—even egalitarian—in the ancient world

(Blanton 2016; Blanton and Fargher 2008; Carballo 2016). And in reference to wealth inequality today, many scholars warn of its negative effects on life and society. Joseph Stiglitz (2012), for example, identifies deleterious changes in norms and institutions, decreasing growth, increasing discrimination and disillusionment, decreasing social mobility, and the digging of ever-deeper poverty traps as consequences of the high levels of inequality in the United States today (see also Wilkinson and Pickett 2009). Other scholars, however, consider such concerns overblown (O'Connell 2010). Finally, there is the disturbing suggestion that inequality rarely declines unless a society is hit by a severe natural or social disaster (Scheidel 2017).

Why are there such divergent views on the extent and significance of social inequality among human societies? One reason is that social scientists and historians have ignored the archaeological record of past societies. By the "dawn of history," when peoples in the Near East began producing written documents, social inequality was already a long-established principle. And by the time European armies, germs, and steel (Diamond 1997) conquered the New World, members of many indigenous societies had experienced inequality for millennia. Disregarding pertinent archaeological evidence permits economists and others to create imaginary, often highly unlikely, scenarios for society and economy in the deep past (Graeber 2011:21–42). Using archaeology to round out our picture of the history and role of inequality in human societies will help scholars understand its origins, nature, and significance (Flannery and Marcus 2012).

By now, archaeologists have identified inequalities in many regions (Price and Feinman 1995; Trigger 2003), but the data have yet to be systematically analyzed and compared. For some archaeologists, sumptuous palaces or big pyramids are evidence enough of social inequality, while for others inequality must be sought at the household level. Diverse approaches and views that too frequently veer toward the subjective do little to advance reliable knowledge of ancient inequality. In general, archaeologists have concentrated on the rise of differential sociopolitical power and have simply assumed (following Marx and Engels [1848] 1969, for example) that wealth differences have been so tightly correlated with power differentials that to study one is to study the other. We think this assumption is premature. The relationship of these two forms of inequality cannot be examined until we develop measures for each individually. Our tasks in this volume are to develop measures of wealth inequality—and see what they yield.

This leads to the second reason for the existence of widely divergent views of inequality among human societies: the scarcity of systematic, comparative data on conditions before the modern era. After reciting the difficulties of studying wealth inequalities in the twentieth century, historian Walter Scheidel remarks, "All these problems pale in comparison to those we encounter once we seek to extend the study of income and wealth inequality farther back in time" (2017:15). Inequality today is analyzed quantitatively (e.g., Bowles 2012; Piketty 2014). Measures like the Gini coefficient, the Theil index, interdecile comparisons, and the Palma measure are routinely employed to describe the distribution of inequality within a population, as well as to compare cities, regions, or nations (Holton 2015; Milanovic 2011). (Use of such measures does not preclude debates and disagreements, as witnessed by the work of Thomas Piketty [2014] and its many critics [King 2016].) Economic historians recently have begun to extend the quantitative study of inequalities into the past (Lindert and Williamson 2016; Milanovic et al. 2011), but few such studies reach deeper than medieval Europe and fewer still examine societies untouched by Western civilization. Quantitative archaeological data are essential if scholars really want to discern how social inequalities originated, how for millennia people created and responded to inequalities of wealth, and how the relationship between wealth and power has varied over the centuries.

This volume contains the first major set of quantitative studies of ancient social inequality using archaeological data. The authors employ the Gini coefficient (and sometimes additional measures) to assess wealth inequality in precapitalist societies over the past several thousand years. Our results suggest that many existing accounts of past inequality are incorrect or overly simplified. In some cases—such as hunter-gatherer societies and early agricultural villages—past inequality was sometimes greater than most scholars typically assume (see chapters 4–7). In other cases—such as early states and empires—we find that specific societies were more egalitarian than prevailing wisdom would allow (see chapters 9 and 10). By using a common metric—the Gini coefficient applied in most cases to the record of house-size distributions—we can compare the level of inequality among very different societies, leading to the novel results emerging in chapter 11. We discuss this metric and warrant its choice as a cross-culturally valid measure of wealth toward the end of this chapter and in several of the chapters that follow.

THREE BIG QUESTIONS ABOUT PAST INEQUALITY

Taken together, the studies in this volume address three key questions about past inequality:

1. How did it originate?
2. How did it persist through time?
3. How can we explain variation in inequality across time and space?

Because of possibilities offered by unique data sets, the authors of a few chapters are also able to address questions such as whether societies tend to flourish in specific ranges of inequality and what sorts of events can lead to declines in inequality.

But a prerequisite to this line of investigation is to consider how wealth inequality differs from the many other types of social difference. To apply the concept of inequality anthropologically—to societies such as hunter-gatherers, who lack social classes and are usually portrayed as relatively "egalitarian"—we need to take a broader approach than is common in the social sciences. Sociologists who focus on contemporary society can define social inequality as "difference that we consider unjust" (Therborn 2006:4). We prefer the more neutral and broadly applicable definition of social inequality provided by Robert Holton, as differences that "create and reproduce systemic inequalities in the life chances of populations over time" (Holton 2015:61).

As archaeologists dealing with contexts that are always more or less time-averaged, though, we must extend Holton's concept of inequalities to account for patterns that persist over long temporal periods. Thus, our focus is on what Charles Tilly (1998) calls "durable inequality," or what Siobhán Mattison and colleagues (2016) refer to as "persistent institutionalized inequality." Although in most cases our chronological sequences preclude fine-grained analyses of change across short intervals, we can boast otherwise unobtainable information about how social phenomena play out over centuries and even millennia. For this reason we are primarily interested in the sorts of inequality that tend to be inherited from generation to generation. In societies not practicing high mobility, differences in wealth often accumulate across generations because of inheritance. Individual differences due to age, sex, and abilities exist in all societies, but recent studies show that these tend to be poorly or only moderately transmissible across generations (Borgerhoff Mulder et al. 2009; Gurven et al. 2010). They do not, by themselves, explain the sorts of sociopolitical hierarchies and marked distinctions in wealth that became common in the post-Pleistocene world. What does?

THE ORIGINS OF SOCIAL INEQUALITY

Homo sapiens colonized most areas of the world during the Pleistocene, in general living in small groups of foragers at low regional population densities. Many factors suppressed wealth differences in such societies, including high mobility in response to low constancy and predictability of food sources. There was little opportunity for intergenerational wealth transmission. Ethnographic analogy suggests the existence of strong norms for resource sharing, while simulation studies demonstrate the desirability of such norms.

In areas where farming developed during the Holocene (and in favored places with high resource abundance, constancy, or predictability where hunter-gatherers or fisher-foragers could develop relatively sedentary communities) population sizes expanded more rapidly than they had ever before (Bocquet-Appel 2002; Kohler and Reese 2014). Reduced mobility improved women's energy balance and decreased interbirth spacing (Sussman and Hall 1972).

It remains to be seen whether the depression of wild resources as a consequence of population growth was fundamentally important to inducing domestication of plants and animals, as many archaeologists have argued (Gremillion et al. 2014; Rosenberg 1998) or whether domestication was led by niche construction activities designed to promote resource security and predictability (Zeder 2012). In either case regional populations grew, beginning to constrain mobility and allow group sizes to scale accordingly (Hamilton et al. 2007). Material-based wealth inequalities are logically impossible when no material resources are scarce (Midlarsky 1999); at best they develop only insofar as individual abilities and household labor pools differ. Thus, development of relative scarcities in productive land or high-ranked wild game likely abetted wealth inequality. Scarcities are dealt with in part by increasing effort, and such intensification seems likely to lead to weakening norms for resource sharing.

Then, too, in chapter 11 we present reasons to believe that (up to thresholds likely determined by communication and transportation cost constraints) larger groups were generally more effective in providing public or common goods (Blanton 2016:40; Dubreuil 2010). This contrasts with the position of Mancur Olson (1965:36) that cooperative behaviors in groups quickly deteriorate as groups increase in size. Models tuned to ancestral human conditions clearly demonstrate the advantages of coordinated punishment (for those not contributing to some public good) in maintaining cooperation. Punishment is individually costly, but if most members of a group cooperate in punishing, the per-individual cost of punishment, as well as the total cost, is reduced, increasing group-average payoffs (Boyd et al. 2010).

Groups unavoidably differentiate internally as they grow, developing segmentations such as kin groups and sodalities. Even such small-scale institutions require someone to speak for them (Durkheim 2014), encouraging development of unequal status and power. Such segments likewise entrain identifications and loyalties; members have a stake in preserving their honor by punishing those who violate their norms (Dubreuil 2010). If such segments are built on an enduring structure, such as kinship, such spokespeople might be able to pass along their status to the next generation.

Recently social scientists have begun to use the tools of social network analysis to describe interactions within groups. Such work suggests an additional but related pathway by which increasing group size might have led to the emergence of inequalities. Reuben Thomas and Noah Mark (2013) present a model in which all individuals in very small groups are connected to all other individuals by personal knowledge and regular interaction (here the network density equals 1). If groups grow for any reason, cognitive and time constraints (e.g., Dunbar 1992; Johnson 1978) at some point dictate that all individuals can no longer interact directly, creating "structural holes" as network density decreases. One result is that individuals begin to rely on indirect reports (reputation) to assess the status of others in their group. The quality of such reports is affected by the relative positions of individuals in the networks, and as network heterogeneities develop, who knows whom becomes increasingly critical. If children tend to inherit the network positions of their parents, then network advantages will persist and perhaps accumulate across generations. Thomas and Mark (2013) tie these network effects to a model for leader selection in small-scale societies to argue that together these processes explain how status can come to be determined more by structural advantage (network position) than by individual ability.

Considering these studies as a group, we can infer that *any* mechanism increasing group size in the past increased the probability of inequalities within the group. Theorists have of course identified numerous mechanisms leading to such group-size increases (collectively resulting in the scaling relationships noted in Hamilton et al. 2007). One is success in intergroup conflict (Bowles 2009; Carneiro 1970; Crabtree et al. 2017; Khaldûn [1377] 1958; Turchin et al. 2013), which leads to an accelerating "big get bigger" dynamic. Intergroup warfare may have additional direct effects on equality beyond its indirect effects via increasing group size. War captives and other booty increase the riches or labor pools of some households; brave warriors and successful war leaders accumulate renown and prestige (Earle 1997; Flannery and Marcus 2012:106, 179). Although the relationship between population size and social complexity is rarely determinant in any simple fashion (Carballo et al. 2014:113–15; Feinman 2013), a variety of pressures and processes in the Holocene have channeled groups toward ever-larger sizes. Size increases created opportunities for the emergence of differential wealth and prestige within groups.

Nevertheless, status or wealth garnered by members of one generation is not automatically transmitted to the next, particularly in small-scale societies. In a comparative analysis of ethnographic data, Monique Borgerhoff Mulder and colleagues (2009; Smith et al. 2010) identify three distinct types of wealth—embodied, relational, and material—that have differing probabilities of cross-generational transmission in societies of different types. Embodied wealth includes body weight, grip strength, practical skills, and reproductive success (in predemographic transition populations). Relational wealth includes social ties in food-sharing networks and other forms of assistance; the social network positions analyzed by Thomas and Mark (2013) are good examples. Material wealth includes those things that today are automatically considered to be wealth: land, livestock, and house and household goods.

Eric Smith and colleagues (2010) note that those kinds of wealth that are most important in hunter-gatherer and horticultural societies—embodied and relational wealth—are the types least likely to be transmitted successfully across generations. Material wealth, in contrast, is the most important basis of wealth in both pastoralist and agricultural societies. Across all twenty-one societies in their sample, the degree of inequality among households was greatest for material wealth, and perhaps not surprisingly, higher degrees of inequality tended to be found among those societies with greater intergenerational transmission of wealth. These are, of course, the sedentary agriculturalists and the pastoralists, not the more mobile horticulturalists and foragers.

These observations can be synthesized to form a plausible sketch of the prerequisites for the emergence of persistent institutionalized inequality, or durable inequality, in small-scale societies. Two essential ingredients are (1) the existence and importance of forms of wealth that are relatively permanent (material wealth, therefore), are not used primarily for signaling purposes (as are many luxury goods), and have economic defensibility (costs of defense are less than benefits of defense). In the context of relatively sedentary societies, these qualities result in (2) wealth that is more likely to be transmitted across generations (Mattison et al. 2016). Because "individually owned and heritable wealth can have major impacts on reproductive success," there is a "clear evolutionary rationale for links among economic defensibility, intergenerational wealth transmission, and persistent institutionalized inequality" (Mattison et al. 2016:190). The model proposed by Mattison and colleagues (2016) is illustrated in figure 1.1. Note that the ability to defend resources likely depends not only on steep resource gradients but also on group size. As long as wealth can be intergenerationally transmitted, the ability to construct a positive correlation between current wealth and expected future income—in this case from the defended resources—is fundamental to differential wealth accumulation.

THE PERSISTENCE OF INEQUALITY

If we now turn from models developed to explain the origins of inequality in ancient or small-scale societies to consider work in the more traditional social sciences, typically among recent or contemporary societies, we see several commonalities. These two bodies of research converge in

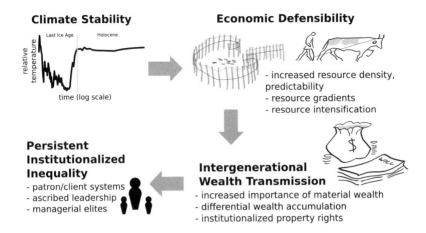

Figure 1.1 Outline of an evolutionary model for the origins of durable inequality. Figure from Mattison et al. 2016:195. Graphic by Bret Beheim, based partly on McNeill 1963; data for the top left are from Petit et al. 1999. Reproduced with permission.

part in their focus on resources and the role of resources in creating and maintaining durable inequality.

Sociologist Gerhard Lenski (1966) presented one of the first comprehensive accounts of the development and maintenance of durable inequality over the long span of cultural evolution and human history. Subsequent scholars tested and extended his work (Haas 1993; Turner 1984). Randall Collins (1988:155–56; 2004) synthesized the results of Lenski and his followers: "Lenski proposes that the surplus wealth beyond subsistence is distributed by power. The concentration of power determines the concentration of wealth. This is a reversal of Marx and is an endorsement of Weber on the autonomous dynamics of politics" (Collins 2004:224).

A generation after Lenski's influential book, Charles Tilly built on its foundation to focus on the specific individual and institutional forces that create and sustain social inequality over time. Although Tilly's examples are mostly drawn from contemporary societies, his model is far more broadly applicable (Tilly 1998, 2001, 2005). He relies on four causal mechanisms that generate inequality, plus the concept of categorical inequality (patterns of inequality that vary systematically with social categories such as race, gender, and occupation). For Tilly, the most powerful mechanisms are *exploitation* (which "occurs when persons who control a resource (a) enlist the effort of others in production of value by means of that resource, but (b) exclude the others from the full value added by their effort" [Tilly 2001:366]) and *opportunity hoarding* (which "operates when members of a categorically bounded network acquire access to a resource that is valuable, subject to monopoly, supportive of network activities, and enhanced by the network's modus operandi" [Tilly 1998:10]). His other mechanisms, which he calls "emulation" and "adaptation," work to cement processes of inequality into durable phenomena.

Tilly's model overlaps considerably with the models outlined above for small-scale societies, particularly as summarized by Mattison and colleagues (2016). Opportunity hoarding is a direct translation of economic defensibility into a context in which future network effects can be anticipated; this once again ties wealth (through the ability it provides to defend resources) to future income. The concept of exploitation adds a Marxian twist that seems more plausible for societies with established inequalities than for cases in which inequalities are beginning to emerge—though this cannot be taken for granted. Tilly's model has been widely discussed in the comparative and historical social science literature (Laslett 2000; Mosse 2010; Voss 2010; Wright 2000) and has been validated quantitatively in several contemporary settings (Tomaskovic-Devey et al. 2009; Vallas and Cummins 2014).

FACTORS AFFECTING DEGREE OF INEQUALITY

Although we have sketched what we view as the key processes structuring inequality above, we wish to more fully acknowledge the long interest in explaining inequality that underlies our efforts. We see these not so much as alternative complete models but as important pieces of an explanation.

RESOURCES AND MODES OF PRODUCTION

Social inequality is all about resources. Inequality derives from the ways that resources are owned, controlled, exchanged, and inherited. The theoretical approaches outlined above focus on the role of defensible resources in generating and maintaining inequality, as do many other approaches to inequality (e.g., Midlarsky 1999). In the broad sweep of cultural evolution from the Pleistocene through the Industrial Revolution, the form of sub-sistence activity has been responsible for major variation in the nature and amount of resources available to a society. Forms of subsistence are often divided into three categories that form an ordinal scale of produc-tivity per unit of land—foraging, horticulture, and intensive agriculture.

Although numerous authors have cited various types of evidence to argue that this scale is positively associated with the degree of inequality in a society (Flannery and Marcus 2012; Johnson and Earle 2000; Smith et al. 2010), no one has yet produced quantitative data on past societies to test this notion. Quantitative production estimates are beginning to become available in selected regions, however (e.g., Kohler and Varien 2012), so such tests may eventually be possible. In chapter 11 we show that the level of inequality does indeed vary systematically with subsistence type. Branko Milanovic and colleagues (2011) explain why this relation-ship is expected, assuming that horticultural production increases the usual surplus over foraging, and agriculture increases the available surplus yet again. They argue that except for recent, rich countries, economic inequality has always risen pretty much as high as it can go without causing (too many of) the poor to starve. They call the maximum level of inequality for a given level of wealth or resources the "inequality pos-sibility frontier." Thus, inequality is limited by whatever surplus exists beyond the basic subsistence needs of all households, as Lenski (1966) also argued. Horticulturalists are less equal than foragers, and farmers less equal than horticulturalists, in large part because the surplus available to be monopolized by a few households increases along that same scale.

POPULATION SIZE

The link between population size and degree of inequality permeates both the evolutionary and the social science literatures, as our review above demonstrates. Whether population is measured as regional pop-ulation, settlement population, or density, there are data to support this relationship and models to explain it. The data in the chapters that fol-low, as synthesized in chapter 11, partly confirm these expectations for our sample of ancient settlements, although we show some surprising divergences from simple expectations that only become obvious in very large-scale, cross-regional comparisons.

POLITICAL COMPLEXITY

Just as subsistence type and population size are commonly associated with the level of inequality among preindustrial societies, so too is the level of political complexity typically held to predict the level of inequality (Flannery and Marcus 2012; Lenski 1966; Scheidel 2017). This relationship is not surprising, as political complexity tends to increase (although not uniformly) with societal scale (e.g., Feinman 2013). Again, our data lend general support to this model for excavated ancient settlements (chapter 11), although we wish to make a distinction between wealth inequality and inequalities of power and status that are too often elided in this literature.

TECHNOLOGY

As noted, a correspondence between mode of production and degree of inequality is expected if greater productivity tends to produce larger surpluses, permitting more-extensive inequities in distribution. In a related vein, the advent of specific technologies can affect the materialization of resources and labor and generate greater concentrations of wealth. For example, development of new transport technologies and the domestication of herd and pack animals (e.g., Diamond 1997) had significant potential impacts on a variety of features: agricultural productivity (Halstead 1995; chapter 8, this volume), size of polities (Turchin 2009), ways that warfare is conducted (Anthony and Brown 2011; White 1943:353), volumes of exchange (Golitko et al. 2012; Santone 1997), and, by implication, concentration of power and wealth (Frankema 2015). The mere presence of domesticated animals or the availability of other new technologies is not necessary and sufficient to generate shifts in each of these domains but leads to greater potential for such changes.

INSTITUTIONAL VARIABILITY

It is not surprising that socioeconomic inequality generally increases with the onset of agricultural production, larger settlements and societal scale, more-hierarchical forms of political complexity, and the development of more-elaborate and more-costly technologies. Each of these shifts fosters disparities in individual and domestic life chances across social networks and within communities, as outlined by Holton (2015:61; see also Pringle 2014). What is perhaps less immediately explicable is the extensive residual variation across time for given regions (Piketty 2014; Turchin and Nefedov 2009), as well as the case-to-case diversity in space and time for specific polities with similar modes of production or degrees of political complexity (e.g., Feinman and Neitzel 1984; Milanovic et al. 2011).

Traditionally, archaeologists have tended to view diversity within economic modes or political formations (e.g., states) as due to idiosyncratic or cultural factors (e.g., Flannery and Marcus 2012), and, of course, these are relevant. Yet cultural factors clearly cannot account for large shifts in degrees of inequality across specific cultural regions or within polities over time (e.g., Blanton et al. 1996; Feinman 2010; Piketty and Saez 2014). Furthermore, cultural traditions are far from immutable, especially when viewed in the realms of political and economic relations as expressed over long periods (Carballo 2016).

In considering both preindustrial contexts (Blanton et al. 1996; Ember et al. 1997; Feinman 1995) and more-contemporary cases (Acemoglu and Robinson 2000; Phillips 2002; Russett 1964; Turchin 2013), researchers have noted consistent correspondences between political formations that afford greater voice to wider segments of society and lower levels of wealth and inequality (Feinman 2012). At the same time, transdisciplinary research that draws on collective action or public goods games approaches (Olson 1965, 1984), while focused on analytical levels below the entire society, has begun to outline key processes and mechanisms (sensu Hedström and Swedberg 1996:281; Smith 2011) that provide potential bases to explain these co-occurrences (Acemoglu and Robinson 2012; Blanton 2016; Blanton and Fargher 2008). In other words, explanations for the extent of inequality require more than a concern with societal scale, political complexity, available technologies, or mode of production; they necessitate a comprehension of societal institutions and their fiscal underpinnings.

The study of socioeconomic institutions has thus become increasingly central in the social sciences over the past scholarly generation (e.g., Ostrom 1986). To paraphrase Douglass North (1990:3), institutions are the rules of the game governing human social, economic, and political interaction in a specific context. They are the basis for different forms of interpersonal cooperation (Blanton 2016:40–41) and consequently establish bases for patterns of governance, trust, and fairness, and hence degrees of inequality (Kohler et al. 2012; Starmans et al. 2017). Institutions are a consistent feature of both small-scale and larger social networks (e.g., Wiessner 2002). Although similar institutional links have been outlined between modes of governance and expressions of inequality and social stratification by different investigators (Acemoglu and Robinson 2012; Blanton 2016; Blanton and Fargher 2008; Turchin and Nefedov 2009), scholars of the preindustrial past have rarely been able to measure inequality quantitatively, and never in a broad comparative context. A major aim of this book is to change that. In establishing the basis for this assessment, we focus most heavily on the research of Richard Blanton and Lane Fargher (Blanton 2016; Blanton and Fargher 2008) because their analysis of preindustrial polities is closest to our own and their comparative sample is the most robust available.

Whereas most prior works in anthropology and archaeology portrayed ancient states as autocratic, with despotic leaders attempting to control the lives of their subjects, Blanton and Fargher (2008) point out that non-autocratic regimes—collective or even democratic—were not uncommon in the ancient world. They created a numerical scale with autocratic regimes at one end and collective regimes at the other. The scale was composed of three subscales, each measured with a series of variables. The subscales are public goods provision, bureaucratization, and control over leaders. Autocratic rulers do not provide public goods for their subjects, and their regimes have little bureaucracy. There are few checks on the rulers. Collective regimes operate under the opposite conditions—with greater expenditures on public goods, larger bureaucracies, and shared power, so that principals are generally somewhat constrained.

Blanton and Fargher (2008) have developed a causal model in which variation in the ways that governing institutions procure the resources and taxes that underpin their activities is a key determinant of that regime's relative autocracy or collectivity (see also Ross 2004). In states where governance depends on the institutionalized taxation of its subjects, public goods are provided to keep subjects from out-migrating as well as to facilitate production and its distribution. A bureaucracy is necessary to collect taxes and ensure compliance with the state, and if there is a perception of bad governance, there are ways for elites or commoners to remove the ruler. Autocratic regimes, in contrast, get their revenues from external sources, by imperial conquest, the control of spot resources, or taxing/controlling trade. Not dependent on their immediate subjects for revenue, they have little motivation to provide public goods.

Although Blanton and Fargher (2008) do not explicitly discuss how wealth inequality fits into their scheme, their findings are in accord with the notion that more-collective regimes should have lower levels of inequality than more-autocratic regimes. In a more recent analysis, Blanton (2016:261–63) finds statistically significant positive correlations both between more-collective governance and larger distributions of public goods, and between the latter and higher estimated standards of living. At the same time, numerous studies of the modern world have illustrated that more-autocratic regimes have higher levels of inequality than do more-democratic regimes (Acemoglu et al. 2004; Lee 2005; Savoia et al. 2010). If contemporary differences between relatively democratic/ republican and nondemocratic regimes parallel the distinction between premodern collective and autocratic regimes, then inequality should associate with Blanton and Fargher's scale.

If the economic foundations of institutions influence the relative concentrations of wealth and power (Blanton 2016; Blanton and Fargher 2008; Levi 1988), then the ways in which governance and power are funded become key to understanding varying degrees of inequality (e.g., D'Altroy and Earle 1985). This parallels the long-standing concern in political science with why contemporary oil states tend toward such high degrees of inequality, despite ample resources—a phenomenon referred to as "the resource curse" (Ross 1999, 2015). The singular focus of certain contemporary states (e.g., those on the Arabian Peninsula) on "spot resources" like petroleum facilitates the concentration of power and hence greater degrees of inequality (Karl 2004). As noted above, the control of trade routes, war booty from raids (if not widely distributed), and the tending of large herds of pack animals can all be pursued without the extensive participation of local labor. Such activities were far more available to governing institutions in Eurasia and Africa than in the Western Hemisphere (Frankema 2015). Thus, the potential for inequality to rise to high degrees was greater in the Old World than the New, although such possibilities did not always occur, as prospective fiscal foundations were not always consistently realized, nor was their availability necessarily stable.

IN SUMMARY (TOWARD A GENERAL MODEL)

To borrow a concept from quantum physics as a metaphor, the "ground state" for protohuman and early human societies throughout most of the Pleistocene must have been small, mobile societies whose levels of inequality would have been low. Inequality was chiefly limited to embodied differences, certainly including sex and age but presumably also involving characteristics such as size, strength, intelligence, and personality factors. Slow average rates of population increase, likely accelerating a few hundred thousand years ago, were made possible by some suppression of predation. Technological improvements riding the crest of a cumulative culture (Boyd and Richerson 1985:chap. 8), perhaps together with shifts in social organization that improved natality, suppressed infant mortality and promoted longer lives for adults (Kaplan et al. 2000). Group structures characterized by relatively high degrees of variation in spatial cohesion, party size, and party composition were likely common by the Upper Paleolithic if not before (Aureli et al. 2008). Opportunities for differentiation along dimensions of skill and knowledge increased with technological sophistication. Similarly, opportunities for differentiation according to the strength and number of relational ties increased with the social complexity of high rates of group fission and fusion. In general, though, Pleistocene societies fulfill Manus Midlarsky's vision of a world with few material resource scarcities and thus little differentiation in material wealth.

Slow processes thus play a role; so too do events. The end of the Pleistocene brought more-stable climates and, in many places, more-abundant and more-predictable resources (Mattison et al. 2016). Steeper gradients between patches that were dense or poor in resources rewarded territorial behavior and reduced mobility, as did increasing population density. Plant and animal domestication likely coevolved with notions of private property, which prompted a decline in demand sharing within groups (Bowles and Choi 2013). Reduced mobility encouraged accumulation of possessions, made transfer of wealth across generations more efficient, increased population growth rates, and demanded resource intensification—all contributing directly or indirectly to differentiation in material wealth. Midlarsky's world of relative scarcity was at hand. With "a shift in the nature of inter-generational wealth transfers from relatively intangible to material property resources and the opportunities these provided for massively increased inequality," the evolutionary imperative of reproductive success was increasingly best achieved through high parental investment in children and high wealth transfers to them (Shennan 2011:918) rather than simply high numbers of offspring.

The world of the hunter-gatherer was in general Malthusian: populations maintained themselves between states of plenty and states of misery, in accordance with the total output of the local natural system. By the late Neolithic (and also among more-sedentary hunter-gatherers actively engaged in niche construction—see, e.g., Hoffman et al. 2016; Yu 2015; chapter 4, this volume), the even division of resources assumed by the Malthusian model was breaking. Some households became markedly wealthier than others. The extent of their departure depended on how strongly households could couple their existing wealth to their expected income; on the total surplus production; and on the degree of efficiency and security with which resources accumulated by one generation could be transferred to the next. As we will see in chapter 11, these in turn depended on the details of production and distribution in specific societies. Whether elites began as wealth categories (as Marx would have it) or as power brokers (as Weber presumed) may not be easy to determine, because wealth can buy power and power can manipulate to achieve wealth. The body of evidence and theory presented above leads us to suggest that societies may follow different historical paths as elites institutionalize their control—one leading to relatively collective outcomes, the other to more-autocratic alternatives. In chapter 11 we explore the extent to which these alternatives have predictable outcomes for wealth differentials. If this general point of view is correct, a key area for future research is to understand the processes, contexts, and transitional forces that favored one path over another.

HOUSING AND WEALTH INEQUALITY

The chapters in this book focus on inequality in ancient wealth. We define wealth as anything that has value for a household. More formally, wealth is "the total of desirable (i.e., valuable) goods, both social and material, possessed by someone or existing in a community" (Schneider 1974:256; see Smith 1987 for discussion). For nonstate societies, classifying wealth into three categories—embodied, relational, and material—has been useful (Borgerhoff Mulder et al. 2009; Bowles et al. 2010). Discussions of wealth in states commonly focus solely on the material, dividing it first into physical and financial components. The former, obviously of greater relevance to archaeologists, is then divided into durable wealth (land and buildings) and portable wealth (Jones 1980), a scheme that has been adopted in archaeological applications (Smith 1987).

In comparison with other types of physical wealth, the value of a house is almost always the strongest indicator of household wealth in monetary economies because it is typically the most expensive item owned (Clark 2002; Dwyer 2009; Forrest and Murie 1995; Jones 1980; Kamp 1987). Parallel relationships between house size and household wealth have been reported for many precapitalist economies. Sizes of elite and commoner houses usually differ greatly in socially stratified societies (Baer 2014; Bodley 2007:97; Ellis 2000; Olson and Smith 2016). Most studies of peasant villages that provide quantitative data have found that house size is a strong index of household wealth (Blanton 1994; Castro et al. 1981; Tax 1953:table 82; Yang 1945). Timothy Kohler and colleagues (2017: supplemental table 1) report twenty-four citations from historians, ethnographers, and archaeologists validating the common positive relationship between house size and wealth in societies of many different types.

There are some technical advantages to basing Ginis on house size. In chapter 2, Peterson and Drennan discuss possible problems in Ginis when many of the units can take on an identical value (zero, in their example) but just one observation has a small, nonzero value. This leads to a very high (and misleading) Gini value. Their example is based on grave goods. House sizes, in contrast, rarely take on identical values (and certainly cannot have zero area), and even without strong wealth differences a certain amount of variability can be expected for any number of reasons, such as position in the household development cycle or in networks of ceremonial responsibilities. This makes it less likely that high Gini values derived from house-size measures are technical anomalies of no research interest.

The positive relationship between house size and household wealth is not universal, however. Timothy Earle (2017), for example, notes that in the chiefdoms of pre-European Hawai'i, house size was not a marker of wealth (although he does not provide quantitative data). Marion Cutting (2006:239) notes that, in general, "building size does not necessarily indicate family wealth. Instead, it may more accurately reflect household size." Household size, however, is a form of embodied wealth, and embodied and relational wealth are especially prominent distinctions in foraging and horticultural societies (Borgerhoff Mulder et al. 2009). In any case, the validity of house size as an index of household wealth is quite widespread in time and space in the preindustrial world, and that relationship underpins our use of it to measure wealth in the archaeological case studies in this volume.

Compared to other types of inequality, wealth has several advantages as a window into past societies. First, wealth inequality plays a key role in most of the theoretical approaches reviewed above. Second, archaeologists can more easily measure ancient wealth, in comparison to other types of inequality (Morris 2005; Smith 1987). We know next to nothing of ancient income, though Kohler and Rebecca Higgins (2016) have suggested that in Pueblo societies, storage area might be considered to measure expected maize yields for a household (an income measure), whereas they consider total residence size (including storage areas) a better measure of household wealth. Although prestige may or may not be considered as a type of wealth, it is typically more difficult to reconstruct in the past than material wealth.

Nevertheless, we do not want to suggest that wealth is the only kind of ancient inequality worth studying. Differential prestige and power are frequently visible in the archaeological record, and the authors of several chapters in this volume describe Gini analyses of burial assemblages that seem to be measuring prestige instead of (or perhaps in addition to) wealth. This is an area that needs methodological attention to follow up on work like that of John Robb and colleagues (2001).

QUALITY OF LIFE

Beyond measuring wealth inequality, scholars are increasingly interested in broader questions of the quality of life or well-being. These definitions are typical: "Quality of life as a general term is meant to represent either how well human needs are met or the extent to which individuals or groups perceive satisfaction or dissatisfaction in various life domains" (Costanza et al. 2007:268); "Quality of life is a broader concept than economic production and living standards. It includes the full range of factors that influences what we value in living, reaching beyond its material side" (Stiglitz et al. 2010:61).

In this domain Amartya Sen (1984, 1987) has been especially influential. In his formulation, well-being has two components: an economic measure (wealth, income, or standard of living) and a broader domain he calls "capabilities." Capabilities reference the degree to which a person can reach his or her goals, participate in community activities, or achieve a level of literacy to participate in political life. For comparisons of nations, standard of living is measured by per capita economic production and capabilities are measured by life expectancy and mean educational levels (Bagolin and Comim 2008).

Archaeologists have begun to explore approaches to measuring quality of life or well-being (Arponen et al. 2016; Hegmon 2016; Smith 2015, 2016). This work is still in its initial phases, and few studies have attempted to quantify the noneconomic components of quality of life. In this volume the study by Rahul Oka and colleagues (chapter 3) comes closest to measuring quality of life by including a wide range of economic and social indicators of wealth and well-being. We see this as a promising avenue of future research. In focusing on wealth differentials, we do not mean to dismiss the importance of these related quality-of-life measures. It would be particularly interesting to understand the relationship between wealth inequality and quality of life over the long spans of time referenced in this volume.

APPLYING THE GINI COEFFICIENT
TO THE DEEP PAST

Of the many quantitative measures of inequality used by economists and sociologists today, the Gini coefficient is the most widespread (Cowell 2011; Lindert and Williamson 2016; Milanovic 2011, 2016). Named for its inventor, Italian sociologist Corrado Gini (Salvemini 1978), this index is both easy to calculate and intuitive. It measures the degree of concentration of a quantity among the units of a population. In studies of contemporary society, the Gini coefficient is used most commonly to characterize distributions of income and wealth. Gini scores range from 0 for complete equality, where all households have the same amount, to near 1 for complete concentration, where one household has nearly *all* of the income or wealth. One approach to calculation is to arrange the income or wealth values of each unit (typically households) from lowest to highest. This permits drawing a Lorenz curve, which plots income or wealth share against the rank-ordered population of households. A reference line at a 45-degree angle marks the special case where each household commands exactly the same amount of wealth, resulting in a Gini index of 0. Concentration of wealth in the richest households on the right end of the x-axis causes the Lorenz curve to drop down away from the diagonal. If the area below the 45-degree line is considered to be 0.5, the Gini index is equal to twice the area between the 45-degree line of equal wealth dispersion and the actual Lorenz curve. The methodological and distributional characteristics of the Gini coefficient are discussed in more detail in chapter 2.

The ease of calculation and intuitive nature of the Gini coefficient make it useful for the quantitative measurement of wealth in the past, and it has become the standard for studies of inequality using historical documents (e.g., Curtis 2013; Lindert and Williamson 2016; Milanovic et al. 2011). Randall McGuire's research on Hohokam burials was the first published archaeological study on inequality using the Gini coefficient (McGuire 1983; McGuire and Schiffer 1982). A decade later, Michael Smith applied the method to Aztec villages in Mexico (Smith 1992, 1994; see also Smith et al. 2014). Since then, a growing number of archaeologists have published studies of ancient inequality (figure 1.2); many of those are authors of the chapters that follow.

Because the quantitative measurement of inequality is a new direction of research in archaeology, the chapters in this book make many diverse contributions: methodological, empirical, and conceptual. Chapters 4–6 describe societies—hunter-gatherers and villagers in the U.S. Southwest—that until fairly recently have been considered to be egalitarian. While archaeologists now accept the existence of inequality in these societies, these chapters (and prior work by their authors) provide crucial data quantifying that degree of inequality. One striking pattern in

A. Published works

	Housing	Domestic artifacts	Burial goods
Foraging			Schulting (1995)
Horticultural	Porčić (2012) Pailes (2014) Kohler & Higgins (2016)	Hayden & Cannon (1984) Peterson et al. (2016)	McGuire (1983) Mitchell (1992) Windler et al. (2013)
Agricultural	Smith (1993) Liendo Stuardo (2002) Smith et al. (2014) Brown et al. (2014) Kron (2011) Ober (2015) Chase (2017)		Castillos (2006)

B. Chapters in this volume

	Housing	Domestic artifacts	Burial goods
Foraging	Ch 4, Prentiss et al.	Ch 4, Prentiss et al.	
Horticultural	Ch 2, Peterson & Drennan Ch 5, Kohler & Ellyson Ch 6, Pailes Ch 7, Betzenhauser Ch 8, Bogaard et al.	Ch 2, Peterson & Drennan Ch 3, Oka et al.	Ch 2, Peterson & Drennan
Agricultural	Ch 8, Bogaard et al. Ch 9, Stone Ch 10, Feinman et al.	Ch 3, Oka et al. Ch 10, Feinman et al.	Ch 9, Stone

Figure 1.2 Archaeological studies of inequality using the Gini coefficient: *A*, published works; *B*, chapters in this volume.

almost all of the chapters is that the level of inequality varied greatly in the past, although the Hohokam study in chapter 6 provides an apparent exception. Levels of inequality typically changed through time within regions, often fluctuating around a mean rather than following a long-term trajectory of continuous change (chapters 4, 9, 10). Inequality was also variable among regions. And in one case, where inequality followed a similar trajectory in two areas, the causal dynamics were distinct in each region (chapter 8). This high level of variability cautions scholars to avoid claiming the existence of "typical" levels of inequality for specific sites, regions, or types of society. This does not mean, however, that there are not large-scale patterns in our data, and we explore these in detail in chapter 11.

Another intriguing finding of some chapters is that social inequality was not always as tightly linked to economic and political institutions as standard social models posit. In chapter 6, for example, Matthew Pailes shows that increases in political hierarchy and complexity in the Hohokam region were apparently not accompanied by expected increases in wealth inequality. In chapter 11 we present data showing that one of the largest cities in ancient central Mexico—the huge imperial capital Teotihuacan—had one of the lowest inequality levels in the region. In other cases, the Gini data confirm long-standing expectations in the literature. Thus, it is no surprise that Chaco Canyon at its apogee had high levels of inequality compared to other nearby regions of the Southwest (chapter 5) or that Cahokia at its peak shows the greatest inequality within the American Bottom area (chapter 7). And in Aztec-period central Mexico it is not at all surprising that towns and cities had far higher levels of inequality than villages (Smith et al. 2014; chapter 11, this volume).

As is appropriate for a new line of research, all the chapters make methodological advances. Most are pertinent to measurement and sampling. Archaeologists—unlike economists studying inequality today— cannot obtain handy online standardized income or wealth data to analyze. We have to go through many steps of fieldwork, analysis, and data transformation before we can calculate a Gini coefficient, and each step in this process raises methodological considerations. This chapter and chapter 2 both have some discussion of the Gini index, but every chapter presents new and important procedures for studying inequality in the past. Chapters 2, 6, and 8 introduce more-sophisticated measures and methods that go beyond calculation of the Gini index. Several chapters (e.g., 9 and 10) present calculated Gini values for more than one type of data. Although collectively these results move us forward in understanding how inequality is expressed in different domains, there is still much to be done. For example, there remain real obstacles to comparing the results of Gini values calculated from burial data to those calculated from architectural and artifactual data. This is a topic in need of more methodological attention by archaeologists.

We should note that the case studies in this volume are far from a random sample of ancient societies. They were selected because their authors had sets of data amenable to calculation of Gini indices and were interested in exploring this approach. Because we lack case studies from important regions—including South America, sub-Saharan Africa, and Southeast Asia—we cannot claim to have sampled all relevant world areas. But the comparative patterns we identify in chapter 11 are clear, and we hope that our work stimulates archaeologists to apply our methods and approach in a wider geographic range of ancient societies.

AIMS OF THE VOLUME

Our primary aim is to present a series of comparable, quantified, empirically based studies of wealth inequality from the deep past to engage the broad transdisciplinary literature on the origins, history, diversity, and causes of inequities in human societies. More specifically, we endeavor to establish a dialogue with current debates over the suite of factors (e.g., mode of production, societal scale, political complexity, technology, institutional variability) postulated to promote or impede shifts in wealth inequality. To achieve these goals we first probe specific times and places in the deep past—in chapters 2 through 10—before turning our attention in chapter 11 to broadly comparative historical trends.

REFERENCES CITED

Acemoglu, Daron, and James A. Robinson. 2000. Why Did the West Extend the Franchise? Democracy, Inequality, and Growth in Historical Perspective. *Quarterly Journal of Economics* 115:1167–99.

———. 2012. *Why Nations Fail.* Crown, New York.

Acemoglu, Daron, Thierry Verdier, and James A. Robinson. 2004. Kleptocracy and Divide-and-Rule: A Model of Personal Rule. *Journal of the European Economic Association* 2(2–3):162–92.

Anthony, David W., and Dorcas R. Brown. 2011. The Secondary Products Revolution, Horse-Riding, and Mounted Warfare. *Journal of World Prehistory* 24:131–60.

Arnold, Jeanne E. 1996. The Archaeology of Complex Hunter-Gatherers. *Journal of Archaeological Method and Theory* 3(1):77–126.

Arponen, V. P. J., Johannes Müller, Robert Hofmann, Martin Furholt, Artur Ribeiro, Christian Horn, and Martin Hinz. 2016. Using the Capability Approach to Conceptualise Inequality in Archaeology: The Case of the Late Neolithic Bosnian Site Okolište c. 5200–4600 BCE. *Journal of Archaeological Method and Theory* 23(2):541–60.

Aureli, Fiolippo, Colleen M. Schaffner, Christophe Boesch, Simon K. Bearder, Josep Call, Colin A. Chapman, Richard Connor, et al. 2008. Fission-Fusion Dynamics: New Research Frameworks. *Current Anthropology* 49(4):627–54.

Baer, William C. 2014. Using Housing Quality to Track Change in the Standard of Living and Poverty for Seventeenth-Century London. *Historical Methods: A Journal of Quantitative and Interdisciplinary History* 47(1):1–18.

Bagolin, Izete Pengo, and Flavio V. Comim. 2008. Human Development Index (HDI) and Its Family of Indexes: An Evolving Critical Review. *Revista de Economia* 34(2):7–28.

Blanton, Richard E. 1994. *Houses and Households: A Comparative Study.* Plenum, New York.

———. 2016. *How Humans Cooperate: Confronting the Challenges of Collective Action.* University Press of Colorado, Boulder.

Blanton, Richard E., and Lane F. Fargher. 2008. *Collective Action in the Formation of Pre-modern States.* Springer, New York.

Blanton, Richard E., Gary M. Feinman, Stephen A. Kowalewski, and Peter N. Peregrine. 1996. Dual-Processual Theory for the Evolution of Mesoamerican Civilization. *Current Anthropology* 37:1–14, 65–68.

Bocquet-Appel, Jean-Pierre. 2002. Paleoanthropological Traces of a Neolithic Demographic Transition. *Current Anthropology* 43(4):637–50.

Bodley, John H. 2007. *Anthropology and Contemporary Human Problems.* 5th ed. AltaMira, Lanham, Md.

Borgerhoff Mulder, Monique, Samuel Bowles, Tom Hertz, Adrian Bell, Jan Beise, Greg Clark, Ila Fazzio, et al. 2009. Intergenerational Wealth Transmission and the Dynamics of Inequality in Small-Scale Societies. *Science* 326:682–88.

Bowles, Samuel. 2009. Did Warfare Among Ancestral Hunter-Gatherers Affect the Evolution of Human Social Behaviors? *Science* 324:1293–98.

———. 2012. *The New Economics of Inequality and Redistribution.* Cambridge University Press, New York.

Bowles, Samuel, and Jung-Kyoo Choi. 2013. Coevolution of Farming and Private Property During the Early Holocene. *PNAS* 110(22):8830–35.

Bowles, Samuel, Eric Alden Smith, and Monique Borgerhoff Mulder. 2010. The Emergence and Persistence of Inequality in Premodern Societies: Introduction to the Special Section. *Current Anthropology* 51(1):7–17.

Boyd, Robert, Herbert Gintis, and Samuel Bowles. 2010. Coordinated Punishment of Defectors Sustains Cooperation and Can Proliferate When Rare. *Science* 328:617–20.

Boyd, Robert, and Peter Richerson. 1985. *Culture and the Evolutionary Process.* University of Chicago Press, Chicago.

Brown, Clifford T., April A. Watson, Ashley Gravlin-Beman, and Larry S. Liebovitch. 2014. Poor Mayapan. In *The Ancient Maya of Mexico: Reinterpreting the Past of the Northern Maya Lowlands*, edited by Geoffrey E. Braswell, pp. 306–24. Routledge, New York.

Carballo, David M. 2016. *Urbanization and Religion in Ancient Central Mexico.* Oxford University Press, New York.

Carballo, David M., Paul Roscoe, and Gary M. Feinman. 2014. Cooperation and Collective Action in the Cultural Evolution of Complex Societies. *Journal of Archaeological Method and Theory* 21:98–133.

Carneiro, Robert L. 1970. A Theory of the Origin of the State. *Science* 169:733–38.

Castillos, Juan José. 2006. Social Stratification in Early Egypt. *Göttinger Miszellen: Beiträge zur ägyptologischen Diskussion* 210:13–18.

Castro, Alfonso Peter, N. Thomas Hakansson, and David Brokensha. 1981. Indicators of Rural Inequality. *World Development* 9(5):401–27.

Chase, Adrian S. Z. 2017. Residential Inequality Among the Ancient Maya: Operationalizing Household Architectural Volume at Caracol, Belize. *Research Reports in Belizean Archaeology* 14:31–39.

Clark, Gregory. 2002. Shelter from the Storm: Housing and the Industrial Revolution, 1550–1909. *Journal of Economic History* 62(2):489–511.

Collins, Randall. 1988. *Theoretical Sociology.* Harcourt, Brace, Jovanovich, New York.

———. 2004. Lenski's Power Theory of Economic Inequality: A Central Neglected Question in Stratification Research. *Sociological Theory* 22(2):219–28.

Costanza, Robert, Brendan Fisher, Saleem Ali, Caroline Beer, Lynne Bond, Roelof Boumans, Nicholas L. Danigelis, et al. 2007. Quality of Life: An Approach Integrating Opportunities, Human Needs, and Subjective Well-Being. *Ecological Economics* 61(2–3):267–76.

Cowell, Frank A. 2011. *Measuring Inequality.* 3rd ed. Oxford University Press, New York.

Crabtree, Stefani A., R. Kyle Bocinsky, Paul L. Hooper, Susan C. Ryan, and Timothy A. Kohler. 2017. How to Make a Polity (in the Central Mesa Verde Region). *American Antiquity* 82(1):71–95.

Curtis, Daniel R. 2013. Is There an "Agro-Town" Model for Southern Italy? Exploring the Diverse Roots and Development of the Agro-Town Structure Through a Comparative Case Study in Apulia. *Continuity and Change* 28(3):377–419.

Cutting, Marion. 2006. More Than One Way to Study a Building: Approaches to Prehistoric Household and Settlement Space. *Oxford Journal of Archaeology* 25:225–46.

D'Altroy, Terrence N., and Timothy K. Earle. 1985. Staple Finance, Wealth Finance, and Storage in the Inka Political Economy. *Current Anthropology* 26:187–206.

Davis, Kingsley, and Wilbert E. Moore. 1945. Some Principles of Stratification. *American Sociological Review* 10(2):242–49.

Diamond, Jared. 1997. *Guns, Germs, and Steel: The Fates of Human Societies.* Norton, New York.

Dubreuil, Benoît. 2010. *Human Evolution and the Origins of Hierarchies: The State of Nature.* Cambridge University Press, New York.

Dunbar, Robin I. M. 1992. Neocortex Size as a Constraint on Group Size in Primates. *Journal of Human Evolution* 22 (6):469–493.

Durkheim, Emile. 2014. *The Division of Labor in Society.* Simon and Schuster, New York. Orig. pub. 1893.

Dwyer, Rachel E. 2009. The McMansionization of America? Income Stratification and the Standard of Living in Housing, 1960–2000. *Research in Social Stratification and Mobility* 27(4):285–300.

Earle, Timothy. 1997. *How Chiefs Come to Power: The Political Economy in Prehistory.* Stanford University Press, Stanford.

———. 2017. Wealth Inequality and the Pristine Hawaiian State: A Political Economy Approach. *Origini* 38:195–210.

Ellis, Simon P. 2000. *Roman Housing.* Duckworth, London.

Ember, Melvin, Carol Ember, and Bruce Russett. 1997. Inequality and Democracy in the Anthropological Record. In *Inequality, Democracy, and Economic Development,* edited by Manus I. Midlarsky, pp. 110–30. Cambridge University Press, New York.

Feinman, Gary M. 1995. The Emergence of Inequality: A Focus on Strategies and Processes. In *Foundations of Social Inequality,* edited by T. Douglas Price and Gary M. Feinman, pp. 255–79. Plenum Press, New York.

———. 2010. A Dual-Processual Perspective on Power and Inequality in the Contemporary United States: Framing Political Economy for the Present and the Past. In *Pathways to Power,* edited by T. Douglas Price and Gary M. Feinman, pp. 255–88. Springer, New York.

———. 2012. Comparative Frames for the Diachronic Analysis of Complex Societies: Next Steps. In *The Comparative Archaeology of Complex Societies,* edited by Michael E. Smith, pp. 21–43. Cambridge University Press, Cambridge.

———. 2013. The Emergence of Social Complexity: Why More Than Population Size Matters. In *Cooperation and Collective Action: Archaeological Perspectives,* edited by David M. Carballo, pp. 35–56. University Press of Colorado, Boulder.

Feinman, Gary M., and Jill Neitzel. 1984. Too Many Types: An Overview of Sedentary Prestate Societies in the Americas. *Advances in Archaeological Method and Theory* 7:39–102.

Flanagan, James G. 1989. Hierarchy in Simple "Egalitarian" Societies. *Annual Review of Anthropology* 18:245–66.

Flannery, Kent V., and Joyce Marcus. 2012. *The Creation of Inequality: How Our Prehistoric Ancestors Set the Stage for Monarchy, Slavery, and Empire.* Harvard University Press, Cambridge, Mass.

Forrest, Ray, and Alan Murie (editors). 1995. *Housing and Family Wealth: Comparative International Perspectives.* Routledge, New York.

Frankema, Ewout. 2015. The Biogeographic Roots of World Inequality: Animals, Disease, and Human Settlement Patterns in Africa and the Americas Before 1492. *World Development* 70:274–85.

Golitko, Mark, James Meierhoff, Gary M. Feinman, and Patrick Ryan Williams. 2012. Complexities of Collapse: Maya Obsidian as Revealed by Social Network Analysis. *Antiquity* 86:507–23.

Graeber, David. 2011. *Debt: The First 5,000 Years.* Melville House, New York.

Gremillion, K. J., L. Barton, and D. R. Piperno. 2014. Particularism and the Retreat from Theory in the Archaeology of Agricultural Origins. *PNAS* 111(17):6171–77.

Gurven, Michael, Monique Borgerhoff Mulder, Paul L. Hooper, Hillard Kaplan, Robert Quinlan, Rebecca Sear, Eric Schniter, et al. 2010. Domestication Alone Does Not Lead to Inequality: Intergenerational Wealth Transmission Among Horticulturalists. *Current Anthropology* 51(1):49–64.

Haas, Ain. 1993. Social Inequality in Aboriginal North America: A Test of Lenski's Theory. *Social Forces* 72(2):295–313.

Halstead, Paul. 1995. Plough and Power: The Economic and Social Significance of Cultivation with the Ox-Drawn Ard in the Mediterranean. *Bulletin on Sumerian Agriculture* 8:11–22.

Hamilton, Marcus J., Bruce T. Milne, Robert S. Walker, Oskar Burger, and James H. Brown. 2007. The Complex Structure of Hunter-Gatherer Social Networks. *Proceedings of the Royal Society of London B: Biological Sciences* 274:2195–2203.

Hayden, Brian, and Aubrey Cannon. 1984. *The Structure of Material Systems: Ethnoarchaeology in the Maya Highlands.* Papers, vol. 3. Society for American Archaeology, Washington, D.C.

Hedström, Peter, and Richard Swedberg. 1996. Social Mechanisms. *Acta Sociologica* 39:281–308.

Hegmon, Michelle (editor). 2016. *Archaeology of the Human Experience.* Archaeological Papers 27. American Anthropological Association, Washington, D.C.

Hoffman, Tanja, Natasha Lyons, Debbie Miller, Alejandra Diaz, Amy Homan, Stephanie Huddlestan, Roma Leon, et al. 2016. Engineered Feature Used to Enhance Gardening at a 3800-Year-Old Site on the Pacific Northwest Coast. *Science Advances* 2:e1601282.

Holton, Robert J. 2015. Global Inequality. In *The Routledge International Handbook of Globalization Studies*, edited by Bryan S. Turner and Robert J. Holton, pp. 60–77. 2nd ed. Routledge, New York.

Johnson, Allen W., and Timothy K. Earle. 2000. *The Evolution of Human Societies: From Foraging Group to Agrarian State.* 2nd ed. Stanford University Press, Stanford.

Johnson, Gregory A. 1978. Information Sources and the Development of Decision-Making Organizations. In *Social Archaeology: Beyond Subsistence and Dating*, edited by Charles L. Redman, pp. 87–112. Academic Press, New York.

Jones, Alice H. 1980. *Wealth of a Nation to Be: The American Colonies on the Eve of the Revolution*. Columbia University Press, New York.

Kamp, Kathryn A. 1987. Affluence and Image: Ethnoarchaeology in a Syrian Village. *Journal of Field Archaeology* 14:283–96.

Kaplan, H. S., K. R. Hill, J. B. Lancaster, and A. M. Hurtado. 2000. A Theory of Human Life History Evolution: Diet, Intelligence, and Longevity. *Evolutionary Anthropology* 9:156–85.

Karl, Terry Lynn. 2004. Oil-Led Development: Social, Political, and Economic Consequences. In *Encyclopedia of Energy*, edited by Cutler Cleveland, 4:661–72. Elsevier, Amsterdam.

Kerbo, Harold R. 2011. *Social Stratification and Inequality: Class Conflict in Historical, Comparative, and Global Perspective*. 8th ed. McGraw-Hill, New York.

Khaldûn, Ibn. 1958. *The Muqaddimah: An Introduction to History*. 3 vols. Translated by Franz Rosenthal. Bollingen Foundation, New York. Orig. pub. 1377.

King, John E. 2016. The Literature on Piketty. *Review of Political Economy* 21(1):1–17.

Kohler, Timothy A., Denton Cockburn, Paul L. Hooper, R. Kyle Bocinsky, and Ziad Kobti. 2012. The Coevolution of Group Size and Leadership: An Agent-Based Public Goods Model for Prehispanic Pueblo Societies. *Advances in Complex Systems* 15(1–2):1150007. doi:10.1142/S0219525911003256.

Kohler, Timothy A., and Rebecca Higgins. 2016. Quantifying Household Inequality in Early Pueblo Villages. *Current Anthropology* 57(5):690–97.

Kohler, Timothy A., and Kelsey M. Reese. 2014. Long and Spatially Variable Neolithic Demographic Transition in the North American Southwest. *PNAS* 111 (28):10101–6.

Kohler, Timothy A., Michael E. Smith, Amy Bogaard, Gary M. Feinman, Christian E. Peterson, Alleen Betzenhauser, Matthew Pailes, et al. 2017. Greater Post-Neolithic Wealth Disparities in Eurasia than in North and Mesoamerica. *Nature* 551:619–22. doi:10.1038/nature24646.

Kohler, Timothy A., and Mark D. Varien (editors). 2012. *Emergence and Collapse of Early Villages: Models of Central Mesa Verde Archaeology*. University of California Press, Berkeley.

Kron, Geoffrey. 2011. The Distribution of Wealth at Athens in Comparative Perspective. *Zeitschrift für Papyrologie und Epigraphik* 179:129–38.

Krugman, Paul. 2014. Why We're in a New Gilded Age. *New York Review of Books*, May 8, 2014. www.nybooks.com/articles/2014/05/08/thomas-piketty -new-gilded-age/.

Laslett, Barbara. 2000. The Poverty of (Monocausal) Theory: A Comment on Charles Tilly's Durable Inequality. *Comparative Studies in Society and History* 42(2):475–81.

Lee, Cheol-Sung. 2005. Income Inequality, Democracy, and Public Sector Size. *American Sociological Review* 70(1):158–81.

Lenski, Gerhard E. 1966. *Power and Privilege: A Theory of Social Stratification.* McGraw-Hill, New York.

Leon-Portilla, Miguel. 1962. *The Broken Spears: The Aztec Account of the Conquest of Mexico.* Beacon Press, Boston.

Levi, Margaret. 1988. *Of Rule and Revenue.* University of California Press, Berkeley.

Liendo Stuardo, Rodrigo. 2002. *La organización de la producción agrícola en un centro Maya del clásico: Patrón de asentamiento en la región de Palenque / The Organization of Agricultural Production at a Classic Maya Center: Settlement Patterns in the Palenque Region, Chiapas, Mexico.* Instituto Nacional de Antropología e Historia, Mexico City; University of Pittsburgh, Pittsburgh.

Lindert, Peter H., and Jeffrey G. Williamson. 2016. *Unequal Gains: American Growth and Inequality Since 1700.* Princeton University Press, Princeton.

Marx, Karl, and Frederick Engels. 1969. *Manifesto of the Communist Party.* In *Marx/Engels Selected Works*, vol. 1, pp. 98–137. Progress Publishers, Moscow. Orig. pub. 1848.

Mattison, Siobhan M., Eric A. Smith, Mary K. Shenk, and Ethan Cochrane. 2016. The Evolution of Inequality. *Evolutionary Anthropology* 25:184–99.

McGuire, Randall H. 1983. Breaking Down Cultural Complexity: Inequality and Heterogeneity. *Advances in Archaeological Method and Theory* 6:91–142.

McGuire, Randall, and Michael B. Schiffer. 1982. *Hohokam and Patayan: Prehistory of Southwestern Arizona.* Academic Press, New York.

McNeill, William H. 1963. *The Rise of the West: A History of the Human Community.* University of Chicago Press, Chicago.

Midlarsky, Manus I. 1999. *The Evolution of Inequality: War, State Survival, and Democracy in Comparative Perspective.* Stanford University Press, Stanford.

Milanovic, Branko. 2011. *The Haves and the Have-Nots: A Brief and Idiosyncratic History of Global Inequality.* Basic Books, New York.

———. 2016. *Global Inequality: A New Approach for the Age of Globalization.* Belknap Press, Cambridge, Mass.

Milanovic, Branko, Peter H. Lindert, and Jeffrey G. Williamson. 2011. Preindustrial Inequality. *Economic Journal* 121:255–72.

Mitchell, Douglas R. 1992. The Pueblo Grande Artifact Analysis: A Search for Wealth, Ranking, and Prestige. In *The Pueblo Grande Project: An Analysis of Classic Period Hohokam Mortuary Practices at Pueblo Grande*, edited by Douglas R. Mitchell, pp. 129–80. Soil Systems Publications, Phoenix.

Morris, Ian. 2005. Archaeology, Standards of Living, and Greek Economic History. In *The Ancient Economy: Evidence and Models*, edited by J. G. Manning and Ian Morris, pp. 91–126. Stanford University Press, Stanford.

Mosse, David. 2010. A Relational Approach to Durable Poverty, Inequality and Power. *Journal of Development Studies* 46(7):1156–78.

North, Douglass C. 1990. *Institutions, Institutional Change, and Economic Performance.* Cambridge University Press, Cambridge.

Ober, Josiah. 2015. *The Rise and Fall of Classical Greece*. Princeton University Press, Princeton.

O'Connell, Michael. 2010. *Affluence Versus Equality? A Critique of Wilkinson and Pickett's Book "The Spirit Level."* Working Papers. Psychology Research Collection, University College Dublin, Dublin.

Olson, Jan Marie, and Michael E. Smith. 2016. Material Expressions of Wealth and Social Class at Aztec-Period Sites in Morelos, Mexico. *Ancient Mesoamerica* 27(1):133–47.

Olson, Mancur. 1965. *The Logic of Collective Action: Public Goods and the Theory of Groups*. Harvard University Press, Cambridge, Mass.

———. 1984. *The Rise and Decline of Nations: Economic Growth, Stagflation, and Social Rigidities*. Yale University Press, New Haven, Conn.

Ostrom, Elinor. 1986. An Agenda for the Study of Institutions. *Public Choice* 48:3–25.

Pailes, Matthew C. 2014. Social Network Analysis of Early Classic Hohokam Corporate Group Inequality. *American Antiquity* 79(3):465–86.

Peterson, Christian E., Robert D. Drennan, and Kate L. Bartel. 2016. Comparative Analysis of Neolithic Household Artifact Assemblage Data from Northern China. *Journal of Anthropological Research* 72(2):200–225.

Petit, Jean-Robert, Jean Jouzel, Dominique Raynaud, Narcisse I. Barkov, J.-M. Barnola, Isabelle Basile, Michael Bender, J. Chappellaz, M. Davis, and G. Delaygue. 1999. Climate and Atmospheric History of the Past 420,000 Years from the Vostok Ice Core, Antarctica. *Nature* 399:429–36.

Phillips, Kevin. 2002. *Wealth and Democracy*. Broadway Books, New York.

Piketty, Thomas. 2014. *Capital in the Twenty-First Century*. Belknap Press, Cambridge, Mass.

Piketty, Thomas, and Emmanuel Saez. 2014. Inequality in the Long Run. *Science* 344:838–43.

Porčić, Marko. 2012. Social Complexity and Inequality in the Late Neolithic of the Central Balkans: Reviewing the Evidence. *Documenta Praehistorica* 39:167–83.

Price, T. Douglas, and Gary M. Feinman (editors). 1995. *Foundations of Social Inequality*. Plenum, New York.

Pringle, Heather. 2014. The Ancient Roots of the 1%. *Science* 344:822–25.

Reeves, Aaron. 2017. The Architecture of Inequality. *Nature* 543:312–13.

Robb, John, Renzo Bigazzi, Luca Lazzarini, Caterina Scarsini, and Fiorenza Sonego. 2001. Social "Status" and Biological "Status": A Comparison of Grave Goods and Skeletal Indicators from Pontecagnano. *American Journal of Physical Anthropology* 115(3):213–22.

Rosenberg, Michael. 1998. Cheating at Musical Chairs: Territoriality and Sedentism in an Evolutionary Context. *Current Anthropology* 39:653–81.

Ross, Michael L. 1999. The Political Economy of the Resource Curse. *World Politics* 51:297–322.

———. 2004. Does Taxation Lead to Representation? *British Journal of Political Science* 34:229–49.

————. 2015. What Have We Learned About the Resource Curse? *Annual Review of Political Science* 18:239–59.

Russett, Bruce M. 1964. Inequality and Instability: The Relation of Land Tenure to Politics. *World Politics* 16:442–54.

Salvemini, Tommaso. 1978. Corrado Gini. In *International Encyclopedia of Statistics*, edited by William H. Kruskal and Judith M. Tanur, 1:394–98. Free Press, New York.

Santone, Lenore. 1997. Transport Costs, Consumer Demand, and Patterns of Intraregional Exchange: A Perspective on Commodity Production and Distribution from Northern Belize. *Latin American Antiquity* 8:71–88.

Savoia, Antonio, Joshy Easaw, and Andrew McKay. 2010. Inequality, Democracy, and Institutions: A Critical Review of Recent Research. *World Development* 38(2):142–54.

Scheidel, Walter. 2017. *The Great Leveler: Violence and the History of Inequality from the Stone Age to the Twenty-First Century*. Princeton University Press, Princeton.

Schneider, Harold K. 1974. *Economic Man*. Free Press, New York.

Schulting, Rick J. 1995. *Mortuary Variability and Status Differentiation on the Columbia-Fraser Plateau*. Archaeology Press, Burnaby, B.C.

Sen, Amartya K. 1984. The Living Standard. *Oxford Economic Papers* 36 (supplement):74–90.

————. 1987. The Standard of Living II: Lives and Capabilities. In *The Standard of Living*, edited by Geoffrey Hawthorn, pp. 20–38. Cambridge University Press, New York.

Service, Elman R. 1966. *Primitive Social Organization*. Random House, New York.

Shennan, Stephen. 2011. Property and Wealth Inequality as Cultural Niche Construction. *Philosophical Transactions of the Royal Society of London, Series B, Biological Sciences* 366:918–926. doi:10.1098/rstb.2010.0309.

Smith, Eric Alden, Monique Borgerhoff Mulder, Samuel Bowles, Michael Gurven, Tom Hertz, and Mary K. Shenk. 2010. Production Systems, Inheritance, and Inequality in Premodern Societies: Conclusions. *Current Anthropology* 51:85–94.

Smith, M. G. 1966. Pre-industrial Stratification Systems. In *Social Structure and Mobility in Economic Development*, edited by Neil J. Smelser and Seymour M. Lipset, pp. 141–76. Aldine, Chicago.

Smith, Michael E. 1987. Household Possessions and Wealth in Agrarian States: Implications for Archaeology. *Journal of Anthropological Archaeology* 6:297–335.

————. 1992. *Archaeological Research at Aztec-Period Rural Sites in Morelos, Mexico*, vol. 1, *Excavations and Architecture / Investigaciones arqueológicas en sitios rurales de la época Azteca en Morelos*, tomo 1, *Excavaciones y arquitectura*. Memoirs in Latin American Archaeology 4. University of Pittsburgh, Pittsburgh.

———. 1994. Social Complexity in the Aztec Countryside. In *Archaeological Views from the Countryside: Village Communities in Early Complex Societies*, edited by Glenn Schwartz and Steven Falconer, pp. 143–59. Smithsonian Institution Press, Washington, D.C.

———. 2011. Empirical Urban Theory for Archaeologists. *Journal of Archaeological Method and Theory* 18:167–92.

———. 2012. *The Aztecs*. 3rd ed. Blackwell Publishers, Oxford, U.K.

———. 2015. Quality of Life and Prosperity in Ancient Households and Communities. In *The Oxford Handbook of Historical Ecology and Applied Archaeology* (online publication), edited by Christian Isendahl and Daryl Stump. Oxford University Press, New York.

———. 2016. *At Home with the Aztecs: An Archaeologist Uncovers Their Domestic Life*. Routledge, New York.

Smith, Michael E., Timothy Dennehy, April Kamp-Whittaker, Emily Colon, and Rebecca Harkness. 2014. Quantitative Measures of Wealth Inequality in Ancient Central Mexican Communities. *Advances in Archaeological Practice* 2(4):311–23.

Starmans, Christina, Mark Sheskin, and Paul Bloom. 2017. Perspective: Why People Prefer Unequal Societies. *Nature Human Behaviour* (online) 1, Article #0082.

Ste. Croix, G. E. M. de. 1981. *The Class Struggle in the Ancient Greek World*. Duckworth, London.

Stiglitz, Joseph E. 2012. *The Price of Inequality: How Today's Divided Society Endangers Our Future*. Norton, New York.

Stiglitz, Joseph E., Amartya Sen, and Jean-Paul Fitoussi. 2010. *Mismeasuring Our Lives: Why GDP Doesn't Add Up*. New Press, New York.

Sussman, Robert W., and Roberta L. Hall. 1972. Addendum: Child Transport, Family Size, and Increase in Human Population During the Neolithic. *Current Anthropology* 13(2):258–67.

Tax, Sol. 1953. *Penny Capitalism: A Guatemalan Indian Economy*. Publication 16. Smithsonian Institution, Institute of Social Anthropology, Washington, D.C.

Therborn, Göran. 2006. Meaning, Mechanisms, Patterns, and Forces: An Introduction. In *Inequalities of the World: New Theoretical Frameworks, Multiple Empirical Approaches*, edited by Göran Therborn, pp. 1–58. Verso, New York.

Thomas, Reuben J., and Noah P. Mark. 2013. Population Size, Network Density, and the Emergence of Inherited Inequality. *Social Forces* 92(2):521–44.

Tilly, Charles. 1998. *Durable Inequality*. University of California Press, Berkeley.

———. 2001. Relational Origins of Inequality. *Anthropological Theory* 1(3):355–72.

———. 2005. Historical Perspectives on Inequality. In *The Blackwell Companion to Social Inequalities*, edited by Mary Romero and Eric Margolis, pp. 15–30. Wiley-Blackwell, Malden, Mass.

Tomaskovic-Devey, Donald, Dustin Avent-Holt, Catherine Zimmer, and Sandra Harding. 2009. The Categorical Generation of Organizational Inequality: A Comparative Test of Tilly's Durable Inequality. *Research in Social Stratification and Mobility* 27:128–42.

Trigger, Bruce G. 2003. *Understanding Early Civilizations: A Comparative Study.* Cambridge University Press, New York.

———. 2006. *A History of Archaeological Thought.* 2nd ed. Cambridge University Press, New York.

Turchin, Peter. 2009. A Theory for Formation of Large Empires. *Journal of Global History* 4:191–217.

———. 2013. Return of the Oppressed. *Aeon,* February 7. https://aeon.co/essays/history-tells-us-where-the-wealth-gap-leads.

Turchin, Peter, Thomas E. Currie, Edward A. L. Turner, and Sergey Gavrilets. 2013. War, Space, and the Evolution of Old World Complex Societies. *PNAS* 110:16384–89.

Turchin, Peter, and Sergey A. Nefedov. 2009. *Secular Cycles.* Princeton University Press, Princeton.

Turner, Jonathan H. 1984. *Societal Stratification: A Theoretical Analysis.* Columbia University Press, New York.

Vallas, Steven, and Emily Cummins. 2014. Relational Models of Organizational Inequalities: Emerging Approaches and Conceptual Dilemmas. *American Behavioral Scientist* 58(2):228–55.

Voss, Kim. 2010. Enduring Legacy? Charles Tilly and Durable Inequality. *American Sociologist* 41:368–74.

White, Leslie A. 1943. Energy and the Evolution of Culture. *American Anthropologist* 45:335–56.

Wiessner, Polly. 2002. The Vines of Complexity: Egalitarian Structure and the Institutionalization of Inequality Among the Enga. *Current Anthropology* 43:233–52.

Wilkinson, Richard G., and Kate Pickett. 2009. *The Spirit Level: Why Greater Equality Makes Societies Stronger.* Bloomsbury Press, New York.

Williamson, Jeffrey G. 2010. Five Centuries of Latin American Income Inequality. *Revista de Historia Económica* 28 (special issue 2):227–52.

Windler, Arne, Rainer Thiele, and Johannes Müller. 2013. Increasing Inequality in Chalcolithic Southeast Europe: The Case of Durankulak. *Journal of Archaeological Science* 40(1):204–10.

Wittfogel, Karl A. 1957. *Oriental Despotism: A Comparative Study of Total Power.* Yale University Press, New Haven, Conn.

Wright, Erik Olin. 2000. Metatheoretical Foundations of Charles Tilly's Durable Inequality. *Comparative Studies in Society and History* 42(2):458–74.

Yang, Martin C. 1945. *A Chinese Village: Taitou, Shantung Province.* Columbia University Press, New York.

Yu, Pei-Lin. 2015. *Rivers, Fish, and the People.* University of Utah Press, Salt Lake City.

Zeder, M. A. 2012. The Broad Spectrum Revolution at 40: Resource Diversity, Intensification, and an Alternative to Optimal Foraging Explanations. *Journal of Anthropological Archaeology* 31(3):241–64.

2

Letting the Gini Out of the Bottle

Measuring Inequality Archaeologically

Christian E. Peterson and Robert D. Drennan

Often used by economists to measure economic inequality between individuals or households in a population, Gini coefficients have considerable potential to contribute to comparative analysis in archaeology by providing a quantitative index of the degrees of inequality present in the contexts we would like to compare. Using Gini coefficients well on various sorts of archaeological observations requires keeping firmly in mind that there are not only different degrees of inequality but also different kinds of inequality (Drennan et al. 2010). Gini coefficients are not inherently a measure of wealth inequality; they are actually a measure of unevenness in the distribution across a population of whatever observations the coefficients are based on. Precisely the same can be said of some other better (or lesser) known measures, such as Atkinson's inequality measure, Kolm's inequality measure, so-called Robin Hood coefficients, and the Theil index (see chapter 6). Even measures of diversity, such as Simpson's index or Shannon's entropy, quantify unevenness of distribution across cases.

When the observations any of these measures are applied to are household annual income or net worth, then they are clearly measures of household wealth inequality. But such coefficients can just as well be calculated, for example, on the distribution of age at death across a population, in which case they are a measure of a completely different kind of inequality—inequality of health and longevity. Inequality of health may well be a result of inequality of wealth, but it cannot be said that inequality of health *is* inequality of wealth. They are two different kinds of inequality whose relationship can be investigated only if they are recognized as different and measured separately. A perfectly reasonable approach would be to calculate a Gini coefficient to measure unevenness in the distribution of age at death and another Gini coefficient to measure unevenness in the distribution of annual income. If these were calculated for several different societies, then one could investigate the extent to which these two kinds of inequality were correlated (and this would not be quite the same thing as investigating whether wealthy people live longer). If the two Gini coefficients did show a strong and significant correlation across societies, then one might entertain the possibility that health inequality is a result of wealth inequality (or, of course, that wealth inequality is a result of health inequality or that both are a result of some other factor).

If Gini coefficients are calculated on observations related to social standing in a community, then they are a measure not of wealth inequality or of health inequality but of prestige differentiation—yet another kind of inequality. Gini coefficients could also be calculated on productive tools of various kinds in different households. These coefficients would measure the degree of productive differentiation, to which it would not be appropriate to apply the term *inequality* at all. Although the utility of calculating Gini coefficients from noneconomic data is widely recognized by economists, archaeologists have tended to view them solely through an economic lens, even when the data from which these coefficients are calculated are not readily interpretable in such terms. This is an understandable consequence of borrowing Gini calculations from economics and of the tight semantic association that has developed between the word *inequality* and economic concerns. It has nonetheless limited the breadth and effectiveness of the application of Gini coefficients in archaeology. Assuming that anything measured with a Gini coefficient is wealth would be a mistake, and mingling observations related to such different things as wealth, prestige, health, and productive differentiation to calculate a single generic index of overall inequality would be muddled thinking. This would be a muddle both because such an overall index would inevitably be taken simply as an index of wealth inequality and because investigating possible relationships between these different kinds of differentiation would be precluded.

In this chapter, we consider various methodological issues surrounding the application of Gini-based analyses to archaeological data, and we provide concrete examples of how to extend the interpretive reach of these measures to the study of inequality of various kinds. We will often use the word *differentiation* in preference to *inequality* when we are not talking about wealth (Drennan and Peterson 2012:76–79).

BRASS TACKS

Gini coefficients (scores, values) range from 0 to 1, with 0 representing a completely uniform distribution of whatever is being measured across the population of units under consideration, and 1 indicating the total concentration of that same something into a single unit. The coefficients themselves are derived from Lorenz curves, which depict the percentage of whatever is under investigation controlled by a given percentage of the population. A 45-degree line running from the lower left to the top right corner of these graphs represents the perfectly even distribution from which the Lorenz curve deviates, and the proportion of the area under the diagonal line that is contained within the curve, divided by the entire area beneath the line, is equivalent to the Gini coefficient. Coefficients should be accompanied by presentations of the Lorenz curves on which they are based for proper interpretation and comparison, as these curves put units of analysis in position from low to high on whatever scale of inequality the observations indicate, making it possible to connect these positions with archaeological evidence for differentiation of various kinds. [*Editors' note: space limitations prevented us from following this good advice throughout this volume.*]

Gini coefficients and Lorenz curves can be produced with relative ease for a given sample using either the "spreadsheet method" (Siegel and Swanson 2004:116–17) or dedicated functions in various statistical software packages (e.g., Signorell 2016). These latter functions regularly incorporate optional "bias correction" that must be disabled if the results obtained are to be comparable to those computed using the spreadsheet method. Some functions also permit the user to calculate Gini coefficients with bootstrapped error ranges for a given level of statistical confidence (discussed further below). Attention should be paid to sample size, because we will have greater confidence in the Gini scores calculated for larger samples than for smaller ones and because small samples often produce low Gini values (Deltas 2003). The size of the samples used should always be presented. The estimated fraction of all units in the population that a sample likely represents may also be relevant to interpretation of Gini scores, particularly in cases where small samples are nonetheless thought to constitute an overwhelming majority of the target population. Altogether apart from this, alertness to sampling bias is essential. It simply will not do to calculate Gini coefficients on a sample produced, for example, by excavating the most monumental burials or the largest house mounds. And finally, we should be cognizant of the fact that differently shaped distributions may yield identical Gini scores, and this distributional data is lost upon conversion into a single numerical value (figure 2.1).

CHALLENGES OF MEASURING INEQUALITY ARCHAEOLOGICALLY

Following on initial work calculating Gini scores to measure wealth inequality from burial assemblages (e.g., McGuire 1983; Schulting 1995; Windler et al. 2013), archaeologists have increasingly experimented with other observations taken to indicate wealth, including house sizes, the sizes of agricultural fields, household faunal assemblages, and household possessions (e.g., Giraldo Tenorio 2013; Kohler and Higgins 2016; Peterson, Drennan, and Bartel 2016; Smith et al. 2014). Various of these approaches have been used by other contributors to this volume. Using these (and other) archaeological data to indicate inequality raises several challenging questions. These questions are easier to answer for some kinds of observations than for others, and the answers are not the same for all regions, periods, or social contexts. Even when answering them seems easy, such questions merit explicit attention.

One fundamental issue is what the observations we focus on indicate inequality between. Individuals? Families? Households? Some yet larger social entity? Do our theoretical or comparative aims imply a need to focus on one of these scales in particular? How convincingly can we establish the connection between the archaeological remains we quantify and one or another of these entities? For example, ownership of agricultural fields (or at least of their products) at a household scale can be difficult to establish if settlement patterns consist of compact local communities; a dispersed farmstead pattern in which household-scale groups live on the land that they farm may be a prerequisite. Household artifact/ecofact assemblages raise the same issue, although forging a connection between a sample of household garbage and a specific residential structure is not usually necessary. Variability in artifact assemblages across a site at a scale that matches the spatial separation of residences can be a good proxy

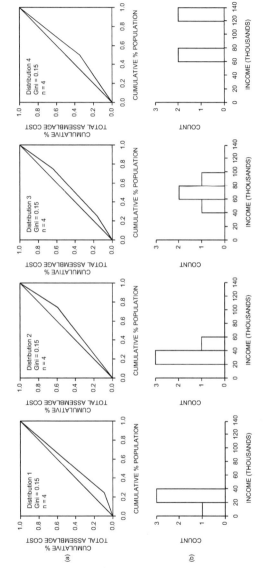

Figure 2.1 (a) Lorenz curves and (b) histograms for four differently shaped distributions of household income yielding identical Gini coefficients.

for household assemblage variability (see below). Burials would seem an ironclad association of inequality-related observations with individuals (except, for example, joint burials of multiple individuals), but determining who invests in funerary treatments may be difficult. It is true that the dead do not bury themselves, but in some societies they do pay for it. Or is it the surviving household of the deceased? Some other related or unrelated household or individual who stands to gain something from being a funeral patron? A yet larger social entity?

Another issue, already raised above, is the kind of inequality, or more generally the kind of differentiation, indicated by the observations a Gini calculation is based on. The distinction between wealth and prestige differentiation is clear as a matter of principle, but in practice the designation of archaeological observations as indicators of one or the other is slippery. A focus on labor costs in burial treatment, residential architecture, or household assemblages does forge a link to economics, but it still makes a difference whether, for example, costly features of a house make it look more impressive to passersby or make it more comfortable for the residents. The number of individuals in a household may have more impact on house size than household wealth does. This issue may be especially complicated in the case of household assemblages, because they certainly have a cost to produce that provides a direct link to wealth, as well as varied social uses that may relate mostly to prestige or even ritual; additionally, many household artifacts are tools connected with potential productive differentiation. The importance of recognizing different kinds (as well as different degrees) of inequality both complicates and enriches working with multiple lines of evidence. If, for a particular society, a Gini coefficient on agricultural plot sizes is high and one on household assemblages is low, we could be dealing with measures of different kinds of inequality that may not be much related to each other. Alternatively, we might have a problem of contradictory results from two lines of evidence that should converge. We need better ways to decide which than just flipping a coin (or, worse yet, picking whichever option suits the theoretical fad of the moment).

Observations on burial treatment and on residential architecture put us at risk of being lied to because both are media in which ancient people made statements about themselves to their contemporaries—statements potentially subject to exaggeration or worse. The very elements that conveyed those messages are among the things that archaeologists observe, complicating our interpretive task. Observing the size of agricultural fields seems pretty well protected against this foible, and household artifacts seem less complicated to interpret from this angle than burials or houses.

All of the kinds of information archaeologists have relied on for calculating Gini scores raise questions about the completeness of our observations or, perhaps more precisely, how to decide when we have reached the point of diminishing returns in attempting to observe more. The size of agricultural fields is obviously central to their productivity. But what about soil depth? Availability of nutrients? Slope? Capacity for moisture retention? Suitability for different crops? House sizes and floor plans are often readily available in observations at excavated sites—the nature of superstructures and their elaboration, less so. This issue thus connects to preservation and taphonomy. A large (as well as highly variable and almost always unknown) proportion of funerary expense may be in funeral ritual itself and in perishables used in funerary ritual. Household artifact assemblages may also include substantial amounts of perishables, although perishable materials are often much easier to work than things like stone and pottery, diminishing the weight that perishables carry in household assemblage labor costs.

Gini coefficients are explicitly designed to exclude the impact of differing levels of societal wealth (that is, different GDP levels) so as to focus solely on how that wealth is distributed within the population. This may make good sense for modern nation-states or even relatively recent historical ones. Whether it does when Gini calculations are carried into the much wider realm of anthropology and archaeology is not necessarily clear. We might make a convincing case that a Gini score on burial goods puts a usefully finer point on a comparison between communities in all of which some burials have no goods, some have modest offerings, and some are more richly endowed. But none of those Gini coefficients will be as high as one calculated on a set of burials that contain no goods at all except for one that has a single poorly made pot. It is probably not meaningful to say that this last set of burials represents wildly greater wealth inequality than the former ones, but that is what a Gini coefficient will purport to tell us. (We unpack this particular point below with a concrete example.) This kind of interpretive difficulty can arise in many guises. If the distribution of agricultural plots of different sizes yields a very high Gini value, does this mean anything interesting in a context where every household has far more agricultural land than needed to raise its food and nothing beyond that is going on in its economic context?

We emphasize that we do not intend this consideration of challenges in using Gini coefficients as just another cautionary tale to take cocksure positivist archaeologists down a notch. We are quite optimistic that Gini coefficients can become a very useful archaeological tool. Like anything else worthwhile in archaeology, however, some clever work will be needed to make that happen, and we hope to make a start on that work here— even though we hasten to add that we do not pretend to resolve even a fraction of these issues in this chapter. Our approach is to try out Gini coefficients on some real data (and some fabricated data too) to see what can go wrong and how that might be avoided.

USING HOUSEHOLD ARTIFACT ASSEMBLAGE DATA

To complement other kinds of observations, we focus especially on calculating Gini scores from household artifact assemblage data. Household artifact assemblages are the archaeologically recoverable garbage the residents of ancient dwellings left behind. Such assemblages may well have been recovered in association with residential architecture, but they need not have been in order to be useful. Artifact samples collected from house floors and pit features are not infrequently the focus of archaeological analysis. But house floor assemblages and pit contents may more often reflect abandonment and postabandonment processes than they do the activities, social roles, and economic well-being of a residence's previous occupants (e.g., LaMotta and Schiffer 1999). Instead, it is usually sufficient (and often more advantageous) to work solely with archaeological midden deposits if these are separated by enough distance that we can be relatively certain they represent the garbage produced by different households (Bayman 1996; Drennan et al. 2010; Hayden and Cannon 1983; Peterson, Drennan, and Bartel 2016). Artifacts from large samples of household middens can very often be obtained in the field without the need for extensive contiguous exposure of archaeological deposits. Distributional analysis of remains recovered through systematic shovel testing, test excavation, or mechanical augering can reveal the locations of ancient households and provide large samples of artifacts for comparative analysis (Bayman 1996; Burks 2004; Drennan 1976; González Fernández 2007a; Hayden and Cannon 1983; McCormack 2002). Under the right conditions, households are even visible as discrete concentrations of artifacts and/or the eroded remains of previously buried features on the surface of archaeological sites (Arnold and Santley 1993; Bayman and Sanchez 1998; Hawkins 1998; Killion et al. 1989; Peterson 2006). Intensive collection of these surface artifact assemblages is both quick and easy (Peterson, Lu, et al. 2016:2–7).

We would argue that uneven distributions of investment in the household possessions that wind up in midden deposits (however these are finally recovered) are more resistant to some challenges as discussed above than are other kinds of archaeological evidence on which Gini coefficients have been based. If we base the Gini calculation on the estimated labor investment in household possessions, then there is a prima facie case that wealth inequality is what is being measured and, thus, that artifact assemblages likely often represent the distribution of wealth across households within a community reasonably accurately.

One issue that arises with use of artifact data, though, is that the overall proportion of household wealth represented may be lower than that invested in other kinds of evidence. Even so, investigating how unequally this portion of a community's wealth is distributed across households can still be meaningful, as a community with great wealth disparities reflected, for example, in residential architecture is unlikely to fail to show considerable disparities in investment in portable possessions. If such a discrepancy is found, one is inclined to wonder what kind of inequality residential architecture really represents or whether it is making a false statement about its inhabitants. Following this line of reasoning—whatever the outcome—produces greater understanding of an ancient community. And this is one way that Gini scores calculated for household artifact assemblages can complement other kinds of archaeological evidence for inequality.

As has frequently been observed, households or families go through a developmental cycle of initial establishment, child bearing and rearing, dispersal of children, and so forth (Goody 1971). Archaeologists have sometimes worried about the impact this can have on conclusions derived from household analysis. This is not just a question of archaeological interpretation; for at least some highly complex societies the argument has been made that this domestic cycle has more to do with economic inequality than class structure does (e.g., Chayanov [1925] 1966; Greenhalgh 1985). Archaeologists studying the emergence and development of social complexity are generally interested in structural society-wide inequalities between households, not in differences in consumption patterns attributable to the stages in the life cycle of a household. Confusion of the two could arise for at least two of the kinds of archaeological data that have been used in attempts to measure economic inequality: household artifact assemblages and house size.

In the case of household artifact assemblages, much of the problem arises from a typical archaeological quest for stratigraphically clean sealed contexts. This thinking is strongly developed in the historical archaeology of quite recent periods, in which privies have become a kind of gold standard of reliable contexts for the recovery of artifact samples that can sometimes result from short depositional episodes that can be quite precisely dated (e.g., LeeDecker 1994). In contrast, jumbled midden or sheet refuse deposits are viewed with suspicion, but these are precisely the contexts we should seek as a source of time-averaged information about a household. By definition such deposits contain materials deposited in a large number of episodes spread through an entire domestic cycle or several of them. Thus, they effectively average out whatever variation in assemblages is produced by different positions in the household's life cycle. This is exactly what is needed if our interest is to assess persistent society-wide structural differentiation between households. It is thus not difficult to guard against the impact of the household life cycle on analysis of artifact assemblages.

The impact of domestic cycling might be harder to avoid when using house size as an indicator of wealth. House structures may be enlarged and additional structures may be added to a group as households go through a developmental cycle. Because many of the houses archaeologists deal with in prehistory may not last even as long as a generation, a considerable amount of construction, destruction, and rebuilding may occur during the life cycle of a household (Howard 1985). If the household area continues in active use, remains of disused structures may well be destroyed without a trace. The particular configuration of an archaeologically recorded household structure or group of structures is more a reflection of a particular moment in time (which is to say, of a particular stage in the household life cycle) than is an artifact sample from a jumbled long-term midden deposit.

We illustrate an approach to calculating Gini coefficients from household artifact data with four communities in the early stages of early complex society development drawn from northern China and Latin America: Late Yangshao period (4000–3000 BC) Dadiwan, in the Qin'an region of China's Gansu Province; Late Dawenkou period (3500–2600 BC) Yuchisi, in the Mengcheng region of Anhui Province; Middle Hongshan period (4000–3500 BC) Fushanzhuang, in the Chifeng region of Inner Mongolia; and the Regional Classic period (AD 1–800) community of Mesitas in the Alto Magdalena region of Colombia. All four appear to have been the central place of a regional-scale polity (Chifeng 2011; Drennan 2006; Liu 2004:87, 96), and each preserves archaeological evidence for social incquality. The Gini coefficients reported for these central places should be considered maximal estimates, as they likely contained higher proportions of wealthier, higher-prestige, or more-productively differentiated households than did outlying settlements. The household artifact data sets used derive from published reports of horizontally extensive excavations (Gansu 2006; Zhongguo 2001, 2007), large-scale systematic shovel testing (González Fernández 2007a, 2007b), and intensive surface collection (Peterson 2006, 2012). Only those assemblages comprising a reasonably large sample of artifacts were selected for inclusion in our Gini calculations. For Dadiwan this amounted to fifteen assemblages; for Yuchisi, seven assemblages; for Fushanzhuang, twenty-two assemblages; and for Mesitas, seventy-five assemblages.

In the calculations presented below, counts of all artifacts per category were divided by the total number of artifacts in each household assemblage, and the resulting proportions were multiplied by 1,000 to "standardize" them (as if each assemblage consisted of a sample of 1,000 artifacts). These numbers were then multiplied by relative quantitative estimates of the labor required to produce different kinds of artifacts, taking into account artifact type, material, and method of manufacture. The estimates we have used for this are educated guesses at relative measures of investment (expressed in generic "units"), anchored to a common baseline and scaled proportionally (see Peterson, Drennan, and Bartel 2016). Estimated energy investment in artifact production was totaled for each 1,000-artifact assemblage, and the total production cost per household was ranked from lowest to highest. Total costs were summed for the entire sample of households in each community, and the proportion of this total represented by each household assemblage was determined. Cumulative percentages of total assemblage production costs were then calculated, from poorest to richest household in each community. These were then graphed, one by one, against the cumulative proportion of households from poorest to richest, to produce the Lorenz curves and Gini coefficients in figure 2.2a.

The Gini scores for these four communities are all very low, indicating only very minimal differences between households in the distribution of community wealth—a result fully consistent with communities in the early stages of complex society development. The Gini score for Mesitas (0.19) jibes well with other evidence interpreted as reflecting only minimal differences in economic well-being between households during Regional Classic times (González Fernández 2007a). Comparative data discussed at length elsewhere (Drennan and Peterson 2006; Drennan et al. 2010) suggest that the Gini scores for Mesitas and Middle Hongshan Fushanzhuang (0.17) ought to be in the same ballpark, and they are. Hongshan communities, like Regional Classic ones, are distinguished by few differences in material well-being between households (Drennan et al. 2017; Peterson 2006; Peterson and Lu 2013). In contrast, the very low Gini coefficients for Dadiwan and Yuchisi do not correspond nearly as well to other kinds of evidence for economic inequality known to archaeologists studying the Middle Neolithic in northern China—evidence such as differences in house size and elaboration, economic specialization, household participation in community feasting and other rituals, and treatment of the dead (Li 2013; Liu 2004; Luan 2013; Peterson, Drennan, and Bartel 2016:203–9; Underhill 2002:89–145). Dawenkou period society in particular is thought to have been characterized by substantial disparities in wealth accumulation between households based on markedly different levels of investment in burial facilities and finely made grave goods (e.g., Fung 2000; Underhill 2000). The Gini coefficient for Late Dawenkou Yuchisi (0.05) is, however, slightly lower than that for Late Yangshao Dadiwan (0.09) and far lower than the scores for Fushanzhuang and Mesitas. These two pairs of cases, then, sort in reverse order to what we might expect based on current understanding of their respective regions' archaeological remains. Given the relatively small sample of artifact assemblages analyzed from Yuchisi and Dadiwan, one wonders whether the Gini scores we calculated are downwardly biased

(Deltas 2003) and thus really ought to be higher. If so, and depending on just how high they should be, the resulting pattern of differences in wealth inequality between all four cases might better conform to conventional thinking about each of the archaeological periods represented.

Because a principal reason for calculating a Gini coefficient of any kind of inequality is for comparison to other communities, regions, or periods, we are likely to rely on data from different sources. It is thus worth considering carefully how different field methods or laboratory approaches to recording data on artifacts could also affect the calculation of Gini coefficients (Peterson, Drennan, and Bartel 2016:218–19). Some particularly rich kinds of artifact data available for Mesitas and Fushanzhuang but not for Dadiwan or Yuchisi may have adversely inflated the first pair of scores, thereby complicating their interpretation. Much larger numbers of vessels were represented in the assemblages from Mesitas and Fushanzhuang, but they were represented and counted differently because they were represented not as whole pots but as sherds. Many classes of lithic and other artifacts absent from the Dadiwan or Yuchisi data constituted a large part of the assemblages analyzed for the other two communities. Although these artifacts were not very costly to make individually, taken together they broaden the array of ways in which household investment in artifacts can differ and thus be unequal.

Insisting that field and laboratory methods be identical is, of course, a prescription for paralysis, since no two projects *really* do these things in identical ways. It is certainly possible, however, to experiment with just how much Gini coefficients are affected by the level of detail in field observations or the number of variables recorded about artifacts. Such an experiment is unfortunately beyond the scope of this chapter. But an assessment of how well each sample of households likely represents the population of households at each settlement we want to compare is not. This can be addressed by determining the statistical confidence we have in differences between Gini coefficients for different samples. Economists have done this, but archaeologists up to now have not.

LIES, DAMNED LIES, AND STATISTICS

Concern with the comparability of Gini coefficients is not limited to those computed using household artifact data sets of differing quality or resolution, because comparability is a subject of much broader scope. The

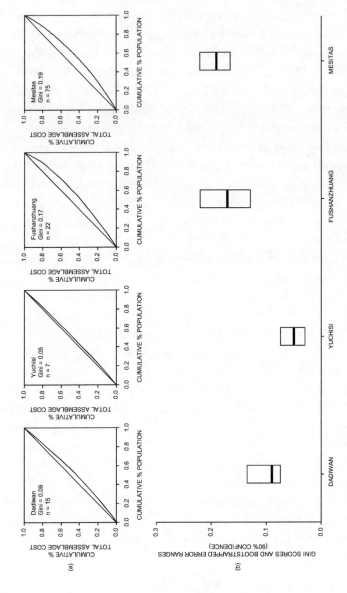

Figure 2.2 (a) Lorenz curves and Gini coefficients for household artifact assemblages from Dadiwan, Yuchisi, Fushanzhuang, and Mesitas, with (b) bootstrapped error ranges for each coefficient.

statistical worry can be summarized as follows: if you have a Gini score of 0.25 for one community and a score of 0.32 for another, you would likely be inclined to say that the second one indicates more inequality than the first, but to do so you also need some measure of confidence that this difference in scores is actually real—because the difference might be due to nothing more than the vagaries of sampling. Economists' quite reasonable solution to this problem has been to attach error ranges to Gini coefficients by way of resampling techniques. The most widely applied of these techniques has been the bootstrap. Bootstrapping takes a sample of something as if it were a population of that same thing and then repeatedly selects a random sample of new samples of the same size as the original from it. The number of resamples selected is usually quite large: at least 1,000. Error ranges for the resulting distribution of samples can then be calculated for a given level of confidence (e.g., 80 percent, 95 percent). The greater the confidence level selected, the larger the error ranges will be.

Figure 2.2b presents bootstrapped error ranges for 90 percent confidence based on a minimum of 1,000 resamples for each of the four Gini coefficients discussed above. All things being equal, bootstrapped error ranges provide us with two additional pieces of information necessary for proper interpretation of Gini values. First, they provide us with a range of possible Gini values for each case wherein the "actual" value lies for a given level of confidence. And second, they allow us to assess just how confident we should be in differences in scores between cases. Because of the lack of overlap between coefficients and opposing error ranges for Dadiwan, Yuchisi, and Fushanzhuang, we can place a high degree of confidence in our previous assessment (and rank ordering) of differences in the degree of inequality represented by these three communities, even though this fails to conform to conventional wisdom about the ways in which the societies these were a part of were unequal. In contrast, substantial overlap of error ranges and coefficients for Fushanzhuang and Mesitas provides support for previous interpretations based on other kinds of evidence that the degree of inequality within these two communities was quite similar. Examination of the error ranges themselves indicates that we should also be quite confident in the relatively low level of inequality represented by the Gini scores calculated for each of these four communities. Of course it might not have worked out this way (for instance, if our samples had been even smaller than some of them were), and that would be important information to have at hand when making either interpretations or comparisons between cases on the basis of Gini coefficients.

Archaeologists have long been in the business of identifying wealthy households as the ones with the highest proportions of decorated pottery or scarce ornamental items or identifying the most prestigious households as the ones near important public buildings. If the households identified by Lorenz curves as being near the top of the scale are also those singled out by these latter kinds of more traditional approaches, then we should feel on relatively solid footing in interpreting the corresponding Gini coefficient as reflecting the same kind of differentiation, and that would help indicate just what kind of differentiation it was. This would be an example of different lines of evidence converging on the same conclusion, and that would make the conclusion more convincing. If this correspondence is not forthcoming, then we are on shakier ground in interpreting Gini scores in these terms.

A great deal of confusion regarding the comparability of multiple Gini scores in archaeology could be avoided by reasoning along similar lines. In some instances, Gini coefficients calculated from different kinds of archaeological remains will reach similar conclusions and thus make a conjoint interpretation more convincing. In others, Gini values calculated on different bases will not agree with each other. This may mean that there are underlying methodological issues of some sort with one or more sets of observations as described above. Or it may be that Gini coefficients based on different sets of observations are providing useful measures of different kinds of differentiation, and the fact that they do not jibe is the valuable conclusion.

A comparison of three Gini coefficients (and corresponding bootstrapped error ranges for 90 percent confidence) calculated for Regional Classic Mesitas household artifact assemblages, house sizes, and burials illustrates these points (figure 2.3). The Gini coefficient based on labor investment in seventy-five household artifact assemblages corresponds to a Lorenz curve that one would be inclined to interpret as putting households in order on a scale of relative wealth. The households near the top of this scale correspond relatively well to those identified as of higher economic standing by the anecdotal presence of rare ornamental

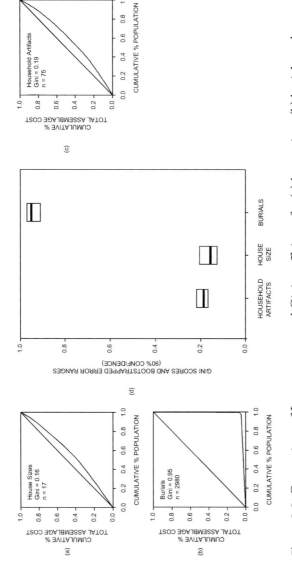

Figure 2.3 Comparison of Lorenz curves and Gini coefficients for (a) house sizes, (b) burials, and (c) household artifact assemblage data from Mesitas. Bootstrapped error ranges for each coefficient are shown in (d).

objects, centrality of location within the community, and persistent long-term occupation. This lends support to the idea that this particular Gini (0.19) is indeed operating as an index of wealth inequality and that the low value indicates that wealth inequality, while recognizably present, was minimal. A Gini coefficient obtained for a sample of seventeen Alto Magdalena house sizes (0.16) does not differ meaningfully from that calculated from household artifact data at the 90 percent confidence level. This high degree of correspondence between scores suggests that both are tracking the same dimension of social variability—differences in the distribution of wealth across households—which again, based on house size, seems minimal.

A different picture emerges when we look at Mesitas burials. The burial sample is composed of 149 stone slab tombs sometimes capped by earthen mounds and accompanied by stone statues carved in supernatural themes. Thought to represent only about 5 percent of the total population of Regional Classic burials, these lavish tombs are most often considered to be those of high-prestige ritual elites (Drennan 1995; Duque Gómez 1964). We estimated the labor expended in their construction, along with that invested in the simple pit graves with few or no artifacts in which the remaining undocumented 95 percent of the population was buried (for a total of 2,980 graves). The Gini coefficient calculated from this sample of burials (0.95) is extremely high and clearly indicates dramatically uneven distribution of investment in burial treatment. Even though labor investment is inherently an economic variable, to interpret this Gini coefficient as evidence of extreme wealth inequality is unconvincing. The labor was invested in architecture and sculpture of religious symbolic importance in the ritual spaces thus created, not in abundance or high quality of personal possessions of any kind. The construction was more likely a collective endeavor than an expenditure or expression of the personal wealth of the deceased or the deceased's survivors (Drennan 1995). The very high degree of inequality is best interpreted as an accurate measure not of wealth inequality at all but of prestige and ritual differentiation.

We should not see the lack of correspondence between these measures as an analytical defect or a contradiction to be resolved, much less erased by rolling all this evidence together. We should instead see it as an opportunity to recognize better differences in the kinds of inequalities whose degrees are being measured. That is to say, discrepancies of this sort are telling us something both interesting and meaningful about the complex composition of Regional Classic communities. Gini coefficients calculated from some kinds of archaeological data will inform us about the degree of inequality in the distribution of social prestige or ritual authority, while those calculated from other kinds of observations will be more revealing of wealth inequality. In short, "egalitarian society" versus "nonegalitarian society" is an overly simplistic idea—for two reasons. First, inequality is most meaningfully considered a continuous variable rather than a dichotomy—a continuous variable that Gini coefficients give us a potentially powerful way to measure. Second, a single society may have dramatic prestige or ritual differentiation but very little inequality of wealth or economic well-being—or vice versa. And there are many other kinds of inequalities worth measuring as well that may (or may not) correlate with prestige or wealth: those based on sex, health, ethnicity, political or religious affiliation, and so forth.

Even when it is recognized that Gini coefficients may indicate differentiation of various kinds, other challenges to their interpretation remain. First, Gini scores calculated from archaeological data can indicate a high degree of inequality when little or none was actually present in an ancient community. Take, for instance, a sample of twenty-five roughly contemporaneous burials excavated from a single cemetery. Imagine that each burial is a simple pit inhumation and none of the deceased are accompanied by any grave goods whatsoever—except for one burial that contains a single poorly made pottery vessel. The difference between this one individual and the rest of the population may truly be an economic difference, but interpreting this minimal difference in grave goods as a dramatic wealth inequality between individuals would be ridiculous. But calculating a Gini coefficient based on this sample results in one (0.96) that indicates just that—no matter what we estimate the effort expended to produce the pot was (figure 2.4a).

This problem pervades the use of all forms of archaeological data, not only that from burials. For instance, using house size without any consideration of architectural elaboration could sometimes cause this problem or its inverse (very low Gini coefficients). And the inverse problem is worth attention in its own right. If all burials have the same large number of low-quality pottery vessels, then it is reasonable to conclude that little

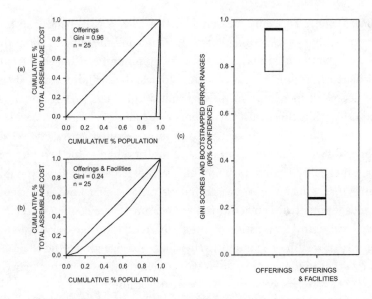

Figure 2.4 Lorenz curves and Gini coefficients for a hypothetical sample of pit burials for which (a) only one grave contained a single low-cost offering and (b) calculations also include estimated investment in imagined burial facilities. Bootstrapped error ranges for each coefficient are shown in (c).

or no wealth inequality is reflected in that sample of burial assemblages. But this conclusion is also an unacceptable half-truth without some consideration of the fact that the average wealth or prosperity represented by this sample of burials is much greater than one in which all burials but one contained no grave goods. One way of keeping both of these perspectives in view at once is to calculate average investment in whatever is being observed for presentation alongside Gini scores, enabling one to deal with both overall prosperity and inequality. Issues of general prosperity and just *how* wealthy the wealthy *are* are inextricably bound up in what we need to know about social and economic change—it is not only about inequality surgically separated from everything else.

THE WHOLE TRUTH AND NOTHING BUT

Measures of inequality like Gini coefficients are, of course, intended to filter out elements like differing levels of prosperity so as to facilitate abstract comparisons of the unevenness of the distribution of something like prestige, well-being, wealth, or income, irrespective of its overall abundance. Mathematical abstractions of this kind make powerful contributions to comparative analysis; they can also bring a risk of making the comparison so abstract that it loses touch with relevant aspects of reality. One effect of this can be to unrealistically exaggerate apparent economic inequality in a technologically and economically very simple setting. Archaeologists who use Gini coefficients in technological and economic contexts wildly different from those of the modern nation-states for which they were developed will need to be especially alert to the impact of this effect on comparisons.

If 90 percent of families live in a structure costing $100,000 and the other 10 percent in a structure costing $1,000,000, a Gini coefficient measures inequality at 0.43. The same distribution and thus the same Gini coefficient is produced when 90 percent of families live in a structure requiring 25 person-days of labor to build and 10 percent in a structure requiring 250 person-days. Concluding that inequality is the same in the two settings might be reasonable and meaningful. Or it might not.

A nuclear family with a couple of relatives can invest 25 person-days of labor in a house in a week's time, and house construction can truly be this minimal in technologically very simple settings, for example, in tropical regions where little shelter is needed and normal daily activities can be carried out mostly outdoors. A nuclear family that marshals four or five relatives might build a 250-person-day house in five or six weeks. One can question how meaningful it is to say that inequality here is the same as that represented by the $900,000 difference between the 90 percent and the 10 percent in the other instance. The example is intentionally simple and extreme to facilitate thinking about fundamental principles. In one instance the gap between "rich" and "poor" represents a total of 225 days' labor; in the other, of 4,500 days' labor. (The U.S. median income is around $50,000, making each day of labor in a five-day workweek worth about $200 on average.) It is true enough to say that inequality of wealth as measured by a Gini coefficient is the same in both contexts. It is equally true to say that the gap between rich and poor is much greater in one than in the other, and to be blinded by identical Gini coefficients and fail to make this latter observation is to miss entirely an important aspect of the comparison.

In sum, a given degree of unevenness of distribution means less when there is very little to distribute unevenly than it does when there is a great deal to be distributed unevenly. As archaeologists compare very different societies in different regions and over long spans of time during which major changes have occurred, keeping track of potentially very different levels of overall prosperity can help make the comparisons more realistic and meaningful. Simply incorporating this as a mathematical modification of the Gini coefficient is not easy, but a measure of the overall level of prosperity can accompany Gini coefficients (see also chapter 1). In this example, it is useful to contemplate the average costs of house structures by dividing the total number of houses by the total labor investment in houses in each instance. The fact that the average house cost is 950 days' labor in one case and 47.5 days' labor in the other means that considerably greater overall prosperity is unevenly distributed in the first. And this makes it unreasonable to say that inequality is the same in both instances. Comparing Gini scores, then, is most likely to be meaningful when the overall prosperity involved in calculating them is in a similar range in all instances compared. To overlook this puts us at risk of making nonsense comparisons.

For our four household artifact data sets, household prosperity varies markedly between Dadiwan and Yuchisi, on the one hand, and Mesitas and Fushanzhuang, on the other. The average investment in household artifact assemblages at Dadiwan is 538,610 "units," only slightly less than the 563,504 "units" at Yuchisi. In contrast, average investment at Mesitas (13,311 "units") and Fushanzhuang (11,415 "units") is nearly identical and an order of magnitude lower than that at Dadiwan or Yuchisi. For each set of communities, this difference parallels that in the Gini coefficients calculated previously. Based on their household assemblage Gini scores (which do seem best interpreted as measures of wealth inequality), Mesitas and Fushanzhuang both evidence higher degrees of inequality between households than do those at Dadiwan or Yuchisi. But these households also enjoyed far less prosperity on average than did those at Dadiwan or Yuchisi. Thus, despite the appearance of a sharper difference between "rich" and "poor" at Mesitas and Fushanzhuang, the real difference between households in overall economic well-being is marginal when compared with that at Dadiwan or Yuchisi—at least when examined on the basis of household artifact assemblages. This greater contextualization of economic inequality produces reconstructions much more in line with conventional thinking among archaeologists about these communities and the regional-scale societies of which they are a part than those provided by looking at Gini scores on their own.

Finally, the issue of average prosperity is connected to the important question of just what domains of evidence should be included in our analyses of inequality in the first place. As illustrated by the hypothetical burial example above, even small differences in grave goods seem like large ones if the range of variability in labor investment is near zero. This problem is compounded as sample size increases. Including in our calculations the labor invested in burial facilities can help to ameliorate this effect, but only a little if even a single labor-intensive object sets one burial off from the others. The Gini score for our hypothetical sample of burials decreases from 0.96 to 0.24 when we incorporate investment in burial facilities; and the burial with the single pot is no longer the "wealthiest," because other graves were imagined as larger and therefore more "costly" to excavate (figure 2.4b). When we are working with houses, overall house size sounds fine in the abstract, but what if some especially large houses (with or without lots of little rooms) functioned as multifamily dwellings? Neither taking the area of each room nor dividing the total area of the structure by the number of families residing in it is a particularly satisfying solution. As previously mentioned, productivity should be taken into account when basing Gini scores on farming plots, but how is this to be measured? And what about the practice of including (as we have here) "income-earning" tools in the household artifact assemblages from which Gini coefficients are computed? Modern auto mechanics, for example, often own tens of thousands of dollars' worth of tools and other equipment used to diagnose and fix problems with automobiles. Should these tools be considered a part of their net worth? What about archaeological artifacts used to make a living, especially those extremely laborious to manufacture? Not including such tools in our calculations of household artifact assemblages from Mesitas decreases its Gini value by nearly two-thirds (from 0.19 to 0.07), and the resulting measure becomes one of investment across households in the most abundant items of daily living, not total portable assets as before. Should certain artifact classes (e.g., ground stone tools and ornaments) be omitted from Gini calculations based on artifact data because taphonomic factors—such as their selective removal from the surface of agricultural fields by modern farmers—and rarity might make their impact on Gini coefficients extremely erratic? There are no prescriptions to which we can look for the answers to these and other difficult questions. Each will need to be considered individually with reference to the regional archaeological record, environment, and social context of specific cases.

LETTING THE GINI OUT OF THE BOTTLE

Measuring inequality is an extremely valuable thing to be able to do well. Lorenz curves and Gini coefficients are solid and useful tools that, for the most part, work well mathematically (although we do need to get in the habit of putting error ranges with Gini scores to know how much statistical confidence we should place in them). The more kinds of data we can apply them to, the better—in search of convergent lines of evidence for inequality but also to recognize and explore different kinds of differentiation. For every case examined we must consider carefully what patterns of evidence are likely to indicate what kinds of differentiation—uncritically ascribing economic interpretations to the Gini scores we calculate simply will not do. Even when inequality of wealth *is* the most plausible interpretation for a particular measurement, recognizing as much represents only one part of the equation needed to fully understand it and place it in comparative perspective. The other part required is a means of estimating the average wealth or general prosperity represented by the sample of whatever units we are working with so as to properly gauge just how wealthy the wealthiest members of the communities we are studying were.

Further exploration of the use of household artifact assemblage data for calculation of Gini coefficients and measures of average prosperity may prove to be especially enlightening, but a few issues remain to be resolved before we can unlock their full potential. One of these is the need for more ethnographic or experimental data on which to base and refine measures of labor expended in artifact manufacture. Another concerns the comparability of household artifact data recovered and recorded in different ways. Experimental studies of Gini scores calculated for some made-up household artifact data that vary in richness of detail may prove useful in assessing how worrisome differences in recovery and recording between cases may be. And finally, the implications of including different kinds of artifacts in our calculations bears some investigation—should, for example, sometimes-expensive productive tools really be treated as "wealth"? As demonstrated above, Gini scores turn out radically different depending on whether or not these are included.

Other issues of application are not so much tied to any particular source of archaeological information. Among these are questions about just what the units of our analyses should be, how best to connect these with empirical observations made of the archaeological record, and how to recognize and avoid sampling bias in our investigations. Another concerns how detailed and comprehensive these investigations need to be in order to be useful—how do we recognize when we have reached the point of diminishing returns in our efforts to combine multiple observations into our analyses? This volume is an important step forward in wrestling with these and other issues involving the application of Gini coefficients in archaeology. We encourage our colleagues to continue exploring them more fully.

REFERENCES CITED

Arnold, Philip J., III, and Robert S. Santley. 1993. Household Ceramics Production at Middle Classic Period Matacapan. In *Prehispanic Domestic Units in Western Mesoamerica: Studies of the Household, Compound, and Residence*, edited by Robert S. Santley and Kenneth G. Hirth, pp. 227–48. CRC Press, Boca Raton, Fla.

Bayman, James M. 1996. Shell Ornament Consumption in a Classic Hohokam Platform Mound Community Center. *Journal of Field Archaeology* 23:403–20.

Bayman, James M., and M. Guadalupe Sanchez. 1998. The Surface Archaeology of Classic Period Hohokam Community Organization. In *Surface Archaeology*, edited by Alan P. Sullivan III, pp. 75–88. University of New Mexico Press, Albuquerque.

Burks, Jarrod D. 2004. Identifying Household Cluster and Refuse Disposal Patterns at the Strait Site: A Third Century A.D. Nucleated Settlement in the Middle Ohio River Valley. PhD dissertation, Ohio State University, Columbus.

Chayanov, A. V. (1925) 1966. Peasant Farm Organization. In *The Theory of Peasant Economy*, edited by Daniel Thorner, Basile Kerblay, and R. E. F. Smith, pp. 29–269. Richard D. Irwin, Homewood, Ill. Orig. pub. Cooperative Publishing House, Moscow.

Chifeng International Collaborative Archaeological Research Project. 2011. *Settlement Patterns in the Chifeng Region*. University of Pittsburgh Center for Comparative Archaeology, Pittsburgh.

Deltas, George. 2003. The Small-Sample Bias of the Gini-Coefficient: Results and Implications for Empirical Research. *Review of Economics and Statistics* 85:226–34.

Drennan, Robert D. 1976. *Fabricá San José and Middle Formative Society in the Valley of Oaxaca*. Memoirs of the Museum of Anthropology 8. University of Michigan, Ann Arbor.

———. 1995. Mortuary Practices in the Alto Magdalena: The Social Context of the "San Agustín Culture." In *Tombs for the Living: Andean Mortuary Practices*, edited by Tom D. Dillehay, pp. 79–110. Dumbarton Oaks, Washington, D.C.

——— (editor). 2006. *Prehispanic Chiefdoms in the Valle de la Plata*, vol. 5: *Regional Settlement Patterns*. Memoirs in Latin American Archaeology 16. University of Pittsburgh, Pittsburgh.

Drennan, Robert D., and Christian E. Peterson. 2006. Patterned Variation in Prehistoric Chiefdoms. *PNAS* 103:3960–67.

———. 2012. Challenges for Comparative Study of Early Complex Societies. In *The Comparative Archaeology of Complex Societies*, edited by Michael E. Smith, pp. 62–87. Cambridge University Press, Cambridge.

Drennan, Robert D., Christian E. Peterson, and Jake R. Fox. 2010. Degrees and Kinds of Inequality. In *Pathways to Power: New Perspectives on the Emergence of Inequality*, edited by T. Douglass Price and Gary M. Feinman, pp. 45–76. Springer, New York.

Drennan, Robert D., Christian E. Peterson, Lu Xueming, and Li Tao. 2017. Hongshan Households and Communities in Neolithic Northeastern China. *Journal of Anthropological Archaeology* 47:50–71.

Duque Gómez, Luis. 1964. *Exploraciones arqueológicas en San Agustín*. Revista Colombiana de Antropología, suplemento no. 1. Imprenta Nacional, Bogotá.

Fung, Christopher. 2000. The Drinks Are on Us: Ritual, Social Status, and Practice in Dawenkou Burials, North China. *Journal of East Asian Archaeology* 2:67–92.

Gansu Sheng Wenwu Kaogu Yanjiusuo. 2006. *Gansu Dadiwan: Xinshiqi Yizhi Fajue Baogao*. 2 vols. Wenwu Chubanshe, Beijing.

Giraldo Tenorio, Hernando Javier. 2013. Midiendo diferenciación en riqueza en el registro arqueológico: Una propuesta aplicada en el área Andina Intermedia. *Revista Chilena de Antropología* 21:39–66.

González Fernández, Victor. 2007a. *Prehispanic Change in the Mesitas Community: Documenting the Development of a Chiefdom's Central Place in San Agustín, Huila, Colombia*. Memoirs in Latin American Archaeology 18. University of Pittsburgh, Pittsburgh.

———. 2007b. Mesitas Community Dataset. Comparative Archaeology Database, University of Pittsburgh. www.cadb.pitt.edu/.

Goody, Jack (editor). 1971. *The Developmental Cycle in Domestic Groups*. Cambridge University Press, New York.

Greenhalgh, Susan. 1985. Is Inequality Demographically Induced? The Family Cycle and the Distribution of Income in Taiwan. *American Anthropologist* 87:571–94.

Hawkins, Rebecca A. 1998. Coming Full Circle: Plowzone Assemblages and the Interpretation of Fort Ancient Settlement Structure. In *Surface Archaeology*, edited by Alan P. Sullivan III, pp. 91–109. University of New Mexico Press, Albuquerque.

Hayden, Brian, and Aubrey Cannon. 1983. Where the Garbage Goes: Refuse Disposal in the Maya Highlands. *Journal of Anthropological Archaeology* 2:117–63.

Howard, Jerry B. 1985. Courtyard Groups and Domestic Cycling: A Hypothetical Model of Growth. In *Proceedings of the 1983 Hohokam Symposium, Part 1*, edited by A. E. Dittert and D. E. Dove, pp. 311–26. Arizona Archaeological Society, Phoenix.

Killion, Thomas W., Jeremy A. Sabloff, Gair Tourtellot, and Nicholas P. Dunning. 1989. Intensive Surface Collection of Residential Clusters at Terminal Classic Sayil, Yucatan, Mexico. *Journal of Field Archaeology* 16:273–94.

Kohler, Timothy A., and Rebecca Higgins. 2016. Quantifying Household Inequality in Early Pueblo Villages. *Current Anthropology* 57:690–97.

LaMotta, Vincent, and Michael B. Schiffer. 1999. Formation Processes of House Floor Assemblages. In *The Archaeology of Household Activities*, edited by Penelope M. Allison, pp. 19–29. Routledge, London.

LeeDecker, Charles H. 1994. Discard Behavior on Domestic Historic Sites: Evaluation of Contexts for the Interpretation of Household Consumption Patterns. *Journal of Archaeological Method and Theory* 1:345–75.

Li, Xinwei. 2013. The Later Neolithic Period in the Central Yellow River Valley Area, c. 4000–3000 B.C. In *A Companion to Chinese Archaeology*, edited by Anne P. Underhill, pp. 213–35. Wiley-Blackwell, Malden, Mass.

Liu, Li. 2004. *The Chinese Neolithic: Trajectories to Early States*. Cambridge University Press, Cambridge.

Luan, Fengxi. 2013. The Dawenkou Culture in the Lower Yellow River and Huai River Basin Areas. In *A Companion to Chinese Archaeology*, edited by Anne P. Underhill, pp. 411–34. Wiley-Blackwell, Malden, Mass.

McCormack, Valerie J. 2002. Sedentism, Site Occupation and Settlement Organization at La Joya, a Formative Village in the Sierra de los Tuxtlas, Veracruz, Mexico. PhD dissertation, University of Pittsburgh.

McGuire, Randall H. 1983. Breaking Down Cultural Complexity: Inequality and Heterogeneity. *Advances in Archaeological Method and Theory* 6:91–142.

Peterson, Christian E. 2006. "Crafting" Hongshan Communities? Household Archaeology in the Chifeng Region of Eastern Inner Mongolia, PRC. PhD dissertation, University of Pittsburgh.

————. 2012. Fushanzhuang Community Dataset. Comparative Archaeology Database, University of Pittsburgh. www.cadb.pitt.edu/.

Peterson, Christian E., Robert D. Drennan, and Kate L. Bartel. 2016. Comparative Analysis of Neolithic Household Artifact Assemblage Data from Northern China. *Journal of Anthropological Research* 72(2):200–225.

Peterson, Christian E., and Lu Xueming. 2013. Understanding Hongshan Period Social Dynamics. In *A Companion to Chinese Archaeology*, edited by Anne P. Underhill, pp. 55–80. Wiley-Blackwell, Malden, Mass.

Peterson, Christian E., Lu Xueming, Robert D. Drennan, and Zhu Da. 2016. Upper Daling Region Hongshan Household and Community Dataset: An Introduction. Comparative Archaeology Database, University of Pittsburgh. www.cadb.pitt.edu/.

Schulting, Richard J. 1995. *Mortuary Variability and Status Differentiation on the Columbia-Fraser Plateau.* Burnaby Archaeology Press, Simon Fraser University, Burnaby, B.C.

Siegel, Jacob S., and David Swanson. 2004. *The Methods and Materials of Demography.* 2nd ed. Elsevier/Academic Press, Boston.

Signorell, Andri. 2016. DescTools: Tools for Descriptive Statistics. R package version 0.99.16.

Smith, Michael E., Timothy Dennehy, April Kamp-Whittaker, Emily Colon, and Rebecca Harkness. 2014. Quantitative Measures of Wealth Inequality in Ancient Mexican Communities. *Advances in Archaeological Practice* 2:311–23.

Underhill, Anne P. 2000. An Analysis of Mortuary Ritual at the Dawenkou Site, Shandong, China. *Journal of East Asian Archaeology* 2:93–127.

————. 2002. *Craft Production and Social Change in Northern China.* Kluwer Academic / Plenum Press, New York.

Windler, Arne, Rainer Thiele, and Johannes Müller. 2013. Increasing Inequality in Chalcolithic Southeast Europe: The Case of Durankulak. *Journal of Archaeological Science* 40:204–10.

Zhongguo Shehui Kexue Kaogu Yanjiusuo. 2001. *Mengcheng Yuchisi—Wanbei Xinshiqi Shidai Juluo Yicun de Fajue yu Yanjiu.* Kexue Chubanshe, Beijing.

————. 2007. *Mengcheng Yuchisi.* Vol. 2. Kexue Chubanshe, Beijing.

3

Dreaming Beyond Gini

Methodological Steps Toward a Composite
Archaeological Inequality Index

*Rahul C. Oka, Nicholas Ames, Meredith S. Chesson, Ian Kuijt,
Chapurukha M. Kusimba, Vishwas D. Gogte, and Abhijit Dandekar*

Understanding inequality has been a fundamental issue in anthropological archaeology for over fifty years (see summaries in Flanagan 1989;
Paynter 1989; Price and Feinman 1995). Traditional narratives of social
evolution describe how human societies transformed from small mobile groups to settled communities with gradually increasing population
levels and social complexity, where population pressure served as a key
driver in the development and institutionalization of social inequality
within and between settlements (Keeley 1988). This model has more recently been questioned on the basis of subsequent observations in many
societies that population growth might have succeeded, and even been
enhanced by, emergent and institutionalized social inequality (Feinman
1995). Other work has focused on inequality as a powerful structuring
and stabilizing mechanism, specifically focusing on the links between
status differentiation, the legitimacy of leadership, and management of
resources (Chesson 2015; Feinman 1995; Frangipane 2007; Joyce 2004;
Kuijt 2008; Paynter 1989; Prentiss et al. 2012).

Recently, however, inequality has become fashionable as the leading explanatory trope across academia, public policy, and contemporary media-scapes, being blamed for all social ills and injustices faced
by marginalized populations in contemporary societies (Deaton 2013,
2014; Piketty 2014). Increasingly scholars posit that high levels of social
inequality accompany structural violence, a combination that ensures
that a large proportion of those born into the lower tiers of society are
condemned to a lifelong lack of access to resources and opportunities,
as well as a general vulnerability to lower physical, emotional, and material well-being (Banerjee and Duflo 2011; Deaton 2013; Farmer 2005;
Kim et al. 2000; Piketty 2014). These findings are in stark opposition

to the neoliberal narratives that drew clear correlations and even causal pathways between equality, globalization, and development and dominated mainstream and development economics between the 1940s and the 1990s, as expressed in the maxims "rising tides float all boats" and "economic growth drives greater equality" (Fukuyama 1992; Hulme et al. 2001; Lindert and Williamson 2003).

These trends in the study of economic differentiation, social inequality, and poverty have occurred within the disciplines of biology, economics, political science, sociology, and the humanities. We argue that these trends open a crucial intellectual space and challenge for archaeologists to develop meaningful questions and answers that also hold relevance for contemporary communities. Specifically, we argue that the field's exclusive access to data on the emergence of inequality in early, prestate, and premodern societies situates archaeology in a far better position to explain the emergence, institutionalization, and endurance of inequality. A clearer understanding of the evolution of inequality would help other social scientists understand the complexities of inequality, including its enduring persistence in contemporary societies despite millions of interventions and billions of dollars expended toward alleviating inequality and its more egregious forms of poverty and marginalization (Easterly 2006, 2007; Escobar 1995; Moyo 2009; Rist 2007; Sen 1992).

Specifically, we argue that this challenge creates two main tasks. First, we must better understand social inequality as a structuring, stabilizing, and destabilizing process across societies and through time, including today. Second, we must investigate "inequality" in ancient and premodern societies with methods that are simultaneously relevant, transferable, and understandable to other disciplines and to contemporary analysis, while recognizing variation in social manifestations of inequality through space and time. Although these two approaches are interrelated, we can best address the first point, which is a more profound question with implications for development, progress, and justice, after answering the second point, which is a methodological question both framed and limited by the nature of archaeological data (see chapters 1, 2, 5, 11).

Thus, we focus on the second charge: developing methods to measure inequality in past societies in meaningful ways. This is a hard task, especially when our primary, and at times only, data source is material-economic archaeological data only occasionally buttressed by historical or ethnographic evidence. As other chapters in this volume and larger critiques of numerical representations of inequality caution, we are aware that measurements of inequality cannot be an end unto themselves. In our minds, however, there is no question that some form of operationalization is crucial if archaeological insights are to be perceived as relevant and useful for other social sciences to consider in their own analyses of inequality. The question is, therefore, how should we proceed? Any attempt at measuring something as complex as inequality leaves us open to charges of reductionism. A number, or even a series of numbers, calculated from social, economic, political, or other data could be interpreted as an exact descriptor of inequality and as a result could become subsumed into traditional classificatory exercises for ranking or categorizing past societies. As various authors in this volume (chapters 2, 4, and 9) assert, such exercises often produce typologies poor in explanation, description, or prediction. We pay attention to these caveats and suggest an alternative use for measurements of inequality as analytical heuristics that enable either the testing of hypothesized changes in inequality derived from *previous* empirical data or the development of hypotheses that may be tested with *future* empirical data.

MEASURING INEQUALITY?

Several researchers in this volume (chapters 1, 2, 5, 10) describe the use of the Gini coefficient (henceforth Gini) as a measure for inequality across the social sciences, including archaeology. However, within economics and development studies, where the Gini coefficient was developed and has found its greatest application, researchers critique single-variable Ginis (Anand and Sen 1994; Haq 1995). They aver that inequality is affected by a complex range of noneconomic and nonmaterial factors within and between societies that lead to different forms of capital (e.g., political, educational, social, ideological) that intersect with economic capital (e.g., wealth, income, assets) (Lin 2000; Ostrom 2005).

We understand these concerns and thus will not produce yet another set of indices or coefficients that claim to capture an *absolute* quantified measurement of inequality. Instead we strive to provide a sound method to evaluate inequality from multiple material data sets that serves either as the beginning of archaeological investigations into the dynamics of inequality at particular sites or a pathway for testing the findings of ongoing investigations. More specifically, our goal is to develop a methodological approach for assessing, hypothesizing, or testing patterns and trends in inequality within and between societies, moving beyond the usual conflation of social strata into monolithic categories of "elites" and "nonelites." This refinement is especially important when the majority of the population might consist of nonelite subgroups who have different forms of capital and access to resources and opportunities (Marcus 1983).

In lieu of the Gini coefficient we propose a Composite Archaeological Inequality (CAI) index, in which we combine available data on all available variables measuring the distribution of materials within a particular society or subgroup. We conceptualize the CAI along the lines of the Human Development Index (HDI), first proposed by Maqbul Haq and Amartya Sen and subsequently refined by the United Nations and the United Nations Development Programme (UNDP) as an alternative to the Gini coefficient. For any nation or state, the HDI is calculated as the geometric mean of the normalized measurements of gross domestic product, life expectancy at birth, and adult literacy rates (UNDP 2010; see also chapter 1). We borrow the methodology used for the HDI to calculate CAI as an indicator of the differential distribution of multiple types of material culture within any society (settlement, groups of settlements, polities, etc.). We believe that our focus on several diverse variables measures both material access and subsequent well-being in archaeological societies, in the spirit of the HDI.

As Peterson and Drennan note (chapter 2), archaeologists enjoy neither the large quantitative data sets of economists nor the behavioral data available to ethnographers. We are necessarily limited to material economic data. Our measurements, hence, must be confined to the material economic variables, such as house size, location, prestige goods, and staple goods. Such material data, however, can provide evidence for actual economic inequalities that might be masked by formal systems of social stratification.

For example, South Asia has long had a formal social hierarchy of a caste system headed by high-born yet impoverished scholars, followed by nobility, merchants, and workers (Kulke and Rothermund 1998). Relevant material data, however, would instead suggest a hierarchical society dominated by nobility and merchants. An even deeper analysis would show that the South Asian political economy was indeed dominated by land-owning nobility and capital-controlling traders, who promoted scholars and priests to the top of the social hierarchy as client dependents. In return, priests and scholars reinforced the legitimacy of their noble/mercantile patrons through ritual and ideology (Altekar 2009; Ghurye 1969). In this case, the material record would be a better indicator of actual distribution of wealth and resource inequality than the textual record. Thus, we argue that a measurement of the distribution of material economic culture such as Gini, HDI, the Robin Hood Index, or the Theil index provides a reliable means to assess the equity of access to wealth, status, and well-being within any society, even if it might not accurately reflect social hierarchy. Whether a single Gini measurement is adequate to these tasks, however, is unclear.

SINGLE OR MULTIPLE GINIS

Various researchers in this volume (chapters 5, 6, 7) use a single Gini measure based on house size as a proxy indicator of wealth. In many societies, a Gini computed on house-size distributions may be indeed the best indicator of status and a good approximation of the inequality within the society. Various households, however, might have differential access to resources and productivity, based on the size and organization of the household, skills, social status, and so forth. These differences could not be captured through a Gini focusing on house size alone (see chapter 9, this volume; Kramer 1982). For example, the house-size Gini for Teotihuacan is 0.12 (Smith et al. 2014). This is an astonishingly low number. If inequality and complexity were correlated, we would expect the Gini of a complex metropolis such as Teotihuacan to be higher.

To understand the problems with a single-variable approach, consider the Soviet period in Russia between the 1960s and the 1980s. This period was characterized by growing hierarchy and well-documented inequality (Sargsyan 1990). Examining the evidence, we could ask whether Ginis for house size or income in Soviet Moscow would adequately reflect the observed and documented hierarchies and inequality, or whether these measurements would suggest low inequality. The majority of the urban Soviet population, both elites and nonelites, lived in government-built apartments whose size was strictly regulated. The income distribution within Soviet society especially after the Stalinist period also highlights a general decline in income difference. The formal salaries for factory workers, scientists, and party functionaries converged between 1955 and 1990 because of major structural changes to salary distribution imposed by the Soviet state (Sargsyan 1990). If we relied on house size or income alone, the Gini values would indeed be low and we would be forced to conclude that Soviet society was markedly equal. However, we know this "egalitarian" distribution of housing was the intentional product of an ideological experiment in communism. Under these regulations, even the suite of residences given to the party elites within the Kremlin was modest, compared with the residences of political elites in other societies, including Western democracies. Also, the mean difference between formal salaries of the upper-status tiers declined from as much as six times to only twice that of lower-status groups between 1955 and 1990 (Karlin 2012; Sargsyan 1990).

It was not house size, however, but location and access to non-income-based wealth that mirrored and approximated inequality in Soviet society. Houses in better locations in Soviet cities, though not markedly larger than those in less-desired locations, usually went to higher-status families, thereby reinforcing inequality (Alexeev 1988). Furthermore, housing in better locations could be "leased" or even "purchased" through a combination of *blat* (bribery, corruption) and access to hard currency. Access to wealth accruing from *blat* in turn provided access to housing in better locations and (for party hierarchs) to villas and *dachas* (country estates). The residences of the wealthier groups, despite the similarities in house size and formal income, also showed higher levels of status in the goods they contained. These could be imported goods purchased from special commissary stores that accepted only Western currencies or imported through informal means such as black markets, or they could be scarce comestibles (eggs, fruit, or vegetables).

Teotihuacan, lacking palaces and closed elite localities, might reflect a complex society with greater equality only if house size were a clear and known reflection of wealth and resources. If, however, a society regulates house sizes (and other forms of consumption) or places upper limits on physical expansion of house space (dense urban dwellings [see chapter 9, this volume]), then a Gini based on house size would potentially mask other systems of inequality. On the basis of our observations, we reiterate that material indicators can be heuristically satisfactory indicators of inequality if, and only if, we use a sufficiently high number and diversity of variables to mitigate against factors such as social regulation and ideology that might limit overt or conspicuous displays of status, wealth, or inequity, while masking deeper material inequalities.

FROM MULTIPLE GINIS TO CAI

We developed the CAI to be an aggregated measure of the maximum number of material variables available. For the purposes of this chapter, we calculate the CAI for one ethnographic case and three archaeological case studies to compare its apparent efficacy across these samples. We first calculate Ginis for n material economic variables within each of the societies and then use the geometric mean of these Ginis to calculate the CAI for each site for each time period and also for comparing within and between subgroups (using the methodology of the HDI):

$$CAI = (G_1 * G_2 * G_3 * \ldots * G_n)^{1/n}$$

Because each Gini (G_n) coefficient is a normalized measurement in which $0 \leq G_n \leq 1$, the resulting CAI will also fall within the same range. As the number of variables increases, both the accuracy and precision of the CAI should also increase. The other main reason for using multiple variables is to ensure comparability between sites and through time. Put another way, how do you compare inequality in pastoral versus agricultural settlements if they have different material culture and differences in social, political, and economic organization? A CAI should determine a replicable measure of general inequality within each settlement that could then be compared and would consider variation in material culture between the sites.

The reasons for using a geometric mean are twofold. First, it gives a "figure of merit" for items that have multiple properties with different numeric ranges, and hence it can be used with ranked or scale data. Second, it is regarded as an ideal method for averaging normalized data such as Gini coefficients. Among the reasons for the UNDP switching to the geometric mean to calculate the HDI is the following: "The geometric mean decreases the level of substitutability between dimensions [being compared] and at the same time ensures that a 1 percent decline in say life expectancy at birth has the same impact on the HDI as a 1 percent decline in education or income. Thus, as a basis for comparisons of achievements, this method is also more respectful of the intrinsic differences across the dimensions than a simple average" (UNDP 2010). While we have considered other methods for measuring central tendencies, including median and principal components analysis, we suggest that the geometric mean is a more conservative and ultimately more useful method for calculating the CAI, as it tends to correct against the effects of a few high values. We considered using the median as an aggregated measure, but it can only work for continuous data where the number of variables is greater than three. We discarded the arithmetic mean as a measure, as it gives consistently higher CAI values because of the greater effect of outliers. For further research, we suggest the development of a range for the CAI with the median as an upper bound and the geometric mean as the lower bound.

The CAI enables two approaches: (1) the testing of hypothesized changes in inequality derived from *previous* empirical data, and (2) the development of hypotheses that may be tested with *future* empirical data. As an illustration of both approaches, we employ three case studies: Kakuma Refugee Camp (forty-four households) in Kenya, Indian Ocean trading ports (Chaul in India, eight areas; Mtwapa in Kenya, ten areas), and Bronze Age Jordan (Numayra, three houses).

We utilized available material data from all of these sites to calculate Ginis for the material data available for these sites and to calculate CAIs for each site as a geometric mean of the material Ginis. We calculated the Gini values using RStudio (DescTools package) with confidence intervals set at 80 percent through bootstrapping (R = 4000). While higher confidence values (95 percent) could be calculated, the range of the calculated Gini made the measurements unusable. We agree with various other authors in this volume that the large ranges for calculated Ginis, even with 80 percent confidence intervals, is problematic. In many cases, we are unable to state with any confidence that Ginis calculated for specific phases are truly statistically different. Also, if the counts of any material across the units in a site are precisely the same, we ignore the calculated Gini value of 0 for that variable. This is necessary since any variable with a value of 0 renders the geometric mean also 0 and hence useless.

However, these limitations would be problematic only if the Ginis or the CAIs were considered as exact measurements of inequality, an approach that we strenuously avoid and caution against in this chapter. Our purpose is to use the calculated Ginis and the resulting CAIs to test hypothesized trends in inequality derived from other data sources and analytical methods, as well as to develop new hypotheses for testing with other methods. To that end, we state our expected findings on inequality from each site as a hypothesis developed by previous work. We then use the CAIs calculated from Ginis of multiple variables to assess different manifestations of and trends in inequality at each site. We first begin with an ethnographic case: understanding inequality within populations uniformly deemed as poor: refugees living in encampment situations.

ETHNOGRAPHIC CASE STUDY: DEEMED POOR VERSUS REALLY POOR IN KAKUMA REFUGEE CAMP

Established in 1992 for refugees fleeing the Sudan conflict, Kakuma Refugee Camp (with a current overall population of 210,000) is one of the largest and oldest relief settlements in the world (see figure 3.1). Kakuma is divided into several subcamps (Kakuma 1, 2, 3, and 4), with people hailing from South Sudan, Sudan, Somalia, Ethiopia, Eritrea, Uganda, Democratic Republic of Congo (DRC), Burundi, and Rwanda. They receive relief in the form of a food basket comprising beans, maize, sorghum, green grams (mung beans), oil, salt, and occasionally flour. While the World Food Program (WFP) considers this a sufficient meal providing between 2,000 and 2,200 calories per person per day, refugees also depend on the commercial economy for culturally appropriate dietary and culinary needs, as well as comforts and luxuries (Oka 2014). Refugees reported gaining access to these goods through cash or credit, largely through remittances (35 percent), jobs (60 percent), and selling food from their relief basket (97 percent) (Oka 2011).

In October 2009 and March 2010, Oka and his team conducted an ethnoarchaeological survey in Kakuma 1 on forty-six Somali households at various distances from the main market area and randomly selected

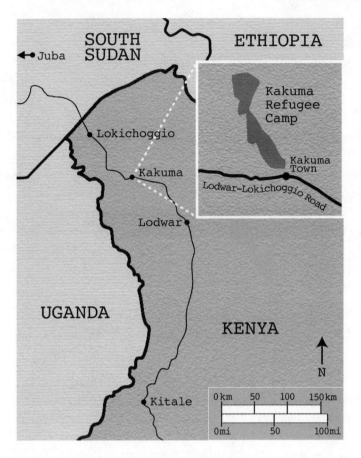

Figure 3.1 Kakuma Refugee Camp (Kenya).

along a transect beginning at the primary market and moving northward. The distance from the market center was plotted using a map generated by the United Nations High Commission for Refugees (UNHCR). Garbage is gathered and discarded every Friday morning for the weekly celebration of Juma. Hence the survey was conducted on Thursdays to capture material remains of weekly consumption. Households were divided into the following groups: Group 1, those that received cash through remittances, jobs, and the sale of rations (n = 14, 30 percent of surveyed households); Group 2, those that received cash through jobs and the sale of rations (n = 15, 33 percent); and Group 3, those that received cash only through the sale of rations (n = 17, 37 percent).

One of the purposes of this study was to ascertain whether archaeological approaches to understanding consumption could also shed light on the complexity of the "poor." Refugees are uniformly seen as poor and destitute. Yet within any settlement of displaced peoples, there are emergent social, ethnic, economic, political, and ideological hierarchies, driven by the cultural behaviors brought in by the refugees and the dynamics of camp life. This study focused on a deceptively simple question: can we distinguish between the "deemed poor" (Group 2) and the "really poor" (Group 3) using material data to extrapolate such methods into the archaeological past (Oka and Bartone 2013)? This is an important question because a significant proportion of those deemed poor (Group 2) have greater access to material consumption than do those who are truly poor (Group 3) although the two groups are indistinguishable in terms of resource ownership. Consequently, those deemed poor are better poised to benefit from policies and actions underlying welfare, development, and poverty alleviation programs (Meyer and Sullivan 2008). The conflation of both groups into one category invariably and disproportionately helps one group and excludes the other.

The results from the prior analysis suggest that Group 2 had significantly more access to consumption of resources than did Group 3 (Oka and Bartone 2013), implying that the CAI showing the distribution of material consumption and access to resources within Groups 2 and 3 would be high. We also hypothesized (after Jantzen and Volpert 2012) that the overall CAIs for Kakuma (All Kakuma) and for the deemed poor of Kakuma (Kakuma "Poor" of Group 2 and Group 3) would be similar to each other, suggesting a scale-free distribution of inequality between the upper and lower levels of society. Subsequently, we calculated Gini coefficients and CAIs for thirty-six material and behavioral indictors of consumption but with the sample divided into two larger groups: All Kakuma (Groups 1, 2, and 3) and Kakuma "Poor" (Groups 2 and 3).

The results from the analysis of Ginis and CAI suggest no significant difference between the overall CAI for all of Kakuma (0.47) and the CAI for the "poor" of Kakuma (Groups 2 and 3) (0.46). The relatively high inequalities within the refugee camp are exacerbated when the CAI is calculated without including the resources given by the relief community, mainly housing (and the location of such) and relief food, for both groups. As expected, the results for All Kakuma (0.52) and Kakuma

"Poor" (0.50) are very similar. Interestingly, the Ginis for house size for both groups are 0.16 and 0.17, both low, despite the overall inequality. This suggests that the observed inequality of Kakuma might be driven by differential access to consumption across the three groups, even as house size is strictly regulated and monitored by authorities.

The ethnographic case study of Kakuma demonstrates the utility of applying CAI from multiple Ginis in a contemporary context, as well as the danger of using house-size Ginis in societies where plot allocations and sizes are strictly controlled by regulating authority. But can we apply this methodology to past societies and develop CAIs to test hypotheses on trends in inequality over time? In the next section, we turn to archaeological case studies, with different data sets and historical contexts ranging from the Indian Ocean Trading Complex (300 BCE–1800 CE) to Early Bronze Age Southwest Asia (2850–2550 BCE), to identify different trajectories in inequality over the duration of settlements.

APPLYING GINI TO ARCHAEOLOGICAL CASE STUDIES

CASE STUDY: INDIAN OCEAN PORT CITIES

The ports of Chaul (300 BCE–1800 CE) and Mtwapa (800–1800 CE) (figure 3.2) were active trade centers in the Indian Ocean world. The rise of these ports, while separated by almost a millennium, transpired during global trade booms: Chaul in the Early Common Era (300 BCE–200 CE) and Mtwapa in the Long Eighth Century (700–900 CE). However, both ports declined almost simultaneously between 1600 and 1800 CE (Oka 2008; Oka et al. 2009). The reasons for this conterminous decline are complex but, between 1500 and 1600 CE, involve the juxtaposition of European presence with the sudden growth of political stability under the large Asian Muslim empires, which led to the trade/commercial boom of the Early Modern Era (ca. 1500–1700 CE), and the emergence of global traders as powerful political and financial brokers. In a drastic break from earlier practices focused on sustainable partnerships, these groups invested in market capture, predatory import substitution, and extraction of raw materials with impunity, especially in smaller ports and peripheral areas (Oka et al. 2009).

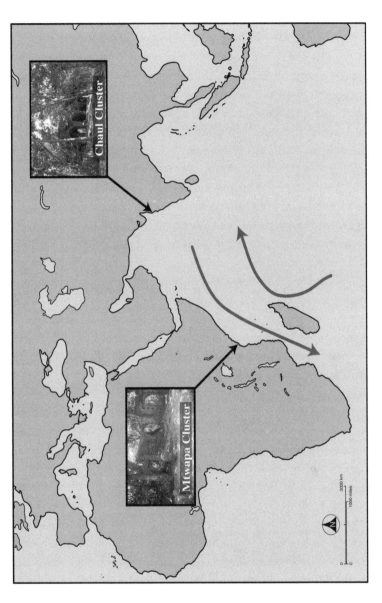

Figure 3.2 Mtwapa and Chaul (Indian Ocean).

To accommodate the changing needs of these traders, port city elites across the Indian Ocean actively disinvested in local production, encouraged market capture by their foreign trade partners, and intensified raw-material extraction (Oka et al. 2009). This led to growing competition between and within the port elites, who in turn transferred investment in former corporate group alliances to networks with foreign traders. There was a drastic increase in public displays of generosity and status through feasting and philanthropy for attracting and reinforcing alliances with foreign traders. Over the long run, this attritional process led to decreasing revenues and a decline in the formerly robust elite-group investment in maintaining the commercial infrastructure of ports. By the mid-seventeenth century, foreign traders were pulling their capital away from smaller ports and investing instead in larger ports that continued to offer required infrastructure and services. As trading activities increasingly became concentrated in megaports such as Mumbai and Mombasa, smaller ports such as Chaul and Mtwapa declined or collapsed (Oka 2008; Oka et al. 2009).

We hypothesized that these changes would be correlated with changes in overall inequality within the elite groups of small ports, namely, Mtwapa and Chaul, and that for small ports the periods of emergence and decline would be characterized by higher inequality and the intermediary period would exhibit low values of CAI. We calculated the CAI for both Mtwapa and Chaul through time, based on multiple Ginis of artifacts recovered from both sites, to test the hypothesized trends in inequality among the port elites. Unlike other chapters in this volume, we did not include house-size Ginis for either port. These are all elite residences, and their horizontal growth was restricted by the dense clustering of houses within the walled city. These houses ranged between 100 and 150 square meters, with low Gini scores. Such relative equality in house sizes would be similar to the aforementioned observations for Soviet cities, our own results from Kakuma Refugee Camp, and Mesopotamia (chapter 9). The house sizes also did not change much over time even as residences changed owners. Because our aim in this chapter was to test hypothesized trends in CAI over time and the house sizes did not change and were not significantly correlated with artifact distribution, we did not include house-size Ginis in our calculation of CAI.

Mtwapa

Mtwapa emerged as a port circa 800 CE and declined/collapsed between 1750 and 1800 CE. Port elites brokered trade between foreign merchants and hinterland producers (Kusimba 1999). To sustain this trade, the elites (in Swahili, *waungwana*) operated as a corporate group that built solidarity and legitimized each other's (and their own) status and control over the commercial economy through publicly performed rituals and communal activities such as monumental construction and feasting (after Blanton et al. 1996; Kusimba 1999; Kusimba and Oka 2009; Robertshaw 2003). These alliances ensured the sustained flow of desired goods between hinterlands and foreign markets between 800 and 1600 CE. During the decline phase, the corporate *waungwana* collapsed because of elite in-between group competition, following the general observed trend across the Indian Ocean.

On the basis of this analysis, we expected the CAI to rise between 800 and 1000 CE, decline between 1000 and 1600, and rise after 1600, with high inequality bookending the rise and demise of Mtwapa as a trading city. The archaeological data for calculating the Ginis are focused on prestige wares prized by Swahili elites: glazed wares, celadons, and blue-and-white as well as white porcelain recovered from ten large households/areas within the old walled city of Mtwapa (100–150 m²). The assemblage was divided into six periods (pre-800, 800–1000, 1000–1200, 1200–1400, 1400–1600, and 1600–1800 CE) using both radiometric and archaeometric dating techniques (Oka et al. 2009). We expected that the rise of the corporate *waungwana* elites between 1000 and 1600 CE would be correlated with a relative decline in CAI, while growing competition within the elite community would be correlated with increasing CAI after 1600 CE. The results are shown in figures 3.3 and 3.4.

The results clearly demonstrate that trends in the CAI follow the expected patterns. On one hand, this should be expected because the hypothesized trends were developed on previous analysis of the distribution of the material. It is important to note, however, that the CAI minimizes the variation within each category to give a more comprehensive figure. Although the differences in CAI are not statistically significant across the periods, the trends do indicate some transformation in elite organization

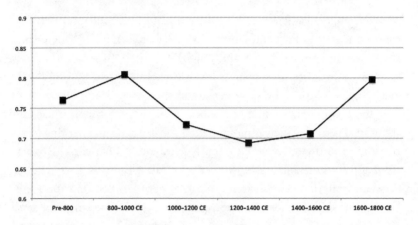

Figure 3.3 Mtwapa CAI (pre-800–1800 CE).

from network to corporate and back to network. Further efforts will include calculating Ginis and CAI based on other material data, including house size, compound area, coarse wares, beads and other prestige crafts products, and faunal and palynological data.

Chaul

Chaul emerged around 300 BCE and continued until 1800, after which it declined. The booming commerce of the Early Common Era (300 BCE–200 CE) promoted open elite competition (Gogte et al. 2006; Ray 1994). The decline of global (but not regional) trade during the so-called Dark Ages (300–600 CE) and the reemergence of large states (600–1200 CE) characterized by volatility and instability led to growing cooperation between various elite groups to maintain their roles and statuses and to ensure autonomy from hinterland states. This autonomy depended on their revenue-generation abilities, which in turn depended on the ports' ability to attract trade, labor, and capital. During these volatile periods, Chaul elites hailing from economic, political, and ideological sectors practiced corporate cooperative strategies and invested in communal solidarity-building rituals, as well as the construction and maintenance of public granaries, warehouses, temples, stupas, monasteries, mosques, synagogues, and churches (Fukuzawa 1991; Gogte et al. 2006; Oka 2018).

These acts facilitated legitimacy of control and also served to successfully attract traders, labor, and capital, thereby providing revenue for maintaining commercial infrastructure. This success reinforced the legitimacy of the elites and attracted more trade, labor, and capital. Between 600 and 1500 CE, the elites of Chaul had institutionalized a tripartite division/sharing of political, economic, and ideological power to negotiate the continuing political instability. Between 1500 and 1800 CE, however, there was increasing competition between and within the elites to attract more clients in the commercial boom of the Early Modern Era. There was a significant shift away from the previous corporate tripartite power sharing toward individual alliance networks between elites and foreign traders. This competition resulted in growing public displays of wealth expenditure as elites sought to outdo each other in competitive displays of their wealth and generosity at public places (Gogte 2003).

This analysis led us to expect that the CAI for Chaul would show decreasing inequality between 0 and 1500 CE and would be bookended by higher inequality during the periods of the early rise (300 BCE–0 CE) and later demise (1500–1800 CE). Archaeological excavations at Chaul resulted in material data from eight houses/areas (100–150 m²) conforming to seven periods of occupation: 300 BCE–0 CE, 0 CE–300 CE, 300–600 CE, 600–900 CE, 900–1200 CE, 1200–1500 CE, and 1500–1800 CE. Ginis were computed for the distribution of beads, bangles, iron nails (a prized commodity), iron pieces, glass (bottles, bowls, shards, and debitage), jewelry (necklaces, rings, etc.), ivory, and art (images, figurines, lamps, and other products of high-end manufacture). The results for the CAI calculation for Chaul over time are shown in figure 3.4.

Unsurprisingly, the results follow the expected trends. Specifically, the data suggest that the emergence of Chaul (300 BCE–0 CE) was marked by high inequality within the elite groups. The volatility of the political and trading landscapes alike between 300 and 1500 CE was mitigated by the emergence/persistence (300–1200 CE) and institutionalization (1200–1500 CE) of corporate elite groups. These groups ensured continuity through their success in port management and trade revenue extraction, thereby contributing to a declining trend in the CAI from

Chaul CAI (300 BCE-1800 CE)

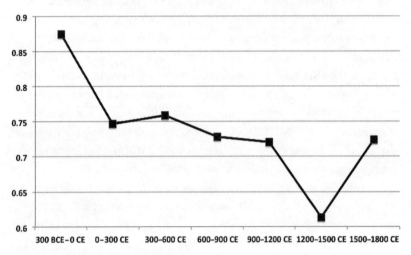

Figure 3.4 Chaul CAI (300 BCE–1800 CE).

300 CE to 1500 CE. The final decline of Chaul was marked by a sudden increase in inequality. Further research includes the use of ceramic and architectural data from the eight households to confirm these trends. Although we do caution against considering individual Ginis and the CAIs for each time period as absolute measurements of inequality, there was a strong agreement between expected and observed trends of inequality over time at both sites.

Parallel Trends in Inequality Across the Western Indian Ocean

The trends in CAI for the two Indian Ocean ports mirror trends observed by other chapters in this volume (chapters 1, 5, 11): that higher inequality might be an indicator of the rise and decline of complex societies, while lower forms of inequality might suggest that elites develop means to reduce within-group competition for the sake of general social stability. We now turn from the historical period to the Early Bronze Age southern Levant to see whether CAI calculated from multiple Ginis enables the testing of hypothesized changes in inequality in small village settlements in the early third millennium BCE.

THIRD-MILLENNIUM POPULATION AGGREGATION IN THE SOUTHERN LEVANT: NUMAYRA

As a third contrastive case study, we turn to the Early Bronze Age III (EB III) fortified town of Numayra (ca. 2850–2550 cal BC), located on the southeastern Dead Sea Plain of the Hashemite Kingdom of Jordan (figure 3.5). The emergence of fortified settlements is a key feature of the Early Bronze Age I–III (ca. 3600–2500 BC) in the southern Levant (Chesson 2015). People abandoned small-scale communities to move into a new type of place—fortified towns—and fundamentally transformed the social, economic, political, and physical geographies of their lives. In the absence of elites, powerful civic and ritual institutions, extensive trade, prestige goods, writing systems, pronounced sociopolitical complexity, and large populations, however, this transformation lacks many of V. Gordon Childe's (1950) hallmarks of urbanism. Instead, people aggregated into large walled towns and villages, intensified agricultural and pastoral production, and invested in non-residential storage facilities, while negotiated growing tensions between rising inequality and more-horizontal relationships within the towns (Chesson 2015; Crumley 1987; Greenberg 2014; Harrison and Savage 2003; Philip 2008).

This reorganization of society necessitated a transformation of people's relationships with material and immaterial resources, especially those linked to land, water, plants, and animals. This widespread aggregation into walled towns required the reorganization of rules governing property, land tenure, water management, and agricultural systems, as well as ritual and craft knowledge, labor, kinship, and economic relationships (Chesson 2003; de Miroschedji 2009; Greenberg 2014; Philip 2008). To feed and support these larger populations, governance structures needed to manage resources, land, and people both inside the settlement and in its immediate hinterlands. This included managerial investment in irrigation systems, orchards, terraces, roads, fortification walls and gates, administrative complexes, ritual compounds, and markets (at larger sites). Differential access to and control over staple goods, land, labor, and water resources acted as the girding underlying Early Bronze Age political, economic, and social power and authority (Chesson and Goodale 2014; Greenberg 2014).

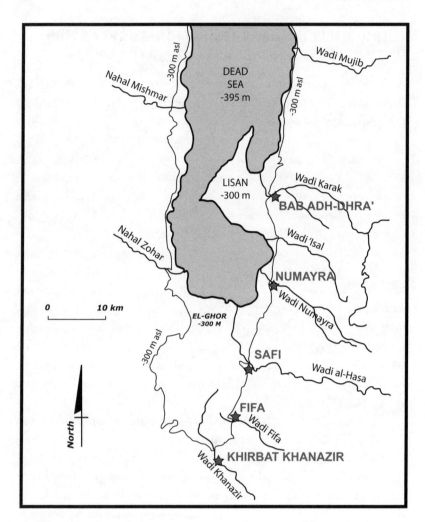

Figure 3.5 Numayra, Jordan.

The EB III site of Numayra, Jordan, is one of numerous smaller fortified towns in the region. Numayra was one hectare in size, of which
1,600 square meters have been excavated, yielding data on household
economies, storage practices, food production, and craft specialization
(Chesson and Goodale 2014; Chesson et al. 2018 (forthcoming); Coogan 1984; Schaub and Chesson 2007). In this study, we focus on three
residential compounds covering approximately 1,000 square meters in

the central area, across two major occupational phases during the walled town's heyday: Phase 2A and Phase 2B (the earlier Phase 1 represents the prefortification settlement). Excellent preservation of artifacts, architecture, and paleoethnobotanical remains offers material evidence to assess variation in socioeconomic organization among the EB III peoples over the two periods of occupation (Chesson and Goodale 2014).

Analysis of social differentiation and inequality at Numayra provides an interesting perspective on differentiation and hierarchy. There are minimal differences in architectural space and materials, ceramic forms, ground stone objects, and inbuilt features within the three households in either of the two periods. All three households over both phases contained food-preparation features, such as hearths, ovens, and grinding slabs, as well as storage features with comparable capacity (Chesson and Goodale 2104). All three households contained concentrated deposits of cereals (emmer wheat or barley) and the same forms of ceramic vessels, chipped stone tools, and ground stone implements. Paleoethnobotanical analysis of grapes and barley shows clear evidence for irrigation (White et al. 2018). The large quantities of grapes also demonstrate a marked investment in managing grape orchards in a challenging arid environment, requiring cooperative management of water and land resources.

Despite these commonalities, the analysis does identify household-level specialization in both phases, to differing degrees. We argue, however, that in these cases specialization does not equal inequality. The distribution of artifacts and plant remains across the three excavated households during Phase 2B (when we have the best evidence) shows patterns of horizontal differentiation between households but no direct evidence of inequality, especially in terms of craft and food production. For example, one residential unit seems to have been associated heavily with textile production. Their next-door neighbors stored remains of wine in storage jars in one room of the compound, with processed barley and wheat to the exclusion of all other plants in an adjacent room. In the third residential compound, inhabitants stored large quantities of grapes (or possibly raisins) in clay bins or baskets but did not leave behind any tools for textile production. In Phases 2A and 2B, excavators recovered chipped stone toolkits in one residential compound, with the other two lacking such a collection of tools and raw materials. The appearance of nonlocal plant-stuffs in all three households, such as discrete and smaller concentrations of chickpeas, suggest exchange relationships with people living in other areas of the region where these plants were commonly grown. In looking at these patterns, we can imagine that residents of certain households managed or had access to certain types of plants (grapes) and animal resources, while their neighbors were more heavily involved in different kinds of craft and food production (weaving and wine making).

With the mixed evidence for social differentiation at EB III Numayra, we expected the CAI to be low (less than 0.50) in Phases 2A and 2B alike and also similar across phases. After calculating the Ginis for various material variables for both phases in Numayra, we determined that the Ginis for both phases are similar to each other across the material categories. The expected household differentiation and specialization is clearly visible in the categories with high Ginis (less than or equal to 0.67) in both phases, especially in the distribution of specialized tools and materials for ceramic, alcohol (wine), stone, and other production activities. Phases 2A and 2B both showed low CAIs that have no statistically significant difference between them, either for the CAI with household specialization (CAI for Phase 2A, 0.32; for Phase 2B, 0.32) or for the CAI without the household specialization (CAI for Phase 2A, 0.19; for Phase 2B, 0.22). The slight difference between the two phases is statistically insignificant, because the actual values suggest relatively low levels of inequality in both phases.

It is possible that the relatively small sample size of households ($n = 3$) might not be representative of the settlement as a whole. Additionally, more than half of the settlement was lost to erosion from the Wadi Numayra: perhaps preservation of the site did not include the nonresidential storage facilities, ritual compounds, or other indicators of greater inequality. Residential compounds at other contemporaneous fortified sites, such as Bâb adh-Dhrâ, lack evidence for marked social differentiation and inequality. However, at larger fortified sites (generally seven hectares or greater) like Tel Bet Yerah (Greenberg et al. 2006), Yarmouth (de Miroschedji 2009), and Khirbat as-Zaraqon (Genz 2002), the presence of nonresidential storage facilities and ritual compounds, evidence for interaction with Egypt, and greater populations likely required more-codified status differentiation (Greenberg 2014). That EB III people assigned different social values to specialized crafts and other production activities is possible. Any social differentiation, however, does not seem to correlate to basic, staple resources, including the size of houses, the number of rooms, ceramics, and tools. Our analysis suggests that a focus on vertical inequality might serve to hide horizontal inequalities, which might have manifested in social and political but not material-economic differentiation.

DISCUSSION AND CONCLUSIONS

We developed the CAI following the methodology of the United Nations Development Programme's HDI, to use Ginis that assess the distributions of material culture within both archaeological and ethnographic sites. However, our concern is not to measure absolute inequality per se but to test trends and patterns in inequality within and between settlements through space and time. We used the CAIs for these societies to test anthropologically derived hypotheses or expectations of trends over time (in Numayra, Mtwapa, and Chaul) and on the complexities of inequality within subgroups arising from differential access to consumption (in Kakuma). Our analysis illustrates the following:

- Comparison of consumption of material culture among the refugees in Kakuma indicates that there is a statistically significant difference in consumption abilities between those "deemed poor" (Group 2) and the "truly poor" (Group 3). The calculated CAI for all of Kakuma and the conflated "poor" of Kakuma indicated a scale-free distribution of the CAI, with a high CAI characterizing both analyzed groups. Specifically, the high CAI value for the conflated category of Groups 2 and 3 confirms the results of the consumption analysis. Both analyses indicate significant social and economic distance between those who have some access to consumption of resources (deemed poor, or Group 2) and those who have none (the truly poor, or Group 3).
- We tested previously inferred and hypothesized shifts in elite alliance formation strategies from network to corporate and back to network in both of the Indian Ocean ports, Mtwapa and Chaul, which would indicate that high inequality characterized the beginnings and ends of each port city as a sustainable settlement. Both ports underwent the generation and institutionalization of

corporate elite groups that functioned to maintain stability of trade, commerce, and revenues for the ports. The decline of the ports was paralleled by a decline in the corporate groups and seems to have preceded larger global changes in commercial and financial systems.

• The Early Bronze Age III site Numayra offered a chance to test the CAI and Gini in a case with low to absent hierarchical inequality but with synchronic differentiation in daily practices. This test demonstrates, supporting expectations from previous archaeological analysis, that economic differentiation does not always equate with status and economic inequality in terms of hierarchical political, economic, and social structures.

In conclusion, while individual Ginis of material data might offer limited accuracy and precision as measures of inequality, rigorous combination of multiple Ginis into an index such as the CAI provides a powerful heuristic tool for more-detailed question-oriented research on the dynamic evolution of inequality in archaeology. Specifically, we argue that the CAIs based on multiple Ginis enable researchers to present hypothesized trends in inequality across and within sites. However, we caution that individual Ginis or the CAI cannot be taken as an absolute measurement of inequality and thus should not be (mis)used to categorize societies. The main strength of the CAI is its dynamic ability to include and incorporate any number of variables (as long as the data are used to show how any material is distributed across a settlement). Our own data suggest that as the number of variables increases, the CAI stabilizes. Does it give a reasonable quantified approximation of inequality at any given time or place? Perhaps, but we discourage such use of the CAI. By looking at the changes in the CAI derived from a high number of material variables, however, we can better understand and operationalize trends in inequality and add to the growing conversation on inequality by analyzing how these trends have emerged and been reproduced in many societies over the past 10,000 years. For archaeologists, that might be the safest approach.

ACKNOWLEDGMENTS

We thank Tim Kohler and Mike Smith for organizing the original panel at the SAA, the Amerind workshop, and this volume. We would also like to thank the University of Notre Dame, Notre Dame Institute for Advanced Studies, NSF (various grants), Wenner-Gren Foundation, National Geographic Society, National Endowment for the Humanities, Carnegie Institute, Pittsburgh Theological Seminary, World Bank, UNHCR, and the governments and research institutes of Jordan, Kenya, and India for support and funding. We would like to thank the Amerind Foundation for accepting our session and hosting us in Dragoon, Arizona.

REFERENCES CITED

Alexeev, Michael. 1988. The Effect of Housing Allocation on Social Inequality: A Soviet Perspective. *Journal of Comparative Economics* 12(2):228–34.

Altekar, Anant Sadashiv. 2009. *State and Government in Ancient India.* Motilal Banarsidas Press, New Delhi, India.

Anand, Sudhir, and Amartya Sen. 1994. *Human Development Index: Methodology and Measurement.* Occasional Paper 12. UN Development Programme, Human Development Report Office, New York.

Banerjee, Abhijit V., and Esther Duflo. 2011. *Poor Economics: A Radical Rethinking of the Way to Fight Global Poverty.* PublicAffairs, New York.

Blanton, Richard E., Gary M. Feinman, Stephen A. Kowalewski, and Peter N. Peregrine. 1996. A Dual-Processual Theory for the Evolution of Mesoamerican Civilization. *Current Anthropology* 37(1):1–14.

Chesson, Meredith S. 2003. Households, Houses, Neighborhoods and Corporate Villages. Modeling the Early Bronze Age as a House Society. *Journal of Mediterranean Archaeology* 16(1):79–102.

———. 2015. Reconceptualizing the Early Bronze Age Southern Levant Without Cities: Local Histories and Walled Communities of EBA II–III Society. *Journal of Mediterranean Archaeology* 28(1):21–79.

Chesson, Meredith S., and Nathan Goodale. 2014. Population Aggregation, Residential Storage, and Socioeconomic Inequality at Early Bronze Age Numayra, Jordan. *Journal of Anthropological Archaeology* 35:117–34.

Chesson, Meredith S., R. Thomas Schaub, and Walter E. Rast. 2018. *Numayra: Excavations at the Early Bronze Age Townsite in Jordan, 1977–1983.* Vol. 4 of *Expedition to the Dead Sea Plain.* Eisenbrauns, Winona Lake, Ind. Forthcoming.

Childe, V. Gordon. 1950. The Urban Revolution. *Town Planning Review* 21:3–17.

Coogan, Michael D. 1984. Numeira 1981. *Bulletin of the American Schools of Oriental Research* 255:75–81.

Crumley, Carole L. 1987. A Dialectical Critique of Hierarchy. In *Power Relations and State Formation,* edited by Thomas C. Patterson and Christine W. Gailey, pp. 155–69. American Anthropological Association, Washington, D.C.

Deaton, Angus. 2013. *The Great Escape: Health, Wealth, and the Origins of Inequality*. Princeton University Press, Princeton.

———. 2014. Inevitable Inequality? *Science* 244:783.

de Miroschedji, Pierre. 2009. Rise and Collapse in the Southern Levant in the Early Bronze Age. *Scienze dell'Antichità: Storia, Archeologica, Antropologia* 15:101–29.

Easterly, William. 2006. *The White Man's Burden: Why the West's Efforts to Aid the Rest Have Done So Much Ill and So Little Good*. Penguin, New York.

———. 2007. Inequality Does Cause Underdevelopment: Insights from a New Instrument. *Journal of Development Economics* 84(2):755–76.

Escobar, Arturo. 1995. *Encountering Development: The Making and Unmaking of the Third World*. Princeton University Press, Princeton.

Farmer, Paul. 2005. *Pathologies of Power: Health, Human Rights, and the New War on the Poor*. University of California Press, Berkeley.

Feinman, Gary M. 1995. The Emergence of Inequality: A Focus on Strategies and Processes. In *Foundations of Social Inequality*, edited by T. Douglas Price and Gary M. Feinman, pp. 255–79. Plenum, New York.

Flanagan, James G. 1989. Hierarchy in Simple "Egalitarian" Societies. *Annual Review of Anthropology* 18:245–66.

Frangipane, Marcella. 2007. Different Types of Egalitarian Societies and the Development of Inequality in Early Mesopotamia. *World Archaeology* 39(2):151–76.

Fukuyama, Francis 1992. *The End of History and the Last Man*. Free Press, New York.

Fukuzawa, Hiroshi. 1991. *The Medieval Deccan: Peasants, Social Systems and States, Sixteenth to Eighteenth Centuries*. Oxford University Press, Delhi.

Genz, Hermann. 2002. *Die frühbronzezeitliche Keramik von Hirbet ez-Zeraqon: Deutsch-jordanische Ausgrabungen in Hirbet ez-Zeraqon 1984–1994*. Abhandlungen des Deutschen Palaestina-Vereins 27, 2. Harrassowitz, Wiesbaden.

Ghurye, G. S. 1969. *Caste and Race in India*. Popular Prakashan, Mumbai, India.

Gogte, Vishwas. 2003. The Archaeology of Maritime Trade at Chaul, Western Coast of India. *Man and Environment* 38:67–74.

Gogte, Vishwas, Shrikant Pradhan, Abhijit Dandekar, Sachin Joshi, Rukhshana Nanji, Shivendra Kadgaonkar, and Vikram Marathe. 2006. The Ancient Port at Chaul. *Journal of Indian Ocean Archaeology* 3:62–80.

Greenberg, R. 2014. Introduction to the Levant in the Early Bronze Age. In *Oxford Handbook of the Archaeology of the Levant*, edited by Margreet L. Steiner and Ann E. Killebrew, pp. 263–71. Oxford University Press, Oxford.

Greenberg, Raphael, Sarit Paz, and Yitzhak Paz. 2006. *Bet Yerah, the Early Bronze Age Mound*. Vol. 1, *Excavations Reports, 1933–1986*. Israel Antiquities Authority, Jerusalem.

Haq, Mahbub ul. 1995. *Reflections on Human Development*. Oxford University Press, Oxford.

Harrison, Timothy P., and Stephen H. Savage. 2003. Settlement Heterogeneity and Multivariate Craft Production in the Early Bronze Age Southern Levant. *Journal of Mediterranean Archaeology* 16(1):33–57.

Hulme, David, Karen Moore, and Andrew Shepherd. 2001. *Chronic Poverty: Meanings and Analytical Frameworks*. CPRC Working Paper 2. Chronic Poverty Research Centre. www.chronicpoverty.org/uploads/publication_files /WP02_Hulme_et_al.pdf.

Jantzen, Robert T., and Klaus Volpert. 2012. On the Mathematics of Income Inequality: Splitting the Gini Index in Two. *American Mathematical Monthly* 119(10):824–37.

Joyce, Rosemary A. 2004. Unintended Consequences: Monumentality as a Novel Experience in Formative Mesoamerica. *Journal of Archaeological Method and Theory* 11:5–29.

Karlin, Anatoly. 2012. Ayn Stalin: Soviet Inequalities in 1929–1954. Webpost in Anatoly Karlin About Economy, June 24, 2012. http://akarlin.com/2012/06 /ayn-stalin/.

Keeley, Lawrence H. 1988. Hunter-Gatherer Economic Complexity and "Population Pressure": A Cross-Cultural Analysis. *Journal of Anthropological Archaeology* 7(4):373–411.

Kim, Jim Yong, Joyce V. Millen, Alec Irwin, and John Gershman. 2000. *Dying for Growth: Global Inequalities and the Health of the Poor*. Common Courage Press, Monroe, Me.

Kramer, Carol. 1982. *Village Ethnoarchaeology: Rural Iran in Archaeological Perspective*. Academic Press, New York.

Kuijt, Ian. 2008. Demography and Storage Systems During the Southern Levantine Neolithic Demographic Transition. In *The Neolithic Demographic Transition and Its Consequences*, edited by Jean-Pierre Bocquet-Appel and Ofer Bar-Yosef, pp. 287–313. Springer, Netherlands.

Kulke, Hermann, and Dietmar Rothermund. 1998. *A History of India*. Routledge, New York.

Kusimba, Chapurukha M. 1999. *The Rise and Fall of Swahili States*. AltaMira Press, Walnut Creek, Calif.

Kusimba, Chapurukha M., and Rahul Oka. 2009. Trade and Polity in East Africa: Re-examining Elite Strategies for Acquiring Power. In *The Changing Worlds of Atlantic Africa*, edited by Toyin Falola and Matt D. Childs, pp. 39–60. Carolina Academic Press, Durham, N.C.

Lin, Nan. 2000. Inequality in Social Capital. *Contemporary Sociology* 29(6):785–95.

Lindert, Peter H., and Jeffrey G. Williamson. 2003. Does Globalization Make the World More Unequal? In *Globalization in Historical Perspective*, edited by Michael D. Bordo, Alan M. Taylor, and Jeffrey G. Williamson, pp. 227–75. University of Chicago Press, Chicago.

Marcus, George E. 1983. Elite as a Concept, Theory and Research Tradition. In *Elites: Ethnographic Issues*, edited by George E. Marcus, pp. 7–27. University of New Mexico Press, Albuquerque.

Meyer, Bruce D., and James X. Sullivan. 2008. Changes in the Consumption, Income, and Well-Being of Single Mother Headed Families. *American Economic Review* 98(5):2221–41.

Moyo, Dambisa. 2009. *Dead Aid: Why Aid Is Not Working and How There Is a Better Way for Africa.* Macmillan, New York.

Oka, Rahul C. 2008. Resilience and Adaptation of Trade Networks in East African and South Asian Port Polities, 1500–1800 CE. PhD dissertation, University of Illinois, Chicago.

———. 2011. Unlikely Cities in the Desert: The Informal Economy as Causal Agent for Permanent "Urban" Sustainability in Kakuma Refugee Camp, Kenya. *Urban Anthropology and Studies of Cultural Systems and World Economic Development* 40(3/4):223–62.

———. 2014. Coping with the Refugee Wait: The Role of Consumption, Normalcy, and Dignity in Refugee Lives at Kakuma Refugee Camp, Kenya. *American Anthropologist* 116(1):23–37.

———. 2018. Trade, Traders, and Trading Systems: Exchange, Trade, Commerce and the Rise/Demise of Civilizations. In *Trade and Civilization,* edited by Kristian Kristiansen, pp. 333–79. Cambridge University Press, Cambridge. Forthcoming.

Oka, Rahul C., and Dianna Bartone. 2013. Reclaiming Poverty for Anthropology: How Archaeology Can Form the Basis for Understanding the Evolution, Endurance, and Ubiquity of Global Poverty. Presented at the 78th Annual Meetings of the Society for American Archaeology, Honolulu, Hawai'i, April 3–7, 2013.

Oka, Rahul C., Chapurukha M. Kusimba, and Vishwas D. Gogte. 2009. Where Others Fear to Trade. In *The Political Economy of Hazards and Disasters,* edited by Arthur Murphy and Eric Jones, pp. 201–32. Monographs in Economic Anthropology. Altamira Press, Walnut Creek, Calif.

Ostrom, Elinor. 2005. *Understanding Institutional Diversity.* Princeton University Press, Princeton.

Paynter, Robert. 1989. The Archaeology of Equality and Inequality. *Annual Review of Anthropology* 18:369–99.

Philip, Graham. 2008. The Early Bronze I–III Ages. In *Jordan: An Archaeological Reader,* edited by Russell Adams, pp. 161–226. Equinox Press, London.

Piketty, Thomas. 2014. *Capital in the Twenty-First Century.* Harvard University Press, Cambridge, Mass.

Prentiss, Anna Marie, Thomas A. Foor, Guy Cross, Lucille E. Harris, and Michael Wanzenried. 2012. The Cultural Evolution of Material Wealth Based Inequality at Bridge River, British Columbia. *American Antiquity* 77:542–64.

Price, T. Douglas, and Gary M. Feinman (editors). 1995. *Foundations of Social Inequality.* Plenum Press, New York.

Ray, Himanshu Prabha. 1994. *The Winds of Change: Buddhism and the Maritime Links of Early South Asia.* Oxford University Press, New Delhi.

Rist, Gilbert. 2007. Development as a Buzzword. *Development in Practice* 17(4–5):485–91.

Robertshaw, Peter. 2003. The Origins of the State in East Africa. In *East African Archaeology: Foragers, Potters, Smiths, and Traders*, edited by Chapurukha M. Kusimba and Sibel B. Kusimba, pp. 149–66. University Museum of Pennsylvania Press, Philadelphia.

Sargsyan, G. S. 1990. Level, Rates and Proportions of Growth of Real Incomes Under Socialism. Central Economics and Mathematics Institute of the USSR. http://50.economicus.ru/index.php?ch=2&le=20&r=5&z=1.

Schaub, R. Thomas, and Meredith S. Chesson. 2007. Life in the Earliest Walled Towns on the Dead Sea Plain: Numeira and Bâb adh-Dhrâ. In *Crossing Jordan: North American Contributions to the Archaeology of Jordan*, edited by Thomas Evan Levy, P. M. Michele Daviau, Randall W. Younker, and May Shaer, pp. 246–52. Equinox Press, London.

Sen, Amartya. 1992. *Inequality Reexamined*. Oxford University Press, Oxford.

Smith, Michael E., Timothy Dennehy, April Kamp-Whittaker, Emily Colon, and Rebecca Harkness. 2014. Quantitative Measures of Wealth Inequality in Ancient Central Mexican Communities. *Advances in Archaeological Practice* 2(4):311–23.

UNDP. 2010. Calculating the Human Development Index. United Nations Development Programme, New York. http://hdr.undp.org/en/content/human-development-index-hdi.

White, Chantel, David McCreery, and Fabian Toro. 2018. Crop Storage, Processing, and Cooking Practices at Numayra: The Plant Remains. In *Numayra: Excavations at the Early Bronze Age Townsite in Jordan, 1977–1983*, edited by Meredith S. Chesson, R. Thomas Schaub, and Walter E. Rast. Eisenbrauns, Winona Lake, Ind. Forthcoming.

4

Testing Hypotheses About Emergent Inequality (Using Gini Coefficients) in a Complex Fisher-Forager Society at the Bridge River Site, British Columbia

Anna Marie Prentiss, Thomas A. Foor, and
Mary-Margaret Murphy

Recent comparative ethnographic and archaeological research (Mattison et al. 2016; Borgerhoff Mulder et al. 2009; Shennan 2011; Smith et al. 2010) has identified what appear to be critical underlying factors conditioning the emergence of institutionalized inequality (Wiessner 2002). These include the presence of resources that are economically defensible and wealth that can be transmitted between generations. In those contexts, inequality must also be acceptable to an emerging subordinate class, typically because of limited options (Kennett et al. 2009; Smith and Choi 2007). Obvious examples to fit these conditions can be found in agricultural and pastoralist societies given the presence of obvious defensible and transmittable wealth. Such patterns are less well represented in horticultural and hunter-gatherer societies (Borgerhoff Mulder et al. 2009). Exceptions occur in hunter-gatherer societies where food resources occur in great abundance with accessibility limited to critical access points during particular times of year (Mattison et al. 2016).

It is clear that while significant progress has been made toward understanding the conditions under which institutionalized inequality develops, less formal attention has been paid to the development and use of rigorous quantitative techniques for measuring inequality and thus testing specific hypotheses. Gini coefficients have been in wide use in the social and economic sciences (e.g., Allison 1978; Cowell 1977; Gastwirth 1972) but have only occasionally made their way into archaeological studies (e.g., Hayden and Cannon 1984; Kohler and Higgins 2016; McGuire 1983; Schulting 1995; Smith et al. 2014; see also chapter 1, this volume). In this chapter, we explore the use of Gini coefficients to test hypotheses about emergent inequality at the Bridge River site, a large housepit village in the Middle Fraser Canyon of British Columbia.

The Mid-Fraser has served as an important context for the study of complex hunter-gatherer societies for several decades (Hayden 1997; Prentiss and Kuijt 2012), yet there remains much that we do not understand. This is partly due to limited archaeological investigations (in comparison to the American Southwest, for example) but also because of limitations in our measuring instruments. Thus, an additional contribution of this paper is a consideration of challenges for the application of Gini coefficients to measuring different forms of inequality in a complex hunter-gatherer context. We begin with a review of archaeological research in the Middle Fraser context that includes explication of specific hypotheses to be tested. We follow with a review of methodological concerns for use of Gini coefficients. We then present our results and conclusions with emphases on defining variation in form and scale of inequality at Bridge River. Interpretations of the Bridge River results are enhanced by comparison to Gini coefficients calculated for artifacts and house sizes for the Ozette site, a well-known Northwest Coast village characterized by inter- and intrahouse ranking (Samuels 2006).

ARCHAEOLOGY OF BRIDGE RIVER AND THE MIDDLE FRASER CANYON CONTEXT

Previous research at the Bridge River housepit village has suggested that wealth-based inequality as measured on an interhousehold basis emerged during a short-lived period of village-wide subsistence stress (Prentiss et al. 2012, 2014). The Bridge River village was initiated circa 1800 cal BP and grew to maximum size during three distinct periods we term Bridge River (BR) 1–3 (Prentiss et al. 2008). BR 1 (ca. 1800–1600 cal BP) is an as-yet poorly understood time in which the village was first established and its storage-based fisher-forager socioeconomic pattern set in place. BR 2 (ca. 1600–1300 cal BP) resulted from rapid growth (figure 4.1) and was for a time a period of demographic stability marked by establishment of geometrically arranged multifamily house groups. BR 3 (ca. 1300–1000 cal BP) is marked by an apparent doubling in village size as measured by numbers of houses (figure 4.1). The growth in numbers of houses between BR 2 and BR 3 was not simply accumulative, because nearly all

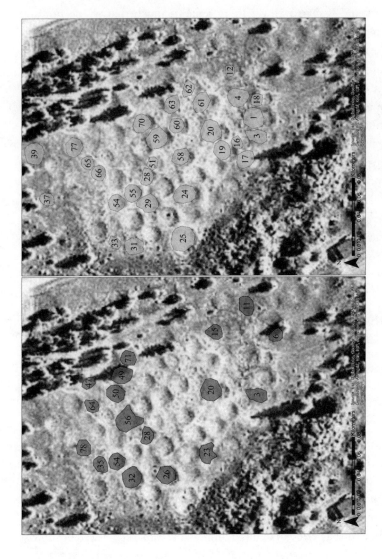

Figure 4.1 Maps of the Bridge River site during the BR 2 (*left*) and BR 3 (*right*) periods. Maps by Matthew Walsh.

BR 2 houses were abandoned when the new ringlike arrangements of BR 3 houses were established. Beginning circa 1150–1200 cal BP, a rapid village-wide abandonment process began that culminated in complete abandonment by circa 1000 cal BP. The Bridge River village was not reoccupied on a consistent basis until circa 400 cal BP at the start of the BR 4 period. The history of the Bridge River site is similar to that of other large villages in the Middle Fraser Canyon area (Hayden and Ryder 1991; Prentiss et al. 2007, 2011; Prentiss and Kuijt 2012).

The BR 2 to 3 transition period was a time of significant socioeconomic and political change. When viewed from a village-wide perspective, two keystone subsistence resources declined. We see a reduction in the density of deer bone and a general shift from a total anatomy signature during BR 2 to one dominated by limb bones in BR 3 times (Prentiss et al. 2014), likely reflecting higher transport costs associated with more-distant foraging (e.g., Broughton 1994). Despite the village-wide shift, select households retained better access to deer compared to others, as marked by higher densities of total deer bone and more-frequent representation of axial and head parts (Prentiss et al. 2014). Access to deer may have been particularly critical if interannual salmon runs were unstable. Houses that combined access to deer and salmon also maintained dogs for consumption and as aids in hunting and gathering (Cail 2011; Prentiss et al. 2014). Simultaneous to changes in interhousehold subsistence economies, we have also recognized variability in household access to a variety of nonsubsistence goods. BR 3 households with the strongest subsistence economies collected particularly significant quantities of nonlocal lithic raw materials, ornamental items (e.g., beads, pendants, and nephrite tools), and raw materials for ornamental or display purposes (steatite, nephrite, and copper). Consequently, we can conclude that as population peaked and key subsistence resources declined, interhousehold inequality emerged as measured from the standpoints of variable access to food items and material goods. Here, we further examine these conclusions using Gini coefficients calculated for house area, subsistence remains, and artifacts.

The results of archaeological research at Bridge River support demographic models that predict population loss, reduction in cooperation, and the possibility of at least short-lived material inequality during a Malthusian crisis (Boone 1998; Hegmon 1991; Puleston and Tuljapurkar

2008; Puleston et al. 2014; Winterhalder et al. 2015). However, significant questions remain regarding how these processes unfolded within individual houses. Given the presence of BR 3 period interhousehold inequality, it is possible to imagine that house groups cooperated internally while competing with other households similarly engaged. In one scenario families within houses cooperated with one another to prepare and store food while presumably sharing access to tools and toolstone. In this context, as food security became more stressful, restrictions against free-riding were loosened to permit those temporarily struggling to survive and remain group members (Angourakis et al. 2015). Under an alternative scenario, competitive conditions gave rise to strategic networking even within houses such that cooperation between family groups declined and inequality arose (Boone 1998). In this context, those suffering reduced access to goods might choose to remain within a household given the very real possibility of worse outcomes external to the house group (Boone 1992).

In this chapter we first conduct additional tests of the hypothesis that interhouse inequality developed during the BR 3 period. We follow with tests of the alternative scenarios for social dynamics within a household persisting under conditions of a Malthusian ceiling, drawing data from our excavations of a single stratified housepit at Bridge River. Housepit (HP) 54 was occupied during both BR 2 and BR 3 times, though it doubled in size slightly after the BR 2–3 transition point, marking that time when the entire village doubled in size and was rearranged on the landscape. Our approach is to review the Housepit 54 stratigraphic sequence, test for changes in household population and access to critical food and material goods, and finally assess the possibility that the nature of intra-household cooperation changed in tandem with that of access to material items. We measure inequality using Gini coefficients calculated on fire-cracked rock, critical food items (salmon and deer), and material items (slate scrapers, ornamental/display ["prestige"] items, and nonlocal raw materials). We measure cooperation in relation to the spatial context of food storage/cache pits and in reference to statistical assessments of tool distributions between domestic activity areas on each house floor. If the data reflect continuous sharing of goods and markers of cooperation in food storage and labor throughout the floor sequence, then we will tentatively conclude that the cooperation scenario is most likely; in contrast, if we recognize increasing intrafloor inequality coupled with indicators of reduced cooperation, then we will accept the competition hypothesis.

MEASURING INEQUALITY IN ARCHAEOLOGICAL CONTEXTS WITH GINI COEFFICIENTS

GENERAL CONCERNS

There are many ways to quantify inequality (chapter 2, this volume; Coulter 1989), with perhaps the most widely used being the Gini coefficient (Allison 1978; Cowell 1977; Gastwirth 1972). The Gini coefficient is most simply defined as a measure of the area between a Lorenz curve derived from empirical sources and a theoretically defined line of equality. As with any measure, variability in the Gini coefficient is impacted by numerous factors. Ideally, the measure reflects differential wealth, when accurately measured. Archaeologists have used Gini coefficients in limited frequency during the past several decades (Ames 2008; Hayden and Cannon 1984; Kohler and Higgins 2016; McGuire 1983: Pailes 2014; Peterson et al. 2016; Schulting 1995; Smith et al. 2014; Windler et al. 2013; Wright 2014). This has led to increasingly sophisticated consideration of issues concerning the application of Gini coefficients using archaeological data (Pailes 2014; Peterson et al. 2016; Windler et al. 2013; see also chapters 2, 6, 8, and 10, this volume). In the following discussion we consider issues regarding variability in the forms of inequality; approaches to quantifying inequality, especially with archaeological data; and appropriate contexts for measuring inequality. Finally, we briefly review our approach to measuring inequality at Bridge River.

Inequality can take many forms. Gini coefficients have been most typically used to measure income inequality (Kuznets 1955; Milanovic 2011). However, inequality can be manifested in other ways, particularly in preindustrial contexts (Milanovic et al. 2011). Access to subsistence resources in nonmonetized places has been shown to be a useful indicator in ethnographic contexts (Smith 1991), though it is not sufficiently studied by archaeologists. Indeed, Christian Peterson and colleagues (2016; see also chapter 2, this volume) outline concerns over the utility of faunal remains in archaeology, given differential preservation and disposal practices. Landholdings, such as orchards (Curtis 2013; Gasco 1996; Smith et al. 2014; see also chapters 6, 8, and 10, this volume), are an additional approach to measuring inequality in food production. House size has been extensively discussed as a useful marker of inequality whether using Gini coefficients (chapters 5, 7, and 9, this volume; Hayden 1997; Smith et al. 2014) or other means (Coupland and Banning 1996 and contributions therein) for quantifying variation under the general assumption that house size reflects aspects of household economy as pertaining to population size and the ability to attract external support for construction, maintenance, and ritual concerns. However, many scholars suggest that house size may reflect demography and not necessarily wealth (e.g., Cutting 2006; Olson and Smith 2016). Artifacts are most commonly used by archaeologists to measure variability in material wealth, given that production of artifacts may depend on the ability to support producers along with the maintenance of trade connections (Ames 2008; Olson and Smith 2016; Peterson et al. 2016; Schulting 1995; Windler et al. 2013; Wright 2014). Peterson and colleagues (2016) offer several concerns regarding artifacts, chiefly that numbers of artifacts could more frequently reflect the effects of archaeological sampling, number of site occupants, and/or length of occupation time. Their alternative to reliance on simple artifact counts is to project estimated production cost per household for its assemblage of artifacts, as they do in chapter 2 of this volume.

Simon Kuznets (1955) presented five specifications for measuring income inequality with Gini coefficients, two of which are particularly relevant to archaeology: indices must measure family income and distributions must be complete (for example, when measuring national income disparity, all income groups in the country should be considered, as opposed to simply upper and lower). Measuring family income implies the use of the category of households, a common practice among archaeologists (Hayden 1997; Hayden and Cannon 1984; Peterson et al. 2016; Smith et al. 2014; Wright 2014). Concern has been raised regarding the measurement of inequality based on artifacts in burials (e.g., Ames 2008; McGuire 1983; Schulting 1995), recognizing that individual burials do not reflect households (Smith et al. 2014). Measurement of complete distributions is a greater challenge in archaeology given the often extreme time and cost investments required to sample archaeological sites made up of dozens to hundreds of house features. When large-scale site excavation (e.g., Peterson et al. 2016; Wright 2014) is not available, this is sometimes accomplished using surface expressions of house forms along with excavated features (Hayden 1997; Smith et al. 2014).

Gini coefficients are affected by sample size, in that small sample sizes generate low Gini scores (Deltas 2003; Dixon et al. 1987). To control for variation in sample size, we calculated an unbiased estimator of the population Gini using the Gini module in StatsDirect. Next, numerous scholars have expressed concerns regarding statistical inference using Gini coefficients and have recommended calculation of confidence intervals to compare variation in samples (Dixon et al. 1987; Mills and Zandvakili 1997; chapter 2, this volume). Following the approach of Jeffrey Mills and Sourushe Zandvakili (1997), we calculated confidence intervals at 95 percent using a bootstrapping approach (100,000 replicates) with StatsDirect. Bootstrapping is particularly effective for calculating confidence intervals from small samples (Mills and Zandvakili 1997).

MEASURING INEQUALITY AT THE BRIDGE RIVER SITE

We measure inequality using Ginis at the Bridge River site using housepit area, fire-cracked rock density, critical subsistence items (deer and salmon remains), and three classes of artifacts: slate scrapers (used for hide production), nonlocal lithic raw materials, and prestige artifacts (tables 4.1 and 4.2). Here we review issues with each of these.

While house size has been typically confirmed as an indicator of status in northwestern North American coastal villages (Sobel et al. 2006 and chapters therein), it is less clear that size alone is an adequate measure within Plateau villages. Brian Hayden (1997) demonstrated significant size disparity in Keatley Creek houses that he argued correlated with differential wealth markers. Independent tests however, have not confirmed the disparity expected (Harris 2012). Likewise, no significant correlations could be found between house size and independent measures of wealth at Bridge River (Prentiss et al. 2012). Many factors could be behind these results, including variability in seasonality, pithouse functions, and household population size. This study provides another opportunity to test for markers of inequality in house size using Ginis calculated on housepit area for the BR 2 (n = 19) and BR 3 (n = 28) periods.

Anna Marie Prentiss and colleagues (2007, 2012) demonstrated the likelihood that fire-cracked rock (FCR) density can serve as a relative

Table 4.1 Gini coefficients for interhousepit variation during the BR 2 and BR 3 periods

Period	Materials	Gini coefficient	Standard error (bootstrap)	Unbiased est. population Gini	Bootstrap confidence interval	
					Low	High
BR 3						
	House area	.18	.02	.19	.16	.25
	Mammals	.34	.09	.43	.40	.48
	Salmon	.40	.14	.50	.41	.54
	Nonlocal raw materials	.42	.12	.51	.40	.70
	Prestige artifacts	.48	.12	.60	.47	.71
BR 2						
	House area	.20	.03	.21	.18	.29
	Mammals	.39	.17	.58	.58	.60
	Salmon	.46	.18	.69	.69	.72
	Nonlocal raw materials	.13	.04	.20	.20	.22
	Prestige artifacts	.48	.12	.60	.47	.71

Note: Data from Prentiss et al. 2012 (for food remains and artifacts) and Prentiss et al. 2005 (for house area).

Table 4.2 Gini coefficients for five Housepit 54 floors

Materials	Floor	Gini coefficient	Standard error (bootstrap)	Unbiased est. population Gini	Bootstrap confidence interval	
					Low	High
Fire-cracked rock						
	IIa	.22	.08	.33	.33	.42
	IIb	.32	.08	.43	.35	.51
	IIc	.17	.05	.23	.22	.29
	IId	.15	.07	.21	.18	.22
	IIe	.40	.14	.59	.59	.66
Slate scrapers						
	IIa	.19	.07	.26	.26	.28
	IIb	.26	.11	.39	.29	.52
	IIc	.45	.16	.68	.68	.75
	IId	.25	.10	.38	.38	.50
	IIe	.45	.16	.67	.67	.72
Deer						
	IIa	.05	.03	.10	0	.10
	IIb	.18	.05	.23	.23	.28
	IIc	.65	.18	.87	.73	.95
	IId	.28	.10	.43	.42	.46
	IIe	.19	.10	.38	0	.38
Salmon						
	IIa		Insufficient data			
	IIb	.05	.02	.09	0	.09
	IIc	.60	.21	.89	.72	1.0
	IId	.46	.12	.61	.53	.79
	IIe	.38	.16	.57	.57	.59
Nonlocal raw materials						
	IIa	.22	.07	.32	.32	.36
	IIb	.31	.09	.42	.38	.49
	IIc	.30	.09	.39	.33	.40
	IId	.38	.11	.51	.45	.58
	IIe	.47	.16	.71	.71	.78
Prestige artifacts						
	IIa	.05	.03	.10	0	.10
	IIb	.18	.05	.23	.23	.28
	IIc	.65	.18	.87	.73	.95
	IId	.28	.10	.42	.42	.46
	IIe	.19	.10	.38	0	.38

proxy for household population size in Mid-Fraser houses. If so, this provides an opportunity to measure demographic variability in multiple households within a single house, as was likely typical during BR 1–3 times at Bridge River and elsewhere in the Mid-Fraser (Hayden 1997; Prentiss and Kuijt 2012). This information could be important if variability in household size relates to economic success and the ability to acquire material goods definable here as wealth. Therefore, we calculate Gini coefficients on FCR density by blocks in each of the upper five floors in Housepit 54 as a means of assessing inequality in household population sizes. We recognize that what we are actually measuring is intensity of cooking with hot stones and that variability in breakage and final discard of these stones could affect the outcome. Our main concern is presence and absence of idiosyncratic features with either abundant or little FCR present. Thus, for these calculations we rely exclusively on FCR embedded in floors but external to cooking and storage features. We control for variability in size by counting pebble- and cobble-size fragments (size distinctions as measured on the Wentworth scale) and excluding smaller pieces.

We have several reasons to believe that faunal remains may be useful measures of inequality in Pacific Northwest villages. First, it is well known that ranking in Northwest Coast and select Plateau villages was reflected in subsistence, as conditioned by differential access to corporeal and noncorporeal property (e.g., whaling gear in the Northwest Coast) required for accomplishing certain hunting and fishing activities (Ames and Maschner 1998). Second, rights of access to select optimal portions of landscapes could be dependent on rank (Ames and Maschner 1998; Hayden 1997; Matson and Coupland 1995; Prentiss and Kuijt 2012). Finally, the Pacific Northwest longhouses and housepits used in this study contain well-preserved faunal remains that include abundant fish parts, thus reducing concern about differential destruction of smaller, less dense elements. Data derive from intensive sampling of house deposits inclusive of roof, floor, and refuse pits, lowering the impact of sampling bias due to differential discard of materials. We test for inequality in access to keystone subsistence resources (deer and salmon) on interhouse (BR 2 and BR 3) and interfloor (Housepit 54) bases.

Artifacts provide critical data for measuring potential wealth-based inequality between BR 2 and BR 3 houses and across the Housepit 54 upper floor sequence. We measure inequality in exchange using nonlocal lithic raw materials (Prentiss et al. 2012) and inequality in accumulated wealth items with Ginis calculated on summed counts of prestige artifacts (ground stone bowls, beads, pendants, jade tools, and so on; Prentiss et al. 2012, 2014). As with faunal remains, we are reasonably confident that assemblages are not unduly biased by sampling, occupation time, and numbers of people per occupation.

Interhousepit variation at Bridge River during BR 2 and BR 3 is the result of sample excavations and could be subject to some bias, though we reduced this by making use of material from all discard contexts. Some bias is undoubtedly present based on the choice of which houses to excavate, because excavating entire villages has not been possible. However, in each case conscious effort was made to excavate a range of house sizes in each neighborhood and time period at the site (Prentiss et al. 2012). We attempt to control for occupation time in several ways. All Bridge River artifact and faunal data are developed as densities, thus controlling for variation in accumulated sediment. All house floors represented in our data likely derive from single-generation occupations. Radiocarbon dating at Housepit 54 at Bridge River confirms approximately twenty-year cycles per floor. A similar assumption is reasonable for other house floors at Bridge River given ethnographic evidence for roof and floor recycling events at similar time frames (Alexander 2000; Prentiss and Kuijt 2012; Teit 1900, 1906) and floors of similar thicknesses to Housepit 54. Finally, we found no significant correlations between measures of household population density and the accumulation of artifacts associated with status at Bridge River (Prentiss et al. 2012). We have nearly complete floor data from Housepit 54, significantly reducing the possibility of sampling bias in those contexts.

VILLAGE-WIDE INEQUALITY AT BRIDGE RIVER

It is well known that wealth-based inequality existed on the Northwest Coast and Middle Fraser Canyon portion of the Plateau during the early colonial periods (Ames and Maschner 1998; Matson and Coupland 1995; Prentiss and Kuijt 2012; Teit 1906). There is some debate, however, as to the degree to which such inequality was present on Middle Fraser Canyon villages predating 1000 BP. Even less is known regarding the forms by which inequalities were manifested. Hayden (1994, 1997, 2000) has long favored a model of stable hereditarily ranked society featuring significant material wealth–based inequality between houses and individuals during what he and June Ryder (Hayden and Ryder 1991) call the Classic Lillooet period (ca. 1000–2000 BP). Prentiss and colleagues (2007, 2008, 2012, 2014; Prentiss and Kuijt 2012) agree that wealth-based inequality existed during this time but suggest that the pattern did not emerge until sometime around 1300 cal BP. Lucille Harris (2012) favors a model of Plateau social organization that assumes egalitarian social structures and unstable village residence patterns. In this study we calculate Gini coefficients for house area, salmon and deer remains, and two classes of artifacts as an additional test of these alternative scenarios.

Gini coefficients for house area are low and change little between the BR 2 and BR 3 occupation periods (figure 4.2). This confirms previous research suggesting that house size is not a good marker of inequality and is probably related to variation in house population size, which was likely a village characteristic from the earliest occupation period (Prentiss et al. 2008, 2012).

We recognize similarly low Gini coefficients for house diameter at Ozette (table 4.3, figure 4.3), though in this case the sample size (three houses) is very small. The examination of artifact Ginis for the housepits in the BR 2 and BR 3 periods illustrates a significant change in prestige items and nonlocal raw materials, indicating the possibility of greater inequality during BR 3 times (figure 4.2). The highest Gini coefficients for artifacts at Ozette are also associated with prestige items, in this case wooden boxes and decorative items, though the confidence intervals on small woodworking tools and woven items also overlap with the former items (table 4.3, figure 4.3). Finally, we find high Ginis for salmon and mammal remains in both BR 2 and BR 3 housepits, with the BR 2 houses featuring the highest scores. We suspect that the history of these houses is complex and best understood with assessment of detailed household histories, because treatment of food remains could vary spatially to a substantial degree on an interhouse basis depending on variation in access to resources but also variation in cleanup and discard practices. These issues are evident at Ozette, where whale bone is concentrated in one house while fish and shellfish are distributed to varying degrees among

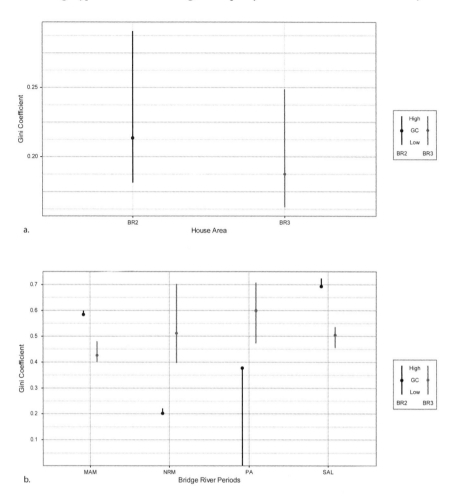

Figure 4.2 Gini coefficients (a) for BR 2 and BR 3 house area and
(b) measures of subsistence and material wealth between houses during
the BR 2 and BR 3 periods, controlled for sample size with bootstrapped
95 percent confidence intervals (MAM = mammals, NRM = nonlocal raw
materials, PA = prestige objects, SAL = salmon).

all houses (Huelsbeck 1988; Wessen 1988). We can explore this issue in
much greater detail by examining interfloor data from Housepit 54 at
Bridge River. This also permits us to further consider the nature of inequality during BR 2 and BR 3 in reference to intrahouse socioeconomic
and political dynamics.

Table 4.3 Gini coefficients for multiple measures from three houses at Ozette

Variable	Gini coefficient	Standard error (bootstrap)	Unbiased est. population Gini	Bootstrap confidence interval	
				Low	High
Long-axis diameter	.04	.02	.06	.06	.06
Short-axis diameter	.09	.03	.09	.06	.09
Woven items	.25	.11	.37	.31	.51
Boxes	.29	.10	.44	.44	.50
Land-hunting tools	.25	.09	.36	.36	.38
Sea-hunting tools	.12	.04	.18	.18	.20
Fishing tools	.07	.03	.10	.10	.11
Small woodworking tools	.23	.11	.35	.31	.50
Large woodworking tools	.13	.05	.20	.20	.23
Decorative items	.30	.18	.45	.44	.78

Note: Data from Samuels 2006.

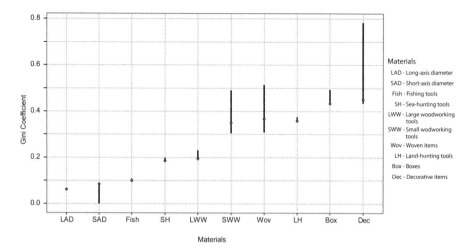

Figure 4.3 Gini coefficients for the Ozette site with bootstrapped 95 percent confidence intervals for house diameters, woven items, boxes, land-hunting tools, sea-hunting tools, fishing tools, small woodworking tools, large woodworking tools, and decorative items.

HOUSEPIT 54 AT THE BRIDGE RIVER SITE

Excavations from 2013 to 2016 exposed a series of anthropogenic floors at Housepit 54 falling within the BR 2 and BR 3 periods. Spatial data were recorded on a grid system that subdivided the floor into four blocks, each composed of sixteen 1-meter squares, each in turn divided into four quads. Housepit strata consist of a series of anthropogenic sedimentary layers interpreted as roof (Stratum V sequence) and floor (Stratum II sequence). Roof deposits reflect instances where all or a portion of a pithouse roof was burned, presumably to eliminate vermin and remove old wood before a new occupation cycle (Alexander 2000). In HP 54, as at most Bridge River houses, collapsed roofs were simply covered by new floor material as the house was revitalized and prepared for another period of occupation. Floor sediments consist of fine clay-loam with small gravels derived from the substrate that underlies all Bridge River valley terraces. Sixteen floors dating to the BR 2 and BR 3 periods (ca. 1150–1450 cal BP) have been at least partially excavated. Horizontal exposure of house floors revealed a consistent pattern of hearth-centered activity areas (accompanied by occasional cache pits and postholes) consistently positioned in each block of the excavation grid. The analysis of lithic artifact variability across all blocks between all floors suggests a high degree of consistency supporting the argument that accumulated materials in each block represent activities of individual families as opposed to special activity areas for accomplishing a narrower range of tasks (Prentiss and Foor 2015).

We also learned that the house effectively doubled in size between the IIf and IIe floors, growing from a rectangular shape (floors III–IIf) to a round shape (IIe to IIa1; Stratum II dates to late BR 4 times [Fur Trade period] and is discussed elsewhere [Prentiss 2017]). The preservation of bone and some plant materials is very good in the Housepit 54 strata. Individual floors appear to have been gently capped with sediments as new floors were created, thus preserving intact the spatial arrangements of materials associated with each occupation. For this study we have distributional data from seven nearly fully excavated floors (2013 and 2014 field season results). Floors IIg and IIf represent transitional BR 2 to early BR 3 occupations, and floors IIe–IIa represent BR 3. The two deeper floors derive from the smaller rectangular-shaped house, and without further study of spatial patterns they do not yet provide appropriate data to permit calculation of adequate Gini coefficients. However, given the smaller house size and constrained space for household activities, we suggest that evidence for persistent inequality as measured across multiple data sets will be limited. We do calculate Gini coefficients from the IIa–IIe floors, thus representing the period of circa 1150–1250 cal BP.

INEQUALITY AND COOPERATION IN HOUSEPIT 54

We assessed variation in household populations by calculating Ginis on FCR densities between floors IIe and IIa (figure 4.4). These results suggest that the maximum variation occurred during IIe and the lowest Ginis during IIc and IId, with moderate coefficients for IIa and IIb. We measured change over time in intrahousehold access to key foods using Gini coefficients calculated for densities of salmon (*Oncorhynchus* sp.) and deer (*Odocoileus* sp.) in each block in floors IIg–IIa (figure 4.4). These results indicate similar patterns for each prey item. We recognize overlapping confidence intervals at 95 percent for all floors with the exception of IIc, with its extraordinarily high score and confidence interval

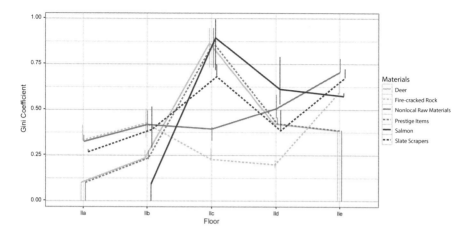

Figure 4.4 Gini coefficients controlled for sample size with bootstrapped 95 percent confidence intervals for fire-cracked rock distributions, salmon, deer, slate scrapers, prestige items, and nonlocal lithic raw materials on five Housepit 54 floors.

that only slightly overlaps with IId for salmon. We calculated Gini co-efficients for densities of slate scrapers as an extra measure of household production activities, given that use-wear on these items nearly always implicates hide working (Prentiss et al. 2015). These results indicate high scores for the IIe and IIc floors compared to lower numbers for the other floors, especially IIa (figure 4.4). Prestige items (ornaments and prestige artifacts) pattern in a manner nearly identical to deer and very close to that of salmon (figure 4.4). Once again floor IIc has by far the highest score and a nonoverlapping 95 percent confidence interval. Nonlocal raw materials pattern quite differently from the other items (figure 4.4); floor IIe has by far the highest score, with others dipping more or less steadily toward a low in floor IIa.

We address variability in Gini coefficients for the Housepit 54 late floors after first examining general trends in subsistence and house pop-ulation size. To address general trends in subsistence we calculated den-sities of salmon and deer for all house floors (table 4.4). We estimated household population (table 4.4) by developing a divisor on fire-cracked rock counts that, in brief, integrated several estimated factors related to cooking in houses (years per floor [20; date sequence from HP 54;

Table 4.4 Estimates of relative variation in estimated population (×10) and densities of critical subsistence items

Floor	Deer	Salmon ÷ 10	Estimated population × 10
IIa	1	2	220
IIb	43	105	120
IIc	49	119	90
IId	20	36	100
IIe	35	19	120
IIf	27	54	100
IIg	20	23	50

Alexander 2000; Teit 1900, 1906], days per year [×365], percentage of year house was occupied [×0.33; Alexander 2000; Teit 1900, 1906], percentage discarded on roofs [÷2; pattern recognized in Housepit 54 roof and floor strata], and number of hearth groups involved [÷15: 3 hearth groups × 5 persons; Hayden et al. 1996]). The results of the latter exercise indicate that the house may have been populated by a range potentially spanning as low as 5 (IIg) up to at least 22 (IIa) persons. Figure 4.5 illustrates an estimated demographic trend with a peak at IIe followed by a trough and a subsequent peak at IIa. The house was abandoned at this point (though likely briefly occupied about a century later, forming the IIaɪ floor, which was then nearly entirely removed by Fur Trade period occupants). Salmon remains pattern in an approximately inverse manner to our demographic estimate, suggesting that salmon declines always preceded human population decline (figure 4.5). An implication here is that instability in salmon led to instability in human numbers on a generational scale. Conversely, enough good salmon years also led to rapid human population growth. The distribution of deer remains is similar to salmon, though slightly different (figure 4.5). Deer are more subject to impacts of human predation pressure. Our data suggest that deer numbers immediately began to decline at the IIe human population peak and then rebounded during the human demographic low. Then they collapsed during the rapid growth period between IIc and IIa. The IId–IIc population trough could reflect the village-wide effects of a Malthusian ceiling, as we have described elsewhere (Prentiss et al. 2014).

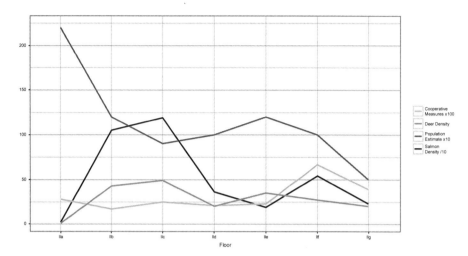

Figure 4.5 Estimates of relative population size and densities for two keystone prey items along with summary coefficient of variation (CV) scores estimating cooperation in lithic tool–related labor across seven Housepit 54 floors.

Ginis for FCR form a pattern that approximates that of the population estimate. It suggests that at a higher density there was often substantial variation, for example, at IIe and IIb. In contrast, the lowest density was matched by the lowest Gini coefficients. While Gini scores are known to be affected by sample size (Deltas 2003), our scores are calculated to control for sample size, and thus these results could possibly mirror some underlying sociodemographic processes. One possibility is that both IIe and IIb represent sudden household demographic growth following a period of lower numbers and that those groups were positioned unevenly around the perimeter of the house. Peak inequality in subsistence measures and prestige objects clearly developed at a time of lower population density within the house and likely the entire village (Prentiss et al. 2012, 2014). That the Gini for nonlocal raw materials is at its maximum on floor IIe, the point at which the house had both doubled in size and also achieved a likely population density peak, is particularly interesting. This could reflect the acceptance of new persons into the house, bringing new trade connections for lithic sources. In contrast, an alternative argument could be that household social order changed significantly at that transition such that select persons or families established new connections not shared by others in the house. If the latter is true, then it could also mean that accepted norms of intrahousehold cooperation changed, resulting in expanding material wealth and subsistence inequality over subsequent generations as reflected in Gini coefficients on food items and prestige artifacts found on floors IIc and IId. Given the presence of inequality strongly on floor IIc but evident to varying degrees on floors IIe and IId, we can now ask whether inequality came about in the context of enhanced or reduced intrahousehold cooperation.

We measure cooperation in two ways: cooperation in storage and in labor. Ethnographies document pit storage as a common strategy for preserving winter foods including dried plants, salmon, and meat from artiodactyls (Alexander 2000; Prentiss and Kuijt 2012; Teit 1900, 1906). We suggest that the spatial organization of food storage could be informative regarding the nature of household cooperation. Household storage that is fully cooperative in nature would likely be reflected in the presence of cache pits clustered in a designated space in the house, not unlike the designated spaces for cooking, toolmaking, and sleeping documented for Fur Trade period occupations (Prentiss 2017; Teit 1900). In contrast, if storage was family specific and use of stored resources was not communal for the entire house, then we would expect to see smaller scattered pits or other evidence for less visible forms of storage. The positioning of cache pits in HP 54 changes significantly between IIg and IIc. Indeed, floors at IIe and lower have volumetrically large cache pits clustered in southern sectors of the house, whereas during IId–IIa cache pits are rarer, smaller, and not consistently concentrated in particular household sectors. We suggest that this could reflect an increasing emphasis on private family property and, thus, loss of household cooperation in food preparation and storage.

If cooperation in food storage during the period reflected in IId and later floors was reduced, it could be that cooperation in overall household work also declined. In this scenario we look for indicators that house floor activity structure was shared, thus permitting some degree of variance in artifact deposition, presuming that some household members specialized in select tasks and shared their products (e.g., hide preparation, projectile point manufacture, etc.). In contrast, if it was not shared, then we would not expect to see evidence for household specialists and thus extreme consistency in activity structure between domestic areas. To test for this we calculated a principal components analysis of tool types by floors (Prentiss and Foor 2015). The tool type components were simple to interpret and reflected woodworking (component 1), ground stone tool production and use (component 2), hide processing and adornment manufacture (component 3), weapons manufacture (component 4), and sewing (component 5). We next calculated component scores for each component to reflect how each domestic area in each floor contributed (table 4.5). Then, to assess the degree to which the activity was shared across each floor, we developed a coefficient of variation (CV) on a distance matrix (technically calculated as a simple difference matrix) calculated from the component loadings (excluding component 5 because of its low variance in the original component solution) for each floor (IIg–IIa) on each component (table 4.6). This allowed us to capture within the CV the maximum degree of diversity in the component scores as it

Table 4.5 Component scores for principal components analysis of tool classes

		Component				
Block	**Floor**	**1**	**2**	**3**	**4**	**5**
A	IIa	−0.65	−0.31	−0.02	0.26	−1.10
	IIb	−0.82	−0.25	−0.78	−0.63	−0.11
	IIc	0.16	−0.59	−0.65	−0.35	0.36
	IId	−0.19	−0.31	−0.88	−0.94	−0.66
	IIe	−1.34	−0.92	−0.18	0.85	1.38
	IIf	−0.92	−0.50	0.89	−1.65	0.44
	IIg	2.12	0.64	−0.16	−0.11	−0.56
B	IIa	0.61	0.04	−0.15	−1.02	1.97
	IIb	−0.81	−0.41	−0.46	0.42	−0.92
	IIc	0.36	−0.56	−0.87	−1.09	1.25
	IId	0.06	−0.26	−0.36	−0.80	−0.79
	IIe	−0.73	0.01	2.36	−0.59	0.98
C	IIa	−1.16	−0.57	−0.05	0.18	−0.73
	IIb	−0.15	0.14	−0.88	−0.77	−0.00
	IIc	−0.54	0.78	−0.74	0.14	−1.64
	IId	0.66	0.00	−0.62	1.90	1.22
	IIe	−0.00	0.18	1.20	1.77	1.10
	IIf	1.41	−0.55	2.77	−0.57	−1.44
	IIg	−0.77	4.06	0.15	−0.14	0.20
D	IIb	2.48	−0.01	−0.84	−0.15	0.18
	IIc	0.36	0.11	0.34	1.54	−0.29
	IId	−0.13	−0.72	−0.11	1.68	−0.85

Table 4.6 Baseline coefficient of variation data by floor and component

Floor	Component	Variance	SD	Mean	N	Coefficient of variation
IIa						
	1	0.47	0.68	1.21	3	0.55
	2	0.03	0.18	0.40	3	0.44
	3	0.00	0.07	0.08	3	0.82
	4	0.45	0.67	0.85	3	0.78
IIb						
	1	2.19	1.48	1.76	6	0.84
	2	0.05	0.22	0.34	6	0.66
	3	0.03	0.17	0.22	6	0.78
	4	0.15	0.38	0.68	6	0.57
IIc						
	1	0.16	0.40	0.48	6	0.82
	2	0.17	0.41	0.85	6	0.49
	3	0.21	0.45	0.55	6	0.82
	4	0.13	0.36	0.61	6	0.59
IId						
	1	0.11	0.34	0.46	6	0.74
	2	0.05	0.23	0.37	6	0.61
	3	0.04	0.21	0.43	6	0.49
	4	1.48	1.21	1.52	6	0.80
IIe						
	1	0.15	0.39	0.89	3	0.44
	2	0.24	0.49	0.73	3	0.68
	3	0.55	0.74	1.70	3	0.44
	4	0.53	0.73	1.57	3	0.44
IIf						
	1	n/a	1.65	0.25	2	0.67
	2	n/a	0.04	0.53	2	0.78
	3	n/a	1.33	1.83	2	0.73
	4	n/a	0.76	1.11	2	0.68
IIg						
	1	n/a	2.05	0.68	2	0.30
	2	n/a	2.40	2.35	2	0.10
	3	n/a	0.05	0.00	2	0.24
	4	n/a	0.03	0.13	2	0.21

Table 4.7 Coefficient of variation data by floors

Floor	Coefficient of variation
IIa	0.28
IIb	0.17
IIc	0.25
IId	0.21
IIe	0.23
IIf	0.67
IIg	0.39

reflects the complete array of relationships between block areas per floor for each activity set. The CV scores for IIf and IIg were calculated directly from the component scores as there were only two variants per floor. We then calculated summary CV scores (table 4.7) from the component-specific CVs to summarize the likelihood of cooperation, assuming that high CV scores raise the possibility of higher cooperation and low CVs the opposite.

These results indicate the highest CV scores for IIg–IIf and very low CVs for IIe–IIa (table 4.7, figure 4.5). These results are similar to those indicated by cache pit distributions with the exception of floor IIe, scoring low cooperation with artifacts but high cooperation with storage features. Clearly the latter floor marks a transition time, as it is the first floor of the expanded full-scale house that comes at a time of declining salmon resources but relatively high human population. The summary CV scores also match the period with best evidence for inequality, suggesting that intrahousehold cooperation, at least in reference to activities involving stone tools and food storage, was not a strong characteristic of life in Housepit 54 during an unstable time.

DISCUSSION

MID-FRASER ARCHAEOLOGY

Although rarely considered together in archaeology, cooperation and inequality are natural bedfellows. We proposed alternative hypotheses regarding intrahousehold cooperation and inequality for a time of emergent interhousehold inequality, at least as measured with food items and material goods. That is, we wondered what happened to social relations between families within houses as village-wide conditions became socially more competitive. One strategy would have been to maintain or increase household cooperation via the sharing of food from common stores and also sharing labor that could include permitting talented craftspeople to specialize in those tasks in exchange for access to goods from other such producers. An alternative strategy would recognize that as the village reached its demographic ceiling, social competition was felt not just at the household level but also at the family and individual level. In this scenario, individuals and families within multifamily households would have networked with others in other houses or even villages to enhance their own livelihood and would not have engaged in the same strategy of open food and goods sharing as proposed for the cooperation hypothesis.

In this study we provide data to further establish evidence for material wealth–based inequality between houses emerging in the Bridge River village (compare with Prentiss et al. 2012 and 2014). In doing so we also confirm a lack of evidence that inequality was manifested in house area; occupation of a large house was not necessarily indicative of social status in the Bridge River village. Given similar results from Ozette, we suggest that this pattern may actually be typical of Interior and Coastal villages in the Pacific Northwest. Additionally, we employed several approaches to measuring inequality and cooperation within floors of a single household that persisted across the transition from village growth (earliest BR 3) to the Malthusian ceiling (mid to late BR 3). Our current results suggest that social approaches to work and food storage changed between the two periods: Earlier floors are characterized by distinct storage spaces and indicators of greater cooperation in work. Later floors either lack evidence for storage or reflect limited decentralized storage features. They also seem to lack evidence for the kind of cooperative labor inferred for earlier floors. Finally, measures of inequality, whether for food items or material goods, point to variation in intrahousehold inequality during occupation of the late floors. In general, therefore, the data point toward the intrahousehold competition and inequality model, though there are some interesting nuances.

This study has numerous implications. These results provide yet another line of evidence that inequality evolved over time in the Mid-Fraser villages rather than simply existing as a characteristic from inception to abandonment (Hayden 1994, 1997; Hayden and Ryder 1991). Further, inequality appears to have been a short-lived phenomenon, because within two to three centuries of its full appearance the Mid-Fraser phenomenon broke down and the high-density villages were abandoned. Ethnographies of the St'át'imc or Upper Lillooet people describe a system of inequality manifested in the form of ranked families and variation in ascribed and achieved statuses (Teit 1900, 1906). But we have yet to find archaeological evidence from the very latest Pre-colonial and Colonial periods for intrahousehold inequality (Prentiss 2017; Smith 2014). Late period (BR 4) interhousehold inequality has not yet been adequately examined. We have suggested that the memory of ancient inequalities may have persisted into the ethnographic period and influenced the writings of ethnographer James Teit, while in day-to-day life Fur Trade and Gold Rush–era groups maintained a relatively high degree of egalitarianism, at least at a level measurable in the archaeological record.

What was the nature of Mid-Fraser material inequality during the BR 3 period? Evidence suggests that it existed on multiple scales. We have recognized material wealth–based inequality that included differential access to keystone food resources between villages, neighborhoods (at Bridge River), and houses. Now we have evidence for it within houses as well. Given the presence of material-based inequality and competitiveness on multiple scales, we infer the operation of a network-like social strategy such as that defined by Richard Blanton and colleagues (1996). To date we have seen no evidence for centralized power as manifested through permanent ritual facilities, the collection of tribute goods from surrounding communities, or central control of specialist labor within or between communities (e.g., Marcus and Flannery 1996). However, we do have evidence for a multitiered settlement system that included large "centers" such as Bridge River and Keatley Creek (Hayden 1997; Prentiss and Kuijt 2012), each likely organized spatially with ring-shaped "neighborhoods" (Prentiss et al. 2014) and mutual exchange networks, as measured by the presence of a common set of lithic raw materials in each village.

We raise the possibility that material wealth–based inequality was predicated on membership within clans that crosscut multiple villages, such that any given village during BR-3 times could have held two or

more ranked clans. In this scenario, inter- and intrahousehold status positions might have been predicated upon ranking and networking ability
within and between clans. Such a social strategy is dimly reflected in the
ethnographies in which James Teit (1906) and Charles Hill-Tout (1905)
describe clans or social groups (respectively) that could exist in more than
one village, which were presided over by the highest-ranking chief in
the original and presumably largest village. If we are correct, then social
power in the Mid-Fraser context was likely simultaneously hierarchical,
as manifested in wealth-based inequality on multiple scales, and heterarchical, in the form of counterbalanced clan groups spread across dozens
of small to very large communities.

Addressing the evolution of such a complex sociopolitical system is
beyond the goals of this chapter. However, we suggest that its foundation
might be seen in the establishment of the first geometric arrangements
of houses as reconstructed here for the BR 2 period at Bridge River. Such
arrangements could have housed the first clan-like social group or groups
under materially more egalitarian conditions. The demographic plateau
we recognize as BR 2 may have been a somewhat more benign Malthusian equilibrium that was interrupted by a period of rapid population
growth that constituted the transition to the BR 3 period. What triggered
that growth pattern is less clear. One possibility is a short-lived cycle of
ultraproductive salmon runs. There are hints of such a possibility in the
record of eastern Pacific marine productivity, which apparently peaked
circa 1200–1400 cal BP (Hay et al. 2007; Patterson et al. 2005; Tunnicliffe
et al. 2001). Alternatively, it could have been a revolutionary rethinking of
the nature of socioeconomic and political strategies at the critical juncture
circa 1300–1350 cal BP, as manifested in the nearly complete rearrange-
ment of the Bridge River village. Such a rethinking of social relationships
could have demanded new capital in the form of intensified harvest of
fish, artiodactyls, and, likely, select plant foods that fed short-lived growth
(the IIe population peak) and eventually the Malthusian ceiling (the IId
and IIc population trough) that is so evident in our data sets.

MEASURING INEQUALITY WITH GINI COEFFICIENTS

Gini coefficients are useful for teasing apart the different components of
inequality. Our study suggests several implications. First, as recognized

elsewhere in this volume (e.g., chapters 2, 3, 6, 8, 10), Gini coefficients are subject to many biases. We have our greatest challenge with sites where incomplete and sparse data make it difficult to control for numerous sampling issues. A particularly difficult challenge for archaeology comes with sampling complete populations. In North American archaeology it is extremely rare that an entire site can be excavated (Ozette is an exception)—much less several—to facilitate Gini-based comparisons. Here we might contrast North American archaeology with that of Japan, for example (e.g., Habu 2004). However, despite many potential problems, careful data management and creative approaches to measurement can still yield informative results.

Second, Ginis are useful for defining variation in the nature of inequality (see also chapter 10, this volume). For example, this study confirms that inequality was manifested in differential access to food sources and material goods, while house area apparently was less important. This is a conclusion that comes in contrast to many other studies, including several in this book. Third, as in chapters 5, 8, and 9 in this volume, temporal trends in Ginis prove useful in our study to address diachronic questions, particularly when additional data sets can be brought to bear. We suggest that demographic and subsistence trends affected social strategies, such that inequalities in food and prestige goods did not co-pattern exactly with inequality in access to nonlocal goods, as measured from lithic raw material types. This raises the distinct possibility that we have more to learn regarding relationships between local demographics, socioeconomic relationships, and social networks.

ACKNOWLEDGMENTS

The Bridge River Archaeological Project is a cooperative partnership between the University of Montana and Xwisten, the Bridge River Indian Band. The project has been generously funded by the National Science Foundation (grant BCS-0713013 funded the 2007–2009 field seasons) and the National Endowment for the Humanities (grant RZ-51287–11 funded the Housepit 54 excavations in 2012–2014). Any views, findings, conclusions, or recommendations expressed in this chapter do not necessarily represent those of the National Endowment for the Humanities. We thank Tim Kohler and Mike Smith for inviting us to participate in the SAA symposium, the Amerind Seminar, and this book project. Finally, we thank the two peer reviewers for their useful comments.

REFERENCES CITED

Alexander, Diana. 2000. Pithouses on the Interior Plateau of British Columbia: Ethnographic Evidence and Interpretation of the Keatley Creek Site. In *The Ancient Past of Keatley Creek*, vol. 2, *Socioeconomy*, edited by Brian Hayden, pp. 29–66. Archaeology Press, Simon Fraser University, Burnaby, B.C.

Allison, Paul D. 1978. Measures of Inequality. *American Sociological Review* 43:865–80.

Ames, Kenneth M. 2008. The Archaeology of Rank. In *Handbook of Archaeological Theories*, edited by R. Alexander Bentley, Herbert D. G. Maschner, and Christopher Chippindale, pp. 487–514. Altamira Press, Lanham, Md.

Ames, Kenneth M., and Herbert D. G. Maschner. 1998. *Peoples of the Northwest Coast: Their Archaeology and Prehistory*. Thames and Hudson, London.

Angourakis, Andreas, Jose Ignacio Santos, Jose Manuel Galan, and Andrea L. Balbo. 2015. Food for All: An Agent-Based Model to Explore the Emergence and Implications of Cooperation for Food Storage. *Environmental Archaeology* 20:349–63.

Blanton, Richard E., Gary M. Feinman, Stephen A. Kowalewski, and Peter N. Peregrine. 1996. A Dual Processual Theory for the Evolution of Mesoamerican Civilization. *Current Anthropology* 37:1–14.

Boone, James L. 1992. Competition, Conflict, and the Development of Social Hierarchies. In *Evolutionary Ecology and Human Behavior*, edited by Eric Alden Smith and Bruce Winterhalder, pp. 301–38. Aldine de Gruyter, New York.

———. 1998. The Evolution of Magnanimity: When Is It Better to Give Than to Receive? *Human Nature* 9:1–21.

Borgerhoff Mulder, Monique, Samuel Bowles, Tom Hertz, Adrian Bell, Jan Beise, Greg Clark, Ila Fazzio, et al. 2009. Intergenerational Wealth Transmission and the Dynamics of Inequality in Small-Scale Societies. *Science* 326:682–87.

Broughton, Jack M. 1994. Late Holocene Resource Intensification in the Sacramento River Valley: The Vertebrate Evidence. *Journal of Archaeological Science* 21:501–14.

Cail, Hannah S. 2011. Feasting on Fido: Cultural Implications of Eating Dogs at Bridge River. MA thesis, University of Montana, Missoula.

Coulter, Phillip B. 1989. *Measuring Inequality: A Methodological Handbook*. Westview Press, Boulder, Colo.

Coupland, Gary, and E. B. Banning (editors). 1996. *People Who Lived in Big Houses: Archaeological Perspectives on Large Domestic Structures*. Monographs in World Archaeology 27. Prehistory Press, Madison, Wis.

Cowell, F. A. 1977. *Measuring Inequality: Techniques for the Social Sciences.* John Wiley and Sons, New York.

Curtis, Daniel R. 2013. Is There an "Agro-Town" Model for Southern Italy? Exploring Diverse Roots and Development of the Agro-Town Structure Through Comparative Case Study in Apulia. *Continuity and Change* 28(3):377–419.

Cutting, Marion. 2006. More Than One Way to Study a Building: Approaches to Prehistoric Household and Settlement Space. *Oxford Journal of Archaeology* 25:225–46.

Deltas, George. 2003. The Small-Sample Bias of the Gini Coefficient: Results and Implications for Empirical Research. *Review of Economics and Statistics* 85:226–34.

Dixon, Philip M., Jacob Weiner, Thomas Mitchell-Olds, and Robert Woodley. 1987. Bootstrapping the Gini Coefficient of Inequality. *Ecology* 68:1548–51.

Gasco, Janine. 1996. Cacao and Economic Inequality in Colonial Soconusco, Chiapas, Mexico. *Journal of Anthropological Research* 52:385–409.

Gastwirth, Joseph L. 1972. The Estimation of the Lorenz Curve and Gini Index. *Review of Economics and Statistics* 54: 306–16.

Habu, Junko. 2004. *Ancient Jomon of Japan.* University of Cambridge Press, Cambridge.

Harris, Lucille. 2012. Heterarchy and Hierarchy in the Formation and Dissolution of Complex Hunter-Gatherer Communities on the Northern Plateau of Northwestern North America, ca. 2000–300 B.P. PhD thesis, University of Toronto, Toronto.

Hay, Murray B., Audrey Dallimore, Richard E. Thomson, Stephen E. Calvert, and Reinhard Pienetz. 2007. Siliceous Microfossil Record of Late Holocene Oceanography and Climate Along the West Coast of Vancouver Island, British Columbia (Canada). *Quaternary Research* 67:33–49.

Hayden, Brian. 1994. Competition, Labor, and Complex Hunter-Gatherers. In *Key Issues in Hunter Gatherer Research*, edited by Ernest S. Burch and Linda L. Ellana, pp. 223–39. Berg Press, Oxford, U.K.

——. 1997. *The Pithouses of Keatley Creek.* Harcourt Brace College Publishers, Fort Worth, Tex.

—— (editor). 2000. *The Ancient Past of Keatley Creek*, vol. 2, *Socioeconomy.* Archaeology Press, Simon Fraser University, Burnaby, B.C.

Hayden, Brian, and Aubrey Cannon. 1984. *The Structure of Material Systems: Ethnoarchaeology in the Maya Highlands.* SAA Papers 3. Society for American Archaeology, Washington, D.C.

Hayden, Brian, Gregory Reinhardt, Richard MacDonald, Dan Holmberg, and David Crellin. 1996. Space Per Capita and the Optimal Size of Housepits. In *People Who Lived in Big Houses: Archaeological Perspectives on Large Domestic Structures*, edited by Gary Coupland and E. B. Banning, pp. 151–64. Prehistory Press, Madison, Wis.

Hayden, Brian, and June Ryder. 1991. Prehistoric Cultural Collapse in the Lillooet Area. *American Antiquity* 56:50–65.

Hegmon, Michele. 1991. The Risks of Sharing and Sharing as Risk Reduction: Interhousehold Food Sharing in Egalitarian Societies. In *Between Bands and States*, edited by Susan A. Gregg, pp. 309–29. Occasional Paper 6. Center for Archaeological Investigations, Southern Illinois University, Carbondale.

Hill-Tout, Charles. 1905. Report on the Ethnology of the Stlatlumh (Lillooet) of British Columbia. *Journal of the Royal Anthropological Institute* 35:126–218.

Huelsbeck, David R. 1988. The Surplus Economy of the Central Northwest Coast. In *Prehistoric Economies of the Pacific Northwest Coast*, edited by Barry L. Isaac, pp. 149–78. Research in Economic Anthropology Supplement 3. JAI Press, Greenwich, Conn.

Kennett, Douglas J., Bruce Winterhalder, Jacob Bartruff, and Jon M. Erlandson. 2009. An Ecological Model for the Emergence of Institutionalized Social Hierarchies on California's Northern Channel Islands. In *Pattern and Process in Cultural Evolution*, edited by Stephen Shennan, pp. 297–314. University of California Press, Berkeley.

Kohler, Timothy A., and Rebecca Higgins. 2016. Quantifying Household Inequality in Early Pueblo Villages. *Current Anthropology* 57(5):690–97.

Kuznets, Simon. 1955. Economic Growth and Income Inequality. *American Economic Review* 45:1–28.

Marcus, Joyce, and Kent Flannery. 1996. *Zapotec Civilization: How Urban Society Evolved in Mexico's Oaxaca Valley*. Thames and Hudson, London.

Matson, R. G., and Gary Coupland. 1995. *Prehistory of the Northwest Coast*. Academic Press, San Diego, Calif.

Mattison, Siobhan M., Eric A. Smith, Mary Shenk, and Ethan E. Cochrane. 2016. The Evolution of Inequality. *Evolutionary Anthropology* 25:184–99.

McGuire, Randall H. 1983. Breaking Down Cultural Complexity: Inequality and Heterogeneity. *Advances in Archaeological Method and Theory* 6:91–142.

Milanovic, Branko. 2011. *The Haves and Have-Nots: A Brief and Idiosyncratic History of Global Inequality*. Basic Books, New York.

Milanovic, Branko, Peter H. Lindert, and Jeffrey G. Williamson. 2011. Preindustrial Inequality. *Economic Journal* 121:255–72.

Mills, Jeffrey A., and Sourushe Zandvakili. 1997. Statistical Inference via Bootstrapping for Measures of Inequality. *Journal of Applied Econometrics* 12:133–50.

Olson, Jan Marie, and Michael E. Smith. 2016. Material Expressions of Wealth and Social Class at Aztec-Period Sites in Morelos, Mexico. *Ancient Mesoamerica* 27:133–47.

Pailes, Matthew C. 2014. Social Network Analysis of Early Classic Hohokam Corporate Group Inequality. *American Antiquity* 79:465–86.

Patterson, R. Timothy, Andreas Prokoph, Arun Kumar, Alice S. Chang, and Helen M. Roe. 2005. Late Holocene Variability in Pelagic Fish Scales and Dinoflagellate Cysts Along the West Coast of Vancouver Island, NE Pacific Ocean. *Marine Micropaleontology* 55:183–204.

Peterson, Christian E., Robert D. Drennan, and Kate L. Bartel. 2016. Comparative Analysis of Neolithic Household Artifact Assemblage Data from Northern China. *Journal of Anthropological Research* 72:200–225.

Prentiss, Anna Marie (editor). 2017. *The Last House at Bridge River: The Archaeology of an Aboriginal Household during the Fur Trade Period.* University of Utah Press, Salt Lake City.

Prentiss, Anna Marie, Hannah S. Cail, and Lisa M. Smith. 2014. At the Malthusian Ceiling: Subsistence and Inequality at Bridge River, British Columbia. *Journal of Anthropological Archaeology* 33:34–48.

Prentiss, Anna Marie, James C. Chatters, Natasha Lyons, and Lucille Harris. 2011. Archaeology of the Middle Fraser Canyon, British Columbia: Changing Perspectives on Paleoecology and Emergent Cultural Complexity. *Canadian Journal of Archaeology* 35:143–74.

Prentiss, Anna Marie, Guy Cross, Thomas A. Foor, Dirk Markle, Matt Hogan, and David S. Clarke. 2008. Evolution of a Late Prehistoric Winter Village on the Interior Plateau of British Columbia: Geophysical Investigations, Radiocarbon Dating, and Spatial Analysis of the Bridge River Site. *American Antiquity* 73:59–82.

Prentiss, Anna Marie, and Thomas A. Foor. 2015. Lithic Tools and Debitage. In Report of the 2014 University of Montana Investigations at the Bridge River Site (EeRl4): Housepit 54 During Bridge River 2 and 3 Periods, edited by Anna Marie Prentiss, pp. 56–94. Report on file, University of Montana (http://hs.umt.edu/bridgeriver/data/default.php), National Endowment for the Humanities, and Bridge River Indian Band.

Prentiss, Anna Marie, Thomas A. Foor, Guy Cross, Lucille E. Harris, and Michael Wanzenried. 2012. The Cultural Evolution of Material Wealth Based Inequality at Bridge River, British Columbia. *American Antiquity* 77:542–65.

Prentiss, Anna Marie, Nathan B. Goodale, Lucille E. Harris, and Nicole Crossland. 2015. The Evolution of the Ground Slate Tool Industry at the Bridge River Site, British Columbia. In *Lithic Technological Systems and Evolutionary Theory*, edited by Nathan Goodale and William Andrefsky Jr., pp. 267–92. Cambridge University Press, Cambridge.

Prentiss, Anna Marie, and Ian Kuijt. 2012. *People of the Middle Fraser Canyon: An Archaeological History.* University of British Columbia Press, Vancouver.

Prentiss, Anna Marie, Natasha Lyons, Lucille E. Harris, Melisse R. P. Burns, and Terence M. Godin. 2007. The Emergence of Status Inequality in Intermediate Scale Societies: A Demographic and Socio-Economic History of the Keatley Creek Site, British Columbia. *Journal of Anthropological Archaeology* 26:299–327.

Prentiss, William C., David S. Clarke, Dirk Markle, Jessica Bochart, Jake Foss, and Sierra Mandelko. 2005. Report of the 2004 University of Montana Investigations at the Bridge River Site (EeRl4). Report on file, Bridge River Indian Band and National Science Foundation.

Puleston, Cedric O., and Shripad Tuljapurkar. 2008. Population and Prehistory II: Space Limited Human Populations in Constant Environments. *Theoretical Population Biology* 74:147–60.

Puleston, Cedric, Shripad Tuljapurkar, and Bruce Winterhalder. 2014. The Invisible Cliff: Abrupt Imposition of Malthusian Equilibrium in a Natural Fertility, Agrarian Society. *PLoS ONE* 9(1) e87541.

Samuels, Stephan R. 2006. Households at Ozette. In *Household Archaeology on the Northwest Coast*, edited by Elizabeth A. Sobel, D. Ann Trieu Gahr, and Kenneth M. Ames, pp. 200–232. Archaeological Series 16. International Monographs in Prehistory, Ann Arbor, Mich.

Schulting, Rick J. 1995. *Mortuary Variability and Status Differentiation on the Columbia-Fraser Plateau.* Archaeology Press, Simon Fraser University, Burnaby, B.C.

Shennan, Stephen. 2011. Property and Wealth Inequality as Cultural Niche Construction. *Philosophical Transactions of the Royal Society B* 366:918–26.

Smith, Courtland L. 1991. Patterns of Wealth Concentration. *Human Organization* 50:50–60.

Smith, Eric Alden, and Jung-Kyoo Choi. 2007. The Emergence of Inequality in Small Scale Societies: Simple Scenarios and Agent Based Simulations. In *The Model-Based Archaeology of Socio-Natural Systems*, edited by Timothy A. Kohler and Sander E. van der Leeuw, pp. 105–20. School of Advanced Research, Santa Fe, N.Mex.

Smith, Eric A., Kim Hill, Frank W. Marlowe, David Nolin, Polly Weissner, Michael Gurven, Samuel Bowles, Monique Borgerhoff Mulder, Tom Hertz, and Adrian Bell. 2010. Wealth Transmission and Inequality Among Hunter-Gatherers. *Current Anthropology* 51:19–34.

Smith, Lisa M. 2014. The Effects of the Fur Trade on Aboriginal Households in the Middle Fraser Region of British Columbia. PhD dissertation, Department of Anthropology, University of Montana, Missoula.

Smith, Michael E., Timothy Dennehy, April Kamp-Whittaker, Emily Colon, and Rebecca Harkness. 2014. Quantitative Measures of Wealth Inequality in Ancient Central Mexican Communities. *Advances in Archaeological Practice* 2:311–23.

Sobel, Elizabeth A., Gahr, D. Ann Trieu, and Kenneth M. Ames. 2006. *Household Archaeology on the Northwest Coast.* Archaeological Series 16. International Monographs in Prehistory, Ann Arbor, Mich.

Teit, J[ames]. 1900. *The Thompson Indians of British Columbia.* Memoirs of the American Museum of Natural History, Jesup North Pacific Expedition 1:63–392.

———. 1906. *The Lillooet Indians*. Memoirs of the American Museum of Natural History, Jesup North Pacific Expedition 2:193–300.

Tunnicliffe, V., J. M. O'Connell, and M. R. McQuoid. 2001. A Holocene Record of Marine Fish Remains from the Northeastern Pacific. *Marine Geology* 174:197–210.

Wessen, Gary C. 1988. The Use of Shellfish Resources on the Northwest Coast: The View from Ozette. In *Prehistoric Economies of the Pacific Northwest Coast*, edited by Barry L. Isaac, pp. 179–210. Research in Economic Anthropology Supplement 3. JAI Press, Greenwich, Conn.

Wiessner, Polly. 2002. The Vines of Complexity: Egalitarian Structures and the Institutionalization of Inequality. *Current Anthropology* 43:233–71.

Windler, Arne, Rainer Thiele, and Johannes Muller. 2013. Increasing Inequality in Chalcolithic Southeast Europe: The Case of Durankulak. *Journal of Archaeological Science* 40:204–10.

Winterhalder, Bruce, Cedric Puleston, and Cody Ross. 2015. Production Risk, Inter-annual Food Storage by Households and Population Level Consequences in Seasonal Prehistoric Agrarian Societies. *Environmental Archaeology* 20:337–48.

Wright, Katherine I. (Karen). 2014. Domestication and Inequality? Households, Corporate Groups, and Food Processing Tools at Neolithic Catalhoyuk. *Journal of Anthropological Archaeology* 33:1–33.

5

In and Out of Chains?

The Changing Social Contract in the
Pueblo Southwest, AD 600–1300

Timothy A. Kohler and Laura J. Ellyson

> *Man was born free, and he is everywhere in chains.*
> —Jean-Jacques Rousseau ([1762] 2006)

Throughout the many decades required to begin building a framework for understanding the pre-Hispanic history of the Puebloan Southwest, almost no one considered that the Pueblo societies still existing in the Southwest, first encountered by Europeans in the 1500s, might not be adequate models for the social and political organization of the predecessors of these societies over the millennium prior to their encounter.

That began to change with the famous Grasshopper/Chavez Pass debate of the 1980s. In one corner was a rather heterarchical view of the large, late prehistoric (Mogollon) Pueblo site of Grasshopper as an independent village internally structured along the lines of coresidential lineages, sodalities, age, and sex. In the other stood a vision of more-hierarchical sociopolitical organizations composed of regional systems spanning numerous large villages, rather loosely anchored on the archaeology of the large Sinagua site known as Chavez Pass (Nuvakwewtaqa) and its region. Even if inadequacies of the data brought to bear on both sides—particularly the spotty nature of the important mortuary data set from Chavez Pass (Whittlesey and Reid 2001)—prevented most archaeologists from declaring a victory for either side, there was one important result. By the 1990s archaeologists of the Pueblo world were open to a larger range of possibilities for ancient organizations than they had been two decades earlier.

Even before this debate was joined, the National Park Service had initiated a long-term project at Chaco Canyon in north-central New Mexico, with fieldwork throughout the 1970s and analysis rather prematurely terminating in the mid-1980s. Important reports directly emanating from this project continued to appear as recently as a decade ago

(Lekson 2006). Virtually all Southwestern archaeologists agree that the Chaco "phenomenon" of late Pueblo I (PI) and Pueblo II (PII) is the expression that most severely confounds the traditional "egalitarian" view of Puebloan sociopolitical organization (Lekson 2015). Most recently it has been reported that nine of the individuals buried in the famous "elite crypt" at Pueblo Bonito (the largest Great House in the canyon) have identical mitochondrial genomes, constituting a matriline seemingly descended from the founding member (Burial 14) interred in the mid–AD 800s along with a vast array of burial goods that is unprecedented in the region (Kennett et al. 2017). The other large project of the late 1970s and the early 1980s—the Dolores Archaeological Program (DAP; Breternitz et al. 1986)—was seemingly safely anchored in the AD 600–900 period (Basketmaker III [BMIII]–PI periods), before Pueblo societies *might* have become more complex. Even here, though, the debate proved to be unavoidable (e.g., Lipe and Kane 1986), because certain late PI villages in the DAP area shared a few features with the contemporaneous Great Houses beginning to appear in Chaco Canyon some two hundred kilometers to the southeast.

Our purpose in this chapter is to bring a slightly different line of evidence to bear on the nature of Pueblo societies. This evidence deals less with the nature of the underlying polities (or, as some would have it, ritualities [Mills 2002; Yoffee et al. 1999]) and more with an aspect of the lived social experience that archaeologists have not adequately considered. Specifically, we present and analyze data sets that we argue are analogous to wealth distributions in contemporary societies. In our reference contexts, we measure wealth using the size distributions of the spaces used by households for living and storage. These data are undoubtedly related to questions of the degree of hierarchy in a society (Gini coefficients for the Roman Empire were almost twice those typical of horticultural societies [Morris 2015:57]) but at the same time engage a slightly different, quasi-independent aspect of life, which we now explore.

PUEBLO HISTORY AND HOW IT MIGHT AFFECT GINIS

Chapters 1 and 2 (this volume) introduce the Gini coefficient as our tool of choice in this volume to measure concentration in a distribution.

Chapter 1 also warrants our use of house size as a reliable indicator of household wealth across societies of very different types (see also Smith et al. 2014:312). Of course, we use *wealth* not in a narrow capitalist sense but in the broadest possible way to encompass dimensions that Monique Borgerhoff Mulder and colleagues (2009) call embodied, relational, and material.

With respect to the taxonomy of economic systems used by Borgerhoff Mulder and colleagues (2009), the societies we consider in this chapter were clearly "horticultural" in at least the seventh through tenth centuries AD. That is, they enjoyed plentiful land per capita (labor likely limited production more than land), derived animal protein almost exclusively from hunting, and practiced relatively high residential mobility (Kohler and Reed 2011; Wills et al. 2012).

Age distributions of human remains (Kohler and Reese 2014) as well as the size and frequencies of archaeological sites through time (Ortman 2014; Schwindt et al. 2016) demonstrate that local and regional populations grew very rapidly during the last half of the first millennium and the first century or two of the second millennium AD. As a result, in the central Mesa Verde region (CMV), where most of the households considered here were located, agricultural land became much more limiting in the PII and PIII periods, so the duration of structure and site use increased markedly. Using sherd accumulation rates calculated from a series of probabilistically sampled and tree-ring-dated sites, Mark Varien and colleagues (Varien and Ortman 2005; Varien et al. 2007) estimate that house use-lives in small CMV sites increased from an average of about eight years in the 600s to about eighteen years in the 800s and 900s, eventually peaking around forty-five years in the 1200s. House use-lives in CMV villages appear to be slightly longer than in hamlets through most of this sequence. By the late AD 1000s, hunting wild game was increasingly less important than turkey raising, and by the mid-thirteenth century (if not before) diets depended on maize to an unhealthy extent (Matson 2016). In short, although no farmers in these societies used plows, in other respects the societies of the PII and PIII periods were "agricultural" as defined by Borgerhoff Mulder and colleagues (2009). The entire northern Pueblo area, including the central Mesa Verde region, was depopulated in the mid- to late AD 1200s, as documented in detail by Dylan Schwindt and colleagues (2016). These generalizations likely apply to the Chaco area too, with the possible exception of its PIII inhabitants, whose numbers and condition are much less well understood than their BMIII–PII precursors.

In chapter 1 we argue that inheritance of wealth from one generation to the next is critical for the cumulation of wealth disparities. Ginis should therefore generally increase during the BMIII–PIII sequence in parallel with a growing continuity of occupation that would have allowed claims to productive land to endure within lineages.

Three considerations, however, temper this simple processual expectation. First, recent examination of Ginis calculated from living and storage areas among BMIII and PI populations in the DAP area (which is in the CMV) documented essentially no change through this three-hundred-year sequence (Kohler and Higgins 2016). We noted, however, that households in villages (where ritual facilities were also generally located) tended to exhibit more variability in their storage areas (and hence higher Ginis) than in their residential areas. If we consider storage areas to be a measure of income (proportional in size to expected or achieved maize harvests) and living area to be a measure of total wealth (including the number of people in the household), we can infer that ritual activity acted like a tax or transfer, levelling households participating in the ritual system. The warrant for this inference is that different amounts of household "income" do not seem to have generated markedly different amounts of household "wealth." Timothy Kohler and Rebecca Higgins (2016) concluded that the best single estimate of the Gini for these populations was 0.28, remarkably similar to the average for fifteen horticulturalist wealth measures of 0.27 reported by Michael Gurven and colleagues (2010:table 3).

The constancy of Ginis reported by Kohler and Higgins is one reason to question whether we should expect gradually rising Ginis throughout the BMIII–PIII sequence, since it suggests that the nature of the ritual (or political) system may be at least as important as duration of occupation in affecting household wealth distributions. Another even larger uncertainty is the rise of Chaco Canyon beginning in the mid-ninth century. This anchored what would clearly become a regional system in the early 1000s, characterized by Great Houses and Great Kivas ostentatiously displaying exaggerated monumental construction, as well as by various architectural characters, road segments, and a great deal of material exchanges mostly within the Southwest but with a few extending to Mesoamerica (Crown and Hurst 2009). By the peak of the Chacoan regional system in the early AD 1100s, these characteristics linked sites as much as 250 kilometers away from Chaco Canyon. The central core of this system, at Chaco Canyon, collapsed in the mid-1100s, but follow-on manifestations complicated the archaeology of the middle San Juan and the CMV (as well as other places outside our present concern) for the following century until they too collapsed.

Thus, we predict that the *events* of the rise and collapse of Chaco will strongly interfere with any monotonic trend of increase in Ginis through time that we might expect solely from increasing durations of structure and site use—at least if the inference of marked differentiation of wealth and power within Chacoan society is correct.

Lastly, the history of Puebloan societies from Basketmaker III through Pueblo III in general is starting to look more episodic and less continuous than it used to. Kyle Bocinsky and colleagues (2016) analyzed the entire available corpus of tree-ring dates from archaeological sites in the upland Southwest. This analysis affirms the presence of four peaks in frequency of tree-ring dates, corresponding to roughly the second halves of each of the Pecos periods from BMIII through PIII. These frequency peaks were noted by Michael Berry some time ago (1982) and continue to be visible despite a much larger database, now generated mostly by cultural resource management priorities rather than by investigator curiosity. Using different series of tree rings to develop annual, spatialized estimates of temperature and precipitation across the upland Southwest, Bocinsky and colleagues were also able to develop maps showing where, in any year, maize could have been grown without water management. It was then possible to estimate whether dry-farmed maize could have been grown on the land immediately surrounding sites during their period(s) of occupation.

It was found that each of the four periods marked by high frequencies of construction activity (periods of "exploitation") terminated with climatic downturns in those areas that were actually occupied. This initiated several decades of "exploration" in which a new configuration of locations, beliefs, and practices was being worked out following the failure of the previous consensus, whose credibility was destroyed by a climatic downturn. Eventually a new consensus (or social contract) emerged, marked by aggressive construction in new locations employing new architectural configurations. These periods of exploitation are distinguished from each other, and from the period of exploration that preceded each of them, by the emergence of the stylistic and organizational canons long recognized as marking distinct Pecos periods. "Large, planned, centralized sites; specialized ceramic production and increased ceramic exchange; homogeneous architectural styles within larger sites; and intensive agriculture" identify these periods (Bocinsky et al. 2016). Climate shocks that we infer caused delegitimation of ritually sanctioned norms and practices then ushered in disaggregation leading to "weak patterns," small sites with more-expedient architecture, less exchange, more-extensive agriculture, and perhaps a more egalitarian and diverse social organization, until a new organization emerged that was sufficiently locally successful to be emulated by, or impose itself on, its neighbors (Kohler and Bocinsky 2017). This analysis assumes that the basis for cooperation in these Neolithic societies (as in archaic states [Feinman 2016]) was fundamentally ritual in nature and that establishing ritual systems as stable bases for cooperation takes longer than does delegitimizing them.

Overall, then, we predict that Ginis will increase through time, mirroring the increasing longevity of site use that enhances cross-generational inheritance of the advantages (or disadvantages) of the previous generations, but that periods of exploitation (especially in the case of Chaco) will tend to support greater wealth inequalities than are seen in the preceding and following periods of exploration.

THE SAMPLE AND ITS LIMITATIONS

The analysis here reports sizes for 177 houses that incorporate the 38 houses recognized under what Kohler and Higgins (2016) called the "Lightfoot protocol" (also adopted here) for inferring spaces used by households. The additional 139 houses analyzed here are largely from the PII and PIII periods in the CMV, as well as from the Chaco area throughout its occupation. Basic data and their sources can be found in table A5.1 in Kohler and Ellyson 2017.

We restrict ourselves to sites in the central Mesa Verde and Chaco areas (figure 5.1) because their sequences are in general well understood. Nevertheless, we encountered numerous difficulties. Many sites were not

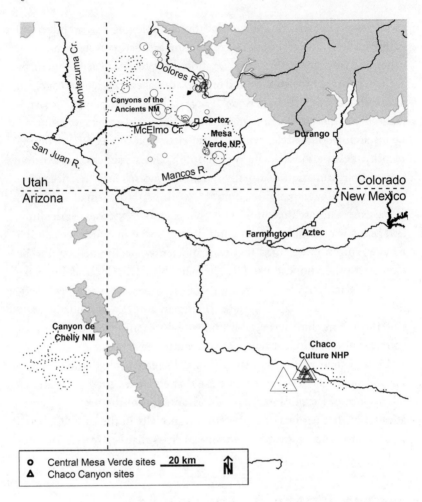

Figure 5.1 Site locations in the two Pueblo regions analyzed. Symbol size is proportional to number of houses in the sample at each site.

excavated sufficiently to identify household suites, which in these areas typically include a pit structure and additional surface rooms or storage features. Even for excavated sites, not all archaeologists are willing to infer social connections among structures, and we have been reluctant to do so, because many subtle characteristics including stratigraphy, artifact joins, poorly visible doors between rooms, and the like are best appreciated by the original investigator. (We made these inferences in a few cases, but where possible we have chosen sites where those inferences were already made.) Some sites are so massive and long-lived (Pueblo Bonito in Chaco Canyon was under construction for almost three centuries) that identification of household suites is difficult, particularly since such Great Houses were typically two or more stories tall and their upper stories are often poorly preserved.

Another issue, identified in many of the chapters in this volume, is how to sample houses to accurately estimate wealth differences in a complex society. Where households are all the same, of course any small sample will do. But like trophic levels, and for very much the same reasons, the nature of stratified societies is that the upper portions of the social pyramid—the elites and their houses—will be much rarer than the lower portions (commoners and their houses). Any sample that does not sample all wealth segments in the same proportion as they existed in the living societies will return an inaccurate estimate of wealth distributions. Although we have done our best, we know that we have not been able to obtain representative samples of all the societies visited here, and we will point out cases along the way where this is most obvious.

In previous work (Kohler and Higgins 2016), we were able to differentiate storage and living areas associated with each house. Here that has not always been possible, in part because in Chacoan Great Houses there is a great deal of space that was neither obviously for living nor for storage. We have had to resort to simply reporting a total area for each house, though elsewhere (Kohler and Ellyson 2017:table A5.1) we separate these into storage and living areas where possible.

Two periods require more discussion. The BMIII Exploration period (AD 500–600) in the Chaco subarea at present includes proveniences only from the famous (and debated) pithouse village Shabik'eschee (Roberts 1929). Frank Roberts divided this site into an early and a late component. A widely cited analysis of social differentiation and leadership development in early pithouse villages seems to have used both components and assigned them both a date of AD 600–700 (Lightfoot and Feinman 1982). More-recent work (Wills and Windes 1989) reports that the site contains considerably more structures than were excavated by Roberts and argues that a trustworthy intrasite chronology of the structures excavated by Roberts cannot be assembled. Wills and Windes assigned the BMIII portions of the site to a date range from the mid–AD 500s until about 700. We retained Roberts's division and assigned the nine pithouses he assigned to his early component to our AD 500–600 period, and those in his later component to our AD 600–700 period. W. H. Wills and Thomas Windes (1989:364) argued that none of the extramural bins can be associated with any specific household, whereas Kent Lightfoot and Gary Feinman (1982) appear to have associated all or most of these external features with specific households. We take a middle path, associating a few of the storage bins reported by Roberts with the closest of these households (see Kohler and Ellyson 2017:table A5.1). That leaves a larger number of bins unassociated with any pit structure that do not enter into our calculations.

For the PII period (and PIII in the CMV) a set of more consequential decisions had to be made. Archaeologists are uncertain how the massive structures called Great Houses were used. Although quite a few have been excavated, much of this work was done in the discipline's early years. Moreover, as mentioned, these structures tend to have long, complex histories. Almost certainly they had multiple uses and meanings for the members of these societies during their existence. Those in Chaco Canyon, as well as the somewhat scaled-down versions throughout and beyond the San Juan basin that are often called outliers, almost certainly had a role in community-integrating ritual activities, including feasting (Cameron 2008:302; Cameron and Toll 2001; Safi and Duff 2016). Many are prominently placed, so it was evidently important for their occupants to see and be seen (Van Dyke et al. 2016). Those in Chaco Canyon, at least, were built with timber coming mostly from forests more than seventy-five kilometers away, at great labor cost (Guiterman et al. 2016). Here we assume that in addition to all these other roles and characteristics, Great Houses were first and foremost the residences of large elite households with lots of storage space. This is in line with Stephen Lekson's (2015:36–40) view but is far from universally accepted. In fact, most archaeologists who discuss Great Houses are conspicuously vague on this essential issue! This decision has obvious consequences for the Ginis we calculate.

Finally, determining the correct spatial and social scope for the calculation of the Gini is difficult. To the extent that the entire Pueblo world would have been aware of itself and internally interacting, perhaps we should simply calculate one Gini for each temporal subdivision for that very large area. However, interactions were surely stronger at more local scales. Ideally we would sample the entire social unit that dictates, or allows, the development of the social heterogeneity encountered. In general, more social heterogeneity signals the presence of a larger system.

We believe, therefore, that "the site" is usually too small to be representative for this computation except in the most homogeneous, smallest-scale societies. "Communities" composed of many sites would be better, though these can be difficult to define, especially prior to the late PI period (see Reese 2014 for a notable recent attempt in Mesa Verde National Park). If many communities all participated in a single ritual or political system, that too is a plausible target for computation. Unfortunately, identifying such systems is as difficult as identifying communities.

Here we decided to calculate Ginis for our entire sample through time and also separately for each of the two regions in which we have collected data. In periods when these regions were largely independent (BMIII and PI), the preferred calculation is for each separately, assuming adequate and representative samples. At the height of Chaco, called the PII Exploitation period below, we believe that the most accurate calculation is to consider both together, as interacting portions of a single polity (Crabtree et al. 2017).

RESULTS

Table 5.1 and figure 5.2 present the Ginis through time separately for these two regions of the Pueblo Southwest and also aggregated together into a single sample, plotted on the eight midpoints of the exploration/exploitation subdivisions of the four Pecos periods, yielding a temporal resolution of about a century on average.

From the mid-500s through the early 800s, Chaco and the CMV display fairly similar house-size distributions (and therefore Gini coefficients). Yet within these broad similarities, by the mid-700s, CMV society had become significantly less equal than Chacoan society, judging by the lack of overlap between the 80 percent confidence intervals for their Ginis. Richard Wilshusen and Ruth Van Dyke (2006:239) also noted that in AD 875, residential hamlets in the Chaco area were much smaller than contemporary northern San Juan villages. Although site size and Gini coefficients are not necessarily related, chapter 8 in this volume demonstrates that mean house area and Gini coefficients often are.

Table 5.1 Sample sizes and Gini coefficients by subperiod and subregion

Subperiod[a]	Dates AD[a]	Chaco N	Chaco Gini	CMV[b] N	CMV[b] Gini	Total Gini
BMIII Explore	500–600	9	0.29	5	0.27	0.29
BMIII Exploit	601–700	14	0.26	14	0.21	0.34
PI Explore	701–790	4	0.22	11	0.30	0.27
PI Exploit	791–890	5	0.65	27	0.28	0.36
PII Explore	891–1035	9	0.47	11	0.23	0.55
PII Exploit	1036–1145	32	0.44	13	0.42	0.43
PIII Explore	1146–1200	0	—	8	0.23	0.23
PIII Exploit	1201–1285	0	—	15	0.36	0.36
Total households		73		104		

[a]After Bocinsky et al. 2016.
[b]CMV = Central Mesa Verde.

The general similarity of the Ginis in these two regions ends in the mid-800s when the first households that can be identified in Pueblo Bonito (Wilshusen and Van Dyke 2006:fig. 7.6A) enter our sample. Wealth disparities in Chaco may have decreased during the following PII Exploration subperiod (essentially the 900s), despite the continued growth of Pueblo Bonito Great House, for which our sample during this period consists of five houses (Wilshusen and Van Dyke 2006:fig. 7.6B). However, the confidence intervals overlap, just barely, for these two periods. In striking contrast to Chaco, in the CMV Ginis remained low throughout the ninth and tenth centuries until the last decades of the eleventh.

The PII Exploitation period (AD 1036–1145) in Chaco—the height of the Chaco regional system—is still marked by high Ginis due to the inclusion in our sample of several suites from Pueblo Alto (Windes 1987), which is unusual in being a Great House excavated recently and in having a relatively short-lived occupation simplifying its interpretation. By around AD 1070 Great Houses also began to appear in the CMV, which in the PII Exploitation period displays household-level inequality almost exactly matching that of Chaco. Our CMV sample includes only one relatively small Great House, Escalante (Hallasi 1979). Even though they are fairly common in the CMV in this period (Glowacki and Ortman

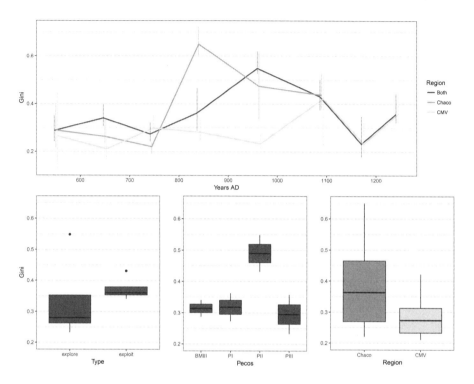

Figure 5.2 Gini coefficients (*top*) derived from house-size distributions in the Central Mesa Verde and Chaco regions, and both regions pooled; (*bottom left*) by the exploration and exploitation subperiod types (all houses, both regions pooled); (*bottom center*) by Pecos periods (all houses, both regions pooled); and (*bottom right*) by region.

2012), no larger Great Houses available to us have been excavated in such a way as to be useable here.

Our measurements for Chaco cease at the end of the PII period. Although a repopulation of Chaco Canyon occurred in the 1200s, following its depopulation in the mid-1100s, we have not succeeded in isolating household suites from that occupation. In the CMV our sample from the PIII Exploration period (1145–1200) is also rather small (eight houses).

Our sample from the PIII Exploitation subperiod (the thirteenth century) in the CMV is dominated by Sand Canyon Pueblo (Kuckelman et al. 2007) and the adjacent, slightly earlier (and likely ancestral)

Albert Porter Pueblo (Ryan 2015). The houses from Albert Porter are represented by kiva suites (Kiva 108 and Kiva 113 with associated rooms) located within the Great House (Block 100). Susan Ryan (2015) reports that Kiva 112 and its associated rooms were constructed first and represent the core of the Great House. Many of the rooms included in these suites were inferred based on evidence from masonry rubble and geophysical testing. Other rooms were left out of our calculations because of their possible association with unexcavated portions of the Great House. The inclusion of two Great House proveniences from Albert Porter (Kiva 108 and its suite, and Kiva 113 and its suite) considerably increases the Ginis in this terminal period.

The bottom left graph of figure 5.2 arrays the Gini coefficients by their membership in either the exploration or the exploitation subperiods, using the more stable calculations derived from all houses in both areas (table 5.1). Although the small sample sizes (only four subperiods in each box) must be kept in mind, the differences between these subperiod types are intriguing. As predicted, exploitation subperiods present higher median Gini scores indicating greater household wealth inequality. We did not, though, predict the much greater range of variability in the exploration subperiods, which appear less standardized than the exploitation subperiods.

The bottom center graph of figure 5.2 also employs the "Both" series (that is, all households from both regions are considered simultaneously in calculating the Ginis), now dividing time into the Pecos periods. Here PII emerges as a strong outlier, with median Ginis approaching 0.5, against the background level of roughly 0.3.

Finally, the bottom right graph of figure 5.2 divides the sequence regionally. The two regions overlap, though both the median Gini and its range through time are higher for Chaco.

DISCUSSION

As the bottom center graph in figure 5.2 shows, the Gini scores for the BMIII, PI, and PIII periods average around 0.3, in line with those expected in horticultural societies (Gurven et al. 2010:61). By contrast, expected Ginis are higher among agricultural societies. Among two historic and six contemporary agricultural societies studied by Shenk and colleagues (2010), material wealth is much more important than embodied or relational wealth, and material wealth is also the most unequally distributed and highly transmitted form of wealth. Ginis for material wealth distributions in these societies average 0.57, somewhat above the median we calculate for PII societies (figure 5.2). Ginis calculated on two measures of relational wealth for these same societies (the number of cattle-loaning partners among the Kipsigis and the size of in-law networks among the Bengaluru), however, average 0.46. The PII values we calculate here approximate the average of these two sources, which is consistent with the notion that variability in house size in these Pueblo societies reflects both variability in material household wealth and the variable positions of households in networks of kin and ceremonial practice (relational wealth).

As anticipated, Gini coefficients tend to increase somewhat through the AD 600–1300 period in these two important subregions of the Pueblo world, though the increase is far from monotonic (figure 5.2). The periods of the florescence of the Chaco regional system (late PI and through late PII) stand out as anomalous, transforming the previously relatively egalitarian Chaco Canyon into a much more unequal society. The Gini coefficients for the two subregions are nearly identical at the height of the Chaco regional system (PII Exploitation subperiod) (table 5.1). Unless our (small) sample is misleading, CMV inequality may decrease in the following period, though the confidence interval for the PIII Exploration period overlaps with that from the prior period (figure 5.2). By the 1200s, inequality appears to have reasserted itself in the CMV, although once again the confidence intervals between this and the next-earlier period slightly overlap.

This possible reassertion of inequality in the thirteenth-century CMV coincides with what Donna Glowacki (2015:164–73) has called the "McElmo Intensification." Using site organization, types of public architecture, and the nature of access to them, Glowacki argues that the degree of social inequality in these large late villages was increasing as power was increasingly consolidated by individuals or groups. The Great Tower Complex at Yellow Jacket Pueblo (Kuckelman 2003) is given as a prime example of how access to critical resources (a spring in this case) was increasingly coming under restricted control. The trends in our Gini analysis seem consistent with Glowacki's assessment.

In general, Ginis were higher in periods of exploitation than in periods of exploration (figure 5.2). Each of the transitions from exploitation to exploration represents a major or a minor collapse of a previously stable set of economic, ceremonial, and organizational practices. The natural question, therefore, is whether (and to what extent) it was a concerted reaction against increasing social inequality that brought on these collapses—or whether these decreases in inequality were simply the indirect result of a collapse of productivity, thereby decreasing the ability of elites to support themselves via taxation (a term we use somewhat metaphorically, following Crabtree et al. 2017 and Drennan and Peterson 2012).

Perhaps in favor of the hypothesis that these collapses were provoked by increasing social inequality is the contrast of this pre-1300 history, discussed here, with the relative continuity of the occupations of the northern Rio Grande (NRG) region that followed the depopulation of the northern Southwest. For the post-1300 occupations of the NRG, we have not tried to make Gini calculations, given the difficulty of identifying household spaces in these sites, their long occupation span, and the relative dearth of recent excavation. It appears, though, that the sorts of boom-and-bust cycles characterizing the earlier northern Southwest were either absent or muted in the post-1300 NRG. We speculate that if we could calculate Ginis for these societies they would be below those we calculated here for the PII periods and probably more in line with the long-term averages seen in both of our subregions. Although the comparison is complicated by many other concurrent changes (such as decreases in the importance of rainfall farming and the incidence of violence, increases in exchange, economic specialization, and aggregate size, and changes to ceremonial organization [see Kohler et al. 2014]), the relative social equality that we speculate existed in this period could have contributed to the stability of the post-1300 northern Rio Grande societies. This line of reasoning supports the notion that episodic increases in inequality might have contributed to episodic collapse.

We tentatively advance another line of evidence suggesting somewhat more directly that any buildup of social inequality in the CMV was regularly challenged, presumably by those who did not benefit from it. Figure 5.3 juxtaposes the time series of violence tabulated from sets of human remains by Sarah Cole (2012) with the time series of Gini coefficients estimated here for the same area. These are calculated at

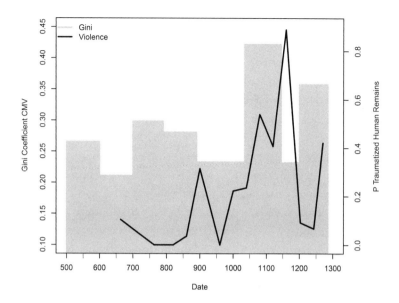

Figure 5.3 Violence (proxied by proportions of sets of human remains with violent trauma) versus wealth inequality (proxied by Gini coefficients on house size through time), Central Mesa Verde region.

different temporal granularities: violence is graphed at the midpoints of the fourteen periods recognized by the Village Ecodynamics Project (Varien et al. 2007; average period length about fifty years), whereas the Gini coefficients are graphed at the midpoints of the eight intersections between the four Pecos periods and the two subperiod types (exploration vs. exploitation) identified by Bocinsky and colleagues (2016; table 5.1, this chapter).

Following Peter Turchin and Andrey Korotayev (2006), Kohler and colleagues (2009) identified some of the variability in CMV violence before circa AD 1000 as due to a lagged dynamic relationship with population growth. We have also argued that some of the variability in violence in this series (especially in later periods) can be attributed to a positive relationship between amount of violence and the standard deviation of potential maize productivity in each period (Kohler et al. 2014). So it may seem uncalled for to suggest yet one more dependency for this series! Yet in any complex system we must acknowledge both the provisionality of interpretation and the inadequacy of any one formalism to capture all the properties of interest (Cilliers et al. 2013; Mikulecky 2007). We must also work with what we have in trying to untangle the highly connected, complex, and multiscalar patterns of change in social systems. We now raise the possibility that some of the episodic violence we see in the CMV may have been intended to challenge high levels of social inequality; each local peak in violence occurred immediately after, or during, a local peak in inequality (figure 5.3). The PI, PII, and PIII Exploitation periods each end with a large increase in violence. Of course, we cannot entirely rule out a different causality: episodes of violence could have been brought on by decreasing productivity causing social chaos as existing social contracts collapsed. In fact, there is no reason to believe that both of these causal paths might not have been effective and mutually constitutive.

In either case, the coincidence of the episodic declines in inequality with the episodic increases in violence is as predicted by Walter Scheidel (2017) but usefully extends his theory to smaller-scale societies in non-Western contexts. Scheidel proposed that social stability tends to favor the growth or maintenance of inequality. Only four processes (his "Four Horsemen of Levelling") have been effective in forcing down inequality, by his analysis: mass-mobilization warfare, transformative revolution, state failure, and pandemics (Scheidel 2017:6). Any warfare in nonstate contexts is potentially "mass mobilization" in the sense that conflict in such societies is not simply the domain of specialists (soldiers). Moreover, the particular case of the Chaco collapse in the mid–AD 1100s (the worst episode of violence in our record) was in fact, by some perspectives, a state collapse. More generally, Scheidel's framework suggests that the declines in inequality seen in the late 800s, mid-1100s, and late 1200s could only be due to disturbances of a far-reaching, radical nature. Thus, the identification of changes in inequality in long-term trajectories such as this is valuable not just in itself but also in what it tells us about lived experiences. In general, stable or increasing inequality speaks to social stability. Reductions in inequality require substantial disruptions. Plausibly, the amount of the decline is an index of the severity of the disruption. However negatively we may view wealth inequalities, the circumstances surrounding their collapse were probably extremely unpleasant even for many who were not among the privileged.

There is some evidence that social inequality in the CMV may have declined during the final years of the PIII Exploitation period. We know of no Great Houses constructed after 1225 (Glowacki and Ortman 2014:table 14.2), and we know of no Great Houses still in use by 1260. The latest households in our sample (see Kohler and Ellyson 2017:table A5.1), from Sand Canyon Pueblo, are not greatly different in size. If high degrees of inequality increased general dissatisfaction and decreased willingness to cooperate, thus helping precipitate often violent collapses, attempts to reverse the situation in this final period were apparently not sufficient.

SUMMARY

> *And they ain't the kind that you can see.*
> —Gerry Goffin and Carole King, "Chains" (1980)

Many of our conclusions here will come as no surprise to Southwestern archaeologists. If we consider Great Houses to be houses of elites, then those places and periods when they were present must be the most unequal in this sequence, as they indeed proved to be. This analysis does yield at least three surprises, however.

First, we show that levels of social inequality during the Chaco era closely approximate those expected in agricultural (as opposed to horticultural) societies. This strengthens the hypothesis that by the height of the Chacoan polity, these farming societies were more land- than labor-limited, and perhaps we should not be surprised that the inequalities we reconstruct first arose in the confines of Chaco Canyon. R. Gwinn Vivian and Adam Watson's (2015) review of farming strategies in the canyon underscores the likelihood that various water-control strategies (especially *akchin* production) were able to significantly increase the production gradient between lands farmed with and without water enrichment and that the resulting production was localized and economically defensible. (Chapter 1 in this volume reviews the theory that identifies the importance of steep resource gradients and economic defensibility to increasing social inequality.) Moreover, high frequencies of corn pollen in Chaco Canyon sites argue against the notion that all or most of Chaco's maize was imported (Geib and Heitman 2015). Chaco's ability to extend a system of control that resulted in tribute flowing to the center (as argued in Crabtree et al. 2017) reinforces the impression that the productive dry-farmable portions of the Southwest were essentially filled up by PII times (Kohler and Reese 2014), since demographic saturation would complicate any possibility of "voting with their feet" for those who might have wished to opt out of Chaco's control.

Second, even though it was established on completely independent grounds, the macro-structure for Southwestern history recently proposed by Bocinsky and colleagues (2016) proves useful for summarizing household-level wealth inequality through time. Considered as a whole, the Pueblo region experienced at least four boom-and-bust cycles. The archaeologists assembled at Pecos in 1927 recognized this structure without knowing its causes or absolute chronology and systematized it using what we now call the Pecos Classification. Beginning at least with BMIII, each Pecos period began with several decades of casting around for areas and ways of life (economic, social, ceremonial, and political modalities) on which to construct successful societies. Out of these explorations came localized kernels of success that either were emulated by their neighbors or encompassed them through growth. In either case, their organizational models spread, and today we recognize the results as BMIII, PI, and so forth. It is not really the entire periods, though, but the exploitation subperiods in which these organizational canons were most widely and clearly expressed.

What we add to this model herein is evidence that wealth inequality generally increased during (or at the outset of) periods of exploitation, perhaps eventually contributing to dissatisfaction with the current organization by those who had the least access to its benefits. (The BMIII period in the CMV may be a counterexample, but as the upper graph in figure 5.2 shows, the confidence interval for the BMIII Exploration period is so large that no firm conclusions should be drawn.) This increase in inequality seems to set the stage for iconoclastic moments during climatic downturns when ritual-political leaders, whose actions were supposed to help maintain production, lost their credibility. Often this led to violence, but even in the absence of violence, disaggregation was probably initiated by those who were most disadvantaged, and such departures further imperiled the current order. As new periods of exploration began, the degree of social inequality was reset in most cases to pre-exploitation levels.

The bottom left graph of figure 5.2 suggests another line of inquiry. Although the median level of inequality is higher in periods of exploitation than in periods of exploration, what really stands out (and this is our third surprise) is the greatly decreased *range* of inequality during the exploitation periods. If we accept that attention to function is valid for characterizing the operation of societies, though not for understanding the origins of social practices (Dubrieul 2010:207–11), this contrast suggests that a fairly narrow range of inequality provided the best conditions for the spread of norms and the development of regional systems and "strong patterns." Going further with the archaeological record in substantiating such a suggestion may be difficult, but some economists (e.g., Stiglitz 2012) recognize a similar phenomenon in contemporary societies. It may be that societies can have levels of inequality that are either too high or too low to be effective in creating wealth and provoking emulation.

This in turn begs a question that builds on the ground gained here. The spurts of major construction and extension of systems (the PI village way of life; the Chacoan regional system as signaled by the Great Houses) represent growth organizations that presumably created wealth and added value to the labor of their members on average, at least for a time. Did such growth *require* increasing inequality, or did it simply *result* in it over several decades of operation? Answering this question will depend on being able to accurately assess, over time, the inputs to and outputs from the public goods games that members of societies play, which in some cases result in increasing returns to scale. Archaeologists are just beginning to consider such topics (Kohler et al. 2012; Ortman et al. 2015).

ACKNOWLEDGMENTS

Our sample incorporates household-area measurements made by Rebecca Higgins and reported in Kohler and Higgins 2016. We thank Bill Lipe, Mark Varien, Chip Wills, and Tom Windes for help identifying or interpreting some of the proveniences used here, as well as the very large number of investigators (see references in Kohler and Ellyson 2017:table A5.1) whose labors over decades have made research like this possible. Some of the analyses herein were made possible by support from National Science Foundation grants DEB-0816400 and SMA-1620462.

REFERENCES CITED

Berry, Michael S. 1982. *Time, Space, and Transition in Anasazi Prehistory*. University of Utah Press, Salt Lake City.

Bocinsky, R. Kyle, Johnathan Rush, Keith W. Kintigh, and Timothy A. Kohler. 2016. Exploration and Exploitation in the Macrohistory of the Prehispanic Pueblo Southwest. *Science Advances* 2, e1501532. doi:10.1126/sciadv.1501532.

Borgerhoff Mulder, Monique, Samuel Bowles, Tom Hertz, Adrian Bell, Jan Beise, Greg Clark, Ila Fazzio, et al. 2009. Intergenerational Wealth Transmission and the Dynamics of Inequality in Small-Scale Societies. *Science* 326:682–88.

Breternitz, David A., Christine K. Robinson, and G. Timothy Gross (compilers). 1986. *Dolores Archaeological Program: Final Synthetic Report*. USDI Bureau of Reclamation, Engineering and Research Center, Denver.

Cameron, Catherine M. (editor). 2008. *Chaco and After in the Northern San Juan: Excavations at the Bluff Great House*. University of Arizona Press, Tucson.

Cameron, Catherine M., and H. Wolcott Toll. 2001. Deciphering the Organization of Production in the Chaco World. *American Antiquity* 66:5–13.

Cilliers, Paul, Harry C. Biggs, Sonja Blignaut, Aiden G. Choles, Jan-Hendrik S. Hofmeyr, Graham P. W. Jewitt, and Dirk J. Roux. 2013. Complexity, Modeling, and Natural Resource Management. *Ecology and Society* 18(3):1. http://dx .doi.org/10.5751/ES-05382-180301.

Cole, Sarah M. 2012. Population Dynamics and Warfare in the Central Mesa Verde. In *Emergence and Collapse of Early Villages: Models of Central Mesa Verde Archaeology*, edited by Timothy A. Kohler and Mark D. Varien, pp. 197–218. University of California Press, Berkeley.

Crabtree, Stefani, R. Kyle Bocinsky, Paul L. Hooper, Susan C. Ryan, and Timothy A. Kohler. 2017. How to Make a Polity (in the Central Mesa Verde Region). *American Antiquity* 82:71–95.

Crown, Patricia L., and W. Jeffrey Hurst. 2009. Evidence of Cacao Use in the Prehispanic American Southwest. *PNAS*. doi:10.1073/pnas.0812817106.

Drennan, Robert D., and Christian E. Peterson. 2012. Challenges for the Comparative Study of Early Complex Societies. In *The Comparative Archaeology of Complex Societies*, edited by Michael E. Smith, pp. 62–87. Cambridge University Press, Cambridge.

Dubreuil, Benoît. 2010. *Human Evolution and the Origins of Hierarchies: The State of Nature*. Cambridge University Press, Cambridge.

Feinman, Gary M. 2016. Variation and Change in Archaic States: Ritual as a Mechanism of Sociopolitical Organization. In *Ritual and Archaic States*, edited by Joanne M. A. Murphy, pp. 1–22. University Press of Florida, Gainesville.

Geib, Phil C., and Carrie C. Heitman. 2015. The Relevance of Maize Pollen for Assessing the Extent of Maize Production in Chaco Canyon. In *Chaco Revisited: New Research on the Prehistory of Chaco Canyon, New Mexico*, edited by Carrie C. Heitman and Stephen Plog, pp. 66–95. University of Arizona Press, Tucson.

Glowacki, Donna M. 2015. *Living and Leaving: A Social History of Regional Depopulation in the Thirteenth-Century Mesa Verde*. University of Arizona Press, Tucson.

Glowacki, Donna M., and Scott G. Ortman. 2012. Characterizing Community-Center (Village) Formation in the VEP Study Area, A.D. 600–1280. In *Emergence and Collapse of Early Villages: Models of Central Mesa Verde Archaeology*, edited by Timothy A. Kohler and Mark D. Varien, pp. 219–46. University of California Press, Berkeley.

Guiterman, Christopher H., Thomas W. Swetnam, and Jeffrey S. Dean. 2016. Eleventh-Century Shift in Timber Procurement Areas for the Great Houses of Chaco Canyon. *PNAS* 113:1186–90.

Gurven, Michael, Monique Borgerhoff Mulder, Paul L. Hooper, Hillard Kaplan, Robert Quinlan, Rebecca Sear, Eric Schniter, et al. 2010. Domestication Alone Does Not Lead to Inequality: Intergenerational Wealth Transmission Among Horticulturalists. *Current Anthropology* 51:49–64.

Hallasi, Judith Ann. 1979. Archaeological Excavation at the Escalante Site, Dolores, Colorado, 1975 and 1976. In *The Archaeology and Stabilization of the Dominguez and Escalante Ruins*, edited by Alan D. Reed, Judith Ann Hallasi, Adrian S. White, and David A. Breternitz, pp. 203–425. Cultural Research Series 7. Bureau of Land Management, Denver.

Kennett, Douglas J., Stephen Plog, Richard J. George, Brendan J. Culleton, Adam S. Watson, Pontus Skoglund, Nadin Rohland, et al. 2017. Archaeogenomic Evidence Reveals Prehistoric Matrilineal Dynasty. *Nature*. doi: 10.1038/ncomms14115.

Kohler, Timothy A., and R. Kyle Bocinsky. 2017. Crises as Opportunities for Culture Change. In *Crisis to Collapse: The Archaeology of Social Breakdown*, edited by Tim Cunningham and Jan Driessen, pp. 263–73. Presses Universitaires de Louvain, Louvain-la-Neuve, Belgium.

Kohler, Timothy A., Denton Cockburn, Paul L. Hooper, R. Kyle Bocinsky, and Ziad Kobti. 2012. The Coevolution of Group Size and Leadership: An Agent-Based Public Goods Model for Prehispanic Pueblo Societies. *Advances in Complex Systems* 15(1–2):1150007. doi:10.1142/S0219525911003256.

Kohler, Timothy A., Sarah Cole, and Stanca Ciupe. 2009. Population and Warfare: A Test of the Turchin Model in Puebloan Societies. In *Pattern and Process in Cultural Evolution*, edited by Stephen Shennan, pp. 297–95. University of California Press, Berkeley.

Kohler, Timothy A., and Laura J. Ellyson. 2017. Table A5.1. Available at https://core.tdar.org/dataset/436268/table-a51.

Kohler, Timothy A., and Rebecca Higgins. 2016. Quantifying Household Inequality in Early Pueblo Villages. *Current Anthropology* 57(5):690–97.

Kohler, Timothy A., Scott G. Ortman, Katie E. Grundtisch, Carly M. Fitzpatrick, and Sarah M. Cole. 2014. The Better Angels of Their Nature: Declining Violence Through Time Among Prehispanic Farmers of the Pueblo Southwest. *American Antiquity* 79:444–64.

Kohler, Timothy A., and Charles Reed. 2011. Explaining the Structure and Timing of Formation of Pueblo I Villages in the Northern U.S. Southwest. In
Sustainable Lifeways: Cultural Persistence in an Ever-Changing Environment,
edited by Naomi F. Miller, Katherine M. Moore, and Kathleen Ryan, pp. 150–
79. University of Pennsylvania Museum of Archaeology and Anthropology,
Philadelphia.

Kohler, Timothy A., and Kelsey M. Reese. 2014. Long and Spatially Variable
Neolithic Demographic Transition in the North American Southwest. *PNAS*.
doi:10.1073/pnas.1404367111.

Kuckelman, Kristin A. 2003. Architecture. In *The Archaeology of Yellow Jacket
Pueblo: Excavations at a Large Community Center in Southwestern Colorado*,
edited by Kristen A. Kuckelman. Crow Canyon Archaeological Center,
Cortez, Colo. Electronic document, www.crowcanyon.org/ResearchReports
/YellowJacket/Text/yjpw_architecture.asp.

Kuckelman, Kristin A., Bruce A. Bradley, Melissa J. Churchill, and James H.
Kleidon. 2007. A Descriptive and Interpretive Summary of Excavations, by
Architectural Block. In *The Archaeology of Sand Canyon Pueblo: Intensive Ex-
cavations at a Late-Thirteenth-Century Village in Southwestern Colorado*, edited
by Kristin A. Kuckelman. Crow Canyon Archaeological Center, Cortez, Colo.
Electronic document, www.crowcanyon.org/sandcanyon.

Lekson, Stephen H. (editor). 2006. *The Archaeology of Chaco Canyon: An Eleventh-
Century Pueblo Regional Center*. School of American Research Press, Santa
Fe, N.Mex.

———. 2015. *The Chaco Meridian: One Thousand Years of Political and Religious
Power in the Ancient Southwest*. 2nd ed. Rowman and Littlefield, Lanham, Md.

Lightfoot, Kent G., and Gary M. Feinman. 1982. Social Differentiation and
Leadership Development in Early Pithouse Villages in the Mogollon Region
of the American Southwest. *American Antiquity* 47:64–86.

Lipe, William D., and Allen E. Kane. 1986. Evaluation of the Models with Dolores Area Data. In *Dolores Archaeological Program: Final Synthetic Report*,
compiled by David A. Breternitz, Christine K. Robinson, and G. Timothy
Gross, pp. 703–7. USDI Bureau of Reclamation, Denver.

Matson, R. G. 2016. The Nutritional Context of the Pueblo III Depopulation of
the Northern San Juan: Too Much Maize? *Journal of Archaeological Science:
Reports* 5:622–31.

Mikulecky, Donald C. 2007. Complexity Science as an Aspect of the Complexity of Science. In *Worldviews, Science and Us: Philosophy and Complexity*,
edited by Carlos Gershenson, Diederik Aerts, and Bruce Edmonds, pp. 30–
52. World Scientific Publishing, Hackensack, N.J. http://dx.doi.org/10.1142
/9789812707420_0003.

Mills, Barbara M. 2002. Recent Research on Chaco: Changing Views on Economy, Ritual, and Society. *Journal of Archaeological Research* 10:65–117.

Morris, Ian. 2015. *Foragers, Farmers, and Fossil Fuels: How Human Values Evolve*.
Princeton University Press, Princeton.

Ortman, Scott G. 2014. Uniform Probability Density Analysis and Population History in the Northern Rio Grande. *Journal of Archaeological Method and Theory*. doi:10.1007/s10816-014-9227-6.

Ortman, Scott G., Andrew H. F. Cabaniss, Jennie O. Sturm, and Luís M. A. Bettencourt. 2015. Settlement Scaling and Increasing Returns in an Ancient Society. *Science Advances* 1:e1400066.

Reese, Kelsey M. 2014. Over the Line: A Least-Cost Analysis of "Community" in Mesa Verde National Park. Master's thesis, Washington State University, Pullman.

Roberts, Frank H. H. 1929. *Shabik'eschee Village: A Late Basket Maker Site in the Chaco Canyon*. Bureau of American Ethnology Bulletin 92. U.S. Government Printing Office, Washington, D.C.

Rousseau, Jean-Jacques. 2006. *The Social Contract*. Translated by Maurice Cranston. Penguin, New York. Orig. pub. 1762.

Ryan, Susan C. (editor). 2015. *The Archaeology of Albert Porter Pueblo (Site 5MT123): Excavations at a Great House Community Center in Southwestern Colorado*. Crow Canyon Archaeological Center, Cortez, Colo. Electronic document, www.crowcanyon.org/albertporter.

Safi, Kristin N., and Andrew I. Duff. 2016. The Role of a Chaco-Era Great House in the Southern Cibola Region of West-Central New Mexico: The Largo Gap Great House Community. *Journal of Field Archaeology* 41:37–56.

Scheidel, Walter. 2017. *The Great Leveler: Violence and the History of Inequality from the Stone Age to the Twenty-First Century*. Princeton University Press, Princeton.

Schwindt, Dylan M., R. Kyle Bocinsky, Scott G. Ortman, Donna M. Glowacki, Mark D. Varien, and Timothy A. Kohler. 2016. The Social Consequences of Climate Change in the Central Mesa Verde Region. *American Antiquity* 81:74–96.

Shenk, Mary K., Monique Borgerhoff Mulder, Jan Beise, Gregory Clark, William Irons, Donna Leonetti, Bobbi S. Low, et al. 2010. Intergenerational Wealth Transmission Among Agriculturalists: Foundations of Agrarian Inequality. *Current Anthropology* 51(1):65–83.

Smith, Michael E., Timothy Dennehy, April Kamp-Whittaker, Emily Colon, and Rebecca Harkness. 2014. Quantitative Measures of Wealth Inequality in Ancient Central Mexican Communities. *Advances in Archaeological Practice* 2:311–23.

Stiglitz, Joseph E. 2012. *The Price of Inequality: How Today's Divided Society Endangers Our Future*. Norton, New York.

Turchin, Peter, and Andrey Korotayev. 2006. Population Dynamics and Internal Warfare: A Reconsideration. *Social Evolution and History* 5(2):112–47.

Van Dyke, Ruth M., R. Kyle Bocinsky, Thomas C. Windes, and Tucker J. Robinson. 2016. Great Houses, Shrines, and High Places: Intervisibility in the Chacoan World. *American Antiquity* 81:205–30.

Varien, Mark D., and Scott G. Ortman. 2005. Accumulations Research in the Southwest United States: Middle-Range Theory for Big-Picture Problems. *World Archaeology* 37:132–55.

Varien, Mark D., Scott G. Ortman, Timothy A. Kohler, Donna M. Glowacki, and C. David Johnson. 2007. Historical Ecology in the Mesa Verde Region: Results from the Village Project. *American Antiquity* 72:273–99.

Vivian, R. Gwinn, and Adam S. Watson. 2015. Revaluating and Modeling Agricultural Potential in the Chaco Core. In *Chaco Revisited: New Research on the Prehistory of Chaco Canyon, New Mexico*, edited by Carrie C. Heitman and Stephen Plog, pp. 30–65. University of Arizona Press, Tucson.

Whittlesey, Stephanie M., and J. Jefferson Reid. 2001. Mortuary Ritual and Organizational Inferences at Grasshopper Pueblo, Arizona. In *Ancient Burial Practices in the American Southwest: Archaeology, Physical Anthropology, and Native American Perspectives*, edited by Douglas R. Mitchell and Judy L. Brunson-Hadley, pp. 68–96. University of New Mexico Press, Albuquerque.

Wills, W. H., and Thomas C. Windes. 1989. Evidence for Population Aggregation and Dispersal During the Basketmaker III Period in Chaco Canyon, New Mexico. *American Antiquity* 54:347–69.

Wills, W. H., F. Scott Worman, Wetherbee Dorshow, and Heather Richards-Rissetto. 2012. Shabik-eschee Village in Chaco Canyon: Beyond the Archetype. *American Antiquity* 77:326–50.

Wilshusen, Richard H., and Ruth M. Van Dyke. 2006. Chaco's Beginnings. In *The Archaeology of Chaco Canyon: An Eleventh-Century Pueblo Regional Center*, edited by Stephen H. Lekson, pp. 211–59. School of American Research Press, Santa Fe, N.Mex.

Windes, Thomas C. 1987. The Identification of Architectural Units (Suites). In *Investigations at the Pueblo Alto Complex, Chaco Canyon*, vol. 1, edited by Thomas C. Windes, pp. 337–82. Publications in Archeology 18F. USDI, National Park Service, Santa Fe, N.Mex.

Yoffee, Norman, Suzanne K. Fish, and George R. Milner. 1999. Comunidades, Ritualities, Chiefdoms: Social Evolution in the American Southwest and Southeast. In *Great Towns and Regional Polities in the Prehistoric American Southwest and Southeast*, edited by Jill E. Neitzel, pp. 261–71. Amerind Foundation and University of New Mexico Press, Albuquerque.

6

Steady Inequality in Changing Times

An Examination of Regional Patterns in Hohokam Structure Data

Matthew Pailes

The Hohokam of southern Arizona, USA, present a useful context in which to evaluate long-held anthropological inferences regarding subsistence economies and the emergence of social inequality. The Hohokam are best known from excavations in the Phoenix basin, including the Salt and Gila Rivers (figure 6.1). The residents of this core region relied heavily on irrigation production throughout a thousand-year sequence that saw mostly population increases before a precipitous decline. Surrounding regions that participated in the Hohokam tradition exhibited varying levels of commitment to irrigation, generally showed evidence of a more expansive and diversified subsistence production, and contained lower population densities.

This contrast suggests potentially differing obstacles to subsistence production management: the core would be more likely to be resource limited, whereas the surrounding basins would be more susceptible to potential labor shortages. This basic categorization, labor shortage versus resource limited, is fundamental to many theories of inequality, with the latter generally thought to allow for greater inequality (Fochesato and Bowles 2017). And, indeed, previous researchers have found the Hohokam an apt case study regarding fundamental dynamics of subsistence production, demographic distributions, and social organization, including Karl Wittfogel's (1957) association of irrigation and political centralization (Abbott 2000; Woodbury 1961), as well as Ester Boserup's (1965) view that population pressure drives intensification (McGuire 1984). This analysis builds on previous research by attempting to evaluate these patterns at a larger scale across the region as reflected in domestic architecture data.

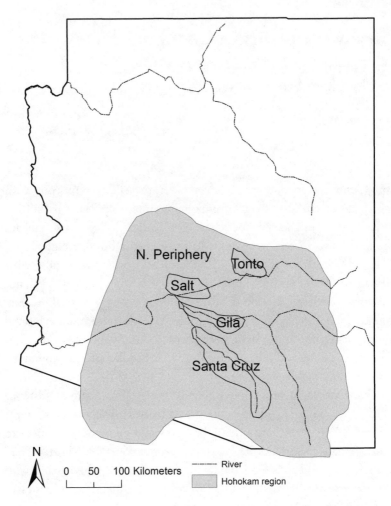

Figure 6.1 The Hohokam region, Arizona, with select basin-level divisions mentioned in text.

HIGH POINTS OF HOHOKAM CULTURAL HISTORY

The Hohokam sequence begins circa AD 400 and is typically defined by ceramic styles, village layouts, and the use of shell adornment (see chapters in S. K. Fish and Fish 2007). The Hohokam did not appear de novo but rather emerged from sedentary, village-based groups present since at least AD 150 (Wallace and Lindeman 2003) and a tradition of domesticated maize use dating over a millennium prior (Mabry 2005).

The emergence of the Hohokam from these earlier sedentary groups is gradual, and the beginning of the Hohokam is a point of continual discussion. Much clearer is the end of the sequence at approximately AD 1450, when there was a significant population decline and a major cultural reorganization (Hill et al. 2004). The sequence is thus approximately a thousand years in length. Prior to the 1450 reorganization, the Hohokam likely reached a maximum population of around forty thousand and occupied an area of approximately 95,000 square kilometers. The vast majority of this population was concentrated in river valleys. Because of this, density estimates for the entire region are of little value. The largest sites likely contained upward of several hundred individuals (Doelle 1995), although significant variance in population size estimates is common to the Hohokam region.

Throughout much of the Hohokam sequence, changes to social organization appear gradually. By the Colonial period (AD 750–950), a standardized village pattern emerged in which multiple structures shared a common courtyard (figure 6.2, left). Some scholars have identified larger groupings called village segments (Henderson 1987; Howard 2000; Huntington 1986). Researchers (S. K. Fish and Fish 2000a, 2000b) have inferred that settlements and multisettlement communities were important levels of affiliation for several aspects of the social contract such as land and water rights. Ritual ballcourt features anchored settlement communities (Doyel 1991a; P. R. Fish and Fish 2007) and served as economic and political focal points from the Colonial through the Sedentary period (AD 950–1150) (Abbott et al. 2007; Scarborough and Wilcox 1991). These venues would seem to be obvious examples of public goods as discussed in chapter 1 of this volume.

A major reorganization of Hohokam society occurred at the onset of the Classic period (Bayman 2001; Doyel 1980; S. K. Fish and Fish 2015), which lasted from approximately AD 1150 to 1450. Courtyard groups were often replaced by, or amalgamated into, compound groups (figure 6.2, right) (Doelle and Wallace 1991; S. K. Fish and Fish 2015). These were larger units than the forerunner courtyard groups. At larger scales of social inclusivity, ballcourts were replaced by a smaller number of platform mound sites (P. R. Fish and Fish 2007; S. K. Fish and Fish 2015). Patterned spacing between platform mound sites suggests that they played important political roles tied to irrigation and other forms of production

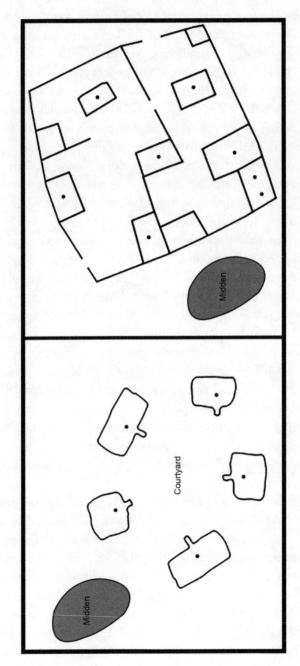

Figure 6.2 A hypothetical pre-Classic courtyard group (*left*) and a hypothetical Classic compound group (*right*).

as well as serving as a venue for ritual integration (Crown 1987). A few researchers (Howard 1987; Wilcox 1991b; Wilcox et al. 2008) have proposed larger levels of social inclusivity for the core Salt and Gila River basins that incorporated multiple platform mound communities along mainline canals and possibly even basin-wide groups. Recent reconstructions postulate that demographic pressure and environmental perturbations necessitated stricter managerial control of subsistence production, leading to the increased social complexity and attendant inequality in the Classic period (Abbott 2003; Bayman 2001; S. K. Fish and Fish 1994, 2015; Wilcox 1991a; Wilcox et al. 2008). Increased subsistence risk and pressure appear to characterize most of this period, though alternative interpretations exist (McClelland 2015). Minimally, increases in the scale and exclusivity of public architecture suggest greater differentiation in regard to the social prestige associated with ideo-political offices (Elson 1996). Simultaneously, there was a decrease in overall regional interaction and likely a balkanization of many relationship patterns (Abbott et al. 2006, 2007; Doyel 1991b).

Despite a clearly shared social identity, there is significant variation in settlement patterns and presumably organizational precepts across the region. The Phoenix basin, with its large flat expanses and perennial streams, relied heavily on irrigation. The corresponding Salt and Gila basins had the densest populations for most of the sequence (Doelle 1995; Hill et al. 2004, 2012). More-expansive settlement patterns with less reliance on irrigation agriculture characterized surrounding basins, most notably the Santa Cruz (e.g., S. K. Fish and Fish 1992). Alternative production techniques including the use of ephemeral drainages, rainfall farming in select topographical settings, and expansive xeric plant cultivation fulfilled a greater role in the subsistence economy of these areas (S. K. Fish and Fish 2004, 2006). These demographic and ecological parameters certainly gave rise to variation in the relative value of land, water, and labor across the region.

RESEARCH FOCUS

The questions this chapter seeks to address are straightforward: Is there spatially synchronic variation or spatially constant diachronic change in inequality, as reflected in domestic structure sizes, through the Hohokam sequence? To the extent that trends are discernable, what kinds of regional deviations are present and how well do they correspond to the inferred demographic and ecological conditions?

To answer these questions I am building a database of habitation-structure areas from published research and in one case my own fieldwork (Pailes 2011). At present, I have collected data on approximately 2,600 structures, but various considerations of chronology, structure completeness, and structure function reduce the present sample to about 1,580. It is my hope to soon make the database available online. The approach utilized here follows a line of research reviewed in chapter 1 arguing that domestic architecture is a good proxy for relative access to labor and thus social and human capital both in regard to the Hohokam (Craig 2001; McGuire 1983) and in society more broadly (Abrams 1989; Feinman and Neitzel 1984). However, a fairly nuanced discussion is warranted to consider exactly what is being measured in this application and what the results are capable of indicating.

To investigate inequality quantitatively, researchers must hold the analytic unit constant and sample the individual units completely in a given dimension (Deininger and Jin 2006). This should be a fairly straightforward set of conditions to meet in the Hohokam region, where decades of research have focused on identifying the nexuses of social rights and associated wealth generation. Following closely on ethnographic models provided by Robert McC. Netting and others (Netting 1982, 1993; Netting et al. 1984), there is wide acceptance that in small-scale horticulture societies the household is the principal locus of decision making regarding production, distribution, and transmission. The household is thus the ideal analytic unit for assessing inequality as experienced by the Hohokam. The current consensus suggests that a Hohokam household corresponds to the entire grouping of structures that surrounds a shared courtyard in the pre-Classic periods (e.g., Craig 2007; Henderson 2001; Howard 1985; Huntington 1986, 1988; Wilcox 1991a). In the Classic period this correspondence is less clear. Either multiroom units or entire compounds could feasibly be the most appropriate unit of household analysis (cf. Doelle and Wallace 1991; S. K. Fish and Fish 2000b; Wilcox 1991a). Alternatively, Craig and Henderson (Craig 2007; Craig and Henderson 2007) argue that courtyards, and presumably compounds, can be conceptualized as *Houses* in the Lévi-Straussian sense. This view allows for more autonomy of constituent family groups within the household. In the remainder of this discussion I associate *households* with the archaeological correlate of compounds/courtyards and *families* with the constituent individual structures.

Accepting the courtyard/compound group (household) as the appropriate unit of analysis is problematic given that the focal unit of archaeological investigation is the structure (family). That is, while most archaeologists believe that courtyard/compound groups are the level at which most of the action is focused, most of our data is complete only for smaller units of affiliation. Consider an analogy: what would we think of an inequality study that randomly measured the size of individual bedrooms in American houses but did not consider the overall structure area? We would potentially regard the data as telling of inequality between individual bedroom occupants and possibly agree that a large enough sample would be informative of town, state, and national patterns, since larger houses often have individually larger bedrooms. However, we should regard any claims made about between-household inequality as questionable, since we have no idea whether the larger structures had three or twenty rooms.

This is much the case with Hohokam data: we have a lot of data on many individual families and relatively little complete data on household-level holdings. This is not the only chapter with such methodological conundrums (see chapters 7 and 9, this volume). There are a few sites for which recording was sufficiently extensive to produce an accurate census of courtyard/compound architectural holdings (e.g., Craig 2001), but these are a decided minority, and discerning contemporaneity between structures of a household is often problematic.

Despite this apparent obstacle, I believe that the family-level data are still highly useful, given the stated research question and broad assumptions regarding internal household organization. Pursuant to the above discussion, the principal dimension of variation I am seeking to explore is the degree to which labor was valued by households, relative to the inferred scarcity of production potential. Among smallholder families that are resource limited, excess population is often forced out of the household through institutions such as primogeniture. This is most common in contexts where a point of diminishing returns is already reached in labor investment, that is, intensification is not an option. In contrast, in frontier, labor-poor contexts, extended family is often enticed to remain through more-equitable distribution and transmission rules. As this concept is applied to the Hohokam, we might expect that the heavily irrigation-reliant Phoenix core of the Salt and Gila Rivers would have been more resource stressed than other regions. Certainly, not all Hohokam archaeologists would accept that Phoenix basin groups were ever in a position of needing to shed excess labor. However, if we think of these scenarios as end points on a continuum, it is reasonable to infer that Phoenix basin groups were normally less worried about labor and more worried about resources than their hinterland counterparts. That is, a household head in the Phoenix basin may have felt substantially less impetus to marshal materials and labor to build a new or larger structure for a nephew who would only challenge their own child's heritable claim to the already conscribed household estate, relative to a Santa Cruz household head hoping to expand the amount of land under production. And indeed, several Hohokam researchers have proposed that individual family units acted as a class of free agents who switched household allegiance or became independent as economic opportunities varied (Ciolek-Torello et al. 2000:86; Doelle et al. 1987; Huntington 1986). It is also important to point out that craft specialization, one way to gainfully employ excess labor, appears to have been more robust as an economic strategy prior to the Classic period (Abbott 2000).

Before presenting the analysis, I should briefly mention how other lines of data might improve this analysis in the future. The distribution of storage space is a common archaeological index of inequality, and interior storage pits are common in the Hohokam region, but so are separate aboveground rooms. The realities of excavation strategies also result in ambiguous relationships between storage structures and the constituent courtyard/compound families. Again, it is rare to excavate all structures in a courtyard/compound. Thus, we cannot reliably re-create this variable at the family or household level. Floor assemblage data offer some potential. Compiling such data would be a much larger task, however, and the floor assemblages would suffer from the same partial analytic unit sampling as structure areas. Most structures also had their contents removed prior to their cessation of use (P. R. Fish and Fish 1991:154). Utilizing the diversity of midden contents would be insightful but often of ambiguous relationship to architectural data (Peterson et al. 2016; see also chapter 2, this volume).

Thus, burial data offer the best complementary source of information. There is appreciable variance in burial offerings in Hohokam populations (McGuire 1992), and detailed inequality analysis of such data has been undertaken for several Salt River sites, with Gini values in the range of 0.77 to 0.7 for pre-Classic La Ciudad (McGuire 1987) and Classic Pueblo Grande, respectively (Mitchell 1994). Recent summaries (Mitchell and Brunson-Hadley 2001) infer that the material accoutrements included with burials are mostly indicative of horizontal differentiation, with some evidence of vertical inequality rooted in the roles of some of the deceased as religious specialists (see also chapter 9, this volume). This is most clear in the Classic period and may indicate lineage-based inequality associated with privileged use of platform mound spaces. The practice of splitting Hohokam cremations between multiple deposits adds some noise to the data set (Cerezo-Román 2015), but this can be controlled. The data do face many of the same group-affiliation hurdles as the architectural data, however. Identification with particular families or households would not be possible for most individuals. The data set would thus speak to individuals and to patterns at the site level and above for which sample size and reliable group ascription would make the data fairly informative. More pressingly, the data seem to speak to a dimension of inequality, social prestige (see chapter 1, this volume), that is not well captured by wealth-based measures and thus would serve as an interesting comparison.

METHODS

The sample is composed of structure areas (i.e., areas putatively housing individual families) reported in numerous site reports. Specific guidelines/assumptions made for the principal analysis of structures are as follows. Any structure smaller than five square meters is assumed to be nonhabitation and was thus excluded from analysis, unless specified as a habitation by the original investigators. Whenever the original investigators interpreted a structure as "nonhabitation," for whatever reason, it was excluded.* The lack of a hearth alone did not lead to exclusion, unless this

---

*This was done reliably when such information was included in tabulated form. Comments made in feature description sections are much less likely to be incorporated.

was the practice of the original investigator.* For structures that spanned only one period boundary, mostly because of mixed assemblages (e.g., Colonial-Sedentary), the structure was counted in the later time period. I also excluded structures whose potential occupation window spanned more than one period boundary and structures with partial floor areas. Corrective estimates to account for rounded corners were applied to data sets for which multiplying length and width was the obvious method of determining area. Given that typical periods in the Hohokam region are often around two hundred years long, it should be assumed that many noncontemporary structures are included in individual temporal subsets. This is unfortunate but essentially unavoidable, given the resolution of architectural dating in the region. I would argue, however, that this should be relatively nonbiasing unless there were substantial shifts in the nature of inequality within a period—as may be the case for the Classic period.

Variable interpretations can be made in regard to what should be included as a domestic space. For example, data for Compound A of the Classic period site of Casa Grande are included in the data set. This set of architecture includes the Great House at Casa Grande, which is arguably the most unequivocal elite residence known in the Hohokam area. This structure is four stories tall, consisting of a filled platform, followed by two floors of five large rooms each, and a final floor of a single room. Oral tradition of the O'odham holds that this was a chief's residence (Bahr 1994). Archaeological interpretations vary between domestic and predominantly ritual functions (Wilcox and Shenk 1977). How should the rooms of this structure be counted: individually like other compound architecture, by floor, or as a complete amalgamation? The top room seems safe to exclude on the grounds of being a special-purpose astronomical observatory room, but what of the others? For the principal analysis I included only the ground-floor rooms of the structure and treat them individually. This is a middle-of-the-road approach that seems most consistent with other assumptions. The potential ramifications of alternative approaches are discussed below.

---

*This is a common interpretive shorthand used by Hohokam archaeologists. However, to the immediate south of the region (in Sonora), hearths are commonly absent from habitation structures. In short, it seems to be a poor criterion.

As a heuristic exercise, amalgamated household- (as opposed to family-) level data are calculated for two sites spanning the temporal range of the Hohokam: Grewe, along the Gila River, which is a pre-Classic site, and Cerro Prieto, along the Santa Cruz River, which is a Classic site. This was done to provide a gauge of comparability to other chapters in this volume for which aggregated household data is the principal topic. Data from Grewe (taken from Craig 2001) were structured to take a Gini of amalgamated courtyard holdings at the point of peak population in various phases of the pre-Classic. The Cerro Prieto sample corresponds to mostly contemporaneous structures of the early Classic.

Gini coefficients were computed as described in chapters 1 and 2 of this volume. Confidence intervals were calculated at the 80 percent level using the bootstrap method with the BCA function of R software. Distributions were sampled one thousand times for period/subregion samples and five thousand times for period/Hohokam region samples. Theil indices (computed as described in Conceição and Ferreira 2000) were normalized by dividing by the natural logarithm of the sample size n. (This is a necessary step when comparing across different sample sizes.) The normed Theil, like the Gini, ranges from a value of 0, indicating pure equality, to 1, indicating pure inequality. The Theil and the Gini do not behave in the same manner, with the Theil being more sensitive to wealth transfers between the poorest half and richest half and approaching 0 faster relative to the Gini throughout most of the upper range of inequality. The Theil's principal advantage is that it is decomposable, such that inequality between and within nonoverlapping subgroups can be calculated separately and summed to produce the overall Theil score. For this to be done appropriately, total wealth and population must be known or estimated for subgroups.

Theil scores, like the Gini, can be calculated easily for subsets of the data, such as Salt-Gila basin Classic period. These indices are valuable but offer little information not already given by the Gini. For the Theil's potential to be maximized, the Theil would need to include the whole sample and decompose inequality between structures at the social grouping levels of families, households, settlements, communities, and basins. All of these levels are thought to be relevant to wealth distribution. As discussed above, this is presently not feasible at the household, site, and community levels for all but a few cases. Because estimates are needed for all such units included in a sample, these levels cannot be considered presently. Basin-level populations estimates are estimated by the Coalescent Communities Database (Doelle 1995; Hill et al. 2012). The research questions chosen for this chapter were selected precisely because they can be meaningfully approached within the bounds of these sample limitations. Many other pressing inequality issues must await further database elaboration, a foreseeable goal given the increased interest in big data projects.

For the present Theil measure to have any validity, the wealth structure must be sampled in proportion to population structure. The *n* of recorded structures included in the present database is not proportional to actual population distributions. This application offers a first approximation by sampling from the existing database, with replacement, in a manner proportional to these areas' estimated population.* No doubt, the numbers presented as a result of this heuristic method will change as the sample size increases. Despite the obstacles posed by sampling, I would argue that this is still a valuable exercise in that it (1) forces a much more overt consideration of the relationship between population and wealth structure and (2) offers a view of the structure of inequality not achievable with the Gini. As to the later point, it is appropriate to interpret the raw Theil score components as indicative of the proportion of inequality expressed at the various levels of analysis.

RESULTS AND INTERPRETATIONS

Table 6.1 reiterates what this approach is most capable of measuring and what it does not address. This table presents the amalgamated household holdings at the sites of Grewe and Cerro Prieto.† Note that the number

---

*The total sample size was set to 1,000; thus, a basin with a population share of 50 percent of the total would be sampled (with replacement) 500 times.

†Note that because of different inclusion/exclusion criteria and other methodological tweaks, these figures will not exactly match those previously reported for these sites. The "compound" measurements for Cerro Prieto are somewhat problematic because a few compounds invested heavily in terraces, so for some units the area measures on which the Ginis are based include just the space occupied for domestic structures plus interstitial clearings, whereas for others it also includes some of their productive capacity (agricultural terraces).

Table 6.1 A heuristic sample of amalgamated "household" holdings in the Hohokam region

Site	Period	Total courtyard/ compound area Gini	Internal structure area Gini[b]	Households (*N*)
Grewe	Pioneer	0.36	0.15	9
Grewe	Colonial	0.24	0.28	6
Grewe	Sedentary	0.12	0.17	4
Cerro Prieto	Classic	0.66[a]	0.42	59

[a]Derived by measuring from the boundaries of feature edges within a house group (compound). Most of these compounds are not walled-off areas; therefore, their boundaries were derived from linking the corners of features to measure the area.
[b]Based on the sum of all interior areas of the structures in a household/compound.

of households is fairly small for the pre-Classic Grewe site, and thus not too much should be made of temporal trends or the lack thereof. The Cerro Prieto results seem to suggest significant inequality; the Ginis are similar in magnitude to those calculated for Chaco to the northeast (discussed in chapter 5, this volume). In the case of "total area of compound," alternative land use requirements tied to alternative production strategies are inflating the index for Cerro Prieto. A thorough examination of the "internal area of structures" data suggests that this category is likely measuring the relative position of households along different stages of the domestic cycle. In many smallholding societies, this is the principal structuring factor of inequality (see chapters in Wilk et al. 1984), and thus seeing it reflected in Hohokam data is hardly surprising. Households that are newly founded, and thus represented by a single structure, appear drastically poorer relative to established households with many members and structures. But does this really reflect how inequality was experienced? As I have argued elsewhere (Pailes 2014), this view of inequality is valuable if we conceptualize the predominant form of inequality as wealth in people (e.g., Nyerges 1992; see also McIntosh 1999) or embodied wealth as discussed in chapter 1. A larger household is likely to enjoy real advantages. Because of the cumulative, intergenerational accumulation of this form of capital, these values are in some ways analogous to modern measures of wealth (an intergenerationally or at least life-span cumulative variable) (e.g., Davies et al. 2008). This investigation,

however, is geared toward examining momentary family wealth inequality—a variable that shares features with, but is certainly not equivalent to,
a modern conception of inequality (which is most commonly calculated
on income, not wealth). That is, the fact that amalgamated household
holdings inequality is significantly higher than those reported below for
individual structure sizes (family wealth) is not surprising or problematic.
Fundamentally different kinds of inequality are being measured in these
approaches. Both are important, but only differential family wealth is the
primary subject of this chapter.

Figure 6.3 presents the Gini values for period and basin subsets of
the data. Table 6.2 presents basic summary statistics. The most telling
aspect of this family-level data analysis is that there was never egregious
inequality in any subset of the Hohokam region or the region as a whole.
Note that far from a steady increase in inequality, there is more of a cyclical trend in the trajectory of several individual basins. The initial high
values of the Pioneer period may be an artifact of smaller sample sizes

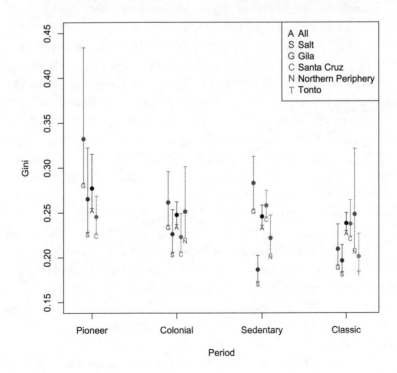

Figure 6.3 Gini coefficients with 80 percent confidence intervals.

Table 6.2 Summary statistics on structure areas (m²) for subsets of the data

Basin	Age	Mean	SD	Structures (N)
Gila	Pioneer	18.28	14.78	49
Gila	Colonial	14.94	7.86	80
Gila	Sedentary	21.44	11.51	73
Gila	Classic	20.95	8.08	81
N. periphery	Pioneer	16.05	NA	1
N. periphery	Colonial	16.91	7.59	25
N. periphery	Sedentary	17.78	7.05	72
N. periphery	Classic	25.34	10.88	15
Salt	Pioneer	15.67	7.48	27
Salt	Colonial	13.13	5.67	99
Salt	Sedentary	14.99	5.21	148
Salt	Classic	16.84	6.3	176
Santa Cruz	Pioneer	13.38	6.16	123
Santa Cruz	Colonial	17.62	7.19	112
Santa Cruz	Sedentary	15.52	7.08	155
Santa Cruz	Classic	16.09	7.97	290
Tonto	Classic	25.95	9.22	60

and the fact that I included "lineage houses" (Wallace and Lindeman 2003) in the sample that may not actually reflect individual family wealth. The significant overlap of most confidence intervals also should not be taken lightly. However, the uniformity of the higher Pioneer period values likely indicates a real trend. A small sample n also most often biases a sample toward equality (Deltas 2003). Conversely, the failure to note significant inequality in the Classic period may partially reflect a lack of sufficiently elite residences or incorrect assumptions about how to amalgamate their areas. Table 6.3 presents alternative assumptions with regard to the treatment of the elite residence of Casa Grande and the results of these alternative assumptions on the Gini of the Classic period, Gila River sample. These differences are nontrivial and should be kept in mind when interpreting further results. Additionally, structure size alone may not capture differential labor investment in variable forms. For example, the mound cost is not considered for structures built on top of platform mounds. I believe that this is appropriate, given that mounds were often constructed generations before domestic architecture was added (Elson and Abbott 2000). Caveats aside, the results clearly run counter to many

Table 6.3 Impacts of alternative assumptions concerning what constitutes an elite residence at Casa Grande in the Gila River Classic sample (*N* = 76 without Casa Grande)

Number of floors included	Rooms amalgamated	Gini
1	Yes	0.26
2	Yes	0.31
1	No	0.21
2	No	0.21

Note: When considered at the Hohokam world scale, the differences become trivial.

common perceptions of the temporal trajectory of inequality in the Hohokam region.

Also of particular note are patterns during the presumed peak of social complexity, in the Classic period (figure 6.3). At this time, the core region presents lower Gini indices than most hinterland basins. The Gila River area appears appreciably more unequal than the Salt until the Classic, suggesting organizational diversity even within this core region. This issue was more fully explored by looking at the decomposition of the Theil (table 6.4) for the entire Hohokam region, appropriately weighted by population estimates as described above. This exercise was undertaken only to examine the Sedentary to Classic transition.* The Theil indices remain essentially unchanged between the Sedentary and Classic, which is still noteworthy given previous suspicions that it would rise. There is, however, a significant change between periods in the relative proportions of between-basin versus within-basin contributions to the overall inequality. A much greater proportion of the total inequality is expressed between basins in the Classic period. Larger average structure areas in the northern periphery and Tonto basin mostly drive this shift. The sample size of the former is worrisomely small, but the Tonto basin is reasonably well represented. The Salt-Gila and Santa Cruz both became relatively less wealthy

---

*As described in the methods section, this is already a tenuous estimate given the small sample sizes of some of the concerned regions. Extending the method back in time to include other, even less well-represented populations seems inappropriate.

Table 6.4 Population-weighted Theil for Hohokam region

Variable and decomposition	Sedentary	Classic
Pop. weighted Theil-normed	0.013	0.012
Within basin %	96	84
Between basin %	4	16

Note: The Salt and Gila basins were amalgamated to one unit for this analysis; otherwise, data subsets follow those in table 6.2.

in this dimension across the Sedentary to Classic transition compared to these more peripheral regions. I believe that these patterns reflect a divergence in social organizational patterns between these regions and the overall balkanization of the region by basins at this time. I suggest that the core region, despite occasionally ostentatious structures like Casa Grande, more effectively enforced leveling mechanisms in the size of domestic architecture. More-peripheral regions allowed for greater variation.

CONCLUSIONS

What are we to make of this compilation of somewhat conflicting data? Several plausible inferences can be made, all of them admittedly post hoc interpretations. This closing section will first draw regionally specific conclusions before turning to the broad theoretical themes of this volume.

This study demonstrated mostly negligible change through time in the degree of inequality experienced by Hohokam families. The Pioneer period at the beginning of the sequence, with its surprisingly higher values, is the one possible exception. There is scant support for my initial proposition that the densely populated Phoenix basin core was able to treat excess population in a more cavalier manner that would lead to greater inequality over time. Instead, inequality appears to have decreased or stayed virtually the same even as populations rose. And throughout time there is, on average, a slight trend toward greater inequality in the less-populated regions of the Hohokam world, as evidenced by the Salt River's consistently low Ginis relative to other basins. Patterns of average house size and its variance through time and across regions are harder to discern but seem to tell a similar story. There is a perceptible relative downturn for the core region and the Santa Cruz in the

Classic compared to the small Tonto and northern periphery samples. These patterns may indicate the presence of more-frontier-like contexts in which less-zero-sum resource allocation systems allowed for greater variance in household and, by extension, familial success. That is, rather than trending toward an equal sharing of resources to retain household labor, there appear to have been more clear winners and losers in these zones. Ethnographically, families often prefer to trade material success for autonomy. If options were greater in less-resource-constricted zones, this could account for the patterns perceived here. That is, a family could go it alone in less-populated areas and survive at the margins, or it could join a larger social grouping, surrender some autonomy, and gain materially. Core regions may have been more constrained, particularly during the environmentally difficult Classic period. Far from my initial starting assumptions, the irrigation networks of the core may have been so labor intensive that equitable distribution of resources and labor investment was always required to prevent the hemorrhaging of population to exterior regions. Prior to the Classic, more salubrious conditions could have contributed to the fairly erratic pre-Classic Gini values.

These interpretations reinforce ideas presented in chapter 1 and attributed to Gerhard Lenski (1966) that the overall potential for surplus production will determine the extent to which inequality can develop. In this view, it is not surprising that the Pioneer period, with its low population, exhibits the greatest inequality whereas the Classic period in the core zone, with potentially marginal conditions, exhibits some of the least. The changing structure of inequality demonstrated by the Theil decomposition with increasing differentiation between basins across the Sedentary/Classic boundary may presage the onset of the post-Classic reorganization. At a minimum, the data suggest that a level of regional variance developed in the Classic period that was appreciably different from that in the pre-Classic. Perhaps these differing organizational patterns helped spur an exodus from the core area that eventually entailed the region-wide reorganization.

In closing, it is worth considering the Hohokam in global contexts. The ecological and demographic qualities of the Hohokam suggest that they should fit comfortably in classic models of social evolution (see chapter 8, this volume) that associate the emergence of significant social complexity with rising inequality. However, while we have reliable indications of increasing social complexity in the Hohokam region, there is only scant evidence of any wealth inequality. The Hohokam sequence thus reinforces the observation that there is no universal rule that increasing political hierarchy will necessarily entail significant increases in economic inequality. This was reflected by both the low overall Gini values of the Hohokam and the between-basin comparisons in which the most irrigation-dependent populations had the lowest Ginis in the Classic period. Similarly, the Hohokam, paragons of intensive-irrigation agriculture, demonstrate that there is no simple causal link between managerially complex production systems and the emergence of substantial wealth inequality. Exploring the peculiarities of the Hohokam case in comparison to these broadly inferred relationships of productive system and inequality (see Bowles et al. 2010) will undoubtedly continue to be a point of active research.

ACKNOWLEDGMENTS

It was a great pleasure to participate in the symposium that facilitated this manuscript. I sincerely thank the organizers, Timothy Kohler and Michael Smith, my fellow session participants, and the Amerind Foundation for supporting our interest. Thank you also to Matt Peeples, who provided access to the population estimates used in this research, which were originally compiled by Archaeology Southwest and the Museum of Northern Arizona as part of the Coalescent Communities Database 2.0. I owe the largest debt to the hundreds of archaeologists who actually did the work and produced the data used in these analyses. All mistakes are, of course, my own.

REFERENCES CITED

Abbott, David R. 2000. *Ceramics and Community Organization Among the Hohokam.* University of Arizona Press, Tucson.

———. 2003. Ceramics, Communities, and Irrigation Management. In *Centuries of Decline During the Hohokam Classic Period at Pueblo Grande*, edited by David R. Abbott, pp. 148–65. University of Arizona Press, Tucson.

Abbott, David R., Scott E. Ingram, and Brent G. Kober. 2006. Hohokam Exchange and Early Classic Period Organization in Central Arizona: Focal Villages or Linear Communities? *Journal of Field Archaeology* 31:285–305.

Abbott, David R., Alexa M. Smith, and Emiliano Gallaga. 2007. Ballcourts and Ceramics: The Case for Hohokam Marketplaces in the Arizona Desert. *American Antiquity* 72(3):461–84.

Abrams, Elliot M. 1989. Architecture and Energy: An Evolutionary Perspective. In *Archaeological Method and Theory*, vol. 1, edited by Michael B. Schiffer, pp. 47–87. University of Arizona Press, Tucson.

Bahr, Donald. 1994. *The Short, Swift, Time of the Gods on Earth*. University of California Press, Berkeley.

Bayman, James M. 2001. The Hohokam of Southwest North America. *Journal of World Prehistory* 15(3):257–311.

Boserup, Ester. 1965. *The Conditions of Agricultural Growth: The Economics of Agrarian Change Under Population Pressure*. George Allen and Unwin, New York.

Bowles, Samuel, Eric Alden Smith, and Monique Borgerhoff-Mulder. 2010. The Emergence and Persistence of Inequality in Premodern Societies. *Current Anthropology* 51:7–17.

Cerezo-Román, Jessica I. 2015. Unpacking Personhood and Funerary Customs in the Hohokam Area of Southern Arizona. *American Antiquity* 80:353–75.

Ciolek-Torello, Richard, Eric E. Klucas, and Stephanie M. Whittlesey. 2000. Hohokam Households, Settlement Structure, and Economy in the Lower Verde Valley. In *The Hohokam Village Revisited*, edited by Suzanne K. Fish, Paul R. Fish, and David E. Doyel, pp. 65–100. Southwestern and Rocky Mountain Division of the American Association for the Advancement of Science, Glenwood Springs, Colo.

Conceição, Pedro, and Pedro Ferreira. 2000. *The Young Person's Guide to the Theil Index: Suggesting Intuitive Interpretations and Exploring Analytical Applications*. University of Texas Inequality Project, Working Paper 14. University of Texas, Austin.

Craig, Douglas B. 2001. Domestic Architecture and Household Wealth at Grewe. In *Grewe Archaeological Research Project*, vol. 3, *Synthesis*, edited by Douglas B. Craig, pp. 115–30. Anthropological Papers 99-1. Northland Research, Tempe, Ariz.

————. 2007. Courtyard Groups and House Estates in Early Hohokam Society. In *The Durable House: House Society Models in Archaeology*, edited by Robin A. Beck, pp. 463–46. Occasional Paper 35. Center for Archaeological Investigations, Carbondale, Ill.

Craig, Douglas B., and Kathleen T. Henderson. 2007. Houses, Households, and Household Organization. In *The Hohokam Millennium*, edited by Suzanne K. Fish and Paul R. Fish, pp. 31–37. School for Advanced Research Press, Santa Fe, N.Mex.

Crown, Patricia L. 1987. Classic Period Hohokam Settlement and Land Use in the Casa Grande Ruins Area, Arizona. *Journal of Field Archaeology* 14(2): 147–62.

Davies, James B., Susanna Sanström, Anthony Shorrocks, and Edward Wolff. 2008. The World Distribution of Household Wealth. UNU-Wider Discussion Paper 2008/03.

Deininger, Klaus, and Songqing Jin. 2006. Tenure Security and Land-Related Investment: Evidence from Ethiopia. *European Economic Review* 50:1245–77.

Deltas, George. 2003. The Small-Sample Bias of the Gini Coefficient: Results and Implications for Empirical Research. *Review of Economics and Statistics* 85:226–34.

Doelle, William H. 1995. Appendix D: A Method for Estimating Regional Population. In *The Roosevelt Community Development Study: New Perspectives on Tonto Basin Prehistory*, edited by Mark D. Elson, Miriam T. Stark, and David A. Gregory, pp. 513–36. Anthropological Papers 15. Center for Desert Archaeology, Tucson, Ariz.

Doelle, William H., Frederick W. Huntington, and Henry D. Wallace. 1987. Rincon Phase Community in the Tucson Basin. In *The Hohokam Village: Site Structure and Organization*, edited by David E. Doyel, pp. 71–95. Southwestern and Rocky Mountain Division of the American Association for the Advancement of Science, Glenwood Springs, Colo.

Doelle, William H., and Henry D. Wallace. 1991. The Changing Role of the Tucson Basin in the Hohokam Regional System. In *Exploring the Hohokam: Prehistoric Desert Peoples of the American Southwest*, edited by George J. Gumerman, pp. 279–345. University of New Mexico Press, Albuquerque.

Doyel, David E. 1980. Hohokam Social Organization and the Sedentary to Classic Transition. In *Current Issues in Hohokam Prehistory*, edited by David E. Doyel and Fred T. Plog, pp. 23–40. Arizona State University Anthropological Research Papers 23. Arizona State University, Tempe.

———. 1991a. Hohokam Cultural Evolution in the Phoenix Basin. In *Exploring the Hohokam: Prehistoric Desert Peoples of the American Southwest*, edited by George J. Gumerman, pp. 231–79. University of New Mexico Press, Albuquerque.

———. 1991b. Hohokam Exchange and Interaction. In *Chaco and Hohokam: Prehistoric Regional Systems in the American Southwest*, edited by Patricia L. Crown and W. James Judge, pp. 225–52. School of American Research Press, Santa Fe, N.Mex.

Elson, Mark D. 1996. An Ethnographic Perspective on Prehistoric Platform Mounds of the Tonto Basin, Central Arizona. PhD dissertation, University of Arizona, Tucson.

Elson, Mark D., and David R. Abbott. 2000. Organizational Variability in Platform Mound–Building Groups of the American Southwest. In *Alternative Leadership Strategies in the Prehispanic Southwest*, edited by Barbara J. Mills, pp. 117–35. University of Arizona Press, Tucson.

Feinman, Gary M., and Jill E. Neitzel. 1984. Too Many Types: An Overview of Prestate Societies in the Americas. In *Advances in Archaeological Method and Theory*, vol. 7, edited by Michael B. Schiffer, pp. 39–102. Academic Press, Orlando, Fla.

Fish, Paul R., and Suzanne K. Fish. 1991. Hohokam Political and Social Organization. In *Exploring the Hohokam: Prehistoric Desert Peoples of the American Southwest*, edited by George J. Gumerman, pp. 151–75. University of New Mexico Press, Albuquerque.

———. 2007. Community, Territory, and Polity. In *The Hohokam Millennium*, edited by Suzanne K. Fish and Paul R. Fish, pp. 39–47. School for Advanced Research Press, Santa Fe, N.Mex.

Fish, Suzanne K., and Paul R. Fish. 1992. The Marana Community in Comparative Contexts. In *The Marana Community in the Hohokam World*, edited by Suzanne K. Fish, Paul R. Fish, and John H. Madsen. Anthropological Papers of the University of Arizona 56. University of Arizona Press, Tucson.

———. 1994. Prehistoric Desert Farmers of the Southwest. *Annual Review of Anthropology* 23:83–108.

———. 2000a. Civic-Territorial Organization and the Roots of Hohokam Complexity. In *The Hohokam Village Revisited*, edited by David E. Doyel, Suzanne K. Fish, and Paul R. Fish, pp. 373–90. Southwestern and Rocky Mountain Division of the American Association for the Advancement of Science, Fort Collins, Colo.

———. 2000b. The Institutional Contexts of Hohokam Complexity. In *Alternative Leadership Strategies in the Prehispanic Southwest*, edited by Barbara J. Mills, pp. 154–67. University of Arizona Press, Tucson.

———. 2004. Unsuspected Magnitudes: Expanding the Scale of Hohokam Agriculture. In *The Archaeology of Global Change: The Impact of Humans on Their Environment*, edited by Charles L. Redman, Steven R. James, Paul R. Fish, and J. Daniel Rogers, pp. 208–23. Smithsonian Books, Washington, D.C.

———. 2006. Cross-Cultural Perspectives on Prehispanic Hohokam Agricultural Potential. In *Environmental Change and Human Adaptation in the Ancient American Southwest*, edited by David E. Doyel and Jeffrey S. Dean, pp. 46–68. University of Utah Press, Salt Lake City.

——— (editors). 2007. *The Hohokam Millennium*. School for Advanced Research, Santa Fe, N.Mex.

Fochesato, Mattia, and Samuel Bowles. 2017. Technology, Institutions, and Wealth Inequality over Eleven Millennia. SFI Working Paper 2017-08-032, pp. 1–21.

Henderson, Kathleen T. 1987. The Growth of a Hohokam Village. In *The Hohokam Village: Site Structure and Organization*, edited by David E. Doyel, pp. 97–125. Southwestern and Rocky Mountain Division of the American Association for the Advancement of Science, Glenwood Springs, Colo.

———. 2001. House Clusters, Courtyard Groups, and Site Structure. In *The Grewe Archaeological Research Project*, edited by Douglas B. Craig, pp. 51–92. Anthropological Papers 99-1. Northland Research, Tempe, Ariz.

Hill, Brett J., Jeffery J. Clark, William H. Doelle, and Patrick D. Lyons. 2004. Prehistoric Demography in the Southwest: Migration, Coalescence, and Hohokam Population Decline. *American Antiquity* 69:689–716.

Hill, Brett J., David R. Wilcox, William H. Doelle, and William J. Robinson. 2012. *Coalescent Communities GIS Database Version 2.0.* Archaeology Southwest, Tucson, Ariz.; Museum of Northern Arizona, Flagstaff.

Howard, Jerry B. 1985. Courtyard Groups and Domestic Cycling: A Hypothetical Model of Growth. In *Proceedings of the 1983 Hohokam Symposium: Part 1,* edited by J. Alfred E. Dittert and Donald E. Dove, pp. 311–26. Arizona Archaeological Society, Phoenix.

———. 1987. The Lehi Canal System: Organization of a Classic Period Irrigation Community. In *The Hohokam Village: Site Structure and Organization,* edited by David E. Doyel, pp. 211–21. Southwestern and Rocky Mountain Division of the American Association for the Advancement of Science, Glenwood Springs, Colo.

———. 2000. Quantitative Approaches to Spatial Patterning in the Hohokam Village: Testing the Village Segment Model. In *The Hohokam Village Revisited,* edited by David E. Doyel, Suzanne K. Fish, and Paul R. Fish, pp. 167–96. American Association for the Advancement of Science, Southwestern and Rocky Mountain Division, Fort Collins, Colo.

Huntington, Frederick W. 1986. West Branch Site: Summary of Household Data. In *Archaeological Investigations at the West Branch Site Early and Middle Rincon Occupation in the Southern Tucson Basin,* edited by Frederick W. Huntington, pp. 349–80. Anthropological Papers 5. Institute for American Research, Tucson, Ariz.

———. 1988. Rincon Phase Community Organization. In *Recent Research on Tucson Basin Prehistory: Proceedings of the Second Tucson Basin Conference,* edited by William H. Doelle and Paul R. Fish, pp. 209–24. Anthropological Papers 10. Institute for American Research, Tucson, Ariz.

Lenski, Gerhard E. 1966. *Power and Privilege: A Theory of Social Stratification.* McGraw-Hill, New York.

Mabry, Jonathan B. 2005. Changing Knowledge and Ideas About the First Farmers in Southeastern Arizona. In *The Late Archaic Across the Borderlands: From Foraging to Farming,* edited by Bradley J. Vierra, pp. 41–83. University of Texas Press, Austin.

McClelland, John A. 2015. Revisiting Hohokam Paleodemography. *American Antiquity* 80:492–510.

McGuire, Randall H. 1983. Breaking Down Cultural Complexity: Inequality and Heterogeneity. In *Advances in Archaeological Method and Theory,* vol. 6, edited by Michael B. Schiffer, pp. 91–142. Academic Press, New York.

———. 1984. The Boserup Model and Agricultural Intensification in the United States Southwest. In *Prehistoric Agricultural Strategies in the Southwest,* edited by Suzanne K. Fish and Paul R. Fish, pp. 327–34. Anthropological Research Papers 33. Arizona State University, Tempe.

———. 1987. Analysis of Grave Lots. In *Death, Society and Ideology in a Hohokam Community: Colonial and Sedentary Period Burials from La Ciudad*, edited by Randall H. McGuire, pp. 63–106. Office of Cultural Resource Management, Department of Anthropology, Arizona State University, Tempe.

———. 1992. *Death, Society, and Ideology in a Hohokam Community*. Westview Press, Boulder, Colo.

McIntosh, Susan Keech. 1999. Pathways to Complexity: An African Perspective. In *Beyond Chiefdoms: Pathways to Complexity in Africa*, edited by Susan Keech McIntosh, pp. 1–30. Cambridge University Press, Cambridge.

Mitchell, Douglas R. 1994. The Pueblo Grande Burial Artifact Analysis: A Search for Wealth, Ranking and Prestige. In *The Pueblo Grande Project*, vol. 7, *An Analysis of Classic Period Mortuary Patterns*, edited by Douglas R. Mitchell, pp. 129–80. Soil Systems, Phoenix.

Mitchell, Douglas R., and Judy L. Brunson-Hadley. 2001. An Evaluation of Classic Period Hohokam Burials and Society: Chiefs, Priests, or Acephalous Complexity? In *Ancient Burial Practices in the American Southwest: Archaeology, Physical Anthropology, and Native American Perspectives*, edited by Douglas R. Mitchell and Judy L. Brunson-Hadley, pp. 45–67. University of New Mexico Press, Albuquerque.

Netting, Robert McC. 1982. Some Home Truths on Household Size and Wealth. *American Behavioral Scientist* 25:641–61.

———. 1993. *Smallholders, Householders: Farm Families and the Ecology of Intensive, Sustainable Agriculture*. Stanford University Press, Stanford, Calif.

Netting, Robert McC., Richard R. Wilk, and Eric J. Arnould. 1984. *Households: Comparative and Historical Studies of the Domestic Group*. University of California Press, Berkeley.

Nyerges, Endre A. 1992. The Ecology of Wealth-in-People: Agriculture, Settlement, and Society on the Perpetual Frontier. *American Anthropologist* 94(4): 860–81.

Pailes, M. C. 2011. Social Organization and Differentiation at a Hohokam Cerros de Trincheras. *Journal of Arizona Archaeology* 1(2):197–209.

———. 2014. Network Analysis of Early Classic Hohokam Corporate-Group Inequality. *American Antiquity* 79:465–86.

Peterson, Christian E., Robert D. Drennan, and Kate L. Bartel. 2016. Comparative Analysis of Neolithic Household Artifact Assemblage Data from Northern China. *Journal of Anthropological Research* (Summer):200–225.

Scarborough, Vernon, and David R. Wilcox (editors). 1991. *The Mesoamerican Ballgame in the American Southwest*. University of Arizona Press, Tucson.

Wallace, Henry D., and Michael W. Lindeman. 2003. Valencia Vieja and the Origins of Hohokam Culture. In *Roots of Sedentism: Archaeological Excavations at Valencia Vieja: A Founding Village in the Tucson Basin of Southern Arizona*, edited by Henry D. Wallace, pp. 371–405. Anthropological Papers 29. Center for Desert Archaeology, Tucson, Ariz.

Wilcox, David R. 1991a. Hohokam Social Complexity. In *Chaco and Hohokam: Prehistoric Regional Systems in the American Southwest*, edited by Patricia L. Crown and W. James Judge, pp. 253–75. School of American Research Press, Santa Fe, N.Mex.

———. 1991b. The Mesoamerican Ballgame in the American Southwest. In *The Mesoamerican Ballgame*, edited by Vernon Scarborough and David R. Wilcox, pp. 101–28. University of Arizona Press, Tucson.

Wilcox, David R., and Lynette O. Shenk. 1977. *The Architecture of Casa Grande and Its Interpretation*. Arizona State Museum Archaeological Series. University of Arizona, Tucson.

Wilcox, David R., Phil C. Wiegand, J. Scott Wood, and Jerry B. Howard. 2008. Ancient Cultural Interplay of the American Southwest in the Mexican Northwest. *Journal of the Southwest* 50:105–210.

Wilk, Richard R., Robert McC. Netting, and Eric J. Arnould (editors). 1984. *Households: Comparative and Historical Studies of the Domestic Group*. University of California Press, Berkeley.

Wittfogel, Karl. 1957. *Oriental Despotism: A Comparative Study of Total Power*. Yale University Press, New Haven, Conn.

Woodbury, Richard B. 1961. A Reappraisal of Hohokam Irrigation. *American Anthropologist* 63(3):550–60.

7

Exploring Measures of Inequality in the Mississippian Heartland

Alleen Betzenhauser

The Mississippian period in the American Bottom region of Illinois, the wide expanse of floodplain along the Mississippi River, dates from approximately AD 1050 to 1400 (Fortier et al. 2006). During this period, tens of thousands of people lived in small to massive settlements in the floodplain and neighboring uplands to the east and west (Milner 2006; Pauketat 2003, 2004; Pauketat and Lopinot 1997). The largest of these precincts is Cahokia, a civic-ceremonial complex measuring 1.8 square kilometers with more than one hundred earthen pyramids (Fowler 1997).

Greater Cahokia, which comprised three connected precincts—the Cahokia, East St. Louis, and St. Louis precincts, covering more than 14 square kilometers—was big from the beginning and may be considered America's first city (Emerson 2017a, 2017b). Mound and plaza construction began rapidly with a planned layout on a monumental scale during the Lohmann phase (AD 1050–1100) (Baires 2017; Betzenhauser and Pauketat 2018; Dalan et al. 2003; Pauketat 2004). The subsequent Stirling phase (AD 1100–1200) is considered the peak of Cahokian influence, with evidence for integration within the region and far-flung contacts with other Mississippian and Woodland peoples throughout the midcontinent and Southeast (Kelly 1991; Pauketat 2004). The following Moorehead (AD 1200–1300) and Sand Prairie (AD 1300–1400) phases are characterized by a decrease in mound construction and a significant depopulation of Cahokia and much of the American Bottom region (Baltus 2014; Emerson and Hedman 2016; Milner 2006; Pauketat and Lopinot 1997).

Widely different interpretations have been posited concerning the sociopolitical organization of Mississippians in the American Bottom, how interconnected or independent different settlements within the region were, and the degree of inequality among and within the various communities (Brown and Kelly 2015; Emerson 1995, 1997; Emerson and Pauketat 2002; Milner 1990, 2006; Pauketat 1994, 2004, 2007; Pauketat and Emerson 1999; Schroeder 2004; Trubitt 2000). In this chapter I briefly review evidence for and interpretations of inequality within the American Bottom region and how inequality has been measured. I then describe how I calculated Gini coefficients using measures of structural floor area of features at Mississippian period sites in the American Bottom region in an attempt to quantify inequality in this Mississippian heartland. Included in the discussion are the difficulties inherent in defining wealth and inequality and determining the criteria by which to measure these with the available data.

MISSISSIPPIAN INEQUALITY

Most researchers studying Mississippian societies in the southeastern and midwestern United States agree that there was inequality but disagree about the degree, how it developed, and when the greatest differences occurred. Few explicitly address how to quantify and compare inequality, and there is limited discussion as to how inequality relates to power and complexity (though a strong positive relationship seems to be assumed). Discussions of inequality are infrequently couched explicitly in terms of wealth or strictly economic factors but typically refer to prestige, rank, status, power, influence, and control over resources.

In the American Bottom region specifically, there have been few attempts to measure inequality quantitatively. Timothy Pauketat (1994) provided a diachronic analysis of the architectural and artifactual patterns in a portion of the Cahokia precinct. Although his analysis included structure floor areas, the buildings were compared in terms of averages and standard deviations and to provide evidence for an increase in population rather than explicitly addressing household inequality. The artifact data were standardized to facilitate comparisons based on the density and distribution of certain classes of artifacts and raw materials. Pauketat suggests that the refuse from features in Tract 15A at Cahokia is indicative of high-status residents, particularly as compared to rural occupants of farmsteads. He also discusses discrete areas where different specialized items (e.g., axe heads, shell beads) were produced, possibly by craft specialists tied to elite households.

Mary Beth Trubitt (2000) attempted to quantify and compare differences in wealth among Mississippian sites in the American Bottom. She used structure size and the density of certain artifact classes she considered as reflecting wealth (e.g., lithic raw materials and finished artifacts, shell-working debris, and decorated ceramics). She divided the sample into high-status and low-status households based on structure size and compared the material remains from the structures and related pit features. She concluded that the greatest differences in wealth occurred during the late Mississippian Moorehead and Sand Prairie phases.

Recently, James Brown and John Kelly (2015) framed their discussion of Mississippian inequality in terms of social relations. They suggest that collective feasting rituals were used to cement relations and that those involved were on equal footing, at least initially. Significant inequality and social stratification could develop over time because of variations in the amount of surplus labor that could be mobilized by different groups in preparation for feasting events. They conclude that Mississippian elite households arose not based on accumulated wealth but based on indebtedness of those who had less surplus to contribute to communal events.

Many others have written of inequality in qualitative rather than quantitative terms. For instance, differences in status or rank have been invoked (or at least referenced) in discussions of differential burial treatments evident in Mound 72 at the Cahokia Precinct (Emerson et al. 2016; Fowler et al. 1999), the differential distribution of faunal remains (Kelly 1997), descriptions of Mississippian settlement patterns (Fowler 1978), and analyses of rural settlements (Betzenhauser 2006; Emerson 1995, 1997; Pauketat 2003). While these prior studies attempted to investigate inequality, they varied in methodology, the samples used, and their interpretations. Although there is interest in documenting inequality, there is little consensus on what criteria and what scales of analysis are appropriate and meaningful.

Here, I calculate Gini indices as an exploratory attempt to measure inequality through variability in architecture. Measurements of floor areas of more than one thousand Mississippian structures are readily accessible from published and unpublished reports and maps of extensive excavations conducted over the past several decades throughout the American Bottom region (see Betzenhauser 2017a for a complete list of references). Analyses of structures in other regions suggest a direct relationship between the size of a structure and wealth, with larger structures associated with wealthier households (chapter 1, this volume; Abrams 1989; Craig 2001). At the very least, the construction of larger buildings required greater resources and possibly the coordination of labor, both of which are suggestive of differences in wealth.

This analysis differs from others based on architectural variability in a few significant ways. Defining Mississippian households and assigning features or artifacts to a specific household is difficult, especially at densely occupied sites (Pauketat 1994:141). Attempts have been made to define Mississippian households, including structures and associated pit features, but these are most successful at small sites with only one or two households (see Mehrer 1995 and various chapters in Rogers and Smith 1995). The density of contemporaneous features and difficulty in assigning specific temporal components to exterior storage pit features at multicomponent sites hinders the assignment of features to a single household unit. Also, many of the exterior storage and refuse pits were likely used by multiple households. In this analysis, each domicile is considered a separate household because of the issues explicated above.

Most Mississippian structures were semisubterranean buildings constructed of wood and thatch that primarily served as residences. Several distinct types of structures are considered special use. These include oversized square and circular buildings; small circular and square structures that served as storage facilities, sweat lodges, or temples; and structures with atypical shapes including T- and L-shaped buildings with alcoves (see Betzenhauser and Pauketat 2018). These structures are included in some of the samples in this analysis because they are part of the community organization and may have had caretakers or people charged with planning and monitoring their construction and/or managing their use on behalf of the community, suggesting differences in status if not wealth.

METHODOLOGY AND EXPECTATIONS

The American Bottom region includes the wide expanse of floodplain and neighboring uplands within three Illinois counties across the Mississippi River from present-day St. Louis (figure 7.1). Floor-area measurements were gathered from published reports, unpublished dissertations, and notes on file at the Illinois State Archaeological Survey (Brennan

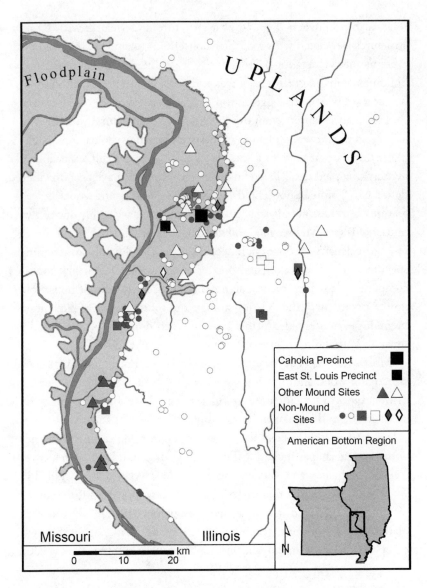

Figure 7.1 Lohmann phase Mississippian sites in the American Bottom and neighboring uplands of Illinois (adapted from Betzenhauser 2011:fig. 7.4).

2017; raw data available at Betzenhauser 2017b). In some cases, areas were measured from plan maps if the floor areas were not reported or were calculated using different methods. Structures that lack floor measurements because they were disturbed or only partially exposed or excavated are necessarily excluded. Other variables recorded include component, site type, and structure class. The sites vary in size, intensity, and duration of occupation. The smallest of these are farmsteads comprising one to three structures. The largest is Cahokia, the biggest mound precinct in the Mississippian world, with more than one hundred mounds. Other site types include nonmound villages and minor mound sites with one or a few mounds. The structure classes consist of residential structures and special-use structures (e.g., council houses, storage structures, sweat lodges, temples).

In addition to the excavated samples with measurable floor areas, a sample of platform mounds at Cahokia was selected to estimate mound-top architectural floor areas. This was done for several reasons. Only one mound-top structure at Cahokia was excavated and documented with controlled methods (Reed 2009; see Pauketat 1993 for partially exposed mound-top structures). However, historical accounts and excavations at other Mississippian mound sites in the Southeast indicate the presence of structures on top of platform mounds (for examples, see Bartram 1791; Bourne 1904; Lewis and Stout 1998). These structures are typically considered the residences of high-status people (including chiefs), but they also likely served as council houses and temples (Anderson et al. 2013; Pauketat 1993).

Estimating the mound-top architecture of all documented mounds at the Cahokia precinct would overinflate the total area of these structures. Only approximately 5 percent of the area encompassed by the Cahokia precinct has been excavated. Therefore, a 5 percent sample of all of the mounds that potentially had residential structures atop them was generated to calculate a comparable sample of mound-top architecture. These mounds were limited to those with flat tops and square or rectangular bases. Two mound-top structure floor areas were estimated by measuring the total surface area of the current mound apex and dividing it in half. This estimate was used for the Stirling phase, because the current dimensions of the mound likely approximate those from that phase (evidence for mound construction greatly decreases in the subsequent Moorehead phase). Because the construction of the selected mounds likely began during the Lohmann phase, the Stirling phase estimate was again divided in half to obtain a Lohmann phase estimate. The estimated values are less than the measured floor area of the structure on Monks Mound but significantly larger than the typical residential structures off-mound and are assumed to be within the actual range of floor areas for mound-top architecture.

Several Gini indices for overlapping subsamples were calculated using a function in the R package DescTools to calculate unbiased estimates, specifying 80 percent confidence intervals derived from 1,000 bootstrap replicates and "BCA" to generate bias-corrected intervals (see chapter 2, this volume). An overall Gini index was not calculated for the entire sample, because there are temporal trends in structure sizes: residential structure floor areas increase over the course of the Mississippian period in the American Bottom (Milner et al. 1984). The structures dated to the final Sand Prairie phase are included with the Moorehead phase structures because of the small sample sizes for these phases and the similarities among the structures and material culture.

Three separate indices were calculated for each of the three phases. One includes all structures in the sample; a second excludes the presumably nonresidential structures; and a third excludes the nonresidential and the mound-top structures. The same three Ginis were calculated using only the structures from sites with mounds, only the structures from sites without mounds, and only the structures from the Cahokia precinct. With these divisions, it is possible to investigate similarities and differences in wealth as reflected in the Gini indices based on component and site type for a variety of sites and throughout the entire Mississippian period.

Although this analysis is somewhat hindered by the incomplete sample and a lack of written records indicating how structures were used and what constituted a household, it is aided by large-scale, contiguous excavations and a large and varied sample. In total, more than 1,000 residential structures and nearly 250 special-use structures from seventy-seven sites are included in the sample. The entire span of Mississippian period occupation is represented. Approximately one-third of these structures date to the Lohmann phase, more than half date to the Stirling phase, and only 14 percent date to the Moorehead / Sand Prairie phases. Special-use structures are most common during the Stirling phase, with 22 percent of the structures classified as nondomestic (compared to 18 percent and 11 percent for the Lohmann and Moorehead phases, respectively). In the following section, I provide an overall comparison of Gini indices for the entire sample by phase and describe the results for each of the subsamples.

It is possible to formulate expectations for this analysis assuming that structure size is related to wealth and based on the data reported from sites throughout the region. The highest indices should be associated with the Cahokia precinct, the largest Mississippian site and that with the greatest population. At least some of Cahokia's residents had easier access to and possibly control over the production and distribution of specialized artifacts and exotic resources (Betzenhauser 2006; Pauketat 1994; Yerkes 1989). Indices calculated on structures associated with the Stirling phase are also likely to be high. At this point in the Mississippian chronology, Cahokians had the greatest influence over local populations and in interactions with other Mississippian and Woodland communities in the Midwest and Southeast. Low indices are expected among structures from the smaller sites that lack mounds, including farmsteads and villages. The smaller number of residents and their distance from Cahokia where wealth was likely concentrated support this notion (Betzenhauser 2006; Emerson 1997; Mehrer 1995).

Several other variables would likely inform on measures of inequality, but they are omitted from this analysis because of the difficulties in obtaining accurate measurements and determining whether they belonged to specific households: these include storage space, mound volume, and agricultural fields. I also did not compare artifact classes that likely indicate differences in wealth, both because of difficulties in quantifying the density per household and because most material items are recovered from secondary contexts. There are very few instances of artifacts found in primary contexts or preserved household assemblages. Most items are recovered from pits or abandoned structure basins that served as refuse receptacles for multiple households. Artifacts associated with burials are not common in the early Mississippian period except for a few well-known, high-status burials (see Baires 2017; Emerson et al. 2016; Fowler et al. 1999), and these are also omitted because of the complications associated with using burial data to measure wealth (see chapters 1 and 2, this volume).

RESULTS

In total, thirty Ginis were calculated for each of the three components using subsamples (table 7.1 and figure 7.2). The Ginis vary considerably depending on which structures are included and excluded from the samples. The lowest Gini is 0.18; it was calculated using only the Stirling phase residential structures from sites that lack mounds. The highest is 0.66, calculated using all of the Stirling phase structures from the Cahokia precinct (for comparison see Gurven et al. 2010 and Shenk et al. 2010). In the remainder of this section I discuss the results of the analysis, focusing on the four sets of calculations beginning with the structures from all of the sites followed by those from mound sites, nonmound sites, and the Cahokia precinct. The section concludes with comparisons between the residential structure samples that include and exclude mound-top architecture in an effort to illustrate the effects of sampling strategies on the Gini results.

ALL SITES

When all of the structures in the sample are included, the Ginis calculated among all of the sites start high in the Lohmann phase (AD 1050–1100) and remain high in the Stirling phase but drop in the Moorehead / Sand Prairie phases (AD 1200–1000) (figure 7.2a). When nonresidential structures are excluded, however, the Ginis are much lower and do not vary much through time. When the mound-top architecture is excluded, the pattern shifts again, most notably during the Stirling phase. In this sequence, the Stirling phase Gini is the lowest while the Gini for the Moorehead / Sand Prairie phases is the highest. The difference between the sample that includes the mound-top structures and the sample that excludes them is greatest during the Stirling phase (0.27 compared to 0.20) but is also significant in the Lohmann phase (0.29 compared to 0.25).

MOUND SITES

The patterns for structures from mound sites, including major settlements like the Cahokia and East St. Louis precincts as well as minor single-mound sites, are similar to the overall sample (figure 7.2b). The

Table 7.1 Gini subsamples and results

| | | Phase and dates (AD) | | | | | | |
| | Lohmann 1050–1100 | | | Stirling 1100–1200 | | | Moorehead / Sand Prairie 1200–1400 | | |
	N	Gini	80% CI	N	Gini	80% CI	N	Gini	80% CI
All sites									
All	457	0.42	.385–.492	686	0.43	.396–.480	180	0.32	.303–.352
Residential+[a]	387	0.29	.256–.335	557	0.27	.229–.321	—	—	—
Residential	385	0.25	.234–.284	554	0.20	.195–.210	161	0.27	.258–.299
Mound centers									
All	321	0.45	.401–.536	427	0.45	.412–.511	51	0.39	.366–.447
Residential+[a]	279	0.30	.268–.365	334	0.28	.237–.362	—	—	—
Residential	277	0.25	.238–.261	331	0.19	.183–.200	46	0.32	.298–.366
Nonmound sites									
All	136	0.33	.289–.418	259	0.29	.254–.337	129	0.28	.260–.310
Residential	108	0.25	.199–.371	223	0.18	.175–.195	115	0.25	.234–.282
Cahokia									
All	97	0.53	.424–.677	58	0.66	.617–.717	32	0.28	.255–.351
Residential+[a]	79	0.35	.285–.477	44	0.57	.448–.669	—	—	—
Residential	77	0.21	.192–.238	41	0.19	.169–.239	29	0.22	.209–.267

[a] The category "Residential+" includes estimated mound-top architecture at Cahokia in the Lohmann and Stirling phases.

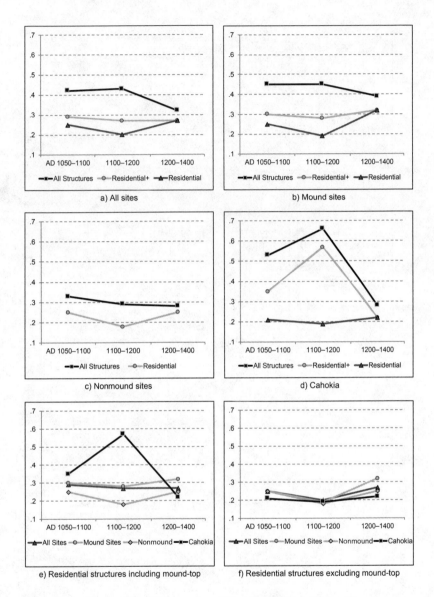

Figure 7.2 Gini results (the category "Residential+" excludes all nonresidential structures and includes estimated mound-top structures in the Lohmann and Stirling phases and for the Monks Mound structure in the Stirling phase).

Ginis that include nonresidential structures begin with high values in the Lohmann and Stirling phases and end with a low value in the Moorehead / Sand Prairie phases. This is the same general pattern observed for all sites, although each of the Ginis is slightly higher and the Moorehead / Sand Prairie decrease is less drastic at mound sites. The greatest difference is associated with the Moorehead / Sand Prairie sample, with an increase from 0.32 to 0.39.

The residential structures exhibit a similar trend in the early phases, but the Gini increases in the Moorehead / Sand Prairie phases. Similar to the sample that includes all structures, the residential structures have a higher Gini in the Moorehead / Sand Prairie phases than that calculated for all sites, but the Lohmann and Stirling phase values are nearly identical. When the mound-top architecture is excluded, the pattern is very similar to the Ginis for all sites, although the Moorehead / Sand Prairie value is higher.

NONMOUND SITES

The Ginis calculated for sites that lack mounds are quite similar to those calculated for all sites (figure 7.2c). The values for all structures decrease through time beginning in the Lohmann phase at 0.33 and ending in the Moorehead / Sand Prairie phases at 0.28. This slight decrease over time is also noted for the sample that includes all structures from all sites but contrasts with the mound sites sample. When the nonresidential structures are excluded, there is an obvious decrease during the Stirling phase, with a subsequent increase during the Moorehead / Sand Prairie phases. A similar pattern is noted for the previous two subsamples, although the Moorehead / Sand Prairie increase is more drastic among the mound sites (+0.13) than the nonmound sites (+0.07).

THE CAHOKIA PRECINCT

The Cahokia samples (figure 7.2d) appear distinct from the previously discussed subsamples. The Ginis calculated for all structures are high in both the Lohmann and Stirling phases but peak in the Stirling phase. This peak is followed by a dramatic decrease during the Moorehead / Sand Prairie phases. A strikingly similar pattern is observed when the nondomestic structures are excluded, although the values are lower for all three components. These are in stark contrast to all three of the previously discussed samples, all of which exhibit a slight increase or decrease during the Stirling phase. However, the pattern is very similar to all of the other samples when the mound-top architecture is excluded. There is only a minute difference between the phases, with a slight decrease during the Stirling phase followed by a slight increase during the Moorehead / Sand Prairie phases.

EFFECTS OF SAMPLE SELECTION ON GINI RESULTS

It became apparent while calculating the Ginis based on the various subsamples that sample selection has a significant impact on the results. When comparing the Ginis calculated for the residential structures including the estimated mound-top architecture with those calculated without the estimates, significantly different patterns emerge (figure 7.2e–f). When the mound-top architecture is excluded, there is virtually no difference between the subsamples: all of the Ginis begin in the Lohmann phase between 0.21 and 0.25, then decrease during the Stirling phase (0.18–0.20), before increasing again during the Moorehead / Sand Prairie phases (0.22–0.32). The least amount of difference between the subsamples is associated with the Stirling phase (range = 0.02), while the greatest difference occurs in the Moorehead / Sand Prairie phases (range = 0.10). The structures with the least amount of difference between phases are those from the Cahokia precinct (range = 0.03), while the greatest differences are among mound sites (range = 0.13).

When the mound-top architecture is included, the Ginis for Cahokia are significantly different for the Lohmann and Stirling phases: the Ginis are high in both phases, reaching a maximum of 0.57 in the Stirling phase. The larger values are due to the inclusion of only two Lohmann and three Stirling mound-top structures. The Gini for the Moorehead / Sand Prairie phases is the same because no mound-top structures were included in the overall sample. This results in a drastic drop (-0.35 difference) between the Stirling and Moorehead / Sand Prairie phases when mound-top architecture is included. The mound center and nonmound site samples exhibit similar trends when mound-top architecture is included, but the Ginis for mound sites are consistently higher throughout all phases. Again, these differences in the Lohmann and Stirling phases are due to the inclusion of only a few mound-top structures, and these structures are necessarily absent from sites that lack mounds. However, the higher value in the Moorehead / Sand Prairie phases is not due to mound-top architecture, because none were included in the sample.

DISCUSSION

The results of this analysis are revealing. When nonresidential structures are included, the indices are generally high in the beginning of the Mississippian period and remain high during the Stirling phase, followed by a decrease during the Moorehead / Sand Prairie phases. The Moorehead / Sand Prairie decrease is more drastic in some of the subsamples (e.g., the Cahokia precinct). The high indices in the Lohmann phase (>0.4) are likely related to the transition to a new architectural style (i.e., wall trench) and the incorporation of disparate groups into the Cahokian community (see Betzenhauser 2011, 2017c). Also reflected in the indices are the new architectural forms that served as communal spaces, temples, and/or storage facilities and mound-top architecture. The increase in indices associated with the Stirling phase, particularly those at Cahokia, is suggestive of greater inequality as well as the increased frequency of special-use structures. The decrease across all subsamples in the Moorehead phase and the drastic decrease at Cahokia in particular suggest the least amount of inequality for the entire Mississippian period in the region (contra Trubitt 2000).

When both nonresidential and mound-top structures are excluded, the temporal trends differ significantly. Clearly evident are the similar patterns but different degrees of variation between site types throughout the Mississippian period when considering only residential structures. These similar historical trajectories in terms of structure size suggest varying degrees of regional integration over time. The larger sites with greater population tend to exhibit more variability at the beginning and end of the Mississippian period (i.e., Lohmann and Moorehead phases) than do smaller sites. In contrast, during the Stirling phase the amount of variation in residential structure size, indicated by low Gini indices, is at a minimum region-wide. This trend is most noticeable at Cahokia, which has one of the lowest Ginis (0.19) calculated for all phases and subsamples. The fact that the low Gini indices are associated with the Stirling phase domestic structures in general and at Cahokia in particular indicate not the least amount of inequality but the greatest amount of standardization and conformity in architectural style. In this case, the calculation of Ginis based on the size of Mississippian residential structures provides further evidence indicating regional integration and possibly data supporting the notion that the structures at Cahokia were built by teams using prefabricated walls (Pauketat and Alt 2005; Pauketat and Woods 1986).

In general, the Ginis calculated using the residential structures including the estimated mound-top structures fall between those calculated using all structures and those calculated using only the residential structures. The chronological patterns, the high value at Cahokia in the Stirling phase, and the higher values at mound sites compared to sites without mounds conform to expectations. It is tempting to say that these Ginis are accurately reflecting measurable differences in wealth, but whether that is indeed the case is unclear given the available data.

It is interesting to note that the least amount of variation among residential structures and the greatest amount of variation when including all structures and mound-top structures both occur during the Stirling phase at Cahokia. The greatest difference between subsamples is also associated with the Stirling phase, suggesting the greatest inequality throughout the region. The large communal structures and temples at Cahokia and other sites in the region likely facilitated or provided spaces for integrative activities. Similarly, as others have suggested (Pauketat and Alt 2003), the act of mound building and participation in large-scale feasting events (Pauketat et al. 2002) would have instilled a feeling of community among the various participants, including those living at nonmound sites throughout the region. Their presence might be indicative of efforts to mask or ameliorate differences in wealth.

CONCLUSIONS AND FUTURE DIRECTIONS

The data presented here offer insight into Cahokian history but not necessarily in terms of economic inequality. For instance, the indices calculated for residential structures excluding mound-top structures appear to be measuring the degree of architectural standardization rather than household inequality. If this is the case, then the similar low degree of variation among residential structure sizes among all of the subsamples during the Stirling phase seems to indicate the greatest degree of regional integration as reflected in standardization of architectural style. This increased degree of uniformity is also observable in other media, including ceramic and lithic production and utilization. During the Stirling phase, nearly all of the pottery is tempered with shell, and jars conform to a limited range of morphological characteristics, surface treatments, and decorative techniques, suggesting greater standardization in pottery production. Similarly, Burlington and Mill Creek cherts dominate lithic assemblages, particularly in terms of formal tools such as projectile points and hoes. Although the calculations including special-use structures result in higher indices, it is not clear that this difference is reflective of diffcrences in wealth, status, power, or influence. The large structures are thought to have served a communal or religious purpose rather than having served as residences for high-status families or individuals.

Sampling affects the results, and in some cases the differences are dramatic. This highlights the importance of sample selection and the utility of calculating and reporting multiple Ginis from subsamples of the overall data set. It is also important to explicitly state which cases are included or excluded and why, to more accurately compare with Ginis from other regions or time periods. Differences in wealth can be expressed in a variety of ways across multiple dimensions. Therefore, it is beneficial to not only calculate Gini coefficients on multiple classes of data (e.g., floor area, storage space, artifact concentration) but also to supplement them with other lines of evidence that might not be amenable to the type of quantification and valuation that Ginis require. Such information might include the locations of structures within a site (e.g., close to or on a mound versus lining a plaza) and between sites (e.g., near Cahokia versus an isolated farmstead).

To this end, the research presented here could be expanded and improved upon with the addition of structures from excavated sites that have yet to be reported and estimates of mound-top architecture from mound sites other than Cahokia. It would also be beneficial to include structures from the Terminal Late Woodland period that immediately preceded the Mississippian period to increase historical depth (see chapter 11, this volume). Ginis could also be calculated on other classes of data, including density of nonlocal materials and specialized objects. Finally, Ginis could be calculated for other Mississippian polities for comparative purposes.

ACKNOWLEDGMENTS

I extend my gratitude to Tim Kohler and Michael Smith for the invitation to participate in the SAA symposium and the Amerind Seminar. Tim was particularly helpful with calculating confidence intervals using R. It was an enlightening week of vigorous discussion, and this chapter benefited greatly from interactions with the other participants. I am also grateful to Timothy Pauketat for encouraging me to contribute. The structure data from East St. Louis were used with permission from the Illinois State Archaeological Survey's director, Thomas E. Emerson. I would also like to thank Dr. Tamira Brennan and my colleagues at the American Bottom Field Station and the Illinois State Archaeological Survey for their support.

REFERENCES CITED

Abrams, E. M. 1989. Architecture and Energy: An Evolutionary Perspective. In *Archaeological Method and Theory*, vol. 1, edited by Michael B. Schiffer, pp. 47–87. University of Arizona Press, Tucson.

Anderson, David G., John E. Cornelison Jr., and Sarah C. Sherwood (editors). 2013. *Archeological Investigations at Shiloh Indian Mounds National Historic Landmark (40HR7), 1999–2004.* Southeast Archeological Center, Tallahassee, Fla.

Baires, Sarah E. 2017. *Land of Water, City of the Dead: Religion and Cahokia's Emergence.* University of Alabama Press, Tuscaloosa.

Baltus, Melissa R. 2014. Transforming Material Relationships: 13th Century Revitalization of Cahokian Religious-Politics. PhD dissertation, University of Illinois, Urbana.

Bartram, William. 1791. *Travels Through North and South Carolina, Georgia, East and West Florida, the Cherokee Country, the Extensive Territories of the Muscogulges or Creek Confederacy, and the Country of the Chactaws.* James and Johnson, Philadelphia.

Betzenhauser, Alleen. 2006. Greater Cahokian Farmsteads: A Quantitative and Qualitative Analysis of Diversity. MA paper, University of Illinois, Urbana.

———. 2011. Creating the Cahokian Community: The Power of Place in Early Mississippian Sociopolitical Dynamics. PhD dissertation, University of Illinois, Urbana.

————. 2017a. Chapter 7 Supplemental References. Available at https://core.tdar .org/document/437491/chapter-7-supplemental-references.

————. 2017b. Betzenhauser American Bottom Structure Metrics. https://uofi .app.box.com/v/ESTL-Data.

————. 2017c. Cahokia's Beginnings: Mobility, Urbanization, and the Cahokian Political Landscape. In *Mississippian Beginnings*, edited by Gregory D. Wilson, pp. 71–96. University of Florida Press, Gainesville.

Betzenhauser, Alleen, and Timothy R. Pauketat. 2018. Elements of Cahokian Neighborhoods. In *Neighborhoods from the Perspective of Anthropological Archaeology*, edited by David Pacifico and Lise Treux. Archeological Papers of the American Anthropological Association. Manuscript under review.

Bourne, Edward G. 1904. *Spain in America, 1450–1580*. Harper and Bros., New York.

Brennan, Tamira K. (editor). 2017. East St. Louis Precinct (11S706) Mississippian Features. Research report draft on file, Illinois State Archaeological Survey, Prairie Research Institute, University of Illinois, Urbana-Champaign.

Brown, James A., and John E. Kelly. 2015. Surplus Labor, Ceremonial Feasting, and Social Inequality at Cahokia: A Study in Social Process. In *Surplus: The Politics of Production and the Strategies of Everyday Life*, edited by Christopher T. Morehart and Kristin De Lucia, pp. 221–44. University of Colorado Press, Boulder.

Craig, Douglas B. 2001. *Grewe Archaeological Research Project*, vol. 3, *Synthesis*. Anthropological Papers 99-1. Northland Research, Tempe, Ariz.

Dalan, Rinita A., George R. Holley, William I. Woods, Harold W. Watters Jr., and John A. Koepke. 2003. *Envisioning Cahokia: A Landscape Perspective*. Northern Illinois University Press, DeKalb.

Emerson, Thomas E. 1995. *Settlement, Symbolism, and Hegemony in the Cahokian Countryside*. PhD dissertation, University of Wisconsin, Madison. University Microfilms, Ann Arbor, Mich.

————. 1997. *Cahokia and the Archaeology of Power*. University of Alabama Press, Tuscaloosa.

————. 2017a. Creating Greater Cahokia: The Cultural Content and Context of the East St. Louis Mound Precinct. In Creating Greater Cahokia: Rediscovery and Large-Scale Excavations of the East St. Louis Precinct, edited by Thomas E. Emerson, Brad Koldehoff, and Tamira K. Brennan. Manuscript on file, Illinois State Archaeological Survey, Champaign.

————. 2017b. Greater Cahokia—Chiefdom, State, or City? Urbanism in the North American Midcontinent, AD 1050–1200. In Creating Greater Cahokia: Rediscovery and Large-Scale Excavations of the East St. Louis Precinct, edited by Thomas E. Emerson, Brad Koldehoff, and Tamira K. Brennan. Manuscript on file, Illinois State Archaeological Survey, Champaign.

Emerson, Thomas E., and Kristin Hedman. 2016. The Dangers of Diversity: The Consolidation and Dissolution of Cahokia, Native North America's First

Urban Polity. In *Beyond Collapse: Archaeological Perspectives on Resilience, Revitalization, and Transformation in Complex Societies*, edited by Ronald K. Faulseit, pp. 147–75. Occasional Paper 42. Center for Archaeological Investigations, Southern Illinois University Press, Carbondale.

Emerson, Thomas E., Kristin M. Hedman, Eve A. Hargrave, Dawn E. Cobb, and Andrew R. Thompson. 2016. Paradigms Lost: Reconfiguring Cahokia's Mound 72 Beaded Burial. *American Antiquity* 81(3):405–25.

Emerson, Thomas E., and Timothy R. Pauketat. 2002. Embodying Power and Resistance at Cahokia. In *The Dynamics of Power*, edited by Maria O'Donovan, pp. 105–25. Occasional Paper 30. Center for Archaeological Investigations, Southern Illinois University at Carbondale.

Emerson, Thomas E., John A. Walthall, Andrew C. Fortier, and Dale L. McElrath. 2006. Advances in American Bottom Prehistory: Illinois Transportation Archaeology Two Decades After I-270. *Southeastern Archaeology* 25(2):155–69.

Fortier, Andrew C., Thomas E. Emerson, and Dale L. McElrath. 2006. Calibrating and Reassessing American Bottom Culture History. *Southeastern Archaeology* 25:170–211.

Fowler, Melvin L. 1978. Cahokia and the American Bottom: Settlement Archaeology. In *Mississippian Settlement Patterns*, edited by Bruce D. Smith, pp. 455–78. Academic Press, New York.

———. 1997. *The Cahokia Atlas: A Historical Atlas of Cahokia Archaeology*. Revised ed. Studies in Archaeology 2. Illinois Transportation Archaeological Research Program, University of Illinois, Urbana.

Fowler, Melvin L., Jerome Rose, Barbara VanderLeest, and Steven R. Ahler. 1999. *The Mound 72 Area: Dedicated and Sacred Space in Early Cahokia*. Illinois State Museum Reports of Investigations 54. Illinois State Museum Society, Springfield.

Gurven, Michael, Monique Borgerhoff Mulder, Paul L. Hooper, Hillard Kaplan, Robert Quinlan, Rebecca Sear, Eric Schniter, et al. 2010. Domestication Alone Does Not Lead to Inequality: Intergenerational Wealth Transmission Among Horticulturalists. *Current Anthropology* 51(1):49–64.

Kelly, John E. 1990. The Emergence of Mississippian Culture in the American Bottom Region. In *The Mississippian Emergence*, edited by Bruce D. Smith, pp. 113–52. University of Alabama Press, Tuscaloosa.

———. 1991. Cahokia and Its Role as a Gateway Center in Interregional Exchange. In *Cahokia and the Hinterlands: Middle Mississippian Cultures of the Midwest*, edited by Thomas E. Emerson and R. Barry Lewis, pp. 61–80. University of Illinois Press, Urbana.

Kelly, Lucretia S. 1997. Patterns of Faunal Exploitation at Cahokia. In *Cahokia: Domination and Ideology in the Mississippian World*, edited by Timothy R. Pauketat and Thomas E. Emerson, pp. 69–88. University of Nebraska Press, Lincoln.

Lewis, R. Barry, and Charles Stout (editors). 1998. *Mississippian Towns and Sacred Spaces: Searching for an Architectural Grammar*. University of Alabama Press, Tuscaloosa.

Mehrer, Mark W. 1995. *Cahokia's Countryside: Household Archaeology, Settlement Patterns, and Social Power*. Northern Illinois University Press, DeKalb.

Milner, George R. 1990. The Late Prehistoric Cahokia Cultural System of the Mississippi River Valley: Foundations, Florescence, and Fragmentation. *Journal of World Prehistory* 4(1):1–43.

———. 2006. *The Cahokia Chiefdom: The Archaeology of a Mississippian Society*. University Press of Florida, Gainesville.

Milner, George R., Thomas E. Emerson, Mark W. Mehrer, Joyce A. Williams, and Duane Esarey. 1984. Mississippian and Oneota Periods. In *American Bottom Archaeology*, edited by Charles J. Bareis and James W. Porter, pp. 158–86. University of Illinois Press, Urbana.

Pauketat, Timothy R. 1993. *Temples for Cahokian Lords*. University of Michigan, Ann Arbor.

———. 1994. *Ascent of Chiefs: Cahokia and Mississippian Politics in Native North America*. University of Alabama Press, Tuscaloosa.

———. 1998. *The Archaeology of Downtown Cahokia: The Tract 15A and Dunham Tract Excavations*. Studies in Archaeology 1. Illinois Transportation Archaeological Research Program, University of Illinois, Urbana.

———. 2003. Resettled Farmers and the Making of a Mississippian Polity. *American Antiquity* 68:39–66.

———. 2004. *Ancient Cahokia and the Mississippians*. Cambridge University Press, Cambridge.

———. 2007. *Chiefdoms and Other Archaeological Delusions*. AltaMira Press, Walnut Canyon, Calif.

———. 2013. *The Archaeology of Downtown Cahokia II: The 1960 Excavation of Tract 15B*. Studies in Archaeology 8. Illinois State Archaeological Survey, University of Illinois, Urbana.

Pauketat, Timothy R., and Susan M. Alt. 2003. Mounds, Memory, and Contested Mississippian History. In *Archaeology of Memory*, edited by R. Van Dyke and S. Alcock, pp. 151–79. Blackwell Press, Oxford, U.K.

———. 2005. Agency in a Postmold? Physicality and the Archaeology of Culture-Making. *Journal of Archaeological Method and Theory* 12(3):213–36.

Pauketat, Timothy R., and Thomas E. Emerson. 1999. Representation of Hegemony as Community at Cahokia. In *Material Symbols: Culture and Economy in Prehistory*, edited by John E. Robb, pp. 302–17. Occasional Paper 26. Center for Archaeological Investigations, Southern Illinois University, Carbondale.

Pauketat, Timothy R., Lucretia S. Kelly, Gayle J. Fritz, Neal H. Lopinot, Scott Elias, and Eve Hargrave. 2002. The Residues of Feasting and Public Ritual at Early Cahokia. *American Antiquity* 67:257–79.

Pauketat, Timothy R., and Neal H. Lopinot. 1997. Cahokian Population Dynamics. In *Cahokia: Domination and Ideology in the Mississippian World*, edited by Timothy R. Pauketat and Thomas E. Emerson, pp. 103–23. University of Nebraska Press, Lincoln.

Pauketat, Timothy R., and William I. Woods. 1986. Middle Mississippian Structure Analysis: The Lawrence Primas Site in the American Bottom. *Wisconsin Archeologist* 67(2):104–27.

Reed, Nelson A. 2009. Excavations on the Third Terrace and Front Ramp of Monks Mound, Cahokia: A Personal Narrative. *Illinois Archaeology* 21:1–89.

Rogers, J. Daniel, and Bruce D. Smith. 1995. *Mississippian Communities and Households*. University of Alabama Press, Tuscaloosa.

Schroeder, Sissel. 2004. Power and Place: Agency, Ecology, and History in the American Bottom, Illinois. *Antiquity* 78:812–27.

Shenk, Mary K., Monique Borgerhoff Mulder, Jan Beise, Gregory Clark, William Irons, Donna Leonettie, Bobbi S. Low, et al. 2010. Intergenerational Wealth Transmission Among Agriculturalists: Foundations of Agrarian Inequality. *Current Anthropology* 51(1):65–83.

Trubitt, Mary Beth. 2000. Mound Building and Prestige Goods Exchange: Changing Strategies in the Cahokia Chiefdom. *American Antiquity* 65:669–90.

Yerkes, Richard W. 1989. Mississippian Craft Specialization in the American Bottom. *Southeastern Archaeology* 8:93–106.

8

Farming, Inequality, and Urbanization

A Comparative Analysis of Late Prehistoric Northern Mesopotamia and Southwestern Germany

Amy Bogaard, Amy Styring, Jade Whitlam, Mattia Fochesato, and Samuel Bowles

V. Gordon Childe's sequence of Neolithic Revolution succeeded by Urban Revolution suggested a progressive narrative of farming development and increasing social inequality (Childe 1929, 1950, 1957) that was influential across the social sciences (e.g., Boserup 1965; Lenski 1966; see also chapter 1). Childe's work was valuable in pointing to the relationship of farming and emergent inequality: farmed land is a key form of unequally held material wealth that is transmitted across generations in many farming societies (e.g., Borgerhoff Mulder et al. 2009; Shenk et al. 2010), and its ownership and use are therefore of fundamental importance for assessing the relation of farming to inequality.

But research since Childe in archaeology and beyond has overturned the notion that farming developed in a sequence of increasingly intensive stages (e.g., Rowley-Conwy 1981; Scott 2009), inexorably unleashing greater inequality (e.g., Gurven et al. 2010; Halstead 1989; Kuijt et al. 2011). Farming is too heterogeneous a phenomenon to play a simple causal role with regard to social inequality: it represents a wide spectrum of practices that, depending on the context, can support or supress wealth disparities (e.g., Halstead 2014; Netting 1971, 1993).

Antonio Gilman (1981) advanced the view that capital-intensive agricultural techniques (e.g., plowing, irrigation) fueled the development of wealth disparity and that aspiring warrior elites offering protection could exploit the unwillingness of farming communities to abandon land made valuable by past labor investment. Gilman's position remains attractive in that it offers an alternative to managerial, top-down perspectives on the role of early elites in agricultural innovation and change (cf. Erickson 2006; Halstead 2014). Gilman followed Childe (1929, 1957) and Ester Boserup (1965) in assuming that the more egalitarian Neolithic cultivators relied on mobile, extensive slash-and-burn techniques, making capital-intensive investment in fixed fields a Bronze Age novelty.

But shifting cultivation as the basis of Neolithic farming in Western Eurasia now seems doubtful given direct bioarchaeological evidence for crop growing conditions in southeastern (Bogaard et al. 2013; Bogaard and Halstead 2015), central (Bogaard 2004; Jacomet et al. 2016), and northwestern Europe (Bogaard and Jones 2007; McClatchie et al. 2016). Neolithic farming in these regions incorporated labor-intensive investment in improving the productivity of land, including manuring and tillage/weeding of long-lived plots, motivating and facilitating claims of land ownership and inheritance (Bogaard et al. 2011, 2013). In these economies wealth could be "banked" in livestock, and stored socially in valued objects or tokens (Halstead and O'Shea 1982). But effective amplification of differential production/debt (Bogucki 1999:205–59) on the basis of salient social categories (Tilly 1998) was evidently rare.

We call this form of farming "labor limited" because its most important input is human effort rather than land, traction animals, or other inputs. In this chapter we present new evidence that labor-limited economies may have been remarkably egalitarian, as observed within the spectrum of recent horticultural societies (e.g., Borgerhoff Mulder et al. 2009; Gurven et al. 2010).

There was a substantial temporal gap, then, between the onset of labor-limited farming, most likely along with family-based ownership and inheritance of land on the one hand and the emergence of substantial and lasting economic inequality on the other. And this gap was not peculiar to Europe. In the rain-fed regions of western Asia, early farmers practiced water management, manuring, and intensive tillage by the ninth millennium cal BC (Bogaard 2005; Styring, Ater, et al. 2016; Wallace et al. 2015). Clear evidence of substantial and persistent economic disparity in agricultural communities emerges much later (e.g., ca. 4200–3850 cal BC, Late Chalcolithic 2 period [Stein 2012]) and appears to have been in some but not all cases associated with a degree of political centralization.

The small-scale, labor-limited farming that was typical of the Neolithic in both western Asia and Europe was not a sufficient cause of the later emergence of inequality. Rather, it was the forerunner of a subsequent and distinctly different kind of farming economy in which land and other forms of material wealth were the limiting factors, an economy that could sustain significant and lasting social inequality.

Far more conducive to some form of centralization and differential accumulation of wealth were crops grown on an expanded scale with the help of specialized plow animals, as attested, for example, in documentary records of strategic elite/institutional involvement in farming in Bronze Age Mesopotamia and the Aegean (Halstead 1995; Postgate 1992:115, 149, 189). The nucleation of a farming population around centers where protection and new institutional services were available—urbanization— would further facilitate the mobilization of these surpluses.

A process of agricultural "extensification" arguably underwrote lasting social inequality in regions of rain-fed farming where arable land was abundant, contrasting with the "intensification" pathway familiar from conventional accounts of irrigation-based societies (e.g., Marcus and Stanish 2006). Figure 8.1 illustrates the classic alternative strategies for increasing agricultural production: to raise labor inputs per unit area (gardens), or to expand the area cultivated (fields). Expansion based on the labor savings made possible through animal traction (extensification) leads to land rather than labor becoming the limiting factor. As a result, labor-limited farming (small-scale, intensive, horticultural) would tend

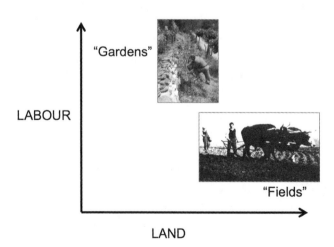

Figure 8.1 Agricultural strategies for increasing production.

to align with relatively low levels of social inequality, and land-limited (extensive) farming with greater inequality.

Here we integrate recent agroecological results from two regional studies—semiarid northern Mesopotamia (Styring, Charles, et al. 2017) and temperate southwestern Germany (Styring, Maier, et al. 2016; Styring, Rösch, et al. 2017)—with estimates of wealth inequality. We focus on key sites offering both architectural data for variation in household size as the basis of our estimates of wealth disparities and archaeobotanical evidence of farming practice. We measure wealth inequality by the Gini coefficient, ranging from 0, indicating the complete absence of wealth differences, to 1, indicating that a single household possesses all of the wealth. Our calculations incorporate a novel way of integrating household living and storage space to assess household wealth (Fochesato and Bowles 2017), an outcome of wider investigation into long-term social inequality (e.g., Bowles et al. 2010).

Our first aim is to assess the expected alignments between intensive versus extensive agrosystems and social inequality in northern Mesopotamia and southwestern Germany using Gini calculations and direct evidence for farming practice. This approach opens the way to assess comparatively the degree and timing of shifts in social inequality relative to agroecological trends. A second aim is to explore the role of settlement morphology, as well as the distinct forms of centralization implied, for shaping both agroecological change and wealth disparity. Early urban centers in northern Mesopotamia and central Europe took very different forms: the tell-centered landscapes of fourth–third millennium cal BC northern Mesopotamia present high-density residential nucleation surrounded by arable fields (Wilkinson 2003). In contrast, the earliest "urban" centers north of the Alps, dating to the early Iron Age (800–450 cal BC), were low-density conglomerations around fortified hilltops (*Fürstensitze*, or chiefly seats), the best documented example being the Heuneburg (Fernández-Götz and Krausse 2013; Fernández-Götz et al. 2014; Kurz 2010).

In these low-density urban systems, population remained sufficiently dispersed not to limit settlement size, in part because inhabitants retained close proximity to arable land (cf. Fletcher 1995). High-density urbanism—large, dense residential cores from which farming residents travel considerable distances to fields—is presumed to entail more radical agricultural extensification than does low-density urbanism. An implication is that extensification under high-density urbanism had a greater accelerating impact on social inequality by fueling land-based wealth disparity.

METHODOLOGICAL BACKGROUND

AGROECOLOGY

We define agricultural intensity in terms of labor inputs per unit area (cf. Brookfield 1972; Morrison 1994), for example, in the form of tillage, manuring, irrigation, and/or weeding. Recent work has refined two complementary methods for inferring the intensity of arable land management: (1) the functional ecology of arable weeds and (2) stable carbon and nitrogen isotope analysis of crop remains.

Weed seeds co-occur with crop remains and provide a basis for reconstructing growing conditions (e.g., Jones 2002; van der Veen 1992). Using functional ecological traits of weed species, we can distinguish between present-day low- versus high-input farming (Bogaard, Hodgson, et al. 2016; Bogaard, Styring, et al. 2016). Stable isotope analysis of crop remains provides a complementary means of assessing agricultural intensity. Stable carbon isotope ($\delta^{13}C$) values of crops reflect water availability during growth (e.g., Wallace et al. 2013) and are useful in regions such as northern Mesopotamia where water was a major limiting factor for crop growth. Crop stable nitrogen isotope ($\delta^{15}N$) values offer a means of assessing possible manuring practice (e.g., Bogaard et al. 2007; Bogaard, Hodgson, et al. 2016; Bogaard, Styring, et al. 2016; Fraser et al. 2011). This approach has been tested in agronomic experiments and in real farming systems where manuring rate is positively associated with cereal grain $\delta^{15}N$ values. In (semi)arid regions, (unmanured) cereal grain $\delta^{15}N$ values tend to increase with aridity, but additional manuring effects can nevertheless be distinguished (Styring, Ater, et al. 2016). Styring and colleagues (Styring, Ater, et al. 2016; Styring, Charles, et al. 2017) have developed methods of imputing cereal manuring levels from $\delta^{15}N$ values under different annual rainfall levels.

MEASURING WEALTH INEQUALITY

Methods for calculating Gini coefficients based on household living and storage areas (in square meters) from archaeological ground plans (after Fochesato and Bowles 2017) are summarized here (see Whitlam and Bogaard 2017b for more detail on measuring room areas from ground plans and the architectural interpretation of each site).

By material wealth we mean an asset that provides a flow of services contributing to the living standard of the holder of the wealth. Housing, for example, is an asset yielding shelter, comfort, and protection, while land and/or livestock (on which we do not have measures) would provide the basis of nutrition.

For each model of each site, Gini coefficients were calculated for living area, storage area, a simple sum of living and storage area, and integration of the two spaces in a single measure of total wealth using an aggregation rule similar to the Cobb-Douglas production function in economics.

In our model, living area is the asset that contributed to what might be called housing well-being, while storage area represents assets proportional to the farming input (or input of any other productive activity) used to produce subsistence. As we can see that both housing and farming assets should be included in the household's wealth, the following question then arises: how should they be aggregated?

Our strategy is to let the value of a particular kind of wealth (dwelling or storage space, for example) be proportional to the amount it contributes to the living standard of the holder. We will show results based on simply adding the areas devoted to housing and storage. Though this is the measure that for comparability with other studies we used elsewhere (Kohler et al. 2017), it fails to take into account that a square meter of storage area when filled may represent orders of magnitude greater value than a similar area of dwelling space. The fact that both are measured in square meters does not provide a good reason to simply add them. Moreover, adding the two does not take account of the fact that the addition to the value of house size or of farming assets associated with additional units of the asset (the marginal value) must diminish as either of the two becomes very large. The additional value to the household of farming 2 hectares rather than 1 is plausibly greater than the additional value of farming 101 hectares rather than 100.

To address these issues, we propose instead to use what we call an aggregation function of the following form:

$$W_i = AH^\alpha F^{1-\alpha}$$

where W_i is the well-being of the i-th household generated by its housing (H_i, the living area) and farming (F_i, measured by the storage area) wealth, with A constant and α being the relative importance of housing compared to farming wealth as a determinant of one's living standard ($0 \leq \alpha \leq 1$). The above aggregation function will be recognized as similar to the Cobb-Douglas production function from economics.

This function has been selected for the following properties: (1) doubling both housing and farming wealth doubles well-being (analogous to constant returns to scale in the production function); (2) increasing either kind of wealth increases well-being but at a decreasing rate (the diminishing marginal contribution of each of the two kinds of wealth, holding constant the other); and (3) the marginal contribution of each type of wealth to the well-being of the household is greater, the larger is the quantity of the other kind of wealth (sometimes expressed in terms of contributors to a household's livelihood, housing and farming wealth being complements rather than substitutes).

The choice of the coefficient α is unavoidably somewhat arbitrary, as it cannot be estimated from any data from the relevant period. We can reason about plausible magnitudes with the following anachronistic thought experiment. If the relative importance of the dwelling services of housing that this coefficient measures were proportional to the household's willingness to pay for housing relative to other things (a plausible assumption) then α would be the fraction of the annual budget (in money, time working, etc.) that one would spend on housing relative to total expenditures.

Where storage area is more unequally distributed than living space (as is typical, if not universal), our aggregated measure will indicate more inequality, the greater the value of α. We aggregated living and storage space using two plausible values for α—0.25 and 0.5—and considered these two values of the resulting Gini coefficient along with that which results when we simply add total housing space without regard to the dwelling/storage distinction. Confidence intervals (95 percent) are reported for all Gini coefficients (based on the 0.025 and 0.975 percentiles of the bootstrapped Gini distribution). All of the bootstrapped Gini distributions were non-normal. We also report the standard errors.

ARCHAEOLOGICAL APPLICATION 1, NORTHERN MESOPOTAMIA

AGROECOLOGICAL CHARACTERIZATION

Styring, Charles, and colleagues (2017) used stable nitrogen and carbon isotope analysis of crop remains across a sequence of Neolithic–Bronze Age sites in Syria to assess the relationship between urbanization and farming practice. A mixed-effects proportional-odds regression model shows a significant effect of settlement size on imputed manuring level, such that the proportion of highly manured cereals is *highest* at the *smallest* sites and *lowest* at the *largest* urban sites (Styring, Charles, et al. 2017:fig. 4). Thus, early cities were sustained through extensification—expansion of low-input arable land surrounding the centers (figure 8.2a)—rather than higher inputs per unit area (intensification). This significant effect of settlement size—a proxy for population size in these high-density tell centers—cannot be explained as an underlying chronological trend (e.g., gradual soil deterioration): the waxing and waning of a major urban cen-

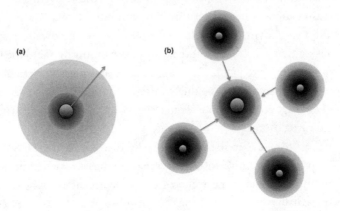

(a)   (b)

Figure 8.2 Schematics representing extensification scenarios in (a) northern Mesopotamia and (b) southwestern Germany. The intensity of the shading corresponds to labor inputs per unit area (e.g., manuring).

ter such as Tell Brak, for example, respects the size/manuring relationship but not a chronological one. The formation of "hollow ways" (routes of human/animal traffic) radiating out from third-millennium centers such as Brak and Hamoukar provides an eventual geoarchaeological correlate of this process (e.g., Ur 2015). Weed ecological comparison of the third-millennium cal BC assemblage from Tell Brak with present-day low- and high-input regimes confirms that a low-input, extensive agrosystem was in place (Bogaard, Styring, et al. 2016).

The farming landscapes of northern Mesopotamia did not lend themselves to large-scale gravity-flow irrigation; opportunities to sow crops in relatively well watered soils depended on proximity to streams/wadis. Crop water management was thus not subject to the same "frictions of distance" as manuring when regional farming populations became aggregated in growing cities. Stable carbon isotope analysis of the same samples/sites reveals strategic planting of wheat in wetter soils (whether naturally or artificially watered) than barley (likely because of its greater drought tolerance) from the Neolithic onward, continuing under urbanization (Styring, Charles, et al. 2017:fig. 5).

WEALTH INEQUALITY

Of the sites suitable for detailed agroecological analysis, three offered wide horizontal exposures of well-preserved living and storage spaces suitable for Gini coefficient calculations; a fourth site with a well-documented settlement layout but without archaeobotanical data was added to broaden the comparison.

Jerf el Ahmar is a mid- to late tenth-millennium cal BC Pre-Pottery Neolithic A settlement of approximately one hectare on the Middle Euphrates in Syria (Stordeur 2015) (figure 8.3a). We selected Phase II/W as a particularly well-preserved horizon. This settlement included several discrete rectangular-ovoid buildings surrounding a circular, semisubterranean structure (EA30) interpreted as a communal storage building (Whitlam and Bogaard 2017a:fig. S1; Stordeur 2015:fig. 91). According to the excavator, the surrounding buildings consisted more or less exclusively of living space (Stordeur 2015:210). The plan poses two challenges: defining households and distributing storage areas among them. Following the excavator's identification of possible household units (Stordeur

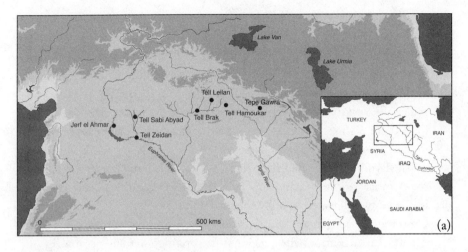

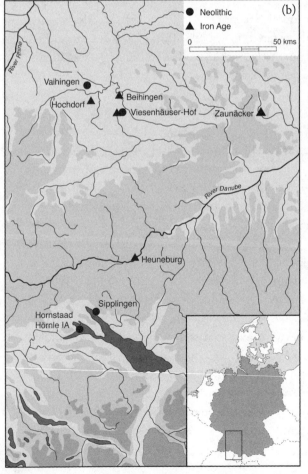

Figure 8.3 (a) Map of northern Mesopotamia showing sites included in Styring, Charles, et al. 2017 and/or this study; (b) map of southwestern Germany showing sites included in Styring, Rösch, et al. 2017 and this study.

2015:263–64, fig. 91), we considered two models: households were defined as (1) five individual buildings or contiguous clusters arranged in an ellipse around the communal storage building, or (2) two groupings of these structures with a shared plan. Individual buildings (if defined as separate households) represent the smallest houses in this study (mean floor area approximately 15 square meters; figure 8.4a).

With regard to the second problem, we considered two solutions: (1) assigning bin compartments within EA30 randomly to the surrounding structures; and (2) assigning bins to structures assorted based on their size (e.g., assigning the largest bin to the largest structure). Table 8.1 shows how Gini coefficients were calculated using methods 1 and 2, for both household models, including confidence intervals where appropriate. Both storage bin assignment strategies, for both models, converge on the inference that inequality levels were low, suggesting minimal wealth disparity.

Stable nitrogen isotope analysis of cereal grains from Jerf el Ahmar (Araus et al. 2014), corrected for aridity (cf. Styring, Ater, et al. 2016; Styring, Charles, et al. 2017), suggests that arable soils were rich in organic matter, plausibly from middening close to the settlement (manuring is unlikely because there is no evidence for animal management at the site). Farming practice here was therefore probably of a small-scale garden type. In sum, Jerf el Ahmar II/W resembles a small community of cultivator-hunter-foragers practicing horticultural crop management and maintaining an egalitarian ethos, powerfully represented by co-storage in communal building EA30.

Sabi Abyad in the Balikh drainage in Syria (figure 8.3a; Whitlam and Bogaard 2017a:fig. S2; Verhoeven and Kranendonk 1996:fig. 2.7) is a tell site extending over approximately one hectare where a late seventh-millennium (pre-Halaf) destruction by fire preserved the so-called Burnt Village horizon (Level 6). To address some ambiguity in the composition of households, two models were considered: a MAX version in which spaces and buildings were merged into households based on the excavators' comments (Verhoeven and Kranendonk 1996); and a MIN version involving minimal grouping of buildings as households.

Especially in the MAX model, household floor area (mean approximately 98 square meters) at Sabi Abyad is much higher than that at Jerf el Ahmar and also considerably higher than that at late eighth to late

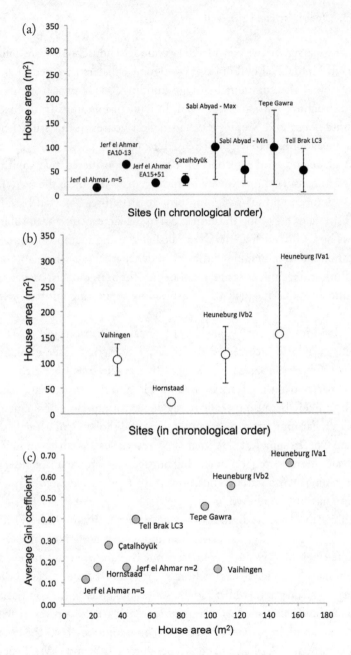

Figure 8.4 Household floor areas (mean m² ±1 SD) (a) in northern Mesopotamia, (b) in southwestern Germany, and (c) in relation to mean Gini coefficients (Cobb-Douglas versions). (In figure 8.4c, Sabi Abyad is excluded because of the problematic definition of households and contrasting results for MIN and MAX models [see table 8.2], illustrating the challenges of some archaeological data sets.)

Table 8.1 Gini coefficients for Jerf el Ahmar Phase II/W

Variable	5 households				2 households		
	Gini (living + storage)	Gini Cobb-Douglas ($\alpha = 0.25$)	Gini Cobb-Douglas ($\alpha = 0.50$)	Gini (living + storage)	Gini Cobb-Douglas ($\alpha = 0.25$)	Gini Cobb-Douglas ($\alpha = 0.50$)
Mean Gini across 10 random assignments	0.152	0.104	0.125	0.193	0.103	0.114
St. error	0.008	0.026	0.035	0.017	0.056	0.067
Gini from size-assorted assignments	0.160	0.097	0.138	0.211	0.160	0.181
Mean between random and size-assorted Gini	0.156	0.100	0.131	0.202	0.130	0.147

Note: Based on alternative assumptions on the relative importance of housing as a form of wealth (α) and using random and size-assorted assignments of bin compartments in a communal storage structure (EA30) to five surrounding structures defined as either five discrete households or two household groupings of the same building type. In the latter, the mean of the two possible random matches is given.

seventh-millennium cal BC Çatalhöyük in central Anatolia (n = 19, mean approximately 30 square meters [data from Green et al. in Demirergi et al. 2014]) (figure 8.4a). Sabi Abyad households may have been more extended. The many seal types in circulation at the time of the fire that destroyed the Burnt Village suggest co-storage of items owned by particular households in rectangular, small-roomed buildings (Akkermans and Schwartz 2003:140–41).

Table 8.2 shows that Gini coefficients for Sabi Abyad (both models) are distinctly higher than those calculated for Jerf el Ahmar, though there is overlap at 95 percent confidence. The Ginis for Sabi Abyad overlap with the range of horticultural ethnographic groups (mean Gini 0.27 [Borgerhoff Mulder et al. 2009:table 2]) and with other archaeological labor-limited economies (Fochesato and Bowles 2017; Kohler and Higgins 2016). Certain Sabi Abyad Ginis are higher, the most extreme being that based on storage area for the MIN model, perhaps reflecting uncertainty in distinguishing living from storage space (see Whitlam and Bogaard 2017b).

Sabi Abyad Level 6 was included in the agroecological study of Styring, Charles, and colleagues (2017), summarized above: at one hectare, it is the smallest of the sites in that study, and crop stable isotope analysis indicates relatively high levels of manuring, as expected for a small-scale community that intensively managed its arable landscape. In sum, the Gini coefficients and agroecological data point to the identification of Sabi Abyad as a community with modest inequality practicing horticultural, labor-limited farming.

The third case study is Tepe Gawra, east of the Tigris (figure 8.3a), in its Round House phase (Level XIA) (ca. 4200–3850 cal BC, Late Chalcolithic 2 period). Gill Stein (2012:135) cites Gawra XIA as an early instance of persistent social disparity and political centralization (Rothman 2002:88–97; Tobler 1950:plate VI). Like Jerf el Ahmar and Sabi Abyad, Tepe Gawra is small (approximately one hectare) and provides a broad horizontal exposure of housing for Gini coefficient calculation (Whitlam and Bogaard 2017a:fig. S3; Rothman 2002:fig. 5.25). The fortified, towerlike Round House contains domestic as well as storage rooms (cf. Rothman 2002:89, fig. 5.25). Two models were considered: (1) the Round House and rooms built against it represent a single household (n = 7 households), and (2) the Round House and abutting rooms are considered to be separate households (n = 8 households). Mean household size

Table 8.2 Gini coefficients for the study sites

Site	Phase	N	Type of wealth	Gini	St. error	Percentile CI Lower	Percentile CI Upper
Tell Sabi	Level 6	4	Living	0.356	0.037	0.256	0.404
Abyad	MAX		Storage	0.276	0.072	0.152	0.399
			Total	0.317	0.052	0.213	0.406
			CD 0.25	0.300	0.061	0.189	0.417
			CD 0.50	0.321	0.055	0.204	0.412
Tell Sabi	Level 6	6	Living	0.268	0.039	0.171	0.329
Abyad	MIN		Storage	0.555	0.057	0.425	0.645
			Total	0.282	0.045	0.182	0.357
			CD 0.25	0.476	0.054	0.344	0.556
			CD 0.50	0.388	0.041	0.287	0.445
Tepe Gawra	Level	7	Living	0.300	0.041	0.197	0.355
	XIA		Storage	0.523	0.054	0.366	0.575
			Total	0.344	0.048	0.210	0.405
			CD 0.25	0.464	0.057	0.302	0.524
			CD 0.50	0.405	0.054	0.254	0.467
Tepe Gawra	Level	8	Living	0.357	0.035	0.267	0.402
	XIA		Storage	0.564	0.055	0.404	0.631
			Total	0.385	0.048	0.261	0.444
			CD 0.25	0.501	0.063	0.329	0.563
			CD 0.50	0.450	0.057	0.288	0.509
Tell Brak	Level 16	4	Living	0.204	0.029	0.125	0.226
			Storage	0.496	0.030	0.393	0.505
			Total	0.361	0.038	0.243	0.375
			CD 0.25	0.432	0.033	0.318	0.442
			CD 0.50	0.360	0.034	0.246	0.374
Vaihingen		11	Living	0.153	0.019	0.110	0.184
			Storage	0.172	0.018	0.126	0.200
			Total	0.154	0.019	0.112	0.186
			CD 0.25	0.165	0.018	0.121	0.194
			CD 0.50	0.160	0.018	0.119	0.190
Hornstaad-	AH2	30	Living	0.171	0.008	0.152	0.187
Hörnle 1A			Storage	0.171	0.009	0.149	0.186
			Total	0.171	0.009	0.151	0.187
			CD 0.25	0.171	0.009	0.151	0.185
			CD 0.50	0.171	0.009	0.148	0.185
Heuneburg	IVb2	11	Living	0.274	0.033	0.186	0.318
			Storage	0.605	0.059	0.481	0.708
			Total	0.255	0.032	0.183	0.298
			CD 0.25	0.566	0.057	0.434	0.678
			CD 0.50	0.536	0.058	0.411	0.638

(*continued*)

Table 8.2 (*continued*)

Site	Phase	N	Type of wealth	Gini	St. error	Percentile CI Lower	Upper
Heuneburg	IVa1	8	Living	0.371	0.040	0.260	0.405
			Storage	0.665	0.074	0.506	0.810
			Total	0.374	0.034	0.285	0.408
			CD 0.25	0.645	0.083	0.473	0.810
			CD 0.50	0.673	0.070	0.523	0.798

Note: Based on the floor area (m²) dedicated to living and storage space per household, total area (living + storage), and the Cobb-Douglas (CD) production function (where α = 0.25 or 0.50); CI = 95% confidence interval, based on 0.025 and 0.975 percentiles from the distribution of the bootstrapped Gini coefficients. For Jerf el Ahmar, see table 8.1.

at Gawra (approximately 96 square meters) is very similar to that at Sabi Abyad (for the MAX model), including in its variability (figure 8.4a).

The Gini coefficients for both models of Gawra XIA households suggest higher levels of inequality than at Jerf el Ahmar and probably also Sabi Abyad, though again there is overlap at 95 percent confidence (tables 8.1–8.2). Ginis based on storage area and on the integrated Cobb-Douglas version approach or exceed mean values for land-limited agricultural communities (mean Gini 0.48 [Borgerhoff Mulder et al. 2009:table 2]), while those based on living or total area per household are intermediate between the mean Ginis of horticultural and land-limited systems.

No direct archaeobotanical evidence for farming practice at Gawra XIA is available. If its small size is interpreted in light of the extensification process identified by Styring, Charles, and colleagues (2017), we can postulate that its agricultural economy was founded on relatively high-intensity land management, at least compared with larger urban centers. In this scenario, the inequality represented in the domestic architecture was based on a form of political centralization that was not associated with radical agricultural extensification.

It could be that Gawra presents an example of a labor-limited agricultural economy with substantial levels of economic inequality, underlining the possible contribution of other aspects—such as a central position in trading networks—to economic differentiation. Alternatively, it could be that farming at Gawra was amplified by specialized animal traction, and thus farming at Gawra may well have been more land-limited than farming at Jerf al Ahmar and Sabi Abyad.

The possibility of a substantially labor-limited economy with significant wealth disparities is a scenario that may be important for understanding the initiation of truly urban centers elsewhere (where the depth of tell stratigraphy prevents direct observation of preurban phases [e.g., Oates et al. 2007]). This is because radical extensification, as observed at sites that grew to an urban size, itself requires a degree of lasting social inequality (i.e., to maintain specialized plow animals and to mobilize additional labor at harvest time [Halstead 1995]). Understanding the sources of inequality in labor-limited economies is therefore essential to an account of the transition to the sustained inequalities of the land-limited economy.

Finally, Tell Brak in the Khabur drainage (figure 8.3a) is a key site for understanding early urbanism in northern Mesopotamia (Oates et al. 2007). Level 20, roughly contemporary with Gawra XIA, included the "basalt threshold" building, a nonritual monumental building constructed when the site extended over fifty hectares and the process of agricultural extensification (Styring, Charles, et al. 2017) was under way. While Level 20 provides insufficient housing data for Gini calculation, Level 16 preserves three domestic buildings and a larger, niched structure (built in Level 18 and subsequently reused) with storage and cooking spaces variously interpreted as a nonritual elite building, contemporary with early phases of the Eye Temple (Whitlam and Bogaard 2017a:fig. S4; Emberling and McDonald 2003; Hald and Charles 2008; Oates et al. 2007).

The resulting Gini coefficients (table 8.2) provide minimal estimates of wealth disparity because the niched building was not completely uncovered and its total area is unknown. Nevertheless, as at Gawra, Gini coefficients based on storage area and the Cobb-Douglas function approach or exceed mean values for land-limited agricultural communities. These data are consistent with the view that extensive agriculture (the LC3 settlement was over 130 hectares) both depended on and fueled considerable wealth disparity among households by increasing pressure on proximate land within the site's growing arable catchment.

Completely excavated houses are lacking for third-millennium cal BC Brak, but the partially excavated oval complex in Area TC (mid-third millennium, Level 6), exceeding 600 square meters and including large-scale baking and storage facilities (Emberling and McDonald 2001, 2003; Hald and Charles 2008), may represent an elite mega-household (Ur and Colantoni 2010).

ARCHAEOLOGICAL APPLICATION 2, SOUTHWESTERN GERMANY

AGROECOLOGICAL CHARACTERIZATION

The analysis of farming practice focused on Neolithic (later sixth to third millennium cal BC) and early Iron Age (ca. 800–450 cal BC) sites in southwestern Germany (figure 8.3b). Relevant results are presented in detail elsewhere (Bogaard 2004, 2011a, 2011b; Bogaard et al. 2013; Bogaard, Hodgson, et al. 2016; Fraser et al. 2013; Styring, Maier, et al. 2016; Styring, Rösch, et al. 2017). Key findings are that Neolithic cultivators practiced intensive garden agriculture, with manuring and intensive tillage of long-established plots. The spatial extent of cultivation was very restricted, being difficult to detect in pollen diagrams (e.g., Kalis et al. 2003). Both ecological analysis of weed flora and stable isotope analysis of crop remains reveal variation in crop growing conditions within this horticultural system, some of which relates to distinct practices by households or household groups managing different plots/parts of the landscape (Bogaard et al. 2011; Styring, Maier, et al. 2016). Some cereal crops were more intensively manured than others, reflecting strategic use of manure/midden material as a limited resource (Styring, Maier, et al. 2016). Use of cattle traction is attested at low levels, especially in the Late Neolithic, but did not have a significant impact on cultivation scale (Bogaard 2011a).

Data from the Bronze Age are comparatively few but consistent with some modest expansion, suggested by both weed ecological analysis of available samples (Bogaard 2011a) and geomorphological evidence for increased erosion (Lang 2003). Clear indications of arable extensification emerge in the early Iron Age (ca. 800–450 cal BC), which in southwestern Germany features the appearance of fortified hilltop centers alongside small rural settlements. There is evidence of extensification from arable weed data (i.e., lower soil fertility and mechanical disturbance compared with the Neolithic) combined with pollen and geomorphological indications of expansion of open anthropogenic landscapes (see Styring, Rösch, et al. 2017). Arable extensification was, however, moderate enough that it did not prevent continued, and even intensified, manuring of fields: crop stable nitrogen isotope results show particularly intensive manuring of hulled six-row barley (Styring et al. 2018), attested in malting ditches for brewing beer on a large scale at Hochdorf (Stika 1996). Consumption of alcoholic beverages, including indigenous beer as well as Mediterranean wine, features in prestigious feasting by Celtic chieftains through this period (Dietler 1990). Figure 8.2b shows a schematic summarizing the agroecological situation in the early Iron Age, with modestly extensive production around rural settlements and mobilization of surplus to fortified hilltop centers (Fischer et al. 2010).

WEALTH INEQUALITY

Two Neolithic settlements and one early Iron Age fortified hilltop were available for Gini coefficient calculation on the basis of household living and storage space; these sites were selected because of their relatively broad horizontal exposures and well-documented architecture.

Vaihingen is a *Linearbandkeramik* settlement (dated to the later sixth millennium); eleven well-defined longhouses (mean area approximately 105 square meters) with traces of raised storage areas at their southern ends were included in Gini calculations (Whitlam and Bogaard 2017a: fig. S5; Bogaard et al. 2017:fig. 9). Hornstaad-Hörnle 1A is a later Neolithic settlement of approximately forty small two-roomed houses (including thirty completely excavated structures averaging approximately 23 square meters), destroyed by fire in 3910 BC (Whitlam and Bogaard 2017a:fig. S6; Styring, Maier, et al. 2016:fig. 2). Charring preserved stores of unthreshed cereals (whole ears) that had fallen from the roof space of each house; the roof storage area was estimated as proportional to the ground (living) floor area, though a more unequal distribution of storage is possible. Both Vaihingen and Hornstaad show direct evidence for intensive garden agriculture as outlined above, and clustering of isotope or weed ecological values from these sites points to farming decisions at the level of the household and/or house group (Bogaard et al. 2011; Styring, Maier, et al. 2016).

Whether based on living, storage, total area, or the Cobb-Douglas integrated version, the Gini coefficients for both sites are remarkably low, suggesting minimal wealth disparity (table 8.2). These values are lower than those reported for wealth inequality in ethnographic cases of labor-limited (forager and horticultural) economies (mean Gini 0.27 [Borgerhoff Mulder et al. 2009:table 2]). They overlap with those calculated for Jerf el Ahmar (table 8.1) and, at 95 percent confidence, with somewhat higher Ginis reported for Çatalhöyük in Turkey and for Early Pueblo communities of southwestern Colorado (Fochesato and Bowles 2017; Kohler and Higgins 2016). Vaihingen and Hornstaad have similar Ginis despite marked differences in absolute house area (figure 8.4b), cultural context, and date.

The Gini coefficients for the Heuneburg Early Iron Age fortified hilltop (Phases IVb2 and IVa1, corresponding with construction/use of the enclosing "Mediterranean" mud-brick wall), present a clear contrast with the Neolithic sites (table 8.2). This analysis uses household clusters (living, [metallurgical] workshop, and raised storage buildings) separated by ditches on the fortified hilltop, as defined by Siegfried Kurz (2010:fig. 10; Whitlam and Bogaard 2017a:fig. S7), and measurements of plans by Egon Gersbach (1996). (Workshops and storage structures were grouped together as assets, distinct from living space—see Whitlam and Bogaard 2017b). As Kurz (2010:figs. 10–11) emphasized, the layout suggests a dominant household set apart from smaller "retainer" households. Mean household area (approximately 154 square meters in phase IVa) is the highest in this study but also highly variable (figure 8.4b). Gini coefficients, especially based on storage areas and the Cobb-Douglas production function (table 8.2), suggest much higher levels of inequality than in the Neolithic cases, well exceeding the mean of ethnographic land-limited agrarian economies (mean Gini 0.480 [Borgerhoff Mulder et al. 2009:table 2]).

The agroecological evidence summarized above, including from the Heuneburg itself, suggests that more-extensive cereal agriculture in the Early Iron Age, relative to the Neolithic, produced the agricultural surpluses mobilized by elites at central sites (figure 8.2b) (cf. Fischer et al. 2010). Moreover, we think it likely that strategic manuring of barley, used in beer brewing, reflected the importance of drinking and feasting to the prevailing political economy (Styring, Rösch, et al. 2017). Weed data pointing to extensification are observed at rural as well as central sites, suggesting that extensification took place regardless of settlement type. It seems, then, that elite involvement in farming practice involved mobilization/extraction (figure 8.2b), plausibly within lineage groups maintaining households on fortified hilltops (cf. Kurz 2010).

While extensification facilitated the emergence of new political centers on fortified hilltops in southwestern Germany, expansion of farming probably both preceded this horizon and also occurred in regions where additional factors such as trade links with the Mediterranean did not precipitate urbanizing phenomena. For example, evidence of earlier extensification, from the Late Bronze Age onward, is emerging in other regions such as the Lower Rhine basin, where "chiefly centers" did not develop in the Early Iron Age (Zerl, forthcoming). Evidence of extensification without elite formation suggests that the expansion of cereal farming may have represented a set of converging factors, including the broadening of crop spectra (through prehistoric "food globalization"—e.g., the spread of millets from East Asia [Jones et al. 2011]), changes in the management of draft animals, and nonelite utilization of farming surpluses.

DISCUSSION

Herein we analyze living and storage space data to assess lasting inequality among households using the Gini coefficient. In agreement with other recent uses of such data (Fochesato and Bowles 2017; Kohler and Higgins 2016), we find that storage areas are typically more unequal than living areas, though there are exceptions (Jerf el Ahmar, Sabi Abyad MAX model), notably, where multiple residential units probably shared storage space. The very low Gini coefficients computed for Jerf el Ahmar and for the two Neolithic sites in southwestern Germany may reflect in part the indirect inference of storage area in these cases, but the strikingly equal living area in these three sites suggests that this cannot be the entire story. Moreover, other evidence points to the possibility of very low inequality, including the fact of communal storage at Jerf el Ahmar and the ecological challenges of early temperate European farming that would have placed a high value on coinsurance and other forms of mutual aid.

Both regions show a tendency for household wealth inequality to increase with household size. Figure 8.4c shows a strong positive relationship between the mean floor area of households and mean Gini coefficients (Cobb-Douglas versions only, as the most plausible estimates of household wealth) (Pearson's $r = 0.78$, t-statistic 3.2321, p-value 0.014).

Figure 8.4c suggests that larger households capable of juggling simultaneous activities (e.g., farming, herding, craft production) are more prone
to the development of lasting inequalities than are smaller units (cf. Flannery 2002), though Vaihingen is an exception.

Table 8.2 and figure 8.4c also raise the possibility of more acute inequality at the Heuneburg than in early urban northern Mesopotamia.
While more data are needed to explore such a comparison further, it may
have implications for the differential sustainability of these social systems.
Urbanization and institutionalized social inequality persisted (albeit in
varying forms) for millennia at Tell Brak (Oates et al. 2007), while the
Heuneburg polity lasted less than two hundred years (Fernández-Götz
and Krausse 2013; Fernández-Götz et al. 2014).

We have largely observed the expected associations between inten-
sive/small-scale horticultural farming and low social inequality, on the
one hand, and more extensive, lower-input farming with higher levels of
social inequality under urbanization, on the other. Identifying exceptions
to this pattern (e.g., horticulture with high inequality, or more-extensive
farming with low inequality) may be crucial for understanding shifts
from one to the other.

We have indeed encountered such useful anomalies, as at Tepe Gawra
Level XIA, where a very small site with an agrosystem that was likely less
land limited than those of huge urban centers was associated with relatively high levels of social inequality. Gawra offers the kind of scenario
that might pertain to the initiation of new political centers that later
attracted demographic nucleation, requiring the development of radically
extensive, land-limited farming.

While lasting inequality was presumably in place prior to radical extensification in northern Mesopotamia (cf. Halstead 1995), the more modest
form of agricultural extensification observed in southwestern Germany
likely did not have the same social prerequisites (cf. Håkansson 2010).
There are indications that processes of modest extensification occurred already during the Bronze Age, the best data set being that from the Lower
Rhine basin, where an extensifying trend seems to begin in the Late
Bronze Age (Zerl, forthcoming), without any radical social corollaries.

Our combination of archaeological and economic methods in this
study has enabled us to refine hypotheses regarding the role of labor- versus land-limited farming economies in the emergence of lasting social in-

equality in two contrasting sequences of urbanization. The specific causal linkages between lasting social inequality and agroecological change appear to have been different in northern Mesopotamia and southwestern Germany. In both regions, agricultural extensification made urbanization possible, but the nature and degree of agroecological change, and its social prerequisites and consequences, were distinct in each region.

Disentangling these factors is necessary for building more-plausible, multicausal accounts of lasting inequality and urbanization (cf. Laslett 2000). This requires an integrated approach combining state-of-the-art methods for assessing inequality from material culture across a range of different types and scales of society (Fochesato and Bowles 2017), with refined approaches to archaeological inference on key variables, including agricultural regimes (e.g., Bogaard, Hodgson, et al. 2016; Bogaard, Styring, et al. 2016; Styring, Ater, et al. 2016; Styring, Charles, et al. 2017; Styring, Maier, et al. 2016; Styring, Rösch, et al. 2017).

ACKNOWLEDGMENTS

We are grateful to the editors for the invitation to take part in the SAA symposium and subsequent Amerind Seminar. The European Research Council funded the agroecological work (AGRICURB project, grant no. 312785; PI Bogaard). Collaborative work with Bowles and Fochesato grew out of a Santa Fe Institute workshop, "Coevolution of Behaviors and Institutions," held in January 2015. We thank Manuel Fernández-Götz, Arno Harwath, and Christiane Krahn-Schigol for plans and/or advice pertaining to the Heuneburg, Hornstaad Hörnle 1A, and Vaihingen, respectively.

REFERENCES CITED

Akkermans, Peter M. M. G., and Glenn M. Schwartz. 2003. *The Archaeology of Syria: From Complex Hunter-Gatherers to Early Urban Societies (c.16,000–300 BC)*. Cambridge University Press, Cambridge.

Araus, José L., Juan P. Ferrio, Jordi Voltas, Mònica Aguilera, and Ramón Buxó. 2014. Agronomic Conditions and Crop Evolution in Ancient Near East Agriculture. *Nature Communications* 5:3953.

Bogaard, Amy. 2004. *Neolithic Farming in Central Europe*. Routledge, London.

———. 2005. "Garden Agriculture" and the Nature of Early Farming in Europe and the Near East. *World Archaeology* 37:177–96.

————. 2011a. Farming Practice and Society in the Central European Neolithic and Bronze Age: An Archaeobotanical Response to the Secondary Products Revolution Model. In *The Dynamics of Neolithisation in Europe: Studies in Honour of Andrew Sherratt*, edited by Angelos Hadjikoumis, Erick Robinson, and Sarah Viner-Daniels, pp. 266–83. Oxbow Books, Oxford, U.K.

————. 2011b. *Plant Use and Crop Husbandry in an Early Neolithic Village: Vaihingen an der Enz, Baden-Württemberg.* Frankfurter Archäologische Schriften. Habelt-Verlag, Bonn.

Bogaard, Amy, Rose-Marie Arbogast, Renate Ebersbach, Rebecca A. Fraser, Corina Knipper, Christiane Krahn, Marguerita Schäfer, Amy Styring, and Rüdiger Krause. 2017. The Bandkeramik Settlement of Vaihingen an der Enz, Kreis Ludwigsburg (Baden-Württemberg): An Integrated Perspective on Land Use, Economy and Diet. *Germania* 94(2016):1–60.

Bogaard, Amy, Rebecca A. Fraser, Tim H. E. Heaton, Michael Wallace, Petra Vaiglova, Michael Charles, Glynis Jones, et al. 2013. Crop Manuring and Intensive Land Management by Europe's First Farmers. *PNAS* 110:12589–94.

Bogaard, Amy, and Paul Halstead. 2015. Subsistence Practices and Social Routine in Neolithic Southern Europe. In *The Oxford Handbook of Neolithic Europe*, edited by Chris Fowler, Jan Harding, and Daniela Hofmann, pp. 385–410. Oxford University Press, Oxford.

Bogaard, Amy, Tim H. E. Heaton, Paul Poulton, and Ines Merbach. 2007. The Impact of Manuring on Nitrogen Isotope Ratios in Cereals: Archaeological Implications for Reconstruction of Diet and Crop Management Practices. *Journal of Archaeological Science* 34:335–43.

Bogaard, Amy, John Hodgson, Erika Nitsch, Glynis Jones, Amy Styring, Charlotte Diffey, John Pouncett, et al. 2016. Combining Functional Weed Ecology and Crop Stable Isotope Ratios to Identify Cultivation Intensity: A Comparison of Cereal Production Regimes in Haute Provence, France, and Asturias, Spain. *Vegetation History and Archaeobotany* 25:57–73.

Bogaard, Amy, and Glynis Jones. 2007. Neolithic Farming in Britain and Central Europe: Contrast or Continuity? In *Going Over: The Mesolithic-Neolithic Transition in North-West Europe*, edited by Alasdair Whittle and Vicki Cummings, pp. 357–75. British Academy, London.

Bogaard, Amy, Rüdiger Krause, and Hans-Christoph Strien. 2011. Towards a Social Geography of Cultivation and Plant Use in an Early Farming Community: Vaihingen an der Enz, South-West Germany. *Antiquity* 85:395–416.

Bogaard, Amy, Amy Styring, Mohammed Ater, Younes Hmimsa, Laura Green, Elizabeth Stroud, Jade Whitlam, et al. 2016. From Traditional Farming in Morocco to Early Urban Agroecology in Northern Mesopotamia: Combining Present-Day Arable Weed Surveys and Crop "Isoscapes" to Reconstruct Past Agrosystems in (Semi-)arid Regions. *Environmental Archaeology.* Published online, December 21, 2016, http://dx.doi.org/10.1080/14614103.2016.1261217.

Bogucki, Peter. 1999. *The Origins of Human Society*. Blackwell, Oxford, U.K.

Borgerhoff Mulder, Monique, Samuel Bowles, Tom Hertz, Adrian Bell, Jan Beise, Greg Clark, Ila Fazzio, et al. 2009. Intergenerational Wealth Transmission and the Dynamics of Inequality in Small-Scale Societies. *Science* 326:682–88.

Boserup, Ester. 1965. *The Conditions of Agricultural Growth*. Aldine, New York.

Bowles, Samuel, Eric Alden Smith, and Monique Borgerhoff Mulder. 2010. The Emergence and Persistence of Inequality in Premodern Societies: Introduction to the Special Section. *Current Anthropology* 51:7–17.

Brookfield, Harold C. 1972. Intensification and Disintensification in Pacific Agriculture: A Theoretical Approach. *Pacific Viewpoint* 13:211–38.

Childe, V. Gordon. 1929. *The Danube in Prehistory*. Clarendon Press, Oxford, U.K.

———. 1950. The Urban Revolution. *Town Planning Review* 21:3–17.

———. 1957. *The Dawn of European Civilization*. Routledge, London.

Demirergi, G. Arzu, Katherine C. Twiss, Amy Bogaard, Laura Green, Philippa Ryan, and Shahina Farid. 2014. Of Bins, Basins, and Banquets: Storing, Handling, and Sharing at Neolithic Çatalhöyük. In *Integrating Çatalhöyük: The 2000–2008 Seasons*, edited by Ian Hodder, pp. 91–108. Cotsen Institute of Archaeology, Los Angeles.

Dietler, Michael. 1990. Driven by Drink: The Role of Drinking in the Political Economy and the Case of Early Iron Age France. *Journal of Anthropological Archaeology* 9:352–406.

Emberling, Geoff, and Helen McDonald. 2001. Excavations at Tell Brak 2000: Preliminary Report. *Iraq* 63:21–54.

———. 2003. Excavations at Tell Brak 2001–2002: Preliminary Report. *Iraq* 65:1–75.

Erickson, Clark L. 2006. Intensification, Political Economy and the Farming Community: In Defense of a Bottom-Up Perspective of the Past. In *Agricultural Strategies*, edited by Joyce Marcus and Charles Stanish, pp. 334–63. Cotsen Institute of Archaeology, Los Angeles.

Fernández-Götz, Manuel, and Dirk Krausse. 2013. Rethinking Early Iron Age Urbanisation in Central Europe: The Heuneburg Site and Its Archaeological Environment. *Antiquity* 87:473–87.

Fernández-Götz, Manuel, Holger Wendling, and Katja Winger. 2014. Introduction: New Perspectives on Iron Age Urbanism. In *Paths to Complexity: Centralisation and Urbanisation in Iron Age Europe*, edited by Manuel Fernández-Götz, Holger Wendling, and Katja Winger, pp. 2–14. Oxbow Books, Oxford, U.K.

Fischer, Elske, Manfred Rösch, Marion Sillmann, Otto Ehrmann, Helga Liese-Kleiber, Ricarda Voigt, A. Stobbe, et al. 2010. Landnutzung im Umkreis der Zentralorte Hohenasperg, Heuneburg und Ipf: Archäobotanische und archäozoologische Untersuchungen und Modellberechnungen zum Ertragspotential von Ackerbau und Viehhaltung. In *"Fürstensitze" und Zentralorte der frühen Kelten: Abschlusskolloquium des DFG-Schwerpunktprogramms 1171 in Stuttgart, 12–15 Oktober 2009*, vol. 2, edited by Dirk Krausse, pp. 195–266. Konrad Theiss, Stuttgart.

Flannery, Kent V. 2002. The Origins of the Village Revisited: From Nuclear to Extended Households. *American Antiquity* 67:417–33.

Fletcher, Roland. 1995. *The Limits of Settlement Growth: A Theoretical Outline.* Cambridge University Press, Cambridge.

Fochesato, Mattia, and Samuel Bowles. 2017. Wealth Inequalities over the Past Eleven Thousand Years. SFI Working Paper 2017-08-032, pp. 1–21.

Fraser, Rebecca, Amy Bogaard, Tim Heaton, Michael Charles, Glynis Jones, Bent T. Christensen, Paul Halstead, et al. 2011. Manuring and Stable Nitrogen Isotope Ratios in Cereals and Pulses: Towards a New Archaeobotanical Inference of Land Use and Dietary Practices. *Journal of Archaeological Science* 38:2790–2804.

Fraser, Rebecca A., Amy Bogaard, Marguerita Schäfer, Rose-Marie Arbogast, and Tim H. E. Heaton. 2013. Integrating Botanical, Faunal and Human Stable Carbon and Nitrogen Isotope Values to Reconstruct Land Use and Palaeodiet at LBK Vaihingen an der Enz, Baden-Württemberg. *World Archaeology* 45:492–517.

Gersbach, Egon. 1996. *Baubefunde der Perioden IIIb–Ia der Heuneburg.* P. von Zabern, Mainz am Rhein.

Gilman, Antonio. 1981. The Development of Social Stratification in Bronze Age Europe. *Current Anthropology* 22:1–23.

Gurven, Michael, Monique Borgerhoff Mulder, Paul L. Hooper, Hillard Kaplan, Rob Quinlan, Rebecca Sear, Eric Schniter, et al. 2010. Domestication Alone Does Not Lead to Inequality: Intergenerational Wealth Transmission Among Horticulturalists. *Current Anthropology* 51:49–64.

Håkansson, N. Thomas. 2010. History and the Problem of Synchronic Models. *Current Anthropology* 51:105–7.

Hald, Mette Mari, and Mike Charles. 2008. Storage of Crops During the Fourth and Third Millennia BC at the Settlement Mound of Tell Brak, North-East Syria. *Vegetation History and Archaeobotany* 17 (Suppl. 1):35–41.

Halstead, Paul. 1989. The Economy Has a Normal Surplus: Economic Stability and Social Change Among Early Farming Communities of Thessaly, Greece. In *Bad Year Economics: Cultural Responses to Risk and Uncertainty*, edited by Paul Halstead and John O'Shea, pp. 68–80. Cambridge University Press, Cambridge.

———. 1995. Plough and Power: The Economic and Social Significance of Cultivation with the Ox-Drawn Ard in the Mediterranean. *Bulletin on Sumerian Agriculture* 8:11–22.

———. 2014. *Two Oxen Ahead: Pre-mechanised Farming in the Mediterranean.* Wiley-Blackwell, Oxford, U.K.

Halstead, Paul, and John O'Shea. 1982. A Friend in Need Is a Friend Indeed: Social Storage and the Origins of Social Ranking. In *Ranking, Resource and*

Exchange, edited by Colin Renfrew and Stephen Shennan, pp. 92–99. Cambridge University Press, Cambridge.

Jacomet, Stefanie, Renate Ebersbach, Örni Akeret, Ferran Antolín, Tilman Baum, Amy Bogaard, Christoph Brombacher, et al. 2016. On-Site Data Cast Doubt on the Hypothesis of Shifting Cultivation in the Late Neolithic (c. 4300–2400 cal BC): Landscape Management as an Alternative Paradigm. *Holocene* 26:1858–74.

Jones, Glynis. 2002. Weed Ecology as a Method for the Archaeobotanical Recognition of Crop Husbandry Practices. *Acta Palaeobotanica* 42:185–93.

Jones, Martin, Harriet Hunt, Emma Lightfoot, Diane Lister, Xinyi Liu, and Giedre Motuzaite-Matuzeviciute. 2011. Food Globalisation in Prehistory. *World Archaeology* 43:665–75.

Kalis, Arie J., Josef Merkt, and Jürgen Wunderlich. 2003. Environmental Changes During the Holocene Climatic Optimum in Central Europe—Human Impact and Natural Causes. *Quaternary Science Reviews* 22:33–79.

Kohler, Timothy A., and Rebecca Higgins. 2016. Quantifying Household Inequality in Early Pueblo Villages. *Current Anthropology* 57:690–97.

Kohler, Timothy A., Michael E. Smith, Amy Bogaard, Gary M. Feinman, Christian E. Peterson, Alleen Betzenhauser, Matthew Pailes, et al. 2017. Greater Post-Neolithic Wealth Disparities in Eurasia than in North and Mesoamerica. *Nature*. doi:10.1038/nature24646.

Kurz, Siegfried. 2010. Zur Genese und Entwicklung der Heuneburg in der späten Hallstattzeit. *"Fürstensitze" und Zentralorte der frühen Kelten: Abschlusskolloquium des DFG-Schwerpunktprogramms 1171 in Stuttgart, 12–15 Oktober 2009*, vol. 2, edited by Dirk Krausse, pp. 239–56. Konrad Theiss, Stuttgart.

Lang, Andreas. 2003. Phases of Soil Erosion-Derived Colluviation in the Loess Hills of South Germany. *Catena* 51:209–21.

Laslett, Barbara. 2000. The Poverty of (Monocausal) Theory: A Comment on Charles Tilly's Durable Inequality. *Comparative Studies in Society and History* 42:475–81.

Lenski, Gerhard E. 1966. *Power and Privilege: A Theory of Social Stratification*. McGraw-Hill, New York.

Marcus, Joyce, and Charles Stanish (editors). 2006. *Agricultural Strategies*. Cotsen Institute of Archaeology, Los Angeles, Calif.

McClatchie, Meriel, Amy Bogaard, Sue Colledge, Nicki J. Whitehouse, Rick J. Schulting, Philip Barratt, and T. Rowan McLaughlin. 2016. Farming and Foraging in Neolithic Ireland: An Archaeobotanical Perspective. *Antiquity* 90:302–18.

Morrison, Kathleen D. 1994. The Intensification of Production: Archaeological Approaches. *Journal of Archaeological Method and Theory* 1:111–59.

Netting, Robert McC. 1971. *The Ecological Approach to Cultural Study*. McCaleb Module in Anthropology. Addison-Wesley Modular Publications, Reading, Mass.

————. 1993. *Smallholders, Householders*. Stanford University Press, Stanford.

Oates, Joan, Augusta McMahon, Philip Karsgaard, Salam Al Quntar, and Jason Ur. 2007. Early Mesopotamian Urbanism: A New View from the North. *Antiquity* 81:585–600.

Postgate, Nicholas. 1992. *Early Mesopotamia*. Routledge, London.

Rothman, Mitchell S. 2002. *Tepe Gawra: The Evolution of a Small, Prehistoric Center in Northern Iraq*. Museum Monograph 112. University of Pennsylvania, Philadelphia.

Rowley-Conwy, Peter. 1981. Slash and Burn in the Temperate European Neolithic. In *Farming Practice in British Prehistory*, edited by Roger Mercer, pp. 85–96. Edinburgh University Press, Edinburgh.

Scott, James C. 2009. *The Art of Not Being Governed: An Anarchist History of Upland South-East Asia*. Yale University Press, New Haven, Conn.

Shenk, Mary K., Monique Borgerhoff Mulder, Jan Beise, Greg Clark, William Irons, Donna Leonetti, Bobbi S. Low, et al. 2010. Intergenerational Wealth Transmission Among Agriculturalists: Foundations of Agrarian Inequality. *Current Anthropology* 51:65–84.

Stein, Gill J. 2012. The Development of Indigenous Social Complexity in Late Chalcolithic Upper Mesopotamia in the 5th–4th Millennia BC—An Initial Assessment. *Origini* 34:125–51.

Stika, Hans-Peter. 1996. Traces of a Possible Celtic Brewery in Eberdingen-Hochdorf, Kreis Ludwigsburg, Southwest Germany. *Vegetation History and Archaeobotany* 5:81–88.

Stordeur, Danielle. 2015. *Le village de Jerf el Ahmar (Syrie, 9500–8700 av. J.-C.): L'architecture, miroir d'une société néolithique complexe*. CNRS, Paris.

Styring, Amy K., Mohammed Ater, Younes Hmimsa, Rebecca Fraser, Holly Miller, Reinder Neef, Jessica A. Pearson, and Amy Bogaard. 2016. Disentangling the Effect of Farming Practice from Aridity on Crop Stable Isotope Values: A Present-Day Model from Morocco and Its Application to Early Farming Sites in the Eastern Mediterranean. *Anthropocene Review* 3:2–22.

Styring, A., M. Charles, F. Fantone, M. M. Hald, A. McMahon, R. H. Meadow, G. Nicholls, et al. 2017. Isotope Evidence for Agricultural Extensification Reveals How the World's First Cities Were Fed. *Nature Plants*. doi:10.1038/nplants.2017.76.

Styring, Amy, Ursula Maier, Elisabeth Stephan, Helmut Schlichtherle, and Amy Bogaard. 2016. Cultivation of Choice: New Insights into Farming Practices at Neolithic Lakeshore Sites. *Antiquity* 90:95–110.

Styring, Amy, Manfred Rösch, Elisabeth Stephan, Hans-Peter Stika, Elske Fischer, Marion Sillmann, and Amy Bogaard. 2017. Centralisation and Long-Term Change in Farming Regimes: Comparing Agricultural Practice in Neolithic and Iron Age South-West Germany. *Proceedings of the Prehistoric Society* 83:357–381. doi: 10.1017/ppr.2017.3.

Tilly, Charles. 1998. *Durable Inequality*. University of California Press, Berkeley.

Tobler, Arthur. 1950. *Excavations at Tepe Gawra*, vol. 2. University of Pennsylvania Museum, Philadelphia.

Ur, Jason A. 2015. Urban Adaptations to Climate Change in Northern Mesopotamia. In *Climate and Ancient Societies*, edited by Susanne Kerner, Rachael J. Dann, and Pernille Bangsgaard, pp. 69–96. Museum Tusculanum Press, Copenhagen.

Ur, Jason A., and Carlo Colantoni. 2010. The Cycle of Production, Preparation, and Consumption in a Northern Mesopotamian City. In *Inside Ancient Kitchens: New Directions in the Study of Daily Meals and Feasts*, edited by Elizabeth A. Klarich, pp. 55–82. University Press of Colorado, Boulder.

van der Veen, Marijke. 1992. *Crop Husbandry Regimes: An Archaeobotanical Study of Farming in Northern England*. J. R. Collis Publications, Sheffield, U.K.

Verhoeven, Marc, and Peter Kranendonk. 1996. The Excavations: Stratigraphy and Architecture. In *Tell Sabi Abyad: The Late Neolithic Settlement*, edited by Peter M. M. G. Akkermans, pp. 25–118. Nederlands Historich-Archaeologisch Instituut, Istanbul/Leiden.

Wallace, Michael, Glynis Jones, Michael Charles, Rebecca Fraser, Paul Halstead, Tim H. E. Heaton, and Amy Bogaard. 2013. Stable Carbon Isotope Analysis as a Direct Means of Inferring Crop Water Status and Water Management Practices. *World Archaeology* 45:388–409.

Wallace, Michael P., Glynis Jones, Michael Charles, Rebecca Fraser, Tim H. E. Heaton, and Amy Bogaard. 2015. Stable Carbon Isotope Evidence for Neolithic and Bronze Age Crop Water Management in the Eastern Mediterranean and Southwest Asia. *PLoS ONE* 10(6): e0127085. doi:10.1371/journal. pone.0127085.

Whitlam, Jade, and Amy Bogaard. 2017a. Supplementary Figures, Chapter 8. https://core.tdar.org/document/437490/supplementary-figures-chapter-8 -bogaard-et-al.

———. 2017b. Supplementary Information, Chapter 8, Bogaard et al. https:// core.tdar.org/document/437489/supplementary-information-chapter-8 -bogaard-et-al.

Wilkinson, Tony J. 2003. *Archaeological Landscapes of the Near East*. University of Arizona Press, Tucson.

Zerl, Tanja. Forthcoming. *Archäobotanische Untersuchungen zur Landwirtschaft und Ernährung während der Bronze- und Eisenzeit in der Niederrheinischen Bucht*. Rheinische Ausgrabungen 78. Phillipp von Zabern, Darmstadt.

9

The Trajectory of Social Inequality in Ancient Mesopotamia

Elizabeth C. Stone

Early complex societies, by definition, are characterized by a ruling elite whose organizational abilities are associated with the development of cities or administrative centers, monumental public buildings, full-time craft specialists, and a bureaucracy to maintain the system. Where scholars disagree is whether this revolution in human organization benefited only the apex of society or whether the economies of scale associated with complexity were harnessed to improve the lot of the majority of the inhabitants in at least some instances (Blanton 1998; Ehenreich et al. 1995; Flannery and Marcus 2012; Trigger 1993). All early civilizations manifest the elaborate public buildings that housed the elites and enabled the bureaucracy to manage these large sociopolitical systems. The question posed here is whether this was universally accompanied by the types of grinding inequality that characterize modern society and is especially reflected in health, stature, and housing to this day (Tilly 1998). If this were not the case, could some of these early societies have maintained a measure of equality in the body politic beneath the institutions associated with the state? Resolving this issue through analyses of housing or perhaps mortuary data should be possible (Smith 1994), although such studies have often been hampered by the predilection of archaeologists to investigate the more elaborate "royal" graves rather than those of the larger population, to prioritize the excavation of public buildings over private houses, and to focus on urban sites instead of small rural villages (table 9.1).

Michael Smith and colleagues (2014) stress that the information provided by household studies differs in significant ways from projects focusing on mortuary data and may therefore result in differing assessments of inequality. Whereas houses were designed to accommodate households, graves were often individual, and while some shelter is an almost

Table 9.1 Public and domestic architecture from excavations and satellite imagery

Source	Public architecture %	Domestic architecture %	Public architecture (ha.)	Domestic architecture (ha.)	Total (ha.)
Excavations	65.12	34.88	64.47	34.53	99.00
Satellite data	34.33	65.67	87.66	167.67	255.33

universal human requirement, disposal of the dead is more culturally sensitive and often reflects prestige, which does not necessarily correlate with wealth. Burials may be individual or collective, may utilize exposure, burial, or cremation, and may or may not include grave goods. Although it has long been argued that grave goods reflect the status of the deceased (Binford 1971; Peebles and Kus 1977; Tainter 1978), this should not be taken for granted.

In many ways, southern Mesopotamia is good place to study social inequality. The mud-bricks used for both public and domestic architecture had no recycle value, and the use of clay tablets has resulted in the preservation of a rich written record that can often be directly associated with the buildings—whether public or private—within which they were found. Moreover, despite the limited field research that has been conducted since Iraq's invasion of Kuwait in 1990, there exists a long history of excavation that did not merely focus on public buildings but also investigated some broad areas of private houses and graves. Following the third millennium, the cuneiform documentation included records generated by private individuals as well as public institutions. Although areas were sometimes set aside as cemeteries, burial within domestic contexts was also common, enabling direct comparison between house size and the grave goods included with the associated burials. Thus texts, houses, and burials can be used together to focus on the issue of social inequality. However, the heyday of Mesopotamian archaeology was in the 1930s, long before modern methods of excavation and analysis were developed, and little archaeological research has been carried out since the First Gulf War (1990–1991). Indeed, whether burials without objects were always reported in the earlier publications remains unclear. The result is that the linkage between house, tablet, and burial can only occasionally be achieved. Moreover, almost no information is provided on why particular areas within the archaeological sites were selected for excavation.

The issue of site selection is a serious problem. Most excavations focused on large urban sites and on the investigation of individual dwellings rather than residential neighborhoods. These houses generally exhibit a more extensive use of baked brick than most examples from the few broad excavation areas, suggesting that many, perhaps all, of these were investigated because, unlike their mud-brick contemporaries, their baked-brick walls were visible on the surface. In our work at Mashkanshapir, we were sometimes able to map whole house plans based on the surface traces of such baked-brick walls (Stone and Zimansky 2004), but this was much less possible for the majority of the domestic architecture, which was made of mud-brick. We also cleared the plan of one example and excavated a sounding within it. Although this building shared the domestic features of the mud-brick houses that we investigated, one of our finds from this small excavation was an unbaked door sealing typical of centralized administrative activities (Stone 1990). These data suggest that the single houses selected by archaeologists for excavation are less likely to be representative of the overall pattern of domestic architecture than those from the investigation of broader residential areas.

But the recent political history of Iraq has had one beneficent effect. The 2003 invasion came shortly after the launch of the Quickbird satellite, and its early missions focused on the route through the ancient Mesopotamian heartland that would be taken by the invading army. In irrigated areas, these images often preserve extraordinary details of subsurface architectural patterns on tell sites because of the concentration of surface salts over the denser mud-brick walls. Moreover, much of the imagery was taken before the destruction of these surface traces by the wave of looting triggered by the U.S. invasion (Stone 2008). These images may well provide as close to a random sample of architecture as we are likely to find anywhere. Extensive architectural traces are visible on forty-six sites of all sizes dated by archaeological survey data (Adams 1968, 1981; Adams and Nissen 1972; Gibson 1972; Wright 1981), including sites dating to almost all periods of centralization between the urban genesis in the fourth millennium to the end of Mesopotamian civilization in the first millennium BCE. These make possible an understanding of the overall organization of settlements of different sizes and dates and in some instances provide a complete view of both public and private architecture throughout an individual site. Especially important here are images of Mesopotamia's earliest cities, those dating to the fourth millennium BCE, where excavations have focused almost exclusively on public buildings.

The combination of data on settlement organization based on satellite imagery, archaeological survey, and excavation demonstrate that Iraq's recent turbulent history is but a continuation of its past. Although the region is credited as the birthplace of urbanism and many of the major sites were occupied over millennia, interruptions in settlement were common, the result of a combination of shifts in the watercourses and fluctuations in political alliances between cities. The highest population estimates are associated with the early second millennium BCE (Adams 1981:142), but this is likely to be due at least in part to an increase in urban settlement and irrigation, whereas less archaeologically visible populations, such as marsh dwellers and pastoral nomads, likely played larger roles in other time periods. Moreover, this peak was followed by a century or so of abandonment of most settlements in the south—probably the result of a failure of the irrigation system (Gasche and Tanret 1998; Stone 1977). As a result, the uppermost and therefore most accessible layers of many of these long-lived settlements date to this time period and may therefore skew the results of surface surveys.

Although architectural traces visible in high-resolution satellite imagery from Mesopotamia arguably provide larger samples of ancient domestic housing than are available for any other early civilization, individual dwellings can be difficult to isolate. After the Neolithic, Mesopotamian houses were combined into blocks sharing party walls, and a combination of the use of mud-brick for their construction and partitive inheritance resulted in the constant reworking of domestic space as houses were divided among heirs, neighboring rooms were bought and sold, and domiciles were reconfigured through the opening or blocking of doorways. This stands in stark contrast with the housing patterns considered by the other contributors to this volume, most of which consisted of isolated structures whose configurations were more or less stable over time. Moreover, a further complicating factor for this study is that the doorways, which provide data on internal circulation and therefore distinguish one house from another, are too small to be visible in the satellite imagery, impeding our ability to isolate individual houses within the dense mass of unexcavated domestic architecture. On the plus side, the strong correlation between courtyard size and house size in excavated houses (table 9.2) means that the variability of space sizes, best measured using Gini coefficients, should reflect the variability of house sizes since courtyards are almost always the largest domestic spaces.

For burial data, we are largely dependent on the results of fieldwork conducted in the 1930s. Although most of this research was good by the standards of the time, only the publication of the burials from Kish (Moorey 1978) includes a record of the skeletal remains associated with the grave goods, and as a result we usually lack the ability to associate the gender, age, or even the number of individuals with the offerings that accompanied them. Moreover, Mesopotamia has a long history of recycling goods, as an early second-millennium letter exemplifies: "If you want to be like a father to me, get me a fine string full of beads, to be worn around the head. . . . If you have none at hand, dig it out of the ground wherever (such objects) are (found) and send it to me" (Oppenheim 1967:87). In the sole publication of more recently excavated graves, Harriet Martin and colleagues (1985) note that the majority of the burials at Abu Salabikh had been disturbed in antiquity. This is also likely to have been the case for burials recovered through earlier excavations at Kish (Moorey 1978) and Ur (Woolley 1934; Woolley and Mallowan 1976). On a more positive note, however, the early second-millennium burials that we excavated recently beneath Leonard Woolley's floors in Area AH at Ur showed no evidence of disturbance, suggesting perhaps that burials in cemeteries were more likely to attract ancient looters.

While house sizes can be measured, evaluating the value of grave goods is more complicated. For this project, weights of objects in the University of Pennsylvania Museum (Baadsgaard 2008) and the rich textual record from Mesopotamia allowed us to translate all gold and copper/bronze grave goods into the currency of the time, shekels of silver (1 shekel = 11 grams) (Snell 1987). The value of more mundane grave goods, such as pots, stone bowls, and cylinder seals, could then be estimated based on the material and labor involved in their creation.

These two data sets, houses and graves, allow an examination of variability in the patterns of domestic architecture obtained from both excavations and high-resolution satellite imagery, of grave goods associated

Table 9.2 Correlations between features of houses from excavated sites

Sample unit	Sample 1	Sample 2	All data		Early Dynastic (3 sites)		Old Babylonian (10 sites)		Neo-Babylonian (6 sites)	
			N	r	N	r	N	r	N	r
House	Courtyard size	House size (with walls)	162	0.99	39	0.67	94	0.88	28	0.99
House	Courtyard size	Wall area	162	0.95	39	0.74	94	0.87	28	0.98
House	Courtyard size	Roofed space	162	0.94	39	0.53	94	0.81	28	0.98
House	Courtyard size	Interior space	162	0.97	39	0.63	94	0.87	28	0.98
House	Mean space size	House size (with walls)	163	0.75	39	0.80	95	0.71	28	0.80
House	Mean space size	Courtyard Size	162	0.74	39	0.47	94	0.75	28	0.81
House	Mean space size	Interior space	163	0.74	39	0.86	95	0.69	28	0.83
Site	House Gini coefficient	Space Gini coefficient	12	0.78						

Note: Only sites with four or more complete house plans were included; p values associated with reported r values are all $<.001$.

with human burials in both cemeteries and domestic contexts, and, when burials were within houses, a comparison between the two. Although both houses and grave goods have been reviewed with the aim of better understanding ancient patterns of inequality, the degree of comparability between these two potential measures of inequality remains less clear (Smith et al. 2014:312). Domestic housing by its very nature has upper and lower size limits. A house must provide space for at least one person to sleep, whereas some of the largest domestic residences excavated, such as the Roman villas of Pompeii, accommodated multiple households of both citizens and slaves (Dickmann 2015). In the case of Mesopotamia, the practice of extended family residence resulted in considerable variation in household size, which waxed as families matured and waned when the houses were divided between male heirs at the death of the paterfamilias, all recorded on cuneiform tablets that are often found in domestic areas. This constant modification of domestic space is reflected in the mass of party-wall structures, with doorways opened and closed as these spaces were reconfigured (Stone 1977). However, the largest areas of excavated domestic housing, investigated during the heyday of Mesopotamian archaeology in the 1930s, only occasionally recorded this practice, focusing more on recovering broad plans of urban blocks.

Graves were much more variable and included simple interments with no grave goods, although most included at least a pot or two that once held food and drink. Some, especially "royal" graves, might include elaborate sepulchers with an extensive inventory of objects and slaughtered attendants. It is also likely that perhaps the most important source of data, excavations within domestic areas at Ur, greatly underestimate the number of graves associated with these houses. Woolley stresses the importance of "chapels" as places of interment. These were spaces within some, but by no means all, houses and featured brick tombs whose tops rose above the floor level. But our recent excavations in Woolley's Area AH found burials wherever we dug beneath the floors of the last occupation, certainly not only in the "chapels." Some rooms had numerous neonates in bowls and jars, others simple inhumations of children and adults. This pattern of intramural burial should facilitate a direct comparison between houses and burials, but the association between houses and graves in the publications can be spotty, and many of these burials were not reached by the early, more-extensive excavations. A comparison of the richness of private graves from early second-millennium Ur and the size of the house they were associated with yielded no more than a very weak positive correlation.

The presence of graves beneath houses does little to mitigate the very different implications of these two data sets. Although houses reflect households, in the case of Mesopotamia these were in constant flux as they waxed through reproduction and waned when divided at the death of the paterfamilias. Graves, in contrast, were individual, but the lack of information on the skeletal remains or whether they were disturbed in antiquity makes these data less reliable.

MESOPOTAMIAN SETTLEMENT HISTORY

SETTLEMENT OVERVIEW

Thanks to the work of Robert Adams and colleagues (Adams 1965, 1972, 1981; Adams and Nissen 1972; Gibson 1972; Wright 1981), we have an almost unparalleled view of the trajectory of settlement in Mesopotamia from the first villages dating to the fifth millennium through the end of Mesopotamian civilization in the first millennium BCE, and indeed into the later Islamic occupation, which is not a focus of this chapter. The settlement area fluctuated considerably over time: site surfaces dating to the fourth millennium based on survey data cover no more than 100 hectares; they rise to nearly 9,000 hectares in the third and mid-second millennia BCE and in the first millennium fall again, to less than 250 hectares (Adams 1981:142, table 13). How much this reflected real changes in settlement density or the percentage of the population living in mud-brick settlements as opposed to reed huts or the tents of pastoralists, however, remains unclear. Published information shows that excavated domestic areas dating to the third millennium cover 0.6 hectares, whereas 2 hectares date to the early second millennium and 1.2 hectares to the first millennium. Some of the major cities and smaller sites were occupied for much of this time, although many were of significance for only a single time period. Settlement was tightly tethered to the availability of water for irrigation; this was provided by the Tigris and Euphrates Rivers, which flowed through the central part of the valley in multiple branches before being pushed toward the edges as the rivers shifted to their current locations as a result of millennia of silt buildup due to irrigation. If we apply the standard population density figure of 125 people per hectare used by Robert McC. Adams (1981:90) to the settlement data, this would suggest an overall population of some 200,000 people in the southern alluvium, perhaps rising to 350,000 during the heyday of Mesopotamian civilization in the late third and early second millennia BCE.

HOUSES

Densely settled urban centers date back to the fourth millennium, but most excavations of these early cities have focused on public rather than private areas. Archaeologists continued to privilege public architecture over domestic remains dating to the late third millennium, but a few extensive domestic areas were also investigated. The best record for domestic architecture dates to the early second millennium BCE, when abundant excavated architectural and artifactual evidence is supplemented by cuneiform tablets left in some of the houses of the southernmost cities as they were abandoned in the face of an abrupt shift of the major watercourses (Charpin 1986; Stone 1977; Van de Mieroop 1992). The recovery of private documents in household contexts is rare in other periods of the Mesopotamian sequence, and such documents are not available to students of other early complex societies. At early second-millennium Ur and Nippur, these data provide a window into the life histories of families living in neighborhoods that accommodated different occupational groups: at Ur, one area was occupied by entrepreneurs (Van de Mieroop 1992) and another by priests (Charpin 1986); and at Nippur, one area was occupied by administrators and the other by small-scale farmers (Stone 1987). Yet even as the texts define differences in occupation, the archaeological remains of the dense blocks of houses sharing party walls manifest very little differentiation between neighborhoods. As indicated above, individual houses expanded and contracted, being broken up at the death of the paterfamilias and recombined through sale and exchange between heirs and neighbors. House size therefore likely reflected a combination of household maturity and household wealth, although these two variables then, as indeed today, were linked. Although the houses were generally small and the neighborhoods crowded, private documents indicate that families often received income from temples and/or owned small date orchards and sometimes agricultural fields. It seems likely that their sons made up part of the agricultural workforce on state lands and were compensated by monthly payments of 60 liters of barley per month (4,000–5,000 calories per day). Broad literacy, at least in the early second millennium, is attested by the presence of scribal schools in most excavated domestic areas and the preservation of school texts in the houses (Postgate 1994b).

These data provide a window into the social conditions that underlay the long trajectory of domestic architecture in Mesopotamia. The low to moderate levels of social differentiation and residential variability can be seen in the archaeological remains of domestic areas at Ur and Nippur dating to the early second millennium and in the private documents found within them (Charpin 1986; Stone 1987; Van de Mieroop 1992), and these can serve as a benchmark against which housing in other contemporary towns and cities—as well as those dating to other periods in Mesopotamian history—can be compared.

MEASURING INEQUALITY

Studies of wealth distributions in modern nation-states commonly make use of the Gini coefficient, which measures the degree of differentiation no matter the scale of the phenomenon and is used to compare inequalities in generally prosperous societies with their more impoverished counterparts. This characteristic of Gini coefficients is especially useful for assessing domestic housing in Mesopotamia, where room and house sizes have long been understood to vary from site to site as a result of differential crowding (Postgate 1994a), even as patterns of variability in mean room sizes within sites remain important. Ginis have already been used by economists and anthropologists to assess preindustrial economies (Milanovic et al. 2011) and to examine how different modes of production affect social organization (Borgerhoff Mulder et al. 2009). They have also been used by archaeologists to evaluate and analyze differentiation in burial data (Windler et al. 2013), housing (Ames 2007; Smith et al. 2014; Stone 2014), and other aspects of the archaeological record (Smith 2014).

MESOPOTAMIAN SETTLEMENT ORGANIZATION

Mesopotamian civilization, which developed abruptly in the fourth millennium, is marked by a remarkably rapid settlement shift away from occupation focused on small villages toward the occupation of large settlements. The survey data (Adams 1968, 1981; Adams and Nissen 1972;

Gibson 1972; Wright 1972) indicate that 78 percent of early third-millennium
settlement was concentrated in sites greater than 80 hectares in size. This
was followed by a slow but consistent trend of increasing ruralization,
until 88 percent of Neo-Babylonian settlement was made up of villages
of less than 10 hectares (Adams 1988:125, table 11). All settlements were
tethered to the irrigation system. In the almost completely flat Mesopotamian plain, silt deposited through irrigation in the center of the plain
pushed the rivers toward its periphery over time; hence the Tigris can
be as far as 140 kilometers from the Euphrates south of Baghdad today.
In the past, however, more or less parallel watercourses were rarely separated by more than 30 kilometers. These rivers provided the key lines
of communication, and the largest urban sites were found beside them.
Although excavations have focused on the remains of these cities, the two
extensive investigations of small sites of around one hectare, Tell Harmel
(Baqir 1959) and Haradum (Kepinski-Lecompte 1992), both dating to
the early second millennium, exposed only minor differences in their
organization and access to resources when compared with their much
larger counterparts.

For most of Mesopotamian history, settlements covered around 1,500
hectares of the 55 square kilometers of alluvium, and the irrigated area
available for agriculture and settlement varied over time. These sites varied in size from less than 5 hectares to large, densely populated cities of
up to 100 hectares in size and very occasionally twice that size (Adams
1981). The main focus of all Mesopotamian cities was the temple, while
smaller places of worship were also scattered throughout the settlements.
These have been identified at sites large and small and dating to all time
periods. Palaces came later and were relatively rare. Some cities also had
areas set aside as cemeteries, although burial within the household was
also common. But Mesopotamian settlements were primarily residential, characterized by dense blocks of party-wall housing from the third
millennium onward. The remains of these houses are what can be investigated to provide data on patterns of inequality.

MESOPOTAMIAN DOMESTIC ARCHITECTURE

The architectural sample from Mesopotamia comes in two parts: one
derived from excavated domestic architecture and the other from high-

resolution satellite imagery. All excavated domestic areas in the southern alluvium of Mesopotamia for which published data exist were included in this project, providing information on both room sizes and house sizes, though the use of party walls means that the latter could be inferred only when doorways were well enough preserved for circulation patterns to be determined. Measurement was effected by creating polygons for each room in ArcGIS, dividing the spaces at the midpoint of the walls. Because of the importance for this project of identifying houses and their component rooms correctly, the detailed analyses of Mesopotamian house plans provided by Peter Miglus (1999) and Laura Battini-Villard (1999) were followed in addition to individual site reports. Excavated data made up 35 percent of the spaces used in the analysis, not all of which could be assigned to actual houses.

The remaining 65 percent of the data was derived from high-resolution Quickbird and WorldView satellite imagery of short-lived sites known otherwise only from survey (Stone 2014). Although doorways cannot be resolved in the 0.5 to 0.6 meter resolution of the imagery, the overall pattern of room sizes can be recorded over much larger areas than is possible from the more limited excavated architecture (figures 9.1 and 9.2). Moreover, whereas excavation areas were selected by archaeologists and are mostly at large urban sites, the preservation of salt concentrations on ancient walls is the result of salinization due to the high saline water table associated with modern irrigation. The beds of the modern rivers have long since shifted considerably over time, such that modern irrigation and settlement areas are largely unrelated to those occupied in the past.

Good samples of surface architectural traces in the imagery exist at sites large and small dating to all of the main periods of Mesopotamian history. Under these circumstances, they should provide a more or less random sample of ancient housing (table 9.1). Where possible, data were recorded from multiple areas within sites, but given the ambiguity of some of the images, only spaces within those areas with especially clear traces were included in the analysis. As was the case for the excavated sample, all spaces were measured from the midpoint of the walls. Because the classic Mesopotamian courtyard house consists of 9 spaces, only samples with at least 40 measurable spaces, comprising between 4 and 8 houses—whether derived from excavations or imagery—were considered for this project, with one exception. Nippur is one of only two sites where more than one

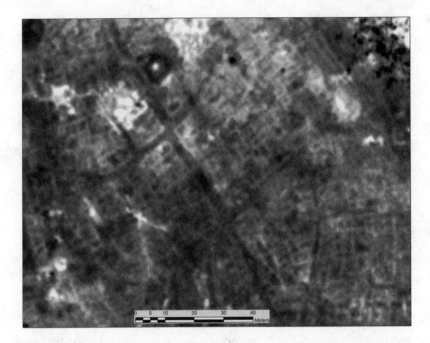

Figure 9.1 Image of Tell Asmar (DigitalGlobe Quickbird Image 1010010005208F00 acquired August 8, 2006). Reproduced courtesy of the DigitalGlobe Corporation.

contemporary residential area was excavated (McCown and Haines 1967), but one of the two areas, TA, consisted of only 34 rooms. Despite its small size, the opportunity to compare different excavated residential districts within a single site led to the inclusion of this data set. Overall the mean number of measured spaces for each area recorded was 139. Because the mean number of rooms per house seen in excavated data is 5.5, and given the bias of archaeologists in favor of excavating large houses, the smallest samples should record data from at least 7 houses, with a mean of 25 for all samples. Streets, open areas other than courtyards, and places where the architecture was unclear in the imagery were omitted from the analysis. Where multiple areas within sites could be measured—whether derived from excavation or satellite imagery—their degree of similarity was assessed through analyses of variance.

Key to this project is the strong correlation in the excavated data between mean space size and house size, between house size and the Gini

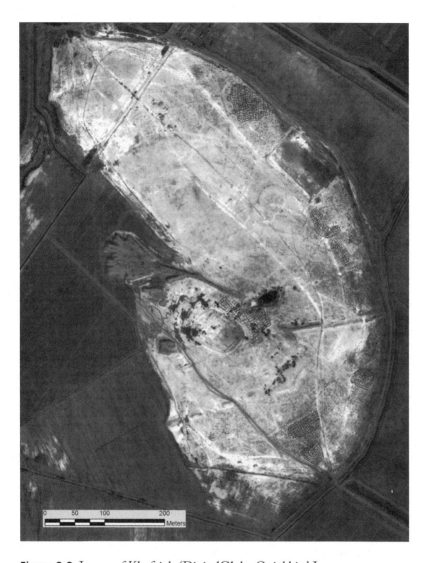

Figure 9.2 Image of Khafajah (DigitalGlobe Quickbird Image
10100100041C5700 acquired March 19, 2005) with sampled housing areas
superimposed (Stone 2013). Reproduced courtesy of the DigitalGlobe
Corporation.

coefficient of the room sizes of that house, and between house size and courtyard size (table 9.2). Especially important is the correlation between the Gini coefficient of spaces (rooms and courtyards) in extensive excavated residential areas with the Gini coefficient of whole houses (table 9.2). Without these correlations, it would not have been possible to expand the limited and likely biased sample based on excavation through the inclusion of a sample derived from satellite imagery, which is nearly three times the size and much more representative. Similar data from villages in the Middle East considered to be largely egalitarian by ethnoarchaeologists, as well as from stratified Roman towns, provide benchmarks for expected ranges of Gini coefficients when measuring house sizes in societies at different levels of stratification. It should be noted, however, that the data from modern villages often generate Gini coefficients that are higher than those from our urban Mesopotamian neighborhoods.

Ideally, all of the rooms of every site would be included in the data used for the calculation of the Gini coefficients, but this was not practicable, for two reasons. The primary reason is the quality of the imagery. At most of the sites used in this project, walls are more or less visible over much of the site, with the result that areas with obviously different densities of housing and the location of public buildings are readily apparent. But for actual measurement of the spaces, exceptional clarity is needed; areas where many but not all of the rooms can be made out clearly would not serve this purpose. The second reason is more practical. Some 50,000 spaces were measured for this project. Because each needed to be traced in ArcGIS, often based on multiple images of the same site and each with multiple enhancements, the recording process was slow. Under these circumstances, it made practical sense to select the best-preserved areas for digitization while ensuring that these were representative of the overall domestic architectural pattern in each site. Where possible I digitized multiple samples within the sites.

ARCHAEOLOGICAL EXAMPLES OF HOUSING BLOCKS

To contextualize these data from Mesopotamia, I developed benchmarks for domestic housing associated with highly differentiated societies and their more egalitarian counterparts. Similar data sets from the stratified Classical Roman cities of Pompeii and Herculaneum and from the more egalitarian Neolithic Çatalhöyük and the Iranian village of Aliabad were subjected to the same analyses as those applied to the data from Mesopotamia. These samples were chosen because, like the Mesopotamian data, they consist of dense blocks of housing, a factor that distinguishes the houses examined in this chapter from those discussed elsewhere in this volume, most of which were stand-alone structures. The Roman houses were frozen at a particular moment as they were destroyed by the eruption of Vesuvius.

Pompeii and Herculaneum, where the poor occupied small houses clustered around the much larger residences of the elites (Wallace-Hadrill 1994), provide excellent examples of domestic architecture associated with a society divided between the wealthy slaveholding elites and the shopkeepers and artisans who helped to support their lifestyle. Obtaining spatial data from societies that lack significant stratification is more difficult. Ethnographers who study simple societies rarely record plans of domestic architecture. An exception was Carol Kramer, who studied the modern village of Aliabad in Iran (Kramer 1982) with the aim of providing ethnoarchaeological data for understanding Neolithic villages. She described it as egalitarian but also noted significant differences in wealth—especially in land—between residents. This settlement differs from our Mesopotamian examples in that it was not walled and was therefore less spatially constrained. It also included spaces for livestock that had to be excluded when used for comparison with Mesopotamian urban dwellings. The other example was the early Neolithic site of Çatalhöyük (Hodder 1996a, 1996b), which was very compact, with little to no space between houses, and, as in Mesopotamia, made no accommodation for domestic animals. However, most houses consisted of no more than one room, whereas single-room structures in Mesopotamia are rare and often interpreted as nonresidential. These data from Aliabad and Çatalhöyük should serve to provide a benchmark for housing variability in less differentiated societies, and they indeed had very similar Gini coefficients despite the differences in their architecture (table 9.3). Unexpectedly, however, their Gini coefficients were generally higher than those obtained from data from Mesopotamian houses.

TRAJECTORIES OF HOUSING INEQUALITY IN MESOPOTAMIA

The available data permit comparison of the four best-documented chronological periods: Uruk and Jemdet Nasr (mid-fourth to early third

Table 9.3 Gini coefficients

Date	N sites	N rooms	Low Gini	High Gini	Mean Gini	Low room size
Gini coefficients on room–size distributions						
UR/JN	3	610	0.32	0.57	0.42	3.26
ED	8	2,187	0.25	0.38	0.32	1.91
OB	23	4,372	0.25	0.39	0.32	1.54
NB	12	1,670	0.28	0.54	0.40	3.07
Aliabad	1	470			0.49	1.34
Çatalhöyük	1	182			0.43	1.29
Pompeii	2[b]	1,369	0.51	0.65	0.63	1.87
Herculaneum	1	393			0.64	2.50
Gini coefficients on room–size distributions within individual houses						
ED	3	39[c]	0.04	0.37	0.22	31.89
OB	24	85[c]	0.07	0.48	0.27	26.70
NB	7	28[c]	0.13	0.50	0.34	82.34
Aliabad	1	67[c]	0.13	0.61		30.28
Çatalhöyük[a]	1	57[c]				5.45
Pompeii	2[b]	78[c]	0.24	0.80	0.52	19.13
Herculaneum	1	44[c]	0.32	0.75		25.19

Abbreviations: Mean Gini = mean coefficient for all sites in each row; low/high Gini = lowest/highest coefficient for all sites in each row; low room size = smallest room size in each row; UR/JN = Uruk and Jemdet Nasr (fourth millennium BCE); ED = late Early Dynastic (mid-third millennium BCE); OB = Isin-Larsa and Old Babylonian (early to mid-second millennium BCE); NB = Neo-Babylonian (mid-first millennium BCE).
[a]Most Çatalhöyük houses have only one or two rooms.
[b]Number of neighborhoods analyzed.
[c]Number of houses.

millennium BCE), late Early Dynastic (mid-third millennium BCE), Old Babylonian* (early to mid-second millennium BCE), and Neo-Babylonian/Achaemenid (mid- to late first millennium BCE) (table 9.3). Data are insufficient for intervening periods. Uruk and Jemdet Nasr data are somewhat limited because the lack of excavated housing precludes

---

*The term "Old Babylonian" is often used for both the Isin-Larsa period, when the center of political power moved from city to city (especially between the cities of Isin and Larsa), and the following period when Babylon held sway. The ceramics did not change significantly after Hammurabi's conquest, and the cities, towns, and villages south of Babylon and north of the marshes were abandoned shortly after, which is why so many sites have surfaces dating to this time.

the comparison between traces visible in satellite imagery and buildings uncovered through excavation.

Despite the limitations outlined above, data from the fourth, mid-third, early second, and first millennia BCE provide a long-term view of similarities and changes in domestic architecture, albeit with significant gaps along the way.

URUK/JEMDET NASR PERIOD (MID-FOURTH TO EARLY THIRD MILLENNIUM BCE)

This is the time when the first urban centers in Mesopotamia—and indeed the world—came into existence. The most extensive excavations have been at Uruk, where a series of temples and other public buildings were uncovered by German excavators in the early twentieth century. But not a single private house dating to this period has been excavated there, nor indeed at any other site in southern Iraq. Domestic architecture has been uncovered at two sites in northern Syria, Habuba Kabira and Jebel Aruda, whose linkage via the Euphrates with southern Mesopotamia has led to their consideration as Uruk trading colonies despite both art historical and trace element connections with the Iranian site of Susa (Blackman 1999). Their distance from Mesopotamia, the question of their possible affiliation with Susa, and the considerable variability in their domestic housing make them unreliable substitutes for the missing excavated houses from the southern alluvium. Therefore, although data on room sizes based on satellite imagery are available for this time period, there are none on the sizes of excavated houses.

URUK/JEMDET NASR PERIOD (FOURTH MILLENNIUM BCE)

Three sites have well-preserved architectural traces visible in satellite imagery of both public buildings (almost certainly temples) and the court-yard houses typical of later Mesopotamian sites. Each site was divided, probably by ancient watercourses, into multiple sectors: two have clear architectural traces on more than one mound, and the third, Tell Uqair, has an excavated temple on one mound and residential traces visible on the other. Room sizes were very variable, as reflected in their high Gini coefficients, and analyses of variance demonstrate that the room sizes

Table 9.4 Analyses of variance of room sizes between different neighborhoods in large sites

Site	Area	Date	Mean	SD	N	F	p	Distance (m)[a]
Uruk Survey 245	NW	UR/JN	30.28	23.02	60	16.42	0.000	260
Uruk Survey 245	West	UR/JN	17.03	13.2	68			
Nippur Survey 1096	North	UR/JN	22.45	16.45	47	6.617	0.001	505
Nippur Survey 1096	South	UR/JN	19.21	12.27	147			
Nippur Survey 1096	West	UR/JN	39.29	73.07	221			580
Khafajah—residential	Center	ED	13.00	4.47	129	0.239	0.787	
Khafajah	North	ED	12.56	5.95	218			
Khafajah	South	ED	12.33	7.09	252			
Khafajah with Sin-Oval area	Sin-Oval	ED	23.45	14.84	117	0.50	0.607	580
Lagash	Far north	ED	20.73	14.44	105	2.57	0.053	2,930
Lagash	North	ED	17.15	15.99	318			
Lagash	Central	ED	18.88	12.52	91			
Lagash	South	ED	21.47	14.99	74			
Mashkan-shapir	West	OB	19.85	19.22	77	1.97	0.117	700
Mashkan-shapir	Center	OB	15.61	12.75	87			
Mashkan-shapir	North	OB	18.44	11.86	272			
Mashkan-shapir	East	OB	16.47	13.31	277			
Asmar	North	OB	14.32	11.30	272	0.167	0.683	360
Asmar	South	OB	14.65	9.42	390			
Nippur	TA	OB	13.65	8.67	34	0.01	0.928	50
Nippur	TB	OB	13.82	8.10	47			
Schmid	N	OB	14.65	11.90	204	0.08	0.781	210
Schmid	S	OB	14.19	8.31	59			
Ur	AH	OB	16.99	12.09	269	0.245	0.621	350
Ur	EM	OB	16.27	11.92	92			

Abbreviations: UR/JN = Uruk and Jemdet Nasr (fourth millennium BCE), ED = late Early Dynastic (mid–third millennium BCE), OB = Isin-Larsa and Old Babylonian (early second millennium BCE).

[a]Maximum distance between neighborhoods.

of the different mounds were statistically different at the 0.05 level (table 9.4). Larger-scale domestic architecture was associated with the part of the site where the temple was located (Stone 2013), an indication that status was likely associated with ties to the main religious institution.

The housing data described above suggest that the initial phase of social complexity in ancient Mesopotamia was associated with significant inequality, a pattern compatible with much of the theoretical writing on the period. Types and sizes of houses differed both within each sector of these settlements and especially between different mounds at the same site. Residents living close to the temples enjoyed more-spacious housing, while more-crowded residential areas were located elsewhere. Overall, the picture is one of a stratified society with significant differences in residential architecture both within each part of the settlement and between them. These data suggest a close relationship between elite residential areas and the main temple.

EARLY DYNASTIC PERIOD (MID-THIRD MILLENNIUM BCE)

During this time, the full institutional complexity of ancient Mesopotamian society was achieved. Most of our evidence—and indeed all of the data available from satellite imagery—comes from the end of this era, slightly later than the date of the famous royal tombs and the associated cemetery excavated at Ur (Woolley 1934), which is discussed below. Although it is customary to call the primary individuals in the elaborate Ur burials kings and queens, whether they were associated with the temple or the palace is not really known—indeed, whether kingship played much of a role at that time is unclear. Our housing data, however, come from somewhat later, the very end of the Early Dynastic period, coincident with an abrupt shift away from small settlements in favor of walled urban sites, often more than one hundred hectares in size, which at this time made up 72 percent of the occupied area (Adams 1981:139). This period is also when we first have evidence for kings and palaces in addition to the priests and temples that characterized the earlier periods and continued to play an important role in later times.

The settlement data, both excavated and from imagery, suggest that the rise of kingship and the movement of people into urban centers at the end of the Early Dynastic period was accompanied by a significant decrease in social differentiation. The mean Gini coefficients for room sizes from both excavated and satellite data (0.31) show a 20 percent drop relative to the Uruk/Jemdet-Nasr period; indeed, this is the lowest level of differentiation seen in any of our data. Variability in the size of excavated houses is also remarkably low, with a mean Gini coefficient of 0.22. It is tempting to associate these changes with the rise of kingship, itself perhaps in part a reaction to the evidence for excessive differentiation of the immediately preceding phase, for which the "Royal Cemetery" at Ur (Woolley 1934), discussed below, is the poster child. Mesopotamian kings always described themselves as the protectors of the weak from the strong and were associated with the popular assembly; indeed, the suggestion has been made that it was the assembly that determined royal succession (Postgate 1994b). Overall, the combination of the (albeit obscure) textual data and the archaeological record suggest less inequality than in the previous period.

The impressive growth of cities at this time was also associated with a dramatic decrease in differences between neighborhoods. Analyses of variance of room sizes from multiple areas within large late Early Dynastic sites indicate remarkable similarity in the scale of domestic architecture within these early cities. Even at Lagash, where traces of residential architecture physically separated by nearly three kilometers can be measured, no significant difference is evident between the occupied mounds (see table 9.4).

OLD BABYLONIAN PERIOD (EARLY SECOND MILLENNIUM BCE)

Nearly 50 percent of our data derive from the Old Babylonian period—a consequence of the extensive abandonment of sites at the end of this period in the south, which left many with their uppermost surfaces dating to this time (Gasche 1989; Stone 1977). As with the more limited data from the late Early Dynastic, the rooms and houses at these sites are characterized by low Gini coefficients, indicating little social inequality. Ten Old Babylonian sites have multiple areas of domestic housing that could be measured, most of them large urban sites with broadly scattered samples, and here too there is no significant variation between each area (see table 9.4).

The few differences in residential architecture that were present can best be understood in the light of data from Mashkan-shapir, where visible architectural traces can be associated with the results of a detailed surface survey (Stone and Zimansky 2004). This city was deliberately created by the construction of a city wall and was divided into five sectors by canals, with the palace in the north, the cemetery in the center, the temple in the south, and manufacturing in the east; all but the religious and cemetery areas have traces of housing visible in DigitalGlobe satellite imagery. These architectural remains exhibit dense housing in all but the southeast, an area where architecture did not reach the city wall and where manufacturing was concentrated. Measurable room sizes from the different mounds at Mashkan-shapir all have similar Gini coefficients. Although the buildings in the southeast were less crowded than those elsewhere at the site, the room sizes are statistically similar. Moreover, wealth objects recovered from the surface—copper/bronze and cylinder seals—were evenly distributed across the site, suggesting that the unique pattern of housing seen in the eastern part was a product of both the newness of the settlement and the specialization of the area in manufacturing rather than of significant differences in wealth.

In addition to the archaeological data, private contracts on cuneiform tablets dating to the Old Babylonian period from several sites describe the division on inheritance and sale of domestic housing. Although the sale documents often deal with parts of houses, especially after a house has been divided after the death of the paterfamilias, the inheritance documents record the entirety of the property owned by the deceased. When the adjoining inherited house shares are added together to represent the original building, both the sizes of houses known only from texts and Gini coefficients of those sizes are very similar to the values obtained from the excavated houses (table 9.5).

In sum, Old Babylonian settlement was consistent both between sites and within them. The overall picture, supported by the extensive excavated areas, which also yielded private cuneiform documents (as discussed at the beginning of this chapter), suggests little in the way of social differentiation within these cities. The architectural pattern shows considerable similarity to that dating to the Early Dynastic period.

NEO-BABYLONIAN DATA (MID-FIRST MILLENNIUM BCE)

No data are available from sites dating to the later second and early first millennia, and both excavated and satellite data from the late first

Table 9.5 Gini coefficients of graves and house sizes

	N	Gini	Min. value	Max. value	Source
Ubaid Eridu graves	161	0.44	0	49.00	Excavations
Early Dynastic Khafajah graves	166	0.77	0	7.44	Excavations
Early Dynastic Ur graves	655	0.80	0	446.00	Excavations
Akkadian Ur graves	413	0.80	0	96.43	Excavations
Old Babylonian Ur graves	76	0.88	0	170.45	Excavations
Neo-Babylonian Ur graves	98	0.88	0	25.20	Excavations
Early Dynastic house sizes	21	0.37	39.22	261.99	Excavations
Old Babylonian house sizes	106	0.40	18.13	546.64	Excavations
Neo-Babylonian house sizes	14	0.40	151.02	1,831.93	Excavations
All Old Babylonian house sizes	33	0.46	18	562.00	Texts
Old Babylonian Nippur house prices	15	0.38			Texts
Old Babylonian Nippur house sizes	15	0.45			Texts
Old Babylonian Ur house prices	8	0.41			Texts
Old Babylonian Ur house sizes	8	0.49			Texts
Inherited houses sizes from Ur	8	0.22			Texts
Inherited houses sizes from Nippur	16	0.40			Texts

millennium are more limited than those from earlier periods. No excavations or images preserve information from multiple areas within sites. Four major cities—Babylon, Nippur, Ur, and Uruk—have excavated houses dating to this time, and there are six sites where high-resolution satellite imagery preserves traces of domestic housing, although all except Sippar are less than six hectares in size. Gini coefficients on room sizes from these data suggest an increase in differentiation from the low levels seen during the Early Dynastic and Old Babylonian periods. Both room and house sizes varied considerably between sites and were higher than those seen in the Early Dynastic and the Old Babylonian data. Most striking is the increase in the size of excavated houses: the average Neo-Babylonian house is more than four times larger than its Early Dynastic or Old Babylonian counterpart, and the satellite imagery suggests that this was a broad pattern, not just the result of the selectivity of the excavators.

Textual data from the Neo-Babylonian period suggest a link between this increase in differentiation and house size with changes in inheritance patterns. In the Old Babylonian period the eldest son received 10 percent more of the estate than his brothers for the maintenance of the family cult, but in the Neo-Babylonian period he received at least 50 percent of the estate (Baker 2010, 2015). The smallest known Neo-Babylonian house was also larger than one-third of Old Babylonian and one-half of Early Dynastic houses, and many houses were very large indeed, often built around multiple courtyards. These differences are explained by textual sources indicating that single houses could be owned by multiple unrelated individuals. In addition, although there are very rare textual references to privately owned slaves in the Old Babylonian period, slaves are much more common in the Neo-Babylonian period, and they too would have needed accommodation within the houses. Although parts of houses could be sold to neighbors in the Old Babylonian period, this always coincided with a modification of the structure, something that does not seem to have been the case for Neo-Babylonian houses. Together, the textual and architectural data suggest significant changes in society encompassing both greater inequality and alterations in residential patterns when compared with earlier times.

The data presented above describe an initial period of highly differentiated settlement associated with the beginnings of complexity in Mesopotamia. However, the dramatic shift in settlement toward urban life dating to the later Early Dynastic period is associated with not only the rise in kingship but also, as manifested in both excavated and satellite-based data on housing, a high degree of equality both between and within residential areas. This pattern continued into the early second millennium BCE until urban life collapsed, especially in the south, probably because of a shift in watercourses (Gasche et al. 1998). Not until the rise of the Neo-Babylonian Empire in the first millennium BCE did cities again become a major feature of the Mesopotamian landscape, and these cities exhibit much greater levels of inequality than their immediate predecessors.

MESOPOTAMIAN MORTUARY DATA

The aim of this chapter is to compare the data available from domestic housing and burials. In analyzing the approximately two thousand Mesopotamian graves examined here, we can compare evidence for inequality both within all levels of society and within nonroyal graves. In the latter case we exclude the data for the royal tombs, which in the Early Dynastic period included sacrificed retainers but are largely unknown (or have been extensively looted) for later periods.

There are many complications involved in working with the mortuary data from Mesopotamia. Much was excavated in the 1930s before the development of modern methods in archaeology, and few publications include information on the age and sex of the individuals who were buried there. Perhaps more significantly, while the one more recent burial publication (Martin et al. 1985) describes almost all burials as disturbed, this is never discussed in the earlier volumes. The early second-millennium burials that my colleagues and I have excavated within residential contexts at Ur and Mashkan-shapir, however, showed no signs of disturbance. Only rarely is the orientation of the burial recorded, but the difficulty is that we are not informed whether this is simply the result of inconsistent note taking or whether the absence of a description means that the burial was too disturbed for these data to be recorded.

By far the most extensive mortuary data comes from Ur. Cemeteries were excavated dating to the mid-third (Early Dynastic), late third (Akkadian), early second (Old Babylonian), later second (Kassite), and first (Neo-Babylonian) millennia, all of which were recorded in the same way and with more detail on the objects (but not the skeletal material) than was common at that time (Woolley 1934, 1956, 1965; Woolley and Mallowan 1976). Four other groups of graves were also examined for this chapter: Those dating to the late Neolithic at Eridu (Safar et al. 1982) provide a window into burial traditions prior to state formation and metallurgy, and indeed this is the only mortuary data set to generate a moderate Gini coefficient. Other Early Dynastic period graves contemporary with or slightly later than those from Ur that have been excavated at the smaller site of Abu Salabikh (Martin et al. 1985) were included, as were those from Kish (Moorey 1978), another major early city—and indeed the place where tradition tells us that kingship first descended from heaven after the flood. Only the Kish and Abu Salabikh publications included data on age and sex. In addition to the early second-millennium graves from Ur (Woolley and Mallowan 1976), the analysis also included contemporary graves from Nippur (McCown and Haines 1967). For the third-millennium burials from Ur, Gini coefficients have been calculated that both include and exclude the royal graves, which contained between two and seventy-three sacrificed retainers in addition to the principal interment. Unlike the comparison of houses, for which measurement is relatively simple, developing a robust method for comparing the wide range of objects found in graves dating to multiple periods is much more complicated. For Mesopotamia, however, the textual data provide a record of the relative value of the metals (Snell 1987)—gold, silver, and copper/bronze—which were often the most valuable items in the graves. Moreover, a dissertation (Baadsgaard 2008)* on objects from the Royal Cemetery at Ur includes weights of all of the metal objects in the University of Pennsylvania Museum (one-quarter of the total from the Royal Cemetery). Weights of metal objects are also included in the publication of the grave goods from Abu Salabikh (Martin et al. 1985). These data were used to determine the mean weight of each type of metal object recorded, which was applied to all objects of that type for which no weights are available. All objects of copper/bronze, gold, and silver were converted into shekels (eleven grams) of silver, the unit of exchange at the time, based on textual information on their relative values (Snell 1987), and the relative value in shekels of the other common objects in the graves (pots, stone bowls, seals, beads, whetstones, and the like) was estimated. These estimates were based on both the nature of the objects themselves and what they were made from. For example, imported beads of lapis and carnelian were clearly more valuable than those of paste, but the reports rarely provided information on the length of the strands or the number of the beads, so only the stones and not their quantity could be used to evaluate their value in most instances. Nevertheless, the similarity between the Gini coefficients generated from the various cemeteries considered, as well as the trend toward slightly increasing levels of inequality over time, suggests that this evaluation should approximate the value of the goods left in these graves.

RESULTS

A striking aspect of our data is the profound difference between the Gini coefficients based on the burial data and those based on the housing data.

---

*I would like to thank William Hafford for bringing this dissertation to my attention and providing me with a copy.

Gini coefficients on houses range from a low of 0.37 to a high of 0.55 regardless of whether the data derive from texts or excavations. In addition, the textual data on house sizes and our excavated examples are reasonably similar, although the smallest Neo-Babylonian houses recorded in the texts are significantly smaller than any known from excavations. Overall, these data suggest a low to moderate level of inequality in Mesopotamia, especially given that house size reflects not only wealth but also the size of the family, which would have varied considerably between nuclear and extended households. These housing data contrast with those derived from burials, which, with the exception of the Neolithic example from Eridu, consistently generate high Gini coefficients. This should not be surprising. Gini coefficients, developed as a means of comparing the distribution of wealth within nations, are best suited for the examination of data that, like incomes or houses, exist within a range of variation. All individuals or households must have enough income to keep body and soul together, while the overall size of the economy will serve to limit the highest incomes. In a similar vein, the smallest house must provide sufficient sheltered space for the inhabitants to be able to sleep, cook, and eat. Most houses are (and were) certainly much larger, but there are also upper limits for those that do not contain large numbers of unrelated servants or slaves. Indeed, the size ranges of our Mesopotamian examples are very similar to those in modern Britain, if smaller than those in countries like the United States and Australia, where ever-increasing house sizes are now common (Wilson 2012).

Burial data, in contrast, have no such limits and may include no grave offerings at all or very large numbers of grave goods; in addition, grave goods are as likely to reflect prestige as wealth. Analyses of grave goods have often focused on the effect of age, sex, and status on both grave goods and the treatment of the body. Unfortunately, with the exception of the data from Kish, the only distinction that was made with regard to the skeletal remains from the major cemeteries was between adults, children, and infants, so no analysis is possible on the effect of gender on grave goods. At Ur, gender was recorded only for the "royal tombs," where the grave of Queen Pu-abi rivaled those of her male counterparts in wealth and elaboration. Moreover, while some of the publications include a clear-eyed assessment of whether or not particular graves had been looted, most—including the burials from Ur, which provide the bulk of the data—omit this information. The frequent lack of information on the orientation of the burials likely indicates that the skeletal material was disturbed, although these data could simply have not been recorded.

CONCLUSIONS

The differences in the Gini coefficients based on domestic housing and grave goods from Mesopotamia reinforce the argument by Smith and colleagues (2014) that the two data sets reflect different aspects of ancient societies. I agree and argue that the distribution of house sizes in the past is comparable to the distribution of incomes in the present in that both have lower and upper limits. This boundedness is what makes Gini coefficients useful for assessing inequality in ancient societies when using house sizes. Grave goods are different in that although there is the lower limit of no grave goods at all, there is no upper limit. Unlike houses, which provide shelter, grave goods have little practical value in themselves and are governed by prestige and ideology, aspects of ancient societies that are perhaps the most difficult for archaeologists to penetrate. Grave goods are also less permanent, in that they were recycled in some societies; it is likely that many, perhaps most, Mesopotamian graves had been disturbed in antiquity.

The differences between the Gini coefficients based on burial and housing data from contemporary sites in Mesopotamia make it clear that any comparison of levels of inequality between sites or societies must be based on analyses of comparable data sets. But sources for residential and burial data are also very different. Whereas the visibility of architectural traces in the satellite imagery results from modern environmental factors that are unrelated to the archaeological landscape, cemeteries were selected for excavation by archaeologists, many of whom were dependent for their funding on museums that would receive a share of the finds. Archaeologists like Leonard Woolley could do fieldwork only if they could export many of the objects to the museums that supported their fieldwork; indeed, this is why Woolley left Iraq when a more restrictive policy for the export of antiquities was enforced. It seems likely that Woolley was able to obtain the funds to explore the domestic areas at Ur only because of the richness of the finds he had recovered from the Royal Cemetery.

ACKNOWLEDGMENTS

I would like to thank Jeroen Smaers, Michael E. Smith, Jason Ur, and Paul Zimansky, who read earlier drafts of this chapter. I would also like to thank Adrian Jaeggi for introducing me to Gini coefficients. Data on which the tables in this chapter are based are available at https://core.tdar.org/project/436029/quantifying-ancient-wealth-inequalities as tDAR ID 439710.

REFERENCES CITED

Adams, Robert McC. 1965. *Land Behind Baghdad*. University of Chicago Press, Chicago.

———. 1968. The Natural History of Urbanism. In *The Fitness of Man's Environment*, edited by the Smithsonian Institution, pp. 39–60. Smithsonian Institution Press, Washington, D.C.

———. 1972. Settlement and Irrigation Patterns in Ancient Akkad. In *City and Area of Kish*, edited by McGuire Gibson, Robert McC. Adams, Henry Field, and Edith M. Laird, pp. 182–208. Field Research Projects, Coconut Grove, Fla.

———. 1981. *Heartland of Cities*. University of Chicago Press, Chicago.

Adams, Robert McC., and H. Nissen. 1972. *The Uruk Countryside: The Natural Setting of Urban Societies*. University of Chicago Press, Chicago.

Ames, Kenneth M. 2007. The Archaeology of Rank. In *Handbook of Archaeological Theories*, edited by R. Alexander Bentley, Herbert D. G. Maschner, and Christopher Chippendale, pp. 487–513. AltaMira Press, Lanham, Md.

Baadsgaard, Aubrey. 2008. Trends, Traditions, and Transformations: Fashions of Dress in Early Dynastic Mesopotamia. PhD dissertation, University of Pennsylvania.

Baker, Heather D. 2010. The Social Dimensions of Babylonian Domestic Architecture in the Neo-Babylonian and Achaemenid Periods. In *The World of Achaemenid Persia*, edited by John Curtis and St. John Simpson, pp. 179–94. IB Tauris, London.

———. 2015. Family Structure, Household Cycle, and the Social Value of Domestic Space in Urban Babylonia. In *House Studies in Complex Societies: (Micro-)Archaeological and Textual Approaches*, edited by Miriam Muller, pp. 371–408. Oriental Institute Seminars 10. Oriental Institute, Chicago.

Baqir, Taha. 1959. *Tell Harmal*. Directorate General of Antiquities, Baghdad.

Battini-Villard, Laura. 1999. *L'espace domestique en Mésopotamie de la IIIe dynastie d'Ur á l'époque paléo-babylonienne*. J. and E. Hedges, Oxford, U.K.

Binford, Lewis R. 1971. Mortuary Practices: Their Study and Their Potential. *Memoirs of the Society for American Archaeology* 25:6–29.

Blackman, M. James. 1999. Chemical Characterization of Local Anatolian and Uruk Style Sealing Clays from Hacinebi. *Paléorient* 25:51–56.

Blanton, Richard E. 1998. Steps Toward a Theory of Egalitarian Behavior in Archaic States. In *Archaic States*, edited by Gary M. Feinman and Joyce Marcus, pp. 135–72. School of American Research, Santa Fe, N.Mex.

Borgerhoff Mulder, Monique, Samuel Bowles, Tom Hertz, Adrian Bell, Jan Beise, Greg Clark, Ila Fazzio, et al. 2009. Intergenerational Wealth Transmission and the Dynamics of Inequality in Small-Scale Societies. *Science* 326:682–88.

Charpin, Dominique. 1986. *Le Clergé d'Ur au siècle d'Hammurabi*. Librarie Droz, Genève-Paris.

Dickmann, Jens-Arne. 2015. Crucial Contexts: A Closer Reading of the Household of the Casa del Menandro at Pompeii. In *Household Studies in Complex Societies: (Micro-)Archaeological and Textual Approaches*, edited by Miriam Muller, pp. 211–28. Oriental Institute Seminars 10. Oriental Institute, Chicago.

Ehenreich, Robert M., Carole L. Crumley, and Janet E. Levy (editors). 1995. *Heterarchy and the Analysis of Complex Societies*. Archaeological Papers of the American Anthropological Association 6. Arlington, Va.

Flannery, Kent, and Joyce Marcus. 2012. *The Creation of Inequality*. Harvard University Press, Cambridge, Mass.

Gasche, Hermann. 1989. *La Babylonie au 17eme siècle avant notre ère*. University of Ghent, Ghent.

Gasche, Hermann, James A. Armstrong, S. W. Cole, and Vahe G. Gurzadyhan. 1998. *Dating the Fall of Babylon: A Reappraisal of Second-Millennium Chronology*. Mesopotamian History and Environment, Series 2, Memoirs 4. University of Ghent, Ghent; University of Chicago Press, Chicago.

Gasche, Hermann, and Michel Tanret. 1998. *Changing Watercourses in Babylonia: Towards a Reconstruction of the Ancient Environment of Lower Mesopotamia*. Mesopotamian History and Environment, Series 2, Memoirs 5. University of Ghent, Ghent; Oriental Institute, Chicago.

Gibson, McGuire. 1972. *City and Area of Kish*. Field Research Publications, Miami, Fla.

Hodder, Ian (editor). 1996a. *On the Surface: Çatalhöyük 1993–95*. McDonald Institute for Archaeological Research, Cambridge, U.K.

———. 1996b. *Excavating Çatalhöyük: South, North and KOPAL Area Reports from the 1995–99 Seasons*. McDonald Institute for Archaeological Research, Cambridge, U.K.

Kepinski-Lecomte, Christine. 1992. *Haradum I: Une ville nouvelle sur le Moyen-Euphrate (XVIIIe–XVIIe siecles av. J.-C.)*. Editions Recherche sur les Civilisations, Paris.

Kramer, Carol. 1982. *Village Ethnoarchaeology*. Academic Press, New York.

Martin, Harriet P. J., J. N. Postgate, and Jane Moon. 1985. *Abu Salabikh Excavations*. Vol. 2, *Graves 1 to 99*. British School of Archaeology in Iraq, London.

McCown, Donald, and Richard C. Haines. 1967. *Nippur I, Temple of Enlil, Scribal Quarter, and Soundings*. Oriental Institute Publications 78. University of Chicago Press, Chicago.

Miglus, Peter A. 1999. *Städtische Wohnarchitektur in Babylonien und Assyrien*. Philipp von Zabern, Mainz am Rhein.

Milanovic, Branko, Peter H. Lindert, and Jeffrey G. Williamson. 2011. Preindustrial Inequality. *Economic Journal* 121:255–72.

Moorey, Peter Roger Stuart. 1978. *Kish Excavations, 1923–1933*. Clarendon Press, Oxford, U.K.

Oppenheim, A. Leo. 1967. *Letters from Mesopotamia*. University of Chicago Press, Chicago.

Peebles, Christopher S., and Susan M. Kus. 1977. Some Archaeological Correlates of Ranked Society. *American Antiquity* 42:421–48.

Postgate, J. Nicholas. 1994a. How Many Sumerians per Hectare? *Cambridge Archaeological Journal* 4:47–65.

———. 1994b. *Early Mesopotamia*. Routledge, London.

Safar, Fuad, Muḥammad 'Alī Muṣṭafá, and Seton Lloyd. 1982. *Eridu*. State Organization of Antiquities and Heritage, Baghdad.

Smith, Michael E. 1994. Social Complexity in the Aztec Countryside. In *Archaeological Views from the Countryside*, edited by Glenn M. Schwartz and Steven E. Falconer, pp. 143–59. Smithsonian Institution Press, Washington, D.C.

———. 2014. Housing in Premodern Cities: Patterns of Social and Spatial Variation. *International Journal of Architectural Research* 8:207–22.

Smith, Michael E., Timothy Dennehy, April Kamp-Whittaker, Emily Colon, and Rebecca Harkness. 2014. Quantitative Measures of Wealth Inequality in Ancient Central Mexican Communities. *Advances in Archaeological Practice* 2(4):311–23.

Snell, Daniel. 1987. *Ledgers and Prices: Early Mesopotamian Merchant Accounts*. Yale Near Eastern Researches 8. Yale University Press, New Haven, Conn.

Stone, Elizabeth C. 1977. Economic Crisis and Social Upheaval in Old Babylonian Nippur. In *Mountains and Lowlands*, edited by T. Cuyler Young Jr. and Louis D. Levine, pp. 267–89. Undena Press, Malibu, Calif.

———. 1987. *Nippur Neighborhoods*. Oriental Institute, Chicago.

———. 1990. The Tell Abu Duwari Project, 1987. *Journal of Field Archaeology* 17:141–62.

———. 2008. Patterns of Looting in Iraq. *Antiquity* 82:125–38.

———. 2013. The Organisation of a Sumerian Town: The Physical Remains of Ancient Social Systems. In *The Sumerian World*, edited by Harriet Martin, pp. 156–78. Routledge, London.

———. 2014. High-Resolution Imagery and the Recovery of Surface Architectural Patterns. *Advances in Archaeological Practice* 3:180–94.

Stone, Elizabeth C., and Paul Zimansky. 2004. *The Anatomy of a Mesopotamian City: Survey and Excavations at Mashkan-shapir*. Eisenbrauns, Winona Lake, Ill.

Tainter, Joseph A. 1978. Mortuary Practices and the Study of Prehistoric Social Systems. *Advances in Archaeological Method and Theory* 1:105–41.

Tilly, Charles. 1998. *Durable Inequality*. University of California Press, Berkeley.

Trigger, Bruce. 1993. *Early Civilizations: Ancient Egypt in Context*. Columbia University Press, New York.

Van de Mieroop, Marc. 1992. *Society and Enterprise in Old Babylonian Ur*. D. Reimer, Berlin.

Wallace-Hadrill, Andrew. 1994. *Houses and Society in Pompeii and Herculaneum*. Princeton University Press, Princeton.

Wilson, Lindsay. 2012. Shrink That Footprint (blog). http://shrinkthatfootprint .com/, accessed April 5, 2015.

Windler, Arne, Rainer Thiele, and Johannes Müller. 2013. Increasing Inequality in Chalcolithic Southeast Europe: The Case of Durankulak. *Journal of Archaeological Science* 40:204–10.

Woolley, C. Leonard. 1934. *Ur Excavations 2: The Royal Cemetery*. British Museum, London.

———. 1956. *Ur Excavations 4: The Early Periods*. British Museum, London.

———. 1965. *Ur Excavations 8: The Kassite Period and the Period of the Assyrian Kings*. British Museum, London.

Woolley, C. Leonard, and Max Mallowan. 1976. *Ur Excavations 7: The Old Babylonian Period*. British Museum, London.

Wright, Henry T. 1972. A Consideration of the Interregional Exchange in Greater Mesopotamia: 4000–3000 BC. *Anthropological Papers* 46:95–105.

———. 1981. The Southern Margins of Sumer: Archaeological Survey of the Area of Eridu and Ur. Appendix in *Heartland of Cities: Surveys of Ancient Settlement and Land Use on the Central Floodplain at the Euphrates*, by Robert McC. Adams, pp. 295–345. University of Chicago Press, Chicago.

10

Assessing Wealth Inequality in the Pre-Hispanic Valley of Oaxaca
Comparative Implications

Gary M. Feinman, Ronald K. Faulseit, and Linda M. Nicholas

"The distribution of wealth is one of today's most widely discussed and controversial issues. But what do we really know about its evolution over the long term?" With these words, Thomas Piketty (2014:1) introduces *Capital in the Twenty-First Century*, a book that Nobel Prize–winning economist Paul Krugman (2014) believes has "transformed our economic discourse" so much that "we'll never talk about wealth and inequality the same way that we used to." Just one year earlier, President Barack Obama (2013) declared, "I believe that [inequality] is the defining challenge of our time." At the forefront of "international conversation," a special issue of *Science* was launched to draw on waves of "data to explore the origins, impact, and future of inequality around the world" (Chin and Culotta 2014:818).

The empirical framing of and well-deserved attention being paid to these issues by a globally visible journal is welcome. Yet given the multi-dimensional frame marshaled to account for contemporary inequality (Piketty and Saez 2014), is a focus on one-dimensional explanations, such as entropy (Cho 2014) or the uneven distributions of resources (Pringle 2014; see also Borgerhoff Mulder et al. 2009), sufficient to make sense of complex patterns of inequality across the world's deep past? How much can archaeology, with its fundamentally material foundations (e.g., Hawkes 1954), contribute to answering, in a systematic and quantitative way, the broad question advanced by Piketty? If we make Piketty's question a priority (e.g., Kintigh et al. 2014:8) and are able to answer it affirmatively, how do we proceed so that we, as investigators, contribute to an understanding of the history and causal underpinnings of inequalities across the broad sweep of the human career? As with the studies of ancient cities that have been undertaken in part to illuminate the broader conditions and consequences of human life, past and present (e.g., Smith

2010), can a greater understanding of past patterns of inequality and its causes help us explain more-contemporary inequities and how we can potentially alleviate them?

Here, our specific empirical focus is the pre-Hispanic Valley of Oaxaca, Mexico, with particular emphasis on the Classic period (ca. AD 200–800). We also briefly consider the earlier San José phase (ca. 1100–800 BC) to provide a diachronic perspective for ancient Oaxaca. As our broader aim is to contribute to understandings of historical trends and diverse patterns of inequality over millennia, we begin with a brief review of the conceptual framing and underlying tenets that guide our examination of the pre-Hispanic era. Although we openly recognize that our perspective and approach reflect current discussions and debates that have emerged mainly from ongoing analyses of contemporary inequality, we do not see this as a serious impediment, as an ultimate goal of this volume is to come to grips with wealth distributions across the broad sweep of time and space. For this reason, we do not see it as appropriate to assume a priori that the fundamental basis for and manifestation of inequality were qualitatively different in the deep past as compared to more-recent times. Rather, to address long-term changes and patterns of variation in global inequality and socioeconomic stratification, we believe that it is necessary to employ approaches and hone concepts that are broadly applicable across temporal eras and empirical specificities (e.g., Bowles et al. 2010; Lindert 1991; Milanovic et al. 2011; Tilly 2005).

INEQUALITY IS RELATIONAL

In the title of his volume *The Haves and the Have-Nots*, Branko Milanovic (2011) aptly captures a fundamental element of inequality. "Inequality is by definition social, since it is a relational phenomenon" (Milanovic 2011:ix). Inequality exists only in the context of interpersonal arrangements and networks. Karl Marx ([1899] 2000:30) recognized this years ago: "A house may be large or small; as long as the neighboring houses are likewise small, it satisfies all social requirements for a residence. But let there arise next to the little house a palace, and that little house shrinks into a hut."

Because inequality is by definition relational, its systematic measurement and examination across different communities or defined social networks requires ways of comparing units within populations to derive a basis to make contrasts between or across them. Although inequality can be examined and measured in numerous ways (and it is useful to integrate various dimensions when we do so), the Lorenz curve and corresponding Gini index provide a widely applied means to assess the distribution of wealth (and income) across populations (Cowell 2011; Milanovic 2011). While Lorenz curves (see chapter 2) provide a means to visually inspect the distribution of wealth or income among segments of a particular population, the associated Gini index, which varies from 0 (perfect equality) to 1 (perfect inequality), provides a relatively straightforward quantitative measure to compare inequality between populations. Widely employed for contemporary settings (e.g., Keister and Moller 2000; Lindert and Williamson 2016; Milanovic 2016), these two analytical measures when examined in tandem provide a basis to define the parameters of inequality in specific contexts. They previously have been used to contrast and compare archaeological (e.g., McGuire 1983; Smith et al. 2014) and historical (e.g., Kron 2011; Milanovic et al. 2011) contexts and thus provide a foundation for the analysis of inequality over the *longue durée*.

Angus Deaton (2014:783) has recognized that "[t]he world is unequal in many dimensions." Certainly since the outset of the Holocene (e.g., Price and Feinman 2010), and possibly well before (Hayden 1995), human networks and aggregations consistently have been characterized by degrees of inequality. But the extent of economic inequality and the specific ways in which wealth has been distributed have not always been consistent. The key axis of wealth disparity may be defined in access to portable goods or currencies, or it may relate to staggering differences in residential construction, or it may pertain to other axes of wealth or to all of the above. In this regard, a further advantage of the Gini index is that it can be employed to assess unequal distributions along a diverse array of different dimensions.

Broad cross-national considerations of inequality (e.g., Kuznets 1955:1; Milanovic 2011:27–28) tend to focus on domestic units as the key elements for comparative investigation. This analytical vantage not only dovetails well with the recognition that households were the basic units of production and exchange in the Classic period Valley of Oaxaca (Feinman and Nicholas 2012), but it also is most suitable for the application of Gini indices to assess the extent of inequality (Deininger and Squire

1996:568). A second principal standard (Deininger and Squire 1996:568–69) for the application of Gini indices requires comprehensive coverage of the target population. Of course, this criterion is difficult to achieve in archaeology, for which the state of knowledge is almost always partial, a sample, and usually a small one. Nevertheless, with the appropriate conceptual frames and tools, archaeology has made and can continue to make significant contributions to the study of inequality and socioeconomic stratification.

THE UNDERPINNINGS OF INEQUALITY EXTEND BEYOND THE ECONOMY

Most explanations that endeavor to account for long-term patterns of inequality have focused intensely on economic variables, such as resource availabilities (and associated scarcities related to expanding population), modes of production, and the cycling or outcomes of economic forces over time (see historical overviews in Milanovic 2011:3–32; Piketty 2014:1–35; Stiglitz 2013:35–103). One conceptual stream of research that endeavors to explain human wealth inequalities across history relies heavily on different production modes (e.g., foraging, horticulture, pastoralism, intensive farming) as the causal foundation (e.g., Borgerhoff Mulder et al. 2009; Bowles et al. 2010). As these studies illustrate (see also Borgerhoff Mulder et al. 2010; Smith et al. 2010), mainly economic variables such as modes of production correlate with (and seemingly help understand) certain broad-brush ranges in the degrees of inequality. Yet notably, across different modes of production, the degrees of inequality also vary from one case to another. Thus, considerable variation cannot be explained by these economic variables alone. In parallel fashion, whether one looks at income inequality for contemporary nation-states (Milanovic 2016:118–54; OECD 2011; World Bank 2016) or for counties in the United States (U.S. Census Bureau 2012), the degrees of inequality are highly variable, so participation in an industrialized economy may account for only so much. Likewise, Gini indices for inequality calibrated for specific historical states and empires, whether deep in the past or more recent, fall within ranges for contemporary polities (e.g., Alfani 2015; Brown et al. 2012; Kron 2011; Milanovic et al. 2011; Scheidel and Friesen 2009).

These empirical patterns are reminiscent of the positive correlation between population size and the hierarchical complexity of political organizations. Although there is a likely causal connection, there also is considerable variation within demographic ranges and parameters of political complexity (e.g., Feinman 2013; Johnson 1982). As with the relationship between population size and political complexity, significant explanations for historical patterns of inequality have to address variation across time and space as well as between cases and contexts that share production modes.

Prominent economists (Milanovic 2011; Piketty 2014; Stiglitz 2013) have begun to challenge and reject long-held ideas that recent inequality is simply the consequence of economic growth, economic complexity, workforce specialization, or the natural outcome of economic cycles (e.g., Kuznets 1955). As Krugman wrote in a 2006 newspaper column, "I've been studying the long-term history of inequality in the United States. And, it's hard to avoid the sense that it matters a lot which political party, or more accurately, which political ideology rules Washington."

Another Nobel Prize winner, Joseph Stiglitz (2013:35), states on the same topic, "American inequality didn't just happen. It was created. Market forces played a role, but it was not market forces alone. Economic laws are universal, but our growing inequality . . . is . . . distinctly American." Adopting a broader historical lens, Piketty (2015:69; see also Piketty 2014:20, 35) declares, "[O]ne should be wary of any economic determinism in regard to inequalities of wealth and income. . . . The history of the distribution of wealth has always been deeply political. . . . How this history plays out depends on how societies view inequalities and what kinds of policies and institutions they adopt." If economists recognize this essential political dimension to inequality, other social scientists should not have difficulty embracing that perspective. As the writings of the authors above outline, trends and degrees of socioeconomic inequality reflect the basic sociopolitical compacts or contracts that bind human cooperative arrangements. In reference to social contracts, we do not consider only specific, often abstract written statements; rather, we also reference the institutions, accepted practices or norms, and interpersonal bonds that underpin and tether our social formations. In other words, multiple causes underpin inequality in wealth (see chapter 1), but institutional (sensu North 1990:3) variation generally is one critically important factor (Boix 2010; Hartmann et al. 2017).

INEQUALITY IN THE VALLEY OF OAXACA

Analytical assessments of household differentials in access, socioeconomic stratification, and inequality focused on the pre-Hispanic Valley of Oaxaca have previously been undertaken. Prior studies have analyzed the roughly three-thousand-year sequence from the first villages to the Spanish conquest (Kowalewski et al. 1992; Kowalewski and Finsten 1983), while others have focused more narrowly on the Classic period (Feinman and Nicholas 2007; Feinman et al. 2008; Haller et al. 2006), when the urban center of Monte Albán (figure 10.1) reached its height in size and monumentality. All of these studies incorporate elements of quantitative information, yet none provides assessments directly comparable with other places and times.

Ideally, we wish it were possible to construct a household-based, quantitative examination of inequality in the Valley of Oaxaca over the entire pre-Hispanic sequence. However, constrained by the available data and the quality standards of sample size and representation (e.g., Deininger and Squire 1996:567–71), the published information at the domestic scale can sustain investigations only for the Classic period and, with less analytical elaboration, the San José phase (during the Early Formative period). We recognize that greater quantitative consideration of the Postclassic period (ca. AD 800–1520) would enhance our investigations, but at this time, because of empirical gaps, we have to rely exclusively on more traditional means to assess the nature of inequality at that time.

Guided by the conceptual frames and constrained by the empirical limitations outlined above, our research aims and expectations are threefold. First, building on previous discussions of Monte Albán and its hinterland during the Classic period (e.g., Feinman and Nicholas 2016), we suspect that in accord with a more collectively organized (see Blanton and Fargher 2008) or "corporate" (e.g., Blanton et al. 1996; Feinman 2001) political formation in the Valley of Oaxaca at that time, wealth inequality would not have been high in a relative sense compared to other urban states in pre-Hispanic Mesoamerica or to archaic states elsewhere. In the context of distributed rather than highly centralized power, wealth inequality was depressed. Furthermore, wealth distributions should not exhibit marked class divisions, with a stark division between a few houses at the top and all others below. Rather, variation in wealth is expected to have followed a somewhat more continuous or gradual gradient. Second, we suspect that earlier during the San José phase (e.g., Marcus and Flannery 1996), when the polities were smaller and the basis of inequality potentially different, we should see distributional patterns that do not necessarily conform to or match those for the Classic period, many centuries later. Third, if expected differences in the degree and nature of inequality also are found for the later Postclassic (Feinman 1996; Feinman and Nicholas 2011, 2016), then we would not find any regular, unidirectional trend or trajectory of change, such as ever-increasing inequality over time; rather, shifting political relations, and their associated norms and institutions, are seen to have a considerable effect on diachronic shifts in the distribution of wealth.

CLASSIC PERIOD INEQUALITY IN
OAXACA: RESIDENTIAL SPACE

To examine wealth distributions for the Classic period, we rely principally on findings from archaeological house excavations, conducted at six pre-Hispanic settlements (Ejutla, El Palmillo, Lambityeco, Macuilxochitl, Mitla Fortress, and Monte Albán), as well as intensive surface-mapping projects implemented at the large secondary center of El Palmillo and the somewhat smaller Mitla Fortress (Feinman and Nicholas 2004). Previously, we (Feinman and Nicholas 2007:145) have argued that variation in residential architecture provides the most marked dimension for wealth differences during the Classic period in the Valley of Oaxaca. The relative sizes of architectural constructions and spaces reflect wealth differences, as these units often endured across generations with only modest shifts and remodeling in size and plan.

Here, we rely on and apply Gini measurements to assess three domestic architectural variables: terrace area (which roughly corresponds to size of residential house lots), house size, and patio area (Classic period residential units in Oaxaca were always composed of a series of rooms that bounded a central patio). In addition, we also examine several artifact distributions, including relative domestic access to obsidian and other rare/valued items. There are no obsidian sources in the state of Oaxaca, so this material—readily transformed into a sharp cutting tool—was clearly valued and broadly procured. The more quantitative comparisons of Classic period houses along these four dimensions are supplemented with other available evidence as relevant and empirically sustainable.

Unfortunately, there is no truly comprehensive or random sample of residential units for the entire Valley of Oaxaca during the Classic period. Instead, as is always the case in archaeology, we draw on the most comprehensive and representative samples available. Such samples come from two settlements at which pre-Hispanic residential terraces have been intensively mapped in detail (Feinman and Nicholas 2004), so that the size of each individual terrace was measured. These terraces, when excavated, have no indications of agricultural plots or spaces on the flat, measured area of these features (Feinman et al. 2007).

The largest sample of terraces comes from El Palmillo (Feinman and Nicholas 2012:fig. 5), a secondary center situated at the eastern limit of the Tlacolula arm of the valley (figure 10.1). The surface distribution of terraces at the site largely reflects the Late Classic period layout of this community, which was occupied for at least five centuries. There was little use of El Palmillo after its Late Classic period occupation, and because of its elevated location, relatively little farming was carried out on the site after its pre-Hispanic use. Such postconquest farming has destroyed terrace boundaries at similar sites in the region, precluding the use of terrace sizes to measure domestic space. There are particular problems at hilltop Monte Albán (Blanton 1978), the largest Classic period site in the region, as well as at Guirún (Feinman and Nicholas 2004), where terrace sizes were found to be much larger at the base of the hill where postoccupation farming and herding was carried out.

At El Palmillo, a total of 1,496 terraces and flat-topped platforms were mapped. At least 1,343 of those terraces and platforms were judged to be large enough to be associated with residences and are included in this analysis (terraces smaller than fourteen square meters were not included). Based on subsequent excavations on a number of terraces (e.g., Feinman and Nicholas 2007; Feinman et al. 2008), larger terraces were always associated with single domestic units and the size of a terrace correlated with the size of the house sustained on the terrace. Thus terrace size

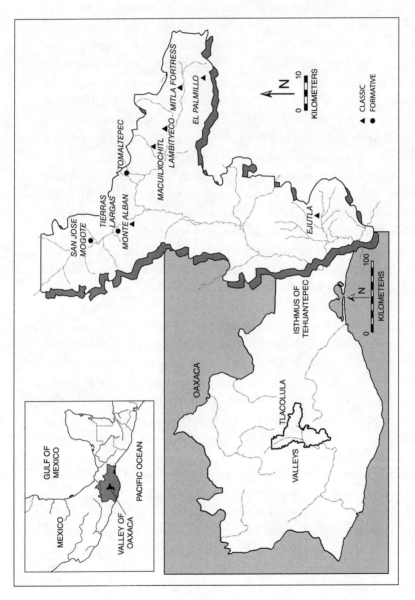

Figure 10.1 The Valley of Oaxaca in southern Mexico and places mentioned in the text.

provides a metric to assess the distribution of domestic space across an entire settlement.

Terrace size (residential space) at El Palmillo was distributed in a continuous manner. That is, there were a few large residential spaces and many smaller ones but also a scattering of residences that were intermediate in size. The Gini value (figure 10.2a) for this distribution is 0.39 with a 95 percent confidence interval between 0.37 and 0.42. Throughout this analysis, all Gini values and confidence intervals were calculated using reldist and boot (Canty and Ripley 2016; Davison and Hinkley 1997; Handcock 2015; Handcock and Morris 1999); the application of these programs produces consistent values for both the larger (such as this one) and smaller sets of data. The confidence intervals presented are always 95 percent.

For the Mitla Fortress, a total of 573 terraces and flat-topped platforms were mapped. We followed the same size considerations as at El Palmillo and found that 517 of these were large enough to consider residential. Using this as our sample, we again found that residential space was distributed more continuously (as opposed to divisible into two discrete size clusters) across the settlement. The Gini value for the Mitla Fortress (0.36) is slightly lower than for El Palmillo (figure 10.2a, 10.2b), although, given the confidence interval for the former, between 0.34 and 0.39, there is overlap between the ranges for the two sites.

CLASSIC PERIOD INEQUALITY IN OAXACA: HOUSE AND PATIO SPACE

We also explored two other dimensions of residential architecture as metrics for the degree of Classic period inequality: house size and patio size. For these analyses, we depended on excavated data, and so our samples were necessarily smaller. Although the size of a house and its patio in the Classic period Valley of Oaxaca are roughly correlated, we examined both variables; by doing so we were able to cobble together slightly different samples because the same sets of information are not necessarily available for each case. For each analysis, we have a representative range of cases: some from large houses and others from smaller dwellings. Large houses are generally more elaborate than smaller ones, with more rooms, thicker walls, larger tombs, and greater use of lime plaster. What we lose in the

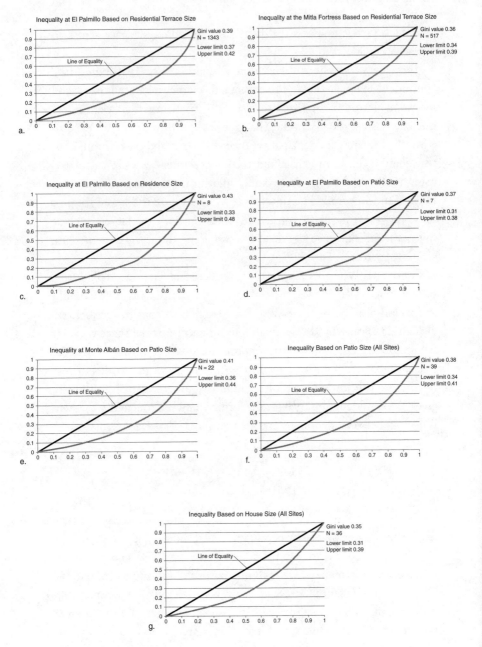

Figure 10.2 Gini values in Classic period Oaxaca, based on (a) residential terrace size at El Palmillo; (b) residential terrace size at the Mitla Fortress; (c) residence size at El Palmillo; (d) patio size at El Palmillo; (e) patio size at Monte Albán; (f) patio size at six sites in the Valley of Oaxaca; (g) house size at six sites in the Valley of Oaxaca.

representation of the sample by focusing on smaller numbers of houses and patios (as compared to the larger sample of terraces) is somewhat balanced by a modest gain in interpretive precision. Simply put, fewer inferences are necessary to envision excavated house and patio sizes as domestic indicators of household wealth when compared with surface assessments of terrace areas (e.g., Blanton 1994:14–15).

We first look at El Palmillo, where an excavated suite of eight pre-Hispanic houses spanned the base to the apex of the hill (Feinman and Nicholas 2007). Generally in Oaxaca, at hilltop terrace settlements, lower-status houses were situated near the base and the socioeconomic standing of residential units increased with elevation (Feinman and Nicholas 2007). Based on house size for this sample of eight, our Gini value is 0.43 (figure 10.2c); however, the confidence interval is broad, between 0.33 and 0.48.

Only seven of these El Palmillo residences had defined patios. We calculated the Gini value for this sample to be 0.37 (figure 10.2d), with a confidence interval between 0.31 and 0.38. The distributions of houses and patios, especially the latter, are continuous. Structure 35 had a palatial plan with rooms on all sides of the patio and L-shaped corner rooms. The size of its patio was intermediate between the two larger palaces and the other residences in the sample. At the same time, the patio for the residence on Terrace 507 was larger than other nonpalatial residences.

We also examined residential patio sizes for twenty-two excavated houses at the Valley of Oaxaca's largest site, Monte Albán (González Licón 2003; Winter 1974; see also Feinman and Nicholas 2007:142). The Gini coefficient for this sample is 0.41, with a confidence range between 0.36 and 0.44 (figure 10.2e). The coefficient for the Monte Albán sample falls between the house and patio Gini indices for El Palmillo, and the ranges overlap.

However, when the excavated sample of twenty-two patios is compared to a larger sample of residential patio sizes recorded (Blanton 1978) during the surface survey of Monte Albán (Feinman and Nicholas 2007:142), the excavated sample appears to be a bit skewed toward larger houses. Slightly fewer than a third of the excavated patios were smaller than twenty square meters in size, while in the larger surface sample, roughly half of the patios were smaller than twenty square meters. Such a bias in the excavated sample is explicable, as the top of Monte Albán has been the focus for most archaeological excavations. A more representative sample that included a greater number of smaller houses might yield a slightly lower Gini value. Nevertheless, even as measured, the confidence intervals overlap. And the excavated and surface patio distributions for Monte Albán are rather continuous and not discretely defined clusters of large and small patios (Feinman and Nicholas 2007:142).

In a final suite of analyses, we examined a set of patio areas and house sizes from Classic period sites across the Valley of Oaxaca. Overall, we had sufficient information to include a total of thirty-nine patios and thirty-six houses, which cumulate data from six Classic period site excavations in the Valley of Oaxaca (figure 10.1): Ejutla (Feinman 1999), El Palmillo (Feinman 2007; Feinman and Nicholas 2007, 2011), Lambityeco (Feinman et al. 2016; Lind and Urcid 1983, 2010), Macuilxochitl (Faulseit 2013), Mitla Fortress (Feinman et al. 2010), and Monte Albán (Blanton 1978; Caso 1935, 1938; González Licón 2003; Marcus 2008; Winter 1974). Both large and small houses were included in this sample, and the respective architectural features were presented in sufficient detail to include in this analysis.

The Gini value for the sample of thirty-nine residential patios from the Classic period Valley of Oaxaca is 0.38, with the confidence interval between 0.34 and 0.41 (figure 10.2f). For the thirty-six houses, the Gini coefficient is 0.35, with the confidence interval between 0.31 and 0.39 (figure 10.2g). Larger houses may be associated with bigger households and spaces for food storage. This is reasonable, as access to labor and the private accumulation of food are two bases of Classic period inequality in Oaxaca.

Although the Gini values for these seven Classic period architectural measures vary between 0.35 and 0.43, the 95 percent confidence ranges for all seven measurements overlap between 0.37 and 0.38. For the architectural metrics of wealth distribution, 0.38 (figure 10.3) seems like a reasonable place to settle, close to the Gini values for the two samples that are most representative: El Palmillo terrace areas (0.39) and the cumulative Valley of Oaxaca patio sample (0.38).

CLASSIC PERIOD INEQUALITY IN OAXACA: ARTIFACT DISTRIBUTIONS

We also adopted a second parameter, residential artifact distributions, to examine wealth differentials in the Classic period Valley of Oaxaca. For

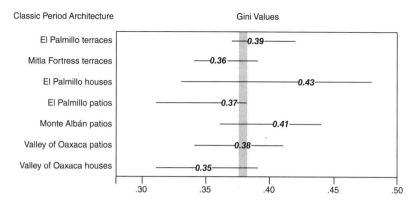

Figure 10.3 Summary of Gini values for Classic period sites in the Valley of Oaxaca based on a range of data types.

this analysis, we examined domestic assemblages for thirteen excavated houses. In each case, we compared residences during their history of use, so the patterns reflect the intergenerational wealth of residential units that were occupied across generations and structure rebuildings. To ensure comparability in the acquisition, recording, and reporting of data, we focused on thirteen houses that were excavated by two of us from the sites of El Palmillo (n = 8), the Mitla Fortress (n = 3), Ejutla (n = 1), and Lambityeco (n = 1).

We assume that any artifacts deposited and recovered in or immediately adjacent to a specific domestic unit had been utilized by the occupants of that house (e.g., Beck 2003; Beck and Hill 2004). For each house, we included objects from both primary and secondary deposits in the analysis. In fact, for Oaxaca, most domestic refuse, and consequently artifacts, in Classic period archaeological contexts come from the latter. We examined three artifact classes for which the sample size was adequate: obsidian, bone ornaments, and total animal bone. As noted above, obsidian was exotic and sufficiently valued to acquire in quantity (e.g., Golitko and Feinman 2015). Bone ornaments were adornments (such as beads and pendants) and required craft labor to prepare. Meat was a critical source of protein that likely could have been acquired through diverse means. We have less confidence in this last metric for that reason and also because the quantity of animal bone is not the most direct or accurate indicator of the quantity and quality of meat resources.

The Gini values (table 10.1) for obsidian (0.38, confidence interval 0.25–0.45) and bone ornament distributions (0.39, confidence interval 0.29–0.45) are very much in accord with the architectural Gini coefficients for the Valley of Oaxaca Classic period. The Gini index for overall animal bone counts (0.34, confidence interval 0.28–0.37) reflects a slightly lower degree of inequality, although the 95 percent confidence interval still overlaps—just barely, at the upper end of the interval—with the ranges of all other Classic period metrics. Despite different variable dimensions and sample components, the overall consistency of these ten Gini measurements for the Classic period Valley of Oaxaca is rewarding. There is no reason that the use of a diversity of variable dimensions that include different sample compositions should lead to or promote analytical consistency in the values reached; in fact, just the opposite.

A Gini value for relative wealth inequality around 0.38 seems to be a reasonable starting estimate for the Classic period Valley of Oaxaca. This value dovetails with previous, less quantitative, interpretations that have seen the degree of inequality for the Classic period Monte Albán polity as relatively muted (e.g., Blanton et al. 1996; Feinman and Nicholas 2007, 2012, 2016) compared to other archaic states, less ostentatious than for contemporaneous Classic period Maya polities, such as Palenque (Gini value 0.44) and Sayil (Gini value 0.71) (Brown et al. 2012). Likewise, not all of the plotted distributions break down into two discrete, easily divisible clusters; there always were some domestic units in the middle ground. Our intent is not to challenge the notion that people in the

Table 10.1 Formative versus Classic: household goods (calculations based on frequency data)

Period and sample size	Good	Gini	Lower	Upper
Formative (San José phase) (16 houses, San José Mogote)	Obsidian	0.61	0.53	0.66
	Mica	0.57	0.49	0.64
	Shell	0.52	0.44	0.58
	Jade	0.71	0.61	0.82
Classic (IIIB–IV phase) (13 houses, El Palmillo, Lambityeco, Mitla Fortress, Ejutla)	Obsidian	0.38	0.25	0.45
	Bone ornament	0.39	0.29	0.45
	Animal bone	0.34	0.28	0.37

Classic period Valley of Oaxaca were born into elite or commoner status. They may have been. Yet if they were, there clearly was enough social mobility that birthright could be somewhat eclipsed by actual socio-economic practice. Wealth distributions (whether measured by architectural space or by household access patterns) were more continuous and do not directly reflect simple, discrete class divisions by birthright or any other factor.

FORMATIVE PERIOD INEQUALITY IN OAXACA

Compared to other preindustrial states (e.g., Brown et al. 2012; Kron 2011:134; Milanovic et al. 2011:263–64; Ober 2010:258–59; Scheidel and Friesen 2009:84–85), wealth inequality was relatively muted in the Valley of Oaxaca during the Classic period when urban Monte Albán dominated the region's landscape. What about inequality in the region before the rise of an urban center and at a time when the regional population was much lower? Was inequality during the San José phase expressed along similar dimensions as during later times? Unfortunately, the suite of available archaeological data published for pre–Monte Albán times makes a quantitative assessment of inequality a bit more challenging, dependent on smaller sample sizes than what we have for the Classic period. Nevertheless, for the San José phase, we were able to compile information on both architecture and artifacts that allowed for preliminary comparisons with later times.

We began with a focus on domestic architecture and compared house size for a total of eight pre-Hispanic dwellings from three sites dating to the San José phase: four from San José Mogote (Flannery and Marcus 2005), the largest settlement in the region at that time; two from Tierras Largas (Winter 1972); and two from Santo Domingo Tomaltepec (Whalen 1981) (figure 10.1). The Gini value (0.25, confidence interval 0.19–0.28) for this sample of house sizes (figure 10.4) is much lower than for any index (architecture or artifacts) pertaining to the Classic period. Clearly, the San José phase houses in the sample were more similar in size than those in our Classic period samples. However, a possible higher-status house (House 13), which was built on an earthen platform at the region's largest settlement (San José Mogote), was not included in this analysis, because it could not be fully excavated (Flannery and Marcus

Inequality in Formative (San José Phase) Oaxaca Based on Structure Size

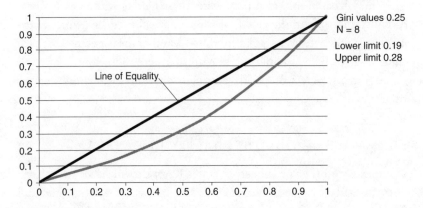

Figure 10.4 Inequality in the Formative period Valley of Oaxaca based on structure size.

2005:396–401). Although the representativeness of our analyzed sample remains in question, domestic architecture does seem to have been less of a marker of wealth differentiation during the San José phase than it was later during the Classic period.

We also examined distributional patterns for a range of portable goods in the San José phase sample. For comparability across the sample, we drew entirely on houses from San José Mogote, where sixteen houses were excavated and consistently reported (Flannery and Marcus 2005). We calculated Gini values (table 10.1) for the distribution of four exotic, portable goods: obsidian, mica, shell, and jade. Each of these goods was consumed more unequally than any of the wealth indicators measured for the Classic period and much more unequally than the San José metrics for house areas. Jade was the most unequally distributed good (Gini value 0.71, confidence interval 0.61–0.82), followed by obsidian (Gini value 0.61, confidence interval 0.53–0.66), mica (Gini value 0.57, confidence interval 0.49–0.64), and shell (Gini value 0.52, confidence interval 0.44–0.58). For this domestic-scale comparison, obsidian was much more unequally consumed than it was in the sample pertaining to the later Classic period.

Although we are reluctant to push these findings too far, several interpretations seem sustainable. First, in the San José phase, the consumption of valued, exotic items was a much more expressed indicator of inequality than were differences in domestic architecture. This finding is consistent with extant interpretations that view access to specific interpersonal networks as a more critical basis of power and wealth in Formative Oaxaca as compared to the Classic period (e.g., Blanton et al. 1996). In contrast to the San José phase, the portable wealth and architectural measures for Classic period Oaxaca yield similar results (Gini values). By the later Classic period, following the rise of more-hierarchical forms of governance (Blanton et al. 1999), entrenched class distinctions may have legitimized multigenerational status-based differences in residential architectural elaboration (palaces vs. commoner residence plans).

A second observation is that even within the same cultural region, inequality may have been expressed along different dimensions over time. We calculated consistent metrics for the degree of inequality during the Classic period regardless of whether we examined distributions of architecture or artifacts. But differential access to portable goods and items of adornment was the clearest marker of inequality earlier during the San José phase.

POSTCLASSIC PERIOD INEQUALITY IN OAXACA

It is unfortunate that we do not have the kinds of systematically reported multicase samples of domestic-scale data for Postclassic Oaxaca that exist for earlier periods. As a result, we cannot calculate Gini values for the Postclassic period. Nevertheless, for the Late Postclassic period, we are able to draw on specific archaeological examples to characterize the nature of inequality and to offer marked contrasts with how inequality was expressed earlier (e.g., Blanton et al. 1996; Feinman 1996; Feinman and Nicholas 2016; Kowalewski and Finsten 1983).

There is no question that the most elaborate funerary assemblages for any pre-Hispanic epoch in the Valley of Oaxaca—Monte Albán Tomb 7 and Zaachila Tomb 1—pertain to the Late Postclassic period (e.g., Caso 1982; Gallegos Ruíz 1978). Of course, most Postclassic burial contexts were much less elaborate (e.g., Herrera Muzgo T. and Winter 2003) than those two famous tombs. Empirically, there is no doubt that Late Postclassic period access to portable wealth was dramatically unequal, at least at death, in the Valley of Oaxaca. This finding corresponds with an assessment of artifact distributions by site, based on regional survey observations, which found much more marked disparities during the Late Postclassic period compared to any other phase subsequent to the founding of Monte Albán (Kowalewski and Finsten 1983:424). In both life and death, inequality may have been greater during the Late Postclassic period than during the earlier Classic period.

In the Valley of Oaxaca, the degree of inequality may have increased from the end of the Classic through the Postclassic period with the fall of the more collectively organized leadership (sensu Blanton and Fargher 2008) of Monte Albán and the rise of petty states. During the Postclassic period, polities were dominated by elite dynasties and woven into larger confederations through interpersonal networks (e.g., Feinman 1996; Feinman and Nicholas 2016; Pohl 2003a). Clearly, over this same transition, inequality became more explicitly expressed through portable, exotic wealth and elaborate items of adornment. These goods served to express status and power, while they also were used to establish and maintain networks across space (e.g., Blanton et al. 2005; Pohl 2003b).

SYNTHETIC PERSPECTIVES ON GINI VALUES, INEQUALITY, AND ANCIENT OAXACA

Where we can apply Gini coefficients for large, representative sets of data that spanned an array of metrics of wealth inequality (the Valley of Oaxaca, Classic period), we achieve tight, consistent values that seem to dovetail with extant interpretations that peg inequality at that time as relatively muted compared to other urbanized, preindustrial settings. For example, at El Palmillo (table 10.2), two of us (Feinman and Nicholas 2007) previously found clear distinctions in access to portable goods and adornments between residences of different sizes, but these distinctions were not extreme or strictly dichotomous. Although the Gini analytical measures produce less consistent results when applied to the earlier San José phase, they do provide a strong case for the recognition that inequality may be expressed in or manifest to variable degrees along different dimensions. This observation resonates for broader comparative analyses because it implies that one Gini value for any time or place may not be sufficient to understand the complexity of inequality, at least until a coincidence of Gini values along multiple axes is empirically demonstrable.

Table 10.2 Portable items from eight residences at El Palmillo

Residence	Patio area	*N* green stone	Obsidian as % of all stone	*N* bone ornaments	*N* stone ornaments	*N* shell ornaments
T.1162	—	3	1.9	2	9	15
T.1163	20.3	2	4.2	4	10	11
T.1147/48	21.0	2	2.1	0	2	10
T.925	21.6	4	7.1	13	15	10
T.507	27.6	4	9.3	10	27	18
St.35	46.2	3	10.0	8	16	15
T.335	97.3	10	8.9	20	15	28
P.11	108.8	11	20.8	12	25	7

For the pre-Hispanic Valley of Oaxaca, we also note that the degree and expression of inequality varied over time. This chronological variance has been recognized for the more contemporary world (e.g., Lindert and Williamson 2016), but it also can now be seen for deeper in the past. At least given what we know now, inequality in the pre-Hispanic Valley of Oaxaca does not appear to have been expressed along one axis or in one way, or change in only one direction over time. Rather, it appears to have been intricately tied to wider politico-economic relations and organization, with the more collectively organized Classic period population less marked by inequities, at least in regard to the distribution of portable wealth goods.

This is a critical point because not all manifestations of inequality are material, nor are they underpinned by strictly economic factors and considerations. For example, during the Classic period in the Valley of Oaxaca, power inequities were in part sustained by greater elite access to public space. Elaborate residential palaces often were situated near central plazas and public buildings where large gatherings and processions were periodically held. Unequal access to ritual seems to have sustained inequities in power but did not translate into great disparities in the consumption and hoarding of portable wealth. Clearly, by the Postclassic period, in the Valley of Oaxaca, these relations had shifted, and public space was reduced. The activities that previously had occurred in public contexts were shifted toward more-private settings, as palaces (e.g., Flannery 1983) and elite networks expanded while the importance of portable wealth in establishing and sustaining alliances and power relations increased (e.g., Feinman 1996; Pohl 2003b).

The consistently low Gini values that we calculated for the Valley of Oaxaca Classic period are informative, especially as indicators of wealth inequality, because they challenge the long-term notion that archaic states were always starkly divisible into the rulers and the ruled, with dramatic differences in resources and quality of life between the two. This coercive/despotic vantage on archaic states is well ensconced in the historical/social sciences for preindustrial times (e.g., Mann 1977; Wittfogel 1957) but now is being challenged as not uniformly applicable (Blanton 2016; Blanton and Fargher 2008), with some historical polities seen as having had a more collective institutional orientation and lower degrees of wealth inequity (e.g., Mann 2016, for a change from his earlier perspective). If the distribution of power and the nature of governance varied across ancient urban states, and even in given states over time, then we might expect to see chronological variance in the degree of inequality and its practical expression as well. Such recognition of variation is important as a check against the acceptance of overly facile or mechanistic models of global history.

In sum, we have utilized a quantitatively informed perspective on preindustrial inequality in the pre-Hispanic Valley of Oaxaca as a basis to start building comparative perspectives that cross both space and time. While we believe that our tack has yielded worthwhile and consistent results that align provocatively with previous interpretations, we also have gained valuable cautions that serve to broaden future comparative applications of Gini values along multiple analytical dimensions (e.g., Milanovic 2016; Ober 2010; Piketty 2014:266). After all, the overarching aim must include not only the quantification or measurement of relative inequality but also an understanding of how specifically it was established in each historical context and, most importantly, the construction of conceptual tools to explain the factors underpinning its degrees and manifestations.

REFERENCES CITED

Alfani, Guido. 2015. Economic Inequality in Northwestern Italy: A Long-Term View (Fourteenth to Eighteenth Centuries). *Journal of Economic History* 75: 1058–94.

Beck, Margaret E. 2003. Ceramic Deposition and Midden Formation in Kalinga Philippines. PhD dissertation, University of Arizona, Tucson.

Beck, Margaret E., and Matthew E. Hill Jr. 2004. Rubbish, Relatives, and Residence: The Family Use of Middens. *Journal of Archaeological Method and Theory* 11:297–333.

Blanton, Richard E. 1978. *Monte Albán: Settlement Patterns at the Zapotec Capital.* Academic Press, New York.

———. 1994. *Houses and Households: A Comparative Story.* Plenum, New York.

———. 2016. *How Humans Cooperate: Confronting the Challenges of Collective Action.* University Press of Colorado, Boulder.

Blanton, Richard, and Lane Fargher. 2008. *Collective Action in the Formation of Pre-modern States.* Springer, New York.

Blanton, Richard, Lane Fargher, and Verenice Y. Heredia Espinoza. 2005. The Mesoamerican World of Goods and Its Transformations. In *Settlement, Subsistence, and Social Complexity: Essays Honoring the Legacy of Jeffrey R. Parsons,* edited by Richard E. Blanton, pp. 260–94. Cotsen Institute of Archaeology, University of California, Los Angeles.

Blanton, Richard E., Gary M. Feinman, Stephen A. Kowalewski, and Linda M. Nicholas. 1999. *Ancient Oaxaca: The Monte Albán State.* Cambridge University Press, Cambridge.

Blanton, Richard E., Gary M. Feinman, Stephen A. Kowalewski, and Peter N. Peregrine. 1996. A Dual-Processional Theory for the Evolution of Mesoamerican Civilization. *Current Anthropology* 37:1–14, 65–68.

Boix, Carles. 2010. Origins and Persistence of Economic Inequality. *Annual Review of Political Science* 13:489–516.

Borgerhoff Mulder, Monique, Samuel Bowles, Tom Hertz, Adrian Bell, Jan Beise, Greg Clark, Ila Fazzio, et al. 2009. Intergenerational Wealth Transmission and the Dynamics of Inequality in Small-Scale Societies. *Science* 326:682–88.

Borgerhoff Mulder, Monique, Ila Fazzio, William Irons, Richard I. McElreath, Samuel Bowles, Adrian Bell, Tom Hertz, and Leela Hazzah. 2010. Pastoralism and Wealth Inequality: Revisiting an Old Question. *Current Anthropology* 51:35–48.

Bowles, Samuel, Eric Alden Smith, and Monique Borgerhoff Mulder. 2010. The Emergence and Persistence of Inequality in Premodern Societies. *Current Anthropology* 51:7–17.

Brown, Clifford T., April A. Watson, Ashley Gravlin Beman, and Larry S. Liebovich. 2012. Poor Mayapan. In *The Ancient Maya of Mexico: Reinterpreting the Past of the Northern Maya Lowlands,* edited by Geoffrey E. Braswell, pp. 306–24. Equinox Publishing, Bristol, Conn.

Canty, Angelo, and Brian Ripley. 2016. boot: Bootstrap R (S-Plus) Functions. R package version 1.3–18.

Caso, Alfonso. 1935. *Las exploraciones en Oaxaca: 1934–1935.* Publicación 18. Instituto Panamericano de Geografía e Historia, Mexico City.

————. 1938. *Las exploraciones en Oaxaca, quinta y sexta temporadas 1936–1937.* Publicación 34. Instituto Panamericano de Geografía e Historia, Mexico City.

————. 1982. *El tesoro de Monte Albán.* Memorias 3. Instituto Nacional de Antropología e Historia, Mexico City.

Chin, Gilbert, and Elizabeth Culotta. 2014. The Science of Inequality: What the Numbers Tell Us. *Science* 344:818–21.

Cho, Adrian. 2014. Physicists Say It's Simple. *Science* 344:828.

Cowell, Frank A. 2011. *Measuring Inequality.* 3rd ed. Oxford University Press, New York.

Davison, Anthony C., and David V. Hinkley. 1997. *Bootstrap Methods and Their Applications.* Cambridge University Press, Cambridge.

Deaton, Angus. 2014. Inevitable Inequality? *Science* 344:783.

Deininger, Klaus, and Lyn Squire. 1996. A New Data Set Measuring Income Inequality. *World Bank Economic Review* 18:565–91.

Faulseit, Ronald K. 2013. *Cerro Danush: Excavations at a Hilltop Community in the Eastern Valley of Oaxaca, Mexico.* Memoirs 54. Museum of Anthropology, University of Michigan, Ann Arbor.

Feinman, Gary M. 1996. The Changing Structure of Macroregional Mesoamerica: With Focus on the Classic-Postclassic Transition in the Valley of Oaxaca. *Journal of World-Systems Research* 27(1):1–18.

————. 1999. Rethinking Our Assumptions: Economic Specialization at the Household Scale in Ancient Ejutla, Oaxaca, Mexico. In *Pottery and People: A Dynamic Interaction*, edited by James M. Skibo and Gary M. Feinman, pp. 81–98. University of Utah Press, Salt Lake City.

————. 2001. Mesoamerican Political Complexity: The Corporate-Network Dimension. In *From Leaders to Rulers*, edited by Jonathan Haas, pp. 151–75. Kluwer/Plenum, New York.

————. 2007. The Last Quarter Century of Archaeological Research in the Central Valleys of Oaxaca. *Mexicon* 29:3–15.

————. 2013. The Emergence of Social Complexity: Why More than Population Size Matters. In *Cooperation and Collective Action: Archaeological Perspectives*, edited by David M. Carballo, pp. 35–56. University Press of Colorado, Boulder.

Feinman, Gary M., and Linda M. Nicholas. 2004. Hilltop Terrace Sites in Oaxaca, Mexico: Intensive Surface Survey at Guirún, El Palmillo, and the Mitla Fortress. *Fieldiana, Anthropology* 37. Field Museum of Natural History, Chicago.

————. 2007. The Socioeconomic Organization of the Classic Period Zapotec State. In *The Political Economy of Ancient Mesoamerica: Transformations During the Formative and Classic Periods*, edited by Vernon L. Scarborough and John E. Clark, pp. 135–47. University of New Mexico Press, Albuquerque.

————. 2011. Monte Albán: Una perspectiva desde los límites del Valle de Oaxaca. In *Monte Albán en la encrucijada regional y disciplinaria: Memoria de la Quinta Mesa Redonda de Monte Albán*, edited by Nelly M. Robles García and

Ángel I. Rivera Guzmán, pp. 241–84. Instituto Nacional de Antropología e Historia, Mexico City.

————. 2012. The Late Prehispanic Economy of the Valley of Oaxaca: Weaving Threads from Data, Theory, and Subsequent History. *Research in Economic Anthropology* 32:225–58.

————. 2016. After Monte Albán in the Central Valleys of Oaxaca: A Reassessment. In *Beyond Collapse: Archaeological Perspectives on Resilience, Revitalization, and Transformation in Complex Societies*, edited by Ronald K. Faulseit, pp. 43–69. Southern Illinois University Press, Carbondale.

Feinman, Gary M., Linda M. Nicholas, and Lindsay C. Baker. 2010. The Missing Femur at the Mitla Fortress and Its Implications. *Antiquity* 84:1089–101.

Feinman, Gary M., Linda M. Nicholas, and Helen R. Haines. 2007. Classic Period Agricultural Intensification and Domestic Life at El Palmillo, Valley of Oaxaca, Mexico. In *Seeking a Richer Harvest: The Archaeology of Subsistence Intensification, Innovation, and Change*, edited by Tina L. Thurston and Christopher T. Fisher, pp. 23–61. Springer, New York.

Feinman, Gary M., Linda M. Nicholas, Heather A. Lapham, Ricardo Higelin Ponce de León, Jorge Ríos Allier, and Christopher Morehart. 2016. Broadening the Context for Classic Period Lambityeco, Oaxaca: New Discoveries from 2013–2015. *Mexicon* 38:46–55.

Feinman, Gary M., Linda M. Nicholas, and Edward F. Maher. 2008. Domestic Offerings at El Palmillo: Implications for Community Organization. *Ancient Mesoamerica* 19:175–94.

Flannery, Kent V. 1983. Major Monte Albán V Sites: Zaachila, Xoxocatlán, Cuilapan, Yagul, and Abasolo. In *The Cloud People: Divergent Evolution of the Zapotec and Mixtec Civilizations*, edited by Kent V. Flannery and Joyce Marcus, pp. 290–95. Academic Press, New York.

Flannery, Kent V., and Joyce Marcus. 2005. *Excavations at San José Mogote 1: The Household Archaeology*. Memoirs 40. Museum of Anthropology, University of Michigan, Ann Arbor.

Gallegos Ruíz, Roberto. 1978. *El Señor 9 Flor en Zaachila*. Universidad Nacional Autónoma de México, Mexico City.

Golitko, Mark, and Gary M. Feinman. 2015. Procurement and Distribution of Pre-Hispanic Mesoamerican Obsidian 900 B.C.–A.D. 1520: A Social Network Analysis. *Journal of Archaeological Method and Theory* 22:206–47.

González Licón, Ernesto. 2003. Social Inequality at Monte Albán, Oaxaca: Household Analysis from Terminal Formative to Early Classic. PhD dissertation, University of Pittsburgh, Pittsburgh.

Haller, Mikael J., Gary M. Feinman, and Linda M. Nicholas. 2006. Socioeconomic Inequality and Differential Access to Faunal Resources at El Palmillo, Oaxaca, Mexico. *Ancient Mesoamerica* 17:39–56.

Handcock, Mark S. 2015. Relative Distribution Methods. Version 1.6-4. www.stat.ucla.edu/~handcock/RelDist.

Handcock, Mark S., and Martina Morris. 1999. *Relative Distribution Methods in the Social Sciences.* Springer, New York.

Hartmann, Dominik, Miguel R. Guevara, Christian Jara-Figueroa, Manuel Aristaran, and César A. Hidalgo. 2017. Linking Economic Complexity, Institutions, and Income Inequality. *World Development* 93:75–93.

Hawkes, Christopher. 1954. Archaeological Theory and Method: Some Suggestions from the Old World. *American Anthropologist* 56:155–68.

Hayden, Brian. 1995. Pathways to Power: Principles for Creating Socioeconomic Inequalities. In *Foundations of Social Inequality,* edited by T. Douglas Price and Gary M. Feinman, pp. 15–86. Plenum Press, New York.

Herrera Muzgo T., Alicia, and Marcus Winter. 2003. *Tres tumbas postclásicas en El Sabino, Zimatlán, Oaxaca.* Arqueología Oaxaqueña 1. Conaculta, Instituto Nacional de Antropología e Historia, Oaxaca.

Johnson, Gregory A. 1982. Organizational Structure and Scalar Stress. In *Theory and Explanation in Archaeology,* edited by Colin Renfrew, Michael J. Rowlands, and Barbara A. Seagraves, pp. 389–412. Academic Press, New York.

Keister, Lisa A., and Stephanie Moller. 2000. Wealth Inequality in the United States. *Annual Review of Sociology* 26:63–81.

Kintigh, Keith W., Jeffrey Altschul, Mary Beaudry, Robert Drennan, Ann Kinzig, Timothy Kohler, W. Frederick Limp, et al. 2014. Grand Challenges for Archaeology. *American Antiquity* 79:5–24.

Kowalewski, Stephen A., Gary M. Feinman, and Laura Finsten. 1992. "The Elite" and Assessment of Social Stratification in Mesoamerican Archaeology. In *Mesoamerican Elites: An Archaeological Assessment,* edited by Diane Z. Chase and Arlen F. Chase, pp. 259–77. University of Oklahoma Press, Norman.

Kowalewski, Stephen A., and Laura Finsten. 1983. The Economic Systems of Ancient Oaxaca: A Regional Perspective. *Current Anthropology* 24:413–41.

Kron, Geoffrey. 2011. The Distribution of Wealth at Athens in Comparative Perspective. *Zeitschrift für Papyrologie und Epigraphik* 179:129–38.

Krugman, Paul. 2006. Wages, Wealth, and Politics. *New York Times,* August 18, 2006. http://sociology101.net/readings/wages-wealth-politics-Krugman.pdf.

———. 2014. Why We're in a New Gilded Age. *New York Review of Books,* May 8, 2014.

Kuznets, Simon. 1955. Economic Growth and Income Inequality. *American Economic Review* 45:1–28.

Lind, Michael, and Javier Urcid. 1983. The Lords of Lambityeco and Their Nearest Neighbors. *Notas Mesoamericanas* 9:78–111.

———. 2010. *The Lords of Lambityeco: Political Evolution in the Valley of Oaxaca During the Xoo Phase.* University Press of Colorado, Boulder.

Lindert, Peter H. 1991. Toward a Comparative History of Income and Wealth Inequality. In *Income Distribution in Historical Perspective,* edited by Y. S. Brenner, Hartmut Kaeble, and Mark Thomas, pp. 212–31. Cambridge University Press, Cambridge.

Lindert, Peter H., and Jeffrey G. Williamson. 2016. *Unequal Gains: American Growth and Inequality Since 1700*. Princeton University Press, Princeton.

Mann, Michael. 1977. States, Ancient and Modern. *European Journal of Sociology* 18:262–98.

———. 2016. Have Human Societies Evolved? Evidence from History and Prehistory. *Theoretical Sociology* 45:203–37.

Marcus, Joyce. 2008. *Monte Albán*. El Colegio de México, Mexico City.

Marcus, Joyce, and Kent V. Flannery. 1996. *Zapotec Civilization: How Urban Society Evolved in Mexico's Oaxaca Valley*. Thames and Hudson, London.

Marx, Karl. (1899) 2000. *Wage-Labor and Capital*. Socialist Labor Party of America. www.slp.org/pdf/marx/wage_labor_capital.pdf.

McGuire, Randall H. 1983. Breaking Down Cultural Complexity: Inequality and Heterogeneity. *Advances in Archaeological Method and Theory* 6:91–142.

Milanovic, Branko. 2011. *The Haves and the Have-Nots: A Brief and Idiosyncratic History of Global Inequality*. Basic Books, New York.

———. 2016. *Global Inequality: A New Approach for the Age of Globalization*. Belknap Press, Cambridge, Mass.

Milanovic, Branko, Peter H. Lindert, and Jeffrey G. Williamson. 2011. Preindustrial Inequality. *Economic Journal* 12:255–72.

North, Douglass C. 1990. *Institutions, Institutional Change and Economic Performance*. Cambridge University Press, Cambridge.

Obama, Barack H. 2013. Remarks by the President on Economic Mobility. www .whitehouse.gov/the-press-office/2013/12/04/remarks-president-economic -mobility#transcript.

Ober, Josiah. 2010. Wealthy Hellas. *Transactions of the American Philological Association* 140:241–86.

OECD (Organisation for Economic Co-operation and Development). 2011. An Overview of Growing Income Inequalities in OECD Counties: Main Findings. www.oecd.org/els/social/inequality.

Piketty, Thomas. 2014. *Capital in the Twenty-First Century*. Belknap Press, Cambridge, Mass.

———. 2015. Putting Distribution Back at the Center of Economics: Reflections on "Capital in the Twenty-First Century." *Journal of Economic Perspectives* 29:67–88.

Piketty, Thomas, and Emmanuel Saez. 2014. Inequality in the Long Run. *Science* 344:838–43.

Pohl, John M. D. 2003a. Royal Marriage and Confederacy Building Among the Eastern Nahua, Mixtecs, and Zapotecs. In *The Postclassic Mesoamerican World*, edited by Michael E. Smith and Frances F. Berdan, pp. 243–48. University of Utah Press, Salt Lake City.

———. 2003b. Ritual Ideology and Commerce in the Southern Mexican Highlands. In *The Postclassic Mesoamerican World*, edited by Michael E. Smith and Frances F. Berdan, pp. 172–77. University of Utah Press, Salt Lake City.

Price, T. Douglas, and Gary M. Feinman. 2010. Social Inequality and the Evolution of Human Social Organization. In *Pathways to Power: New Perspectives on the Emergence of Social Inequality*, edited by T. Douglas Price and Gary M. Feinman, pp. 1–14. Springer, New York.

Pringle, Heather. 2014. The Ancient Roots of the 1%. *Science* 344:822–25.

Scheidel, Walter, and Steven J. Friesen. 2009. The Size of the Economy and the Distribution of Income in the Roman Empire. *Journal of Roman Studies* 99:61–91.

Smith, Eric Alden, Monique Borgerhoff Mulder, Samuel Bowles, Michael Gurven, Tom Hertz, and Mary K. Shenk. 2010. Production Systems, Inheritance Systems, and Inequality in Premodern Societies: Conclusions. *Current Anthropology* 51:85–94.

Smith, Michael E. 2010. Sprawl, Squatters and Sustainable Cities: Can Archaeological Data Shed Light on Modern Urban Issues? *Cambridge Archaeological Journal* 20:229–53.

Smith, Michael E., Timothy Dennehy, April Kamp Whittaker, Emily Colon, and Rebecca Harkness. 2014. Quantitative Measures of Wealth Inequality in Ancient Central Mexican Communities. *Advances in Archaeological Practice* 2:311–23.

Stiglitz, Joseph E. 2013. *The Price of Inequality: How Today's Divided Society Endangers Our Future*. W. W. Norton, New York.

Tilly, Charles. 2005. Historical Perspectives on Inequality. In *The Blackwell Companion to Social Inequalities*, edited by Mary Romero and Eric Margolis, pp. 15–30. Blackwell, Malden, Mass.

U.S. Census Bureau. 2012. Household Income Inequality Within U.S. Counties: 2006–2010. www.census.gov/prod/2012pubs/acsbr10-18.pdf.

Whalen, Michael. 1981. *Excavations at Santo Domingo Tomaltepec: Evolution of a Formative Community in the Valley of Oaxaca, Mexico*. Memoirs 12. Museum of Anthropology, University of Michigan, Ann Arbor.

Winter, Marcus C. 1972. Tierras Largas: A Formative Community in the Valley of Oaxaca. PhD dissertation, University of Arizona, Tucson.

———. 1974. Residential Patterns at Monte Albán, Oaxaca, Mexico. *Science* 186:981–87.

Wittfogel, Karl. 1957. *Oriental Despotism*. Yale University Press, New Haven, Conn.

World Bank. 2016. GINI Index, World Bank Estimate. http://data.worldbank.org/indicator/SI.POV.GINI.

11

Deep Inequality

Summary and Conclusions

Timothy A. Kohler, Michael E. Smith, Amy Bogaard, Christian E. Peterson, Alleen Betzenhauser, Gary M. Feinman, Rahul C. Oka, Matthew Pailes, Anna Marie Prentiss, Elizabeth C. Stone, Timothy J. Dennehy, and Laura J. Ellyson

The chapters in this volume describe patterns of wealth inequality among households in the deep past. Unlike some contemporary studies of inequality, which rely on readily available, well-understood data, we had to detail the methods, contexts, and settings for each study. Context is important, and archaeological contexts require extensive discussion before analysis can take place. But now that we have presented numerous case studies pertaining to multiple regions, periods, and sites, it is time to step back from the detailed local contexts and look at broader patterns and conclusions.

In this chapter we use data compiled in the previous chapters, with a few additions, to point up findings that only emerge out of comparison. The ability to conduct such comparisons is, after all, one of the key advantages of calculating an index such as the Gini, on an identical basis, across a number of societies. Of course we do not believe that a comparison across any one dimension (such as the house-size distributions on which we focus) exhausts the interesting cross-cultural variability in our sample. Nor must we believe that differences in house size *mean* exactly the same thing in each society to explore such variability for the shared information it contains about inequality in human prehistory. Although we have found some of the trends we anticipated, just as frequently we have been surprised by expectations not met in these data. Frankly, we did not anticipate our most interesting findings, although recent theory helps us make sense of them (in hindsight!). Such surprises are the happy rewards of cross-cultural research, while the more routine nature of finding expected patterns reassures us that the individual histories and idiosyncrasies of particular societies do not obscure pervasive underlying structural commonalities.

The foregoing chapters raise several interesting points. Among those that we are not going to pursue here (though perhaps we might elsewhere) is the question of how measures of Gini coefficients based on artifacts, burials, and house size tend to differ. In this chapter we simply employ the Ginis calculated on house sizes. Were we working in a contemporary society, we could calculate the elasticity of house sizes to changes in income or wealth in a fairly straightforward fashion. Much indirect evidence, cited throughout the volume, has convinced us that houses were typically a "normal good" in the sense that their sizes would increase given increases in income or wealth. We would not be surprised to find that their responsiveness to changes in income or wealth is different through time, or across societies, however, and we certainly cannot claim to hold such responsiveness constant across the huge spans of time, and cultures, represented here. We might also point out, though, that even attempts to measure wealth in contemporary societies are fraught with difficulties. Competing methods yield divergent results; "available evidence on [wealth] is much more scant and conflicting than that on income and earnings" (Kopczuk 2015).

Theory, as reviewed in chapter 1, leads us to expect that wealth disparities (measured throughout this chapter as Gini indices computed over house-size distributions) tend to increase as

1. climatic stability promotes increased resource density, predictability, and strong gradients in resource values;
2. group size or regional population density increases;
3. mobility decreases sufficiently to allow resources to be transmitted across generations, potentially accumulating;
4. one or more transmissible resources becomes scarce;
5. norms of private or corporate property in resources develop, placing limits on resource sharing within groups;
6. production beyond the subsistence needs of households—expected to be most prevalent in agricultural societies—presents opportunities for exploitation and opportunity hoarding, as Charles Tilly (2001) uses these terms, such that Ginis measuring wealth inequal-

ity should in general increase with increases in surplus (Lenski 1966); and

7. more-exclusionary governance institutions dominate.

All the societies considered here date to the Holocene, so differences in the degree of climatic stability they experienced were probably fairly minor even though climatic variability undoubtedly affected individual sequences.

In a number of places in the early Holocene, increases in group size and regional population size tended to co-occur with decreased mobility and resource intensification, in some cases leading to agriculture. More generally, the factors labelled 2–5 above are so enmeshed in co-causality that it is easier to pick out modal categories resulting from their interactions than it is to place societies on scales denoting each dimension separately, especially given the uncertainties inherent in the archaeological record. For example, hunter-gatherers are often (though not invariably) organized in small groups with low regional population densities and employ relatively high mobility to prevent local resource depression. Resource sharing is often more common in such groups than among horticulturalists and agriculturalists. Horticulturalists are typically less mobile than foragers but more mobile than agriculturalists (though some of the Chinese Neolithic societies included in table 11.1, labeled as "horticulturalists," appear to have been fully sedentary). Monique Borgerhoff Mulder and colleagues (2009) consider horticulturalists to be labor- rather than land-limited, with greater levels of investment in embodied and relational wealth than in material wealth. Because these types of wealth are less transmissible across generations than material wealth (Big Men, for example, cannot transfer alliances they built to their children [Binford 1983:chap. 9]), horticulturalists are likely to be more equal than agriculturalists, though they also tend to be somewhat less equal than foragers given their generally reduced mobility. For these reasons, as well as the likelihood that agriculturalists are more commonly able to produce surpluses subject to unequal distribution and even monopolization, we expect our sample to show the greatest wealth equality for foragers and the highest inequality for agriculturalists, with horticulturalists in an intermediate position—as found in both ethnographic (Smith et al. 2010) and historical (Lenski 1966) studies.

METHODS

In table 11.1 we present a few key variables for the sixty-two cases analyzed in this chapter, and we locate these societies in figure 11.1.* Thirty-seven of these are presented in the preceding chapters; the other twenty-five were provided by various chapter authors drawing on a variety of sources listed by Kohler and colleagues (2017: Supplementary Materials).

EFFECTS OF ADAPTATION TYPE AND SITE TYPE ON INEQUALITY

As noted above, theory and data from ethnography and history point to a rank ordering in expected wealth inequality among societies practicing foraging, horticulture, and agriculture. These expectations are generally borne out in our sample. Gini coefficients are generally lower for foragers than for horticulturalists, whereas agricultural societies tend to have the highest coefficients (figure 11.2a). We note, however, a fair amount of overlap in the Ginis among these groups, especially given the great range of values among agriculturalists. Some of the variability in Gini values among agricultural societies is due to the fact that some settlements in our sample do not exhibit the full range of social variability in their society. For example, a village in a state—such as the Aztec village Capilco (table 11.1)—may not house any elites and might therefore have a low Gini value (as Capilco does). This problem is more pronounced as settlements become increasingly differentiated by size and function within their regions, explaining the increasing variance in Ginis from foragers to agriculturists. These results parallel an ethnographic study that compared Gini values among three groups of villages labeled as egalitarian or exhibiting status inequality or exhibiting hyper-inequality

---

*Since this chapter was written, Kohler and colleagues (2017) analyzed a slightly different data set. That publication added two hunter-gatherer cases and revised several of the values contributed from chapter 8 to use the versions of those Ginis that were calculated on the total house size (residence + storage) rather than the versions using an aggregation rule similar to the Cobb-Douglas production function in economics. This last change was done to make those Ginis more comparable to those calculated elsewhere in this volume. These modifications do not change the conclusions presented in this chapter.

Table 11.1 Selected variables for cases analyzed in this chapter

Site	Period	Date AD	Gini	Lower bound	Upper bound	Region	Site type	Total site pop (HH)	No. of households in sample
Jerf el Ahmar	PPNA	−9200	0.13	0.10	0.15	Middle Euphrates	Village	4	2
Çatalhöyük	Neolithic	−6500	0.28			Anatolia	Town	4,250	19
Tell Sabi Abyad L. 6	Neolithic	−6000	0.30	0.19	0.42	Balikh drainage, Syria	Village	8	4
Nantaizi	Xinglongwa	−5400	0.15	0.12	0.20	Inner Mongolia	Village	165	32
Vaihingen	LBK (Neolithic)	−5200	0.17	0.12	0.19	SW Germany	Village	40	11
Zhaobaogou	Zhaobaogou	−5150	0.35	0.29	0.43	Inner Mongolia	Village	325	17
Jiangzhai	Early Yangshao	−4550	0.46	0.40	0.53	Henan	Village	350	65
Baiyinchanghan	Hongshan	−4250	0.20	0.15	0.27	Inner Mongolia	Village	80	17
Tepe Gawra	Late Chalcolithic 2	−4000	0.46	0.30	0.52	Tigris, Iraq	Village	16	7
Hornstaad-Hornle 1A	Late Neolithic Hornstaad	−3900	0.17	0.15	0.19	Lake Constance, Germany	Village	40	30
Tell Brak L. 16	Middle Northern Uruk/LC3	−3800	0.43	0.32	0.44	Khabur drainage, Syria	City	2,167	4
Wangmushan	Middle Yangshao	−3750	0.33	0.25	0.43	Inner Mongolia	Village	20	20
Dadiwan	Late Yangshao	−3200	0.53	0.46	0.61	Gansu	Town	500	30
Jianxin	Middle–Late Dawenkou	−3050	0.35	0.32	0.40	Shandong	Village	10	10
Yuchisi	Late Dawenkou	−2700	0.37	0.32	0.48	Anhui	Town	400	11
Various	Early Dynastic	−2700	0.37			S Mesopotamia	City		21
Yinjiacheng	Longshan	−2300	0.13	0.10	0.17	Shandong	Village		6
Kahun	Middle Kingdom	−1930	0.68			Egypt	Town	500	137
Various	Old Babylonian	−1700	0.40			S Mesopotamia	City		106
San José Mogote	San José phase	−1100	0.25	0.19	0.28	Oaxaca	Town	1,000	8
Various	Neo-Babylonian	−600	0.40			S Mesopotamia	City		14

(*continued*)

Table 11.1 Selected variables for cases analyzed in this chapter

Site	Period	Date AD	Gini	Lower bound	Upper bound	Region	Site type	Total site pop (HH)	No. of households in sample
Heuneburg IVb2	Early Iron Age/Late Hallstatt	–600	0.57	0.43	0.68	Danube, Germany	Town	270	11
Heuneburg IVa1	Early Iron Age/Late Hallstatt	–550	0.65	0.47	0.81	Danube, Germany	Town	270	6
Pompeii	Pompeii	79	0.54			Italy	City	2200	78
Herculaneum	Herculaneum	79	0.52			Italy	City	1,000	44
Teotihuacan	Classic	300	0.12			Central Mexico	City	14,485	14,485
Bridge River	Bridge River 2	500	0.20	0.18	0.29	Canadian Plateau—Middle Fraser Canyon	Village	125	19
Various	BMIII	550	0.31	0.12	0.40	CMV	Village		5
Grewe	Early Pioneer	600	0.36			Hohokam	Village	57	9
Various	Pioneer	600	0.28	0.26	0.32	All Hohokam	Village		200
Various	BMIII	650	0.21	0.17	0.29	CMV	Village		15
Caracol	Classic	700	0.34			Maya	City	17,860	4,058
Various	Classic	700	0.38			Oaxaca	City		36
Various	PI	746	0.30	0.27	0.36	CMV	Village		11
Various	Patrick	750	0.19	0.18	0.21	American Bottom	Village		86
Bridge River	Bridge River 3	750	0.18	0.16	0.25	Canadian Plateau—Middle Fraser Canyon	Village	226	28
Tikal	Classic	765	0.62			Maya	City	11,070	756
Various	PI	841	0.28	0.25	0.33	CMV	Village		27
Various	Colonial	850	0.25	0.24	0.26	All Hohokam	Village		316

Site	Period	Date				Region	Settlement		
Grewe	Middle Colonial	850	0.24			Hohokam	Village	188	6
Various	PII	963	0.25	0.21	0.27	CMV	Town		9
Various	TLW	975	0.35	0.33	0.37	American Bottom	Town		351
Various	Besant & Late Prehistoric	1000	0.16			Wyoming	Village		144
Various	Sedentary	1050	0.25	0.24	0.26	All Hohokam	Town		448
Grewe	Middle Sedentary	1050	0.12			Hohokam	Town	117	4
Cahokia	Lohmann	1075	0.35	0.29	0.48	American Bottom	City	2,221	79
Greater Cahokia	Lohmann	1075	0.29	0.26	0.34	American Bottom	Town		387
Various	PII	1091	0.44	0.24	0.53	Various	Town		12
Cahokia	Stirling	1150	0.57	0.45	0.67	American Bottom	City	803	44
Greater Cahokia	Stirling	1150	0.27	0.23	0.32	American Bottom	City		557
Various	PIII	1173	0.23	0.19	0.33	CMV	Village		8
Various	PIII	1243	0.36	0.31	0.44	CMV	Village		15
Various	Classic	1300	0.24	0.23	0.25	All Hohokam	Town		622
Cahokia	Moorehead/Sand Prairie	1300	0.22	0.21	0.27	American Bottom	Town	425	29
Greater Cahokia	Moorehead/Sand Prairie	1300	0.27	0.26	0.30	American Bottom	Town		161
Mayapan	Postclassic	1330	0.41			Maya	City	4,031	4,031
Capilco	LPC-A	1370	0.10			Central Mexico	Village	13	7
Cuexcomate	LPC-A	1370	0.48			Central Mexico	Town	43	43
Capilco	LPC-B	1480	0.16			Central Mexico	Village	21	21
Cuexcomate	LPC-B	1480	0.25			Central Mexico	Town	139	135
Yautepec	LPC-B	1480	0.21			Central Mexico	City	1,900	1,619
Tenochtitlan	Contact	1500	0.30			Central Mexico	City	30,006	30,006

Note: Cases sorted by date.

Abbreviations: BMIII = Basketmaker III; CMV = central Mesa Verde region; LBK = Linearbandkeramik; LC₃ = Late Chalcolithic 3; LPC–A = Late Postclassic A; LPC–B = Late Postclassic B; PI = Pueblo I; PII = Pueblo II; PIII = Pueblo III; PPNB = Pre-Pottery Neolithic B; TLW = Terminal Late Woodland.

Figure 11.1 Locations of samples analyzed in this chapter. Points on the map often locate more than one data point.

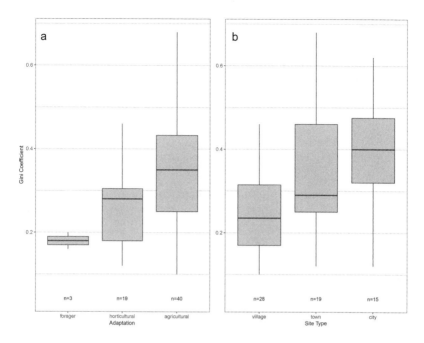

Figure 11.2 Boxplots of Gini coefficients: (a) by adaptation type; (b) by site type. Data points encompassing more than one site are assigned according to the largest site in the group.

(Smith 1991). The central tendencies for these Ginis follow the expected order, despite considerable overlap in their range.

The patterning of Gini coefficients by site type displays similar trends and variance (figure 11.2b). Our site typology of villages, towns, and cities is based on both site size and a concept of urban function. An urban function is an activity or institution in a settlement that affects a larger hinterland (Trigger 1972). Here we identify urban functions as features or facilities whose likely use extended beyond the settlement to a hinterland; we call them "central features." Examples would include a chief's house, a temple of a type found only in larger settlements (and thus presumably serving a population larger than its own settlement), and a feature whose design and construction required knowledge or labor beyond the individual settlement. Based on an analogy with central place theory (Lloyd and Dicken 1977; Trigger 1972), central features can be classified into levels. Lower-level features are more widespread within a settlement system and pertain to a smaller catchment area, while higher-level features are more infrequent and tend to be found only in the largest settlements, where they pertain to a larger catchment area or hinterland. Our typology is not intended to be a comprehensive classification that will work cleanly for all ancient settlement systems; rather, it is a rough approximation of the extent to which settlements operated on a social scale beyond that of the daily lives of their own residents.

On the basis of these considerations, a village is defined as any settlement of one thousand or fewer residents that lacks a central feature. A town is defined as either a settlement with more than a thousand residents but lacking a central feature or a settlement of more than two hundred residents that has one or two lower-level (typically small or moderately sized) central features. A city is any settlement with more than one thousand residents and one or more high-level (i.e., large and prominent) central features.

Although the central tendencies of Ginis for villages, towns, and cities increase in the expected direction (figure 11.2b), the categories overlap considerably. In agrarian states, the wealthiest elites typically live in cities, which also usually house the ruler or highest-ranking leader and the regional institutions. Therefore, we might expect higher levels of inequality in cities than in towns. This is certainly the case in the modern world: large cities have higher levels of inequality than smaller cities and towns (Baum-Snow and Pavan 2013; Behrens and Robert-Nicoud 2014a, 2014b), and they are also the settings for more inequality than is found in their country as a whole (Behrens and Robert-Nicoud 2014a). But the link between urbanization and inequality may have been different in the distant past. While house size is generally a good measure of wealth (as attested in the chapters in this book), this relationship may weaken in an urban settlement if building a house proportionate to the wealth of the wealthiest residents (typically members of the elite class) is difficult or impossible. This may reflect both energetic limits on wealth concentration in the ancient world and high land values in the centers of cities.

Sometimes quantitative associations that are weak in cross-cultural samples are expressed more strongly within a specific region or cultural tradition. To facilitate further exploration of the relationship between inequality and settlement type, table 11.2 presents data on this relationship for a single regional tradition, Aztec-period central Mexico. While both archaeological and historical data record extreme wealth

Table 11.2 Gini coefficients by site type in central Mexico

Site	Period	Type	Population	Gini
Tenochtitlan	LPC-B	City	212,500	0.30
Yautepec	LPC-B	City	1,900	0.21
Cuexcomate	LPC-B	Town	139	0.25
Cuexcomate	LPC-A	Town	39	0.48
Capilco	LPC-A	Village	13	0.10
Capilco	LPC-B	Village	21	0.16

Abbreviations: LPC-A = Late Postclassic A; LPC-B = Late Postclassic B.

variation within Tenochtitlan (Smith and Hicks 2016), evidently the large number of quite similar households to some extent balances the great wealth of the emperor and the top elites, since the value we compute (0.30, using procedures described in Kohler et al. 2017: Methods) is somewhat lower than that for the town of Cuexcomate in the LPC-A. The limitations of house size in cities as a measure of wealth for the rich, pointed out above, may also contribute to the lower Ginis for these contexts. Factors such as location, presumably connected with prestige, may have been as important as house size in distinguishing households from each other.

INEQUALITY AND DEMOGRAPHIC SCALE

In chapter 1 we identify several reasons why increases in inequality within groups might be expected with increases in the group population sizes. Somewhat to our surprise, for the entire sample there is no relationship between the Ginis and regional population size (r^2 = 0.04; $p > F_{(1, 41)}$ = 0.19). Figure 11.3a, on which the New and Old World linear models are plotted separately, illustrates that whereas the relationships between Gini coefficients and regional population size trend in the expected direction, the linear fit (especially for the New World) is obscured by a very high level of variability; neither relationship is significant. Although this variability could be taken to indicate that no relationship exists, it could equally be due to the difficulty of accurately estimating regional populations in this sample, as well as variability in how the regions themselves are defined. Indeed, for the eleven Old World cases in which we have estimates of both regional population size and area of region, the

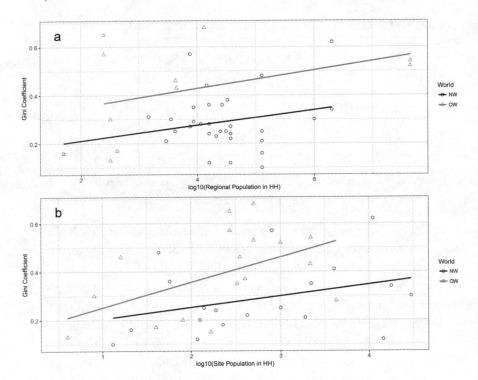

Figure 11.3 Gini coefficients versus measures of demographic scale, by hemisphere: (a) Gini coefficients versus estimated regional populations in households (n = 41); (b) Gini coefficients versus estimated site populations in households (n = 35). HH = number of households; NW = New World; OW = Old World.

relationship between Ginis and population density is strongly positive (r^2 = 0.62; p > $F_{(1, 9)}$ = 0.004) although no such linear relationship exists among the twenty-eight available cases in the New World sample (r^2 = 0.003; p > $F_{(1, 26)}$ = 0.76).

As illustrated by figure 11.3b, the relationship between Ginis and site population size is also positive. Here again these variables are more strongly related in the Old World (r^2 = 0.25; p > $F_{(1, 16)}$ = 0.04) than in the New World (r^2 = 0.11; p > $F_{(1, 17)}$ = 0.17).

Note that in each of the three ways we have measured demographic scale, the relationship between scale and degree of inequality is always more strongly positive in the Old World than in the New. So far as we are aware, this difference has not been previously noted. Below, we present reasons to believe that this pattern contains important information about the factors structuring inequality in these two world regions.

COMPARING THE EVOLUTION OF
INEQUALITY IN THE OLD AND NEW WORLD

As implied by figure 11.3 (a and b), there is a tendency for Ginis in the Old World to be higher than in the New World. To attempt to understand this difference we now examine how it developed through time (figure 11.4a). The Old World series sampled here (mostly from the Near East and Europe; see table 11.1) begins much earlier than the New World series but by circa 4000 BC exhibits higher Gini values than were ever typical of the New World.

A possible confounding factor in this comparison, though, is the presence of foragers in the New (but not the Old) World sample. In figure 11.4b we look more closely at the past three millennia by subregions, isolating the North American foragers and other small-scale societies in the sample, to better understand the sources of the differences in figure 11.4a. (The linear fits in figure 11.4b are not of substantive interest but are displayed to make the central tendencies visible.) This allows us to see that although the North American foragers included here were indeed relatively equal in wealth, as expected, the other major groups in the New World sampled here were also more equal than the contemporaneous societies we sampled from the Old World. Perhaps the largest surprise here is that the Gini values for the Mesoamerican states are so low in general, though values for Mayan centers do tend to be higher. Overall, households in the Mesoamerican states were only slightly more unequal on this measure than were contemporaneous horticultural and agricultural societies in North America, though all three were markedly less equal than the foragers. In the Old World, societies passing through the Neolithic into the Bronze and Iron Age were marked by generally increasing wealth inequalities. Unfortunately we lack household-size data for the early villages in Mesoamerica, although the U.S. Southwest provides some hints for what it might have looked like.

What factors enabled states in the Old World, but not in the New World in most cases, to develop greater inequality than was experienced

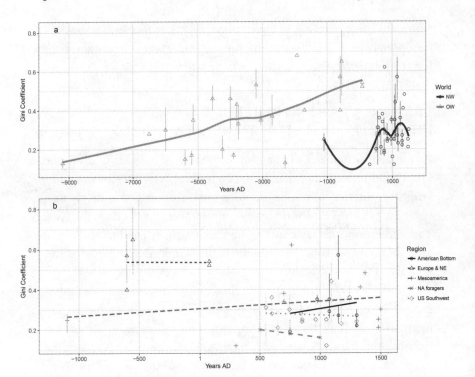

Figure 11.4 Gini coefficients through time: (a) robust regression of Gini coefficients through time by hemisphere (New World versus Old World) with 80 percent CIs where available (alpha = 0.5, *n* = 60); (b) Gini coefficients for the past three millennia by region with linear trends and 80 percent CIs where available (*n* = 41). Villages in states (*n* = 2, both Aztec) have been removed from both samples; fits are not weighted by number of households. NW = New World; NE = Near East; NA = North American; OW = Old World; US = United States.

by households living within earlier, or smaller-scale, social and political formations?

ACCOUNTING FOR DIFFERENCES IN WEALTH EQUALITY AMONG STATES

Figure 11.4b demonstrates that ancient states in general, including New World states, supported quite variable degrees of inequality. One factor that might account for some of the variation is the nature of the political regimes. Scholars have found that among contemporary nations, more-autocratic regimes have higher levels of inequality than do more-democratic regimes (e.g., Acemoglu et al. 2004; Savoia et al. 2010). Anthropologists Carol Ember and colleagues (1997:116) reported a similar finding, concluding that "inequality is associated with less political participation in the ethnographic record, just as in the cross-national record." These findings suggest that Richard Blanton and Lane Fargher's (2008) scale of autocratic-to-collective regimes for premodern states might be correlated with the degree of inequality in this sample and, if our sample of Old World states tends to be more autocratic, might help explain the Old/New World differences we have noted. As discussed in chapter 1, Blanton and Fargher define autocratic states as providing few public goods for their subjects, possessing little bureaucracy, and suffering few checks on rulers' actions. Collective regimes have the opposite characteristics. These differences are hypothesized to stem from differences in how the state is financed. In states where the regime depends on taxation of its subjects, public goods have to be provided to keep subjects happy, and a bureaucracy is needed to collect taxes and ensure compliance with the state. Autocratic regimes, in contrast, gain most revenues from outside the polity by conquest or by taxing trade. Because they are not dependent on their immediate subjects for revenue, there is less motivation to provide public goods. Blanton and Fargher's scheme was developed out of the distinction made between "corporate" and "network" strategies by Blanton and colleagues (1996).

Blanton and Fargher do not discuss how their scheme relates to levels of inequality, but the studies cited above suggest that more-autocratic ancient regimes may have higher levels of inequality than do more-collective regimes. Here we explore the relationship between political regimes and inequality in our sample, to determine whether this axis of variability can help explain the variability we see among states in general, and between New and Old World states in particular. Unfortunately there is no recognized method for scoring polities known primarily from archaeology along Blanton and Fargher's autocratic-collective continuum. We employ an ordinal scale—autocratic, intermediate, and collective—for categorizing regimes. Michael Smith (chapter 1, this volume), Gary Feinman (chapter 10, this volume), and Elizabeth Stone (chapter 9, this volume) provided subjective judgments for each of their cases. In Smith's case the judgment was aided by an independent quantitative analysis of this continuum for several of the regimes included in this chapter (Smith et al. 2016). We derive our assessment of Rome in the first century AD as collective directly from the work of Blanton and Fargher (2008). Kohler et al. 2017 (Supplementary Materials) contains the resultant codes for the states in our sample.

In figure 11.5 we compare Gini coefficients to that taxonomy. Not surprisingly, Gini values tend to be highest for the three autocratic states in our sample (Tikal and Caracol, capitals of Classic Maya city-states, and Kahun, a town housing workers while they constructed a Middle Kingdom pyramid in Egypt). We assumed that by contrast the collectively organized states (Teotihuacan and the early Roman Empire represented

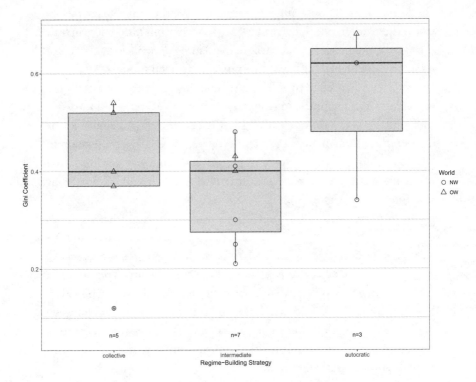

Figure 11.5 Boxplots of Gini coefficients by inferred regime-building strategies of states in the sample. Cases in each box are identified as New or Old World. Two villages from states (both Aztec) are not included in the analysis (n = 15).

here by Herculaneum and Pompeii) would exhibit the lowest Ginis. In fact, our "intermediate" and "collective" states have identical medians and largely overlapping ranges.

Noting that all but two of the societies coded as "intermediate" are in the New World, whereas all but one of the "collective" states are in the Old World, we examine the possibility that regime type and inequality may be associated *within* particular regions or cultural traditions but not cross-culturally. Table 11.3 shows the data for all Mesoamerican cases except the village of Capilco (omitted for comparability with other sites, all of which likely included some elite residents). These data support the hypothesis that, within Mesoamerica at least, more-collective regimes have a lower level of inequality than do more-autocratic regimes. Therefore, the unanticipated ordering of societies classified by regime type on Ginis in figure 11.5 is likely due to the interaction of the regime-building strategies with the origins of these societies in either the Old or the New World. This then returns us to the question of why societies in the Old and New Worlds appear to have developed markedly different degrees of wealth inequality.

Table 11.3 Inequality by regime type in Mesoamerican states

Site[a]	Period	Gini	Mean Gini	Contributor
Caracol	Classic	0.34		Dennehy
Tikal	Classic	0.62		Dennehy
Settlements in autocratic states (n = 2)			0.48	
Tenochtitlan	Late Postclassic	0.30		Smith
Yautepec	Late Postclassic	0.21		Smith
Cuexcomate	Late Postclassic, B	0.25		Smith
San José Mogote	Formative	0.25		Feinman
Various	Classic	0.38		Feinman
Mayapan	Late Postclassic	0.41		Dennehy
Cuexcomate	Late Postclassic, A	0.48		Smith
Settlements in intermediate states (n = 7)			0.33	
Teotihuacan	Classic	0.12		Smith
Settlements in collective states (n = 1)			0.12	

[a] The Late Postclassic village of Capilco is not included.

OLD WORLD VERSUS NEW WORLD DIFFERENCES, REVISITED

Subjection enters the house with the plough.
—attributed to the Prophet Mohammed by Gellner (1988:10)

If regime-building strategies do not adequately account for differences among states in the Old and New Worlds, what else could explain these differences? Why, even before the emergence of states (ca. 4000 BC in the Old World), do typical levels of wealth inequality there already surpass those typical of the preconquest New World?

Generalizing the argument introduced by Bogaard and her co-authors in chapter 8, we propose that the best single explanation of these wealth differences is the presence after circa 8000 BC of a variety of large domesticated animals in the Old World, coupled with their general absence in the New World. The most important (but not the sole) effect of this difference, we suggest, was to make agricultural extensification possible and profitable in many portions of the Old World. Draft animals were the engines behind profitable extensification, acting as a multiplier on human labor (White 1949:367ff.), enabling some farmers to travel farther to fields and to work much larger fields. If not all farmers owned draft animals, as seems likely (Halstead 2014:318–19), or if only some households could maintain large oxen at peak strength (Halstead 2014:20, 53), then those who did could loan them out in return for a share of the production they enabled. Such flows of rents would provide an additional source of economic disparity. We propose that animal husbandry permitted Old World households to generate greater agricultural surpluses than their New World counterparts, and this in turn enabled processes leading to their higher level of inequality, as anticipated by Gerhard Lenski's (1966) model. The absence of draft animals made profitable agricultural extensification more difficult for New World societies. (South America is unfortunately not included in our sample, but Andean camelids were useful for carrying goods for exchange, not for plowing.)

But if some households profited directly from extensification, over long enough periods others suffered. Agricultural extensification is a land-hungry strategy that would eventually, in the Old World, result in a class of landless peasantry that never (or rarely) appeared in the preconquest New World. So extensification levers up a few households but in the long run depresses many others, and both actions increased Gini coefficients by magnifying the difference between rich and poor.

The contributions of large domesticated animals to the Gini differential in Old and New World contexts did not stop with the advantages of draft animals for agricultural extensification, however. The cases in our sample from Asia illustrate this clearly. For most of the Chinese Neolithic and Bronze Age, until circa 2000 BC, stone hand plows, hoes, and digging sticks were used without the benefit of animal traction. Nevertheless, the Chinese cases in our sample exhibit Ginis in line with contemporaneous samples from Europe and the Near East. These Chinese societies did rely heavily on domesticated animals for meat as a complement to the cultivation of crops—generally pig in the earlier sites, sheep/goats at some of the later sites, though these animals were not used for plowing. The China cases therefore suggest that "food on the hoof" was also centrally important to the creation of wealth disparities, perhaps because very unequal numbers of animals may have been maintained by contemporaneous households in these societies (Cucchi et al. 2016:15; Kim 1994; Ma 2005:74–99; Peterson and Shelach 2012:281–83).

Cow and goat milk are also useful infant foods, allowing mothers to wean their children and resume bearing earlier. As discussed in chapter 1 and documented in several figures above, the resulting increased demographic scale tends to accompany increasing wealth differentials. Large domesticated mammals also produced valuable manure and numerous other "secondary products" such as milk and fiber (Sherratt 1981). Paul Halstead (2014:319, 348, 352) emphasizes that as the variety of domesticated crops and animals increased, feasting events could take on a competitive dimension. Well-fed animals would have made signal contributions to such "diacritical commensality." By the Bronze Age in Europe, domestic animals were the prime source of animal products, enabling societies to pass through lean seasons more easily, raising the demographic floor. Pastoralists were able to inhabit areas such as central Sweden (for example) in numbers that would not have been possible given other adaptations (Vretemark 2010). Horse harnesses, appearing for the first time in Europe in the Middle Bronze Age, mark the emergence of a new mounted warrior elite, contributing directly to higher Ginis through their large rich houses and indirectly through territorial conquests that greatly increased polity scale (Earle and Kristiansen 2010). Horses and other pack animals (in some areas, camels) were potent offensive weapons (Turchin 2010) allowing successful polities to expand farther than was possible in the New World. Rein Taagepera (1978) studied the time and space evolution of the thirty largest states and empires between 3000 and 600 BC. All were in the Old World.

Though monuments and papyri are especially explicit about the role of cattle as wealth in Dynastic Egypt, the centrality of cattle in Egypt extends to the Predynastic period and earlier. Andrew Gordon and Calvin Schwabe (2004) report that bull skulls (bucrania) were often depicted above doorways as early as Hierakonopolis—recalling their importance at an even earlier site in our sample, Çatalhöyük (Hodder and Doherty 2014)—and surmounting some First Dynasty mastabas. Egypt's first king, Narmer, "recorded the capture of 120,000 prisoners, 400,000 cattle, and 1,422,000 sheep and goats" (Gordon and Schwabe 2004:52). Even if these numbers are exaggerated, similar boasts were made by later kings. Richard Lobban Jr. (1989) believed that livestock wealth financed the construction of the impressive monuments distinguishing Egyptian civilization. Gordon and Schwabe (2004:53) remind us that our words *capital* (not forgetting its importance in our *stock* markets) and *chattel* derive from "head of cattle."

More generally yet, animal traction, eventually in conjunction with the wheel and more technologically advanced shipping, reduced the friction in moving people and products in the Old World relative to the New World. This also contributes to the stronger response of Ginis to increasing demographic scale in the Old World than in the New. Through trade, raiding, and conquest warfare, large portions of the Old World were already tied together into a fairly integrated world economy by the Bronze Age (Kristiansen and Suchowska-Ducke 2015)—in considerable contrast to the New World. This world economy favored economies of scale with respect to infrastructure such as roads, but just as important it favored increasing returns to scale such as the development of technology via relatively wealthy artisans, whose products also marked wealth for others (see contributions to Brysbaert and Gorgues 2017). Such increasing returns to scale have been established for some individual pre-Hispanic settlements included in our sample, from the Basin of Mexico (Ortman et al. 2015) and the central Mesa Verde region (Ortman and Coffey 2017).

We suggest that this concept can be extended to networks of settlements (societies), and that for the reasons given above, beginning in the Old World Bronze Age, such networks were able to produce greater returns to scale than were typically possible in the New World.

Branko Milanovic and colleagues (2011) proposed the concept of the "inequality possibility frontier," which follows directly from Lenski's (1966) model but helps explain these Old and New World differences by putting them into a more quantitative framework. Milanovic and colleagues start with the assumption that the commoners in an agrarian state have the minimum level of production needed to ensure their subsistence. The elites will then divide up the surplus beyond commoner requirements. "The maximum attainable inequality [the inequality possibility frontier] is an increasing function of mean overall income. Whether the elite fully exploit that maximum or allow some trickle-down is, of course, another matter entirely" (Milanovic et al. 2011:256). Our results suggest that beyond a certain point—already attained by regional polities— New World states, in contrast to those in the Old World, could not significantly increase overall mean income by increasing their populations or area.

This impression is reinforced by another way of looking at the Ginis through time, now portraying time as relative to the local arrival or development of domesticated plants in each region (figure 11.6). This puts the time scale in the different hemispheres on a more equal footing, enabling us to more easily compare their rates of change through time. The three data points in the New World from areas in which agriculture never developed indigenously were assigned a date of AD 1500 for "first local domesticated plants," giving them negative dates on the x-axis.

In both hemispheres, Ginis start very low but begin to increase immediately, presumably in tandem with increasing cultigen productivity, residential stability, and size of social groups. For about the first two millennia after the local appearance of cultigens, the rate of increase in Ginis is similar in the two hemispheres.

At that point, however, Ginis in the New World flatten out and even decline. In the Old World, in contrast, Ginis stagnate for a bit around three millennia after the local appearance of cultigens but then renew their rapid increase. Old World wealth differentials were still increasing rapidly by the relative time represented by two of our most recent data

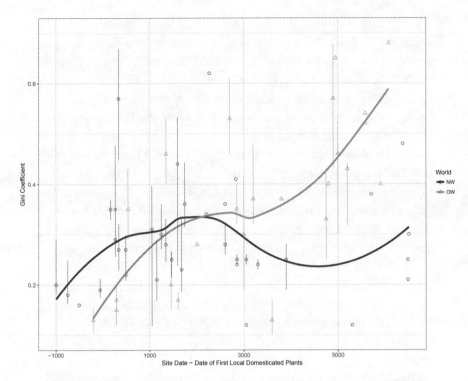

Figure 11.6 Robust regression of Gini coefficients through time relative to local arrival of Neolithic, by hemisphere (alpha = 0.5, *n* = 60). Two villages in states, both Aztec, are not included in the analysis. Temporal placement for each site was determined by subtracting the date of the earliest domesticated plants used locally from the site date. In the New World, we used either maize dates (rather than squash dates) or dates on other members of the Eastern Agricultural Complex. NW = New World; OW = Old World.

points, Pompeii and Herculaneum, more than five millennia after the appearance of domesticated plants in their region. Even though we now know that that trend was soon to collapse (as illustrated in schematic fashion in Scheidel 2017:fig. 3.1), both the long duration of its increase and its contrast with the trajectory of Ginis in the New World are quite remarkable.

We suggest that the second notable increase in the Old World Gini trend line marks the point at which agricultural extensification in conjunction with traction animals, bronze metallurgy, horses and mounted warriors, and a large suite of sociopolitical changes, reviewed briefly above, effectively appear in a number of local records. Except for some parallel sociopolitical changes such as the development of states, these are precisely the changes in which the New World did not participate. To be clear, we are not glorifying these high Ginis in the Old World; they entrained a great deal of misery for many segments of the population. (Not to mention that by some analyses, the profligate luxury enjoyed by the upper classes at the height of the Roman Empire helped precipitate its demise.) We present the contrast between the higher Ginis in the Old World states than in the New World states as fundamental facts that have so far gone unrecognized.

CONCLUDING THOUGHTS

Comparing our results with data on inequality in the modern world is a complicated task given its great variability in contemporary societies (Milanovic 2011), as well as the variation we report in this book. Still, one striking finding is that the levels of wealth inequality we reconstruct are systematically lower than those reported for the United States today, which as Scheidel (2017:421) notes increased from about 0.81 in 2001 to 0.85 in 2010. To answer one of the questions raised in the preface, such wealth inequalities are indeed historically unusual, though they rival those reconstructed for Paris and London on the eve of the Black Death (Sussman 2006), a few cities in northern Italy in the nineteenth century (Alfani 2014), and Britain in the late nineteenth century. Only two of our Gini coefficients approach such heights—that based on the early Iron Age chiefly center of Heuneburg in Germany (0.65), and that from Kahun (0.68). Daron Acemoglu and James Robinson (2012) and Joseph Stiglitz (2012) argue that such high levels of wealth inequality undermine the social fabric of democracies by limiting social mobility and reducing inclusiveness and political equality. Interestingly, as Bogaard and colleagues note in chapter 8 of this volume, the Heuneburg polity lasted less than two hundred years.

Our findings can also put to rest some older views that still find expression in the social sciences. One such idea is that wealth inequality was pronounced and rigid in all ancient states, permitting little or no mobility (Sjoberg 1960:137). According to this view, inequality did not decline until after the Industrial Revolution. Although scholars from Lenski (1966) on have argued against this notion, empirical data on inequality in the distant past have been lacking before now.

Milanovic and colleagues (2011:268), in contrast, assert on the basis of a rather poor sample that wealth inequality in preindustrial societies was "not very different" from inequality in the developing world today, with an average Gini of approximately 0.45. As several figures in this chapter demonstrate, that depends on when and where we look! In the New World, typical Ginis never got that high, even in states. Typical Ginis were below 0.45 in Old World as well before circa 4000 BC.

Another lesson from this analysis is that it is important to differentiate between sociopolitical hierarchies and wealth differentials, which are socioeconomic phenomena. Although these should be generally correlated (figure 11.2b), we have also shown that wealth differences expressed in house sizes are much more pronounced in Old World than in New World states, though by any account all were differentiated by hierarchies of status and power. Economic power (wealth) is, after all, only one of four major sources of social power, along with ideological, military, and political power (Mann 2013). Perhaps there was a greater tendency to mark status in the New World in ways not related to house size—for example, by differences in house placement, access to secret knowledge, or position within kin networks (though certainly such social markers were also employed in Old World states). If so, however, this tendency in turn needs to be explained, and the analyses here will have been instrumental in raising this issue.

How do the various theories and empirical generalizations forwarded by current economists fare against our findings here?

Let's begin by briefly reviewing what recent theorists of inequality have claimed, keeping in mind that for the most part they have dealt with the recent capitalist West, and therefore, portions of their arguments are difficult to generalize to the often smaller-scale societies we emphasize. Milanovic (2011) suggests that the possible level of inequality is based on total income, as that affects the total size of the surplus. Our data support this, albeit indirectly, since we cannot measure total income.

In general our data speak to broad patterns and usually reveal little about the shorter-term dynamics of inequality within societies. Focusing primarily on these higher-frequency dynamics, Milanovic (2016) asserts that inequality in the past responded primarily to noneconomic factors such as wars and epidemics, whereas economic drivers became prominent more recently. Our data strongly suggest, however, that there were systematic economic drivers of inequality in the distant past. Wars and epidemics may explain small-scale variation within recent history, but these are inadequate to explain Gini variability across the range of societies included in this book.

Yet the highest-temporal-resolution Gini sequence presented in this volume (see figure 5.3) demonstrates that in the central Mesa Verde region, high levels of violence always occur toward the end of periods when inequality was unusually high. If the sometimes extreme violence in this region was responsible for periodically resetting wealth inequalities to much lower levels, as this figure suggests, then Milanovic's position is reinforced, as is Walter Scheidel's argument that the only potent forces leveling inequality have always been major upheavals and disasters such as mass-mobilization warfare, transformative revolutions, state collapse, and catastrophic plagues (Scheidel 2017).

Finally, though, we recognize that we have barely cracked open the door to a new and powerful way of looking at human prehistory in a comparative fashion that at this point raises as many questions as it answers. How and when did inequality arise in other major world regions not sampled here, such as South Asia, sub-Saharan Africa, and South America? Are there general relationships between technological innovation and wealth inequality, as the discussions in this chapter suggest? Does the causal relationship between the creation of wealth and its inequality of distribution typically flow in the direction suggested by Lenski, or can wealth inequalities sometimes stimulate surpluses? Do wealth inequalities generally precede inequalities in power, or is the reverse more common? When markets form in societies not influenced by the recent economies of Eurasia, how do they affect wealth inequalities? As our chronologies improve, do we find further support for the suggestions of Milanovic and Scheidel on the factors capable of decreasing inequality?

Above all, we present this volume as evidence that contemporary archaeology must embrace approaches that do not retreat from large questions of current concern in order to pursue ever deeper contextualization of particular ancient societies. We still have much to learn from the archaeological record if we are willing to think quantitatively and comparatively. Archaeologists can, and should, contribute to understanding the factors structuring human history, providing empirical grounds to guide future philosophical historians as they revisit the concerns animating thinkers from Jean-Jacques Rousseau through Karl Marx to Thorstein Veblen. Better yet, we can begin to forge our own narratives.

ACKNOWLEDGMENTS

We all thank the Amerind Foundation for its stimulation of this research and this volume. The first two authors are also grateful to the Santa Fe Institute for its support and encouragement. Finally, Tim Kohler thanks Bill Lipe for references he contributed to this chapter and our highly enjoyable discussions of these materials.

REFERENCES CITED

Acemoglu, Daron, and James A. Robinson. 2012. *Why Nations Fail: The Origins of Power, Prosperity, and Poverty*. Profile Books, London.

Acemoglu, Daron, Thierry Verdier, and James A. Robinson. 2004. Kleptocracy and Divide-and-Rule: A Model of Personal Rule. *Journal of the European Economic Association* 2(2–3):162–92.

Alfani, Guido. 2014. Economic Inequality in Northwestern Italy: A Long-Term View (Fourteenth to Eighteenth Century). Dondena Working Paper 61, Bocconi University, Milan. //ftp.dondena.unibocconi.it/WorkingPapers/Dondena_WP061.pdf.

Baum-Snow, Nathaniel, and Ronni Pavan. 2013. Inequality and City Size. *Review of Economics and Statistics* 95(5):1535–48.

Behrens, Kristian, and Frédéric Robert-Nicoud. 2014a. Urbanisation Makes the World More Unequal. *VOX: CEPR's Policy Portal July 24, 2014*. http://voxeu.org/article/inequality-big-cities.

———. 2014b. Survival of the Fittest in Cities: Urbanisation and Inequality. *Economic Journal* 124(581):1371–1400.

Binford, Lewis R. 1983. *In Pursuit of the Past: Decoding the Archaeological Record*. Thames and Hudson, New York.

Blanton, Richard E., and Lane Fargher. 2008. *Collective Action in the Formation of Pre-modern States*. Springer Science and Business Media, New York.

Blanton, Richard E., Gary M. Feinman, Stephen A. Kowalewski, and Peter N. Peregrine. 1996. A Dual-Processual Theory for the Evolution of Mesoamerican Civilization. *Current Anthropology* 37(1):1–14.

Borgerhoff Mulder, Monique, Samuel Bowles, Tom Hertz, Adrian Bell, Jan Beise, Greg Clark, Ila Fazzio, et al. 2009. Intergenerational Wealth Transmission and the Dynamics of Inequality in Small-Scale Societies. *Science* 326:682–88.

Brysbaert, Ann, and Alexis Gorgues. 2017. *Artisans Versus Nobility? Multiple Identities of Elites and "Commoners" Viewed Through the Lens of Crafting from the Chalcolithic to the Iron Ages in Europe and the Mediterranean*. Sidestone Press, Leiden.

Cucchi, Thomas, Lingling Dai, Marie Balasse, Chunqing Zhao, Jiangtao Gao, Yaowu Hu, Jing Yuan, and Jean-Denis Vigne. 2016. Social Complexification and Pig (*Sus scrofa*) Husbandry in Ancient China: A Combined Geometric Morphometric and Isotopic Approach. PLoS ONE 11(7):e0158523. doi: 10.1371/journal.pone.0158523.

Earle, Timothy, and Kristian Kristiansen. 2010. Organising Bronze Age Societies: Concluding Thoughts. In *Organising Bronze Age Societies*, edited by Timothy Earle and Kristian Kristiansen, pp. 218–56. Cambridge University Press, Cambridge.

Ember, Carol R., Melvin Ember, and Bruce Russett. 1997. Inequality and Democracy and the Anthropological Record. In *Inequality, Democracy, and Economic Development*, edited by Manus I. Midlarsky, pp. 110–30. Cambridge University Press, Cambridge.

Gellner, Ernest. 1988. *Plough, Sword, and Book: The Structure of Human History*. University of Chicago Press, Chicago.

Gordon, Andrew H., and Calvin W. Schwabe. 2004. *The Quick and the Dead: Biomedical Theory in Ancient Egypt*. Vol. 4. Egyptological Memoirs. Brill, Styx, Leiden.

Halstead, Paul. 2014. *Two Oxen Ahead: Pre-mechanised Farming in the Mediterranean*. Wiley-Blackwell, Oxford, U.K.

Hodder, Ian, and Chris Doherty. 2014. Human-Thing Entanglements. In *Integrating Çatalhöyük: Themes from the 2000–2008 Seasons*, edited by Ian Hodder, pp. 221–31. BIAA Monograph 49. British Institute at Ankara, London; Cotsen Institute of Archaeology, University of California, Los Angeles.

Kim, Seung-Og. 1994. Burials, Pigs, and Political Prestige in Neolithic China. *Current Anthropology* 35:119–41.

Kohler, Timothy A., Michael E. Smith, Amy Bogaard, Gary M. Feinman, Christian E. Peterson, Alleen Betzenhauser, Matthew Pailes, et al. 2017. Greater Post-Neolithic Wealth Disparities in Eurasia than in North and Mesoamerica. *Nature*. doi:10.1038/nature24646.

Kopczuk, Wojciech. 2015. What Do We Know About Evolution of Top Wealth Shares in the United States? *Journal of Economic Perspectives* 29:47–66.

Kristiansen, Kristian, and Pauline Suchowska-Ducke. 2015. Connected Histories: The Dynamics of Bronze Age Interaction and Trade, 1500–1100 BC. *Proceedings of the Prehistoric Society* 81:361–392. doi:10.1017/ppr.2015.17.

Lenski, Gerhard E. 1966. *Power and Privilege: A Theory of Social Stratification*. McGraw-Hill, New York.

Lloyd, Peter E., and Peter Dicken. 1977. *Location in Space: A Theoretical Approach to Economic Geography*. 2nd ed. Harper and Row, New York.

Lobban, Richard A., Jr. 1989. Cattle and the Rise of the Egyptian State. *Anthrozoös* 2(3):194–201.

Ma, Xiaolin. 2005. *Emergent Social Complexity in the Yangshao Culture: Analyses of Settlement Patterns and Faunal Remains from Lingbao, Western Henan, China.* British Archaeological Reports, Oxford.

Mann, Michael. 2013. *The Sources of Social Power.* Vol. 4, *Globalizations, 1945–2011.* Cambridge University Press, Cambridge.

Milanovic, Branko. 2011. *The Haves and the Have-Nots: A Brief and Idiosyncratic History of Global Inequality.* Basic Books, New York.

———. 2016. Income Inequality Is Cyclical. *Nature* 537(7621):479–82.

Milanovic, Branko, Peter H. Lindert, and Jeffrey G. Williamson. 2011. Preindustrial Inequality. *Economic Journal* 121(551):255–72.

Ortman, Scott G., Andrew Cabaniss, Jennie O. Sturm, and Luís M. A. Bettencourt. 2015. Settlement Scaling and Increasing Returns in an Ancient Society. *Science Advances* 1e00066. doi:10.1126/sciadv.00066.

Ortman, Scott G., and Grant D. Coffey. 2017. Settlement Scaling in Middle-Range Societies. *American Antiquity* 82(4):662–82.

Peterson, Christian E., and Gideon Shelach. 2012. Jiangzhai: Social and Economic Organization of a Middle Neolithic Chinese Village. *Journal of Anthropological Archaeology* 31(3):265–301.

Savoia, Antonio, Joshy Easaw, and Andrew McKay. 2010. Inequality, Democracy, and Institutions: A Critical Review of Recent Research. *World Development* 38(2):142–54.

Scheidel, Walter. 2017. *The Great Leveler: Violence and the History of Inequality from the Stone Age to the Twenty-First Century.* Princeton University Press, Princeton.

Sherratt, Andrew. 1981. *Plough and Pastoralism: Aspects of the Secondary Products Revolution.* Cambridge University Press, Cambridge.

Sjoberg, Gideon. 1960. *The Preindustrial Society: Past and Present.* Free Press, Glencoe, Ill.

Smith, Courtland. 1991. Patterns of Wealth Concentration. *Human Organization* 50(1):50–60.

Smith, Eric Alden, Monique Borgerhoff Mulder, Samuel Bowles, Michael Gurven, Tom Hertz, and Mary K. Shenk. 2010. Production Systems, Inheritance, and Inequality in Premodern Societies: Conclusions. *Current Anthropology* 51:85–94.

Smith, Michael E., Timothy Dennehy, April Kamp-Whittaker, Benjamin Stanley, Barbara L. Stark, and Abigail York. 2016. Conceptual Approaches to Service Provision in Cities Through the Ages. *Urban Studies* 53(8):1574–90.

Smith, Michael E., and Frederic Hicks. 2016. Inequality and Social Class. In *Oxford Handbook of the Aztecs*, edited by Deborah L. Nichols and Enrique Rodríguez-Alegría, pp. 425–36. Oxford University Press, New York.

Stiglitz, Joseph E. 2012. *The Price of Inequality: How Today's Divided Society Endangers Our Future.* Norton, New York.

Sussman, Nathan. 2006. Income Inequality in Paris in the Heyday of the Commercial Revolution. DEGIT conference paper. http://degit.sam.sdu.dk/papers/degit_11/C011_043.pdf (accessed July 1, 2017).

Taagepera, Rein. 1978. Size and Duration of Empires' Growth-Decline Curves, 3000 to 600 BC. *Social Science Research* 7(2):180–96.

Tilly, Charles. 2001. Relational Origins of Inequality. *Anthropological Theory* 1(3):355–72.

Trigger, Bruce G. 1972. Determinants of Urban Growth in Pre-industrial Societies. In *Man, Settlement, and Urbanism*, edited by Peter J. Ucko, Ruth Tringham, and G. W. Dimbleby, pp. 575–99. Schenkman, Cambridge, Mass.

Turchin, Peter. 2010. Warfare and the Evolution of Social Complexity: A Multilevel-Selection Approach. *Structure and Dynamics* 4(3):Article 2.

Vretemark, Maria. 2010. Subsistence Strategies. In *Organising Bronze Age Societies*, edited by Timothy Earle and Kristian Kristiansen, pp. 155–84. Cambridge University Press, Cambridge.

White, Leslie A. 1949. *The Science of Culture: A Study of Man and Civilization.* Grove Press, New York.

CONTRIBUTORS

Nicholas Ames is a PhD student at the University of Notre Dame. His research interests focus on historic Irish migration and the development of transnational communities among immigrant populations. He has participated in archaeological projects in California, Ireland, Italy, Oman, Sudan, and Jordan. His current research investigates community connections between western Ireland and Pittsburgh, Pennsylvania.

Alleen Betzenhauser is a senior research archaeologist with the Illinois State Archaeological Survey (ISAS), Prairie Research Institute. Her research interests focus on Late Woodland and Mississippian archaeology in the Midwest and the American Bottom region of southwestern Illinois. She contributed to the fieldwork, analysis, and reporting of ISAS's investigations at the East St. Louis precinct. Her interests in ceramic analysis, geophysical survey, and urbanization structure her investigation of the Mississippian transition near Cahokia, the largest Mississippian site in America. She has written several reports and contributed chapters to edited volumes on topics ranging from the Mississippian transition to archaeological approaches to neighborhoods.

Amy Bogaard is a professor of Neolithic and Bronze Age archaeology at the University of Oxford. Her research centers on the ecological characterization of farming regimes to address issues ranging from resilience to inequality. Recently she led the European Research Council–funded project The Agricultural Origins of Urban Civilization (AGRICURB), which framed comparative analysis of late prehistoric farming in western Asia and Europe using novel archaeobotanical approaches.

Samuel Bowles heads the Behavioral Sciences Program at the Santa Fe Institute. Bowles's research includes theoretical and empirical studies of political hierarchy and wealth inequality and their evolution over the very long run. His recent books include *The Moral Economy: Why Good Laws Are No Substitute for Good Citizens* (2016) and *A Cooperative Species: Human Reciprocity and Its Evolution* (with Herbert Gintis, 2011). His next book will be *Equality's Moment: The Origins and Future of Economic Disparity and Political Hierarchy*. With CORE (Curriculum Open-Access Resources for Economics), he has produced a new university-level introduction to economics (www.core-econ.org).

Meredith S. Chesson is an associate professor of anthropology at the University of Notre Dame. She is an archaeologist focusing on two major research themes: the materiality of daily life and the construction of difference and identity. She co-directs the following projects: Expedition to the Dead Sea Plain Project's research on the Early Bronze Age of the southern Levant with Dr. Morag Kersel (http://expeditiondeadseaplain .org); late prehistory and the postmedieval in Calabria, Italy, with the Bova Marina Archaeological Project (www.arch.cam.ac.uk/research/ projects/bova-marina/); and life in nineteenth- and twentieth-century rural western Ireland with Notre Dame's Cultural Landscapes of the Irish Coast (www.facebook.com/Cultural-Landscapes-of-the-Irish-Coast -Project-ND-246146295491973/).

Abhijit Dandekar is an assistant professor in the Department of Archaeology and a research associate in the Department of Epigraphy and Numismatics at Deccan College. His research interests include trade and commerce in the Indian Ocean. He is currently the director of the Chaul Archaeological Research Project.

Timothy J. Dennehy is a PhD candidate in the School of Human Evolution and Social Change at Arizona State University, Tempe. His dissertation research uses evidence from three Archaic period Belizean rockshelters to examine changes in human mobility during the shift from foraging to food production. Other research interests include urban spatial inequities, the origin of social inequality, and the pre-Maya occupants of Mesoamerica. His involvement in the Urban Organization through the Ages project has led to co-authorship on several peer-reviewed publications, including a chapter in *Archaeology of the Human Experience*, a special issue of the Archaeological Papers of the AAA.

Robert D. Drennan pursues comparative analysis aimed at delineating patterns of variation in the developmental trajectories of early complex societies worldwide. He has carried out archaeological field research with a focus on regional settlement demography, communities, and households in Mesoamerica, northern South America, and northeastern China. He is Distinguished Professor of Anthropology and the director of the Center for Comparative Archaeology at the University of Pittsburgh, as well as a member of the U.S. National Academy of Sciences.

Laura J. Ellyson is a PhD student in the Department of Anthropology at Washington State University. Her research centers on Ancestral Pueblo settlement and subsistence in the northern San Juan region in the American Southwest. Other research interests include archaeological applications of agent-based modeling, the emergence of wealth inequalities, and human-environment interactions. She has presented her research at annual meetings of the Society for American Archaeology, the Society of Ethnobiology, and the Pecos Conference, as well as at the International Congress of Archaeozoology meeting in San Rafael, Argentina.

Ronald K. Faulseit is an assistant professor of anthropology at Pierce College in Los Angeles. He is an archaeologist with a research focus on complex societies. He currently directs a long-term field project in the Tlacolula Valley of Oaxaca, Mexico, with the goal of understanding cultural resilience in the wake of political fragmentation. As a visiting scholar at Southern Illinois University, Faulseit organized and edited the volume *Beyond Collapse: Archaeological Perspectives on Resilience, Revitalization, and Transformation in Complex Societies* (2016). He also authored *Cerro Danush: Excavations of a Hilltop Community in the Eastern Valley of Oaxaca, Mexico* (2013).

Gary M. Feinman is the MacArthur Curator of Anthropology at the Field Museum of Natural History, Chicago, Illinois. He has co-directed long-term archaeological research programs in Oaxaca (Mexico) and Shandong (China). In the Valley of Oaxaca, Feinman has co-directed excavations at four Classic period settlements. Over his career, he has focused investigations on the causes and consequences of the emergence of large-scale cooperative formations, the cycling or transformations of these complex societies, and economic relations at multiple scales. Feinman is a Fellow of the American Association for the Advancement of Science and received the Presidential Recognition Award from the Society for American Archaeology.

Mattia Fochesato is a postdoctoral associate of economic history in the Social Sciences Division at New York University Abu Dhabi. His research focuses on the long-run determinants of income and wealth distribution across different world regions. He is currently working on the institutional causes of the late medieval and early modern Europe's North-South economic divide and the analysis of the determinants of trends of wealth inequality from prehistory to the present.

Thomas A. Foor is a professor emeritus of anthropology at the University of Montana in Missoula. He has three main theoretical interests: quantitative analysis, measurement theory, and their applications to anthropology; ethnological theory; and the archaeology and ethnohistory of the northern Plains and Rocky Mountain regions. He has directed field projects in his regions of interest over his thirty-five-year career. He has authored or co-authored over forty articles as well as numerous technical contracted reports.

Vishwas D. Gogte is currently an emeritus professor and was previously a professor and joint director at the Deccan College Post Graduate and Research Institute, Pune University. His interests include trade, exchange, and interactions in ancient South Asia and the archaeological chemistry of ancient materials. He is directing ongoing archaeological work at the ports of Palshet and Chaul in Western India.

Timothy A. Kohler is Regents Professor of Anthropology at Washington State University, an external professor at the Santa Fe Institute, and a research associate at Crow Canyon Archaeological Center. From 2001 to 2012 he coordinated the NSF-funded Village Ecodynamics Project in the northern U.S. Southwest. His most recent book is the co-edited volume *Emergence and Collapse of Early Villages: Models of Central Mesa Verde Archaeology* (2012). He is a Fellow of the American Association for the Advancement of Science and in 2014 was recognized with the Alfred

Vincent Kidder Award for Eminence in American Archaeology by the American Anthropological Association.

Ian Kuijt is a professor and archaeologist at the University of Notre Dame who works on the emergence of social differentiation and the materialization of identity, the origins of agriculture, and the forager-farmer transition. His most recent book is the co-edited volume *Transformation by Fire: The Archaeology of Cremation in Cultural Context* (2014). In 2016 he was named a Distinguished Fellow of the Notre Dame Institute for Advanced Study.

Chapurukha M. Kusimba is a professor of anthropology at American University. His research focuses on the development of complex societies along the Kenyan coast during precolonial times. His current archaeological field research addresses the ancient maritime trade between East Africa, South Asia, and East Asia. He is excavating the ancient port city of Manda in the Lamu Archipelago on the Kenyan coast.

Mary-Margaret Murphy is a lead technician for the 3D Imaging Lab (SSRL—3DI) of the University of Montana in Missoula. She applies her background in arts, technology, and quantitative analysis to her research interests in anthropology and intersecting sciences. She is currently applying digital and historic data for human identification. She has produced content for several reports and publications. For the article "The Coarse Volcanic Rock Industry at Rio Ibáñez 6 West, Aisén Region, Patagonian Chile" (*Lithic Technology*, 2015), she contributed print images from 3D models that accurately communicate modification to lithic artifacts that are not possible with photography.

Linda M. Nicholas is an adjunct curator of anthropology at the Field Museum of Natural History, Chicago, Illinois. She has co-directed long-term archaeological field projects in Oaxaca (Mexico) and Shandong (China). In both regions, she has co-directed systematic regional surveys and also has co-led excavations at four Classic period settlements in the Valley of Oaxaca. Her research interests include settlement pattern studies, household archaeology, ancient economies, and the processes associated with early urbanization and the transformation of complex societies over time. She has published extensively on her fieldwork in Mexico and China.

Rahul C. Oka is Ford Family Assistant Professor of Anthropology at the University of Notre Dame. His research interests include the evolution and impact of trade and traders on social, political, and cultural infrastructures. He is currently investigating the evolution of trade and commerce in the Indian Ocean, circa 1000 BCE–1800 CE, and the impact of socioeconomic interactions on contemporary relief and development processes.

Matthew Pailes is an assistant professor of anthropology at the University of Oklahoma. His research focuses on the social organization of middle-range societies, including topics such as the emergence of inequality, exchange relationships, and the resilience of different political structures. Most of his research is conducted in the U.S. Southwest and northwestern Mexico, as exemplified by his most recent publication, "Northwest Mexico: The Prehistory of Sonora, Chihuahua, and Neighboring Areas," in the *Journal of Archaeological Research* (2017). He is currently developing a collaborative research program with Mexican colleagues to explore the diverse political structures of prehistoric communities in the Sierra Madre.

Christian E. Peterson is an associate professor and the chair of anthropology at the University of Hawaiʻi at Manoa. He specializes in the comparative study of early complex societies; regional settlement patterns and demography; household archaeology; and quantitative and spatial analysis. His current field research focuses on the emergence and development of Neolithic Hongshan period chiefly communities in northeastern China. He is the (co-)author of numerous scholarly articles and monographs, including "Hongshan Households and Communities in Neolithic Northeastern China" (with Robert D. Drennan, Lu Xueming, and Li Tao, *Journal of Anthropological Archaeology*, 2017), and "Comparative Analysis of Neolithic Household Artifact Assemblage Data from Northern China" (with Robert D. Drennan and Kate L. Bartel, *Journal of Anthropological Research*, 2016).

Anna Marie Prentiss is a professor of archaeology at the University of Montana in Missoula. She is also editor of the *SAA Archaeological Record*, magazine of the Society for American Archaeology. Her research interests include the archaeology of indigenous hunting and gathering societies of North America, lithic technology, and the cultural evolutionary process. She has published six books and many journal articles, book chapters, and technical reports of archaeological investigations. Her most recent book, *The Last House at Bridge River* (2017), is an archaeological examination of a traditional Salishan (St'át'imc) household during the Canadian Fur Trade period.

Michael E. Smith is a professor of archaeology at Arizona State University, Tempe, and the director of the ASU Teotihuacan Research Laboratory in Mexico. He is an archaeologist with two main research themes: the Aztecs and Teotihuacan in central Mexico; and the comparative analysis of ancient cities and societies. He has directed fieldwork projects at sites in the provinces of the Aztec empire, excavating houses to study daily life. He has published twelve books and numerous scholarly articles; his latest book, *At Home with the Aztecs: An Archaeologist Uncovers Their Daily Life* (2016), won the 2017 Award for Best Book, Popular Category, by the Society for American Archaeology. He is a Fellow of the American Association for the Advancement of Science.

Elizabeth C. Stone is a professor of anthropology at the State University of New York at Stony Brook. Her research has focused on the social and economic structure and evolution of Mesopotamian society through both textual analysis and excavation, with an emphasis on the role played by the larger population. In addition to projects in Turkey and Syria, she has directed survey and excavations at Mashkan-shapir and Ur in Iraq. She has also used high-resolution satellite imagery to map the architectural configuration of some fifty Mesopotamian archaeological sites. Her books include *Nippur Neighborhoods* and *The Anatomy of a Mesopotamian City: Survey and Soundings at Mashkan-shapir.*

Amy Styring is a Humboldt Research Fellow at Goethe University, Frankfurt. She is an archaeological chemist with a specialty in crop isotope geochemistry and an interest in ancient agriculture, human-environment interactions, and adaptation to societal and environmental changes. She has published papers on past farming practice in Europe and the Near East, including a recent article in *Nature Plants* titled "Isotope Evidence for Agricultural Extensification Reveals How the World's First Cities Were Fed."

Jade Whitlam is an Early Career Fellow at the University of Oxford who specializes in the analysis of charred plant macroremains from prehistoric sites in western Asia. Her research focuses on reconstructing early plant management strategies and farming systems from the Neolithic to the Bronze Age, and she is currently involved in projects in Iraq, Iran, Jordan, Syria, and Italy. Her research has been published in site monographs and as peer-reviewed articles, and she co-edited the *Environmental Archaeologies of Neolithisation* (2014, 2015) special issues of *Environmental Archaeology*.

INDEX

Page numbers with *f* appended indicate figures. Page numbers with *t* appended indicate tables

AMERIND SERIES IN ANTHROPOLOGY

Series Editor **Christine Szuter**

Trincheras Sites in Time, Space, and Society
Edited by Suzanne K. Fish, Paul R. Fish, and M. Elisa Villalpando

Collaborating at the Trowel's Edge: Teaching and Learning in Indigenous Archaeology
Edited by Stephen W. Silliman

Warfare in Cultural Context: Practice, Agency, and the Archaeology of Violence
Edited by Axel E. Nielsen and William H. Walker

Across a Great Divide: Continuity and Change in Native North American Societies, 1400–1900
Edited by Laura L. Scheiber and Mark D. Mitchell

Leaving Mesa Verde: Peril and Change in the Thirteenth-Century Southwest
Edited by Timothy A. Kohler, Mark D. Varien, and Aaron M. Wright

Becoming Villagers: Comparing Early Village Society
Edited by Matthew S. Bandy and Jake R. Fox

Hunter-Gatherer Archaeology as Historical Process
Edited by Kenneth E. Sassaman and Donald H. Holly Jr.

Religious Transformation in the Late Pre-Hispanic Pueblo World
Edited by Donna M. Glowacki and Scott Van Keuren

Crow-Omaha: New Light on a Classic Problem of Kinship Analysis
Edited by Thomas R. Trautmann and Peter M. Whiteley

Native and Spanish New Worlds: Sixteenth-Century Entradas in the American Southwest and Southeast
Edited by Clay Mathers, Jeffrey M. Mitchem, and Charles M. Haecker

Transformation by Fire: The Archaeology of Cremation in Cultural Context
Edited by Ian Kuijt, Colin P. Quinn, and Gabriel Cooney

Chaco Revisted: New Research on the Prehistory of Chaco Canyon
Edited by Carrie C. Heitman and Stephen Plog

Ancient Paquimé and the Casas Grandes World
Edited by Paul E. Minnis and Michael E. Whalen